WORKSHOPS IN COMPUTING

Series edited by C. J. van Rijsbergen

Also in this series

Women into Computing: Selected Papers 1988–1990
Gillian Lovegrove and Barbara Segal (Eds.)

3rd Refinement Workshop (organised by BCS-FACS, and sponsored by IBM UK Laboratories, Hursley Park and the Programming Research Group, University of Oxford), Hursley Park, 9–11 January 1990
Carroll Morgan and J. C. P. Woodcock (Eds.)

Designing Correct Circuits, Workshop jointly organised by the Universities of Oxford and Glasgow, Oxford, 26–28 September 1990
Geraint Jones and Mary Sheeran (Eds.)

Functional Programming, Glasgow 1990, Proceedings of the 1990 Glasgow Workshop on Functional Programming, Ullapool, Scotland, 13–15 August 1990
Simon L. Peyton Jones, Graham Hutton and Carsten Kehler Holst (Eds.)

4th Refinement Workshop, Proceedings of the 4th Refinement Workshop, organised by BCS-FACS, Cambridge, 9–11 January 1991
Joseph M. Morris and Roger C. Shaw (Eds.)

AI and Cognitive Science '90, University of Ulster at Jordanstown, 20–21 September 1990
Michael F. McTear and Norman Creaney (Eds.)

Software Re-use, Utrecht 1989, Proceedings of the Software Re-use Workshop, Utrecht, The Netherlands, 23–24 November 1989
Liesbeth Dusink and Patrick Hall (Eds.)

Z User Workshop, 1990, Proceedings of the Fifth Annual Z User Meeting, Oxford, 17–18 December 1990
J.E. Nicholls (Ed.)

IV Higher Order Workshop, Banff 1990
Proceedings of the IV Higher Order Workshop, Banff, Alberta, Canada, 10–14 September 1990
Graham Birtwistle (Ed.)

ALPUK91 Proceedings of the 3rd UK Annual Conference on Logic Programming, Edinburgh, 10–12 April 1991
Geraint A. Wiggins, Chris Mellish and Tim Duncan (Eds.)

Specifications of Database Systems,
1st International Workshop on Specifications of Database Systems, Glasgow, 3–5 July 1991
David J. Harper and Moira C. Norrie (Eds.)

7th UK Computer and Telecommunications Performance Engineering Workshop,
Edinburgh, 22–23 July 1991
J. Hillston, P.J.B. King and R.J. Pooley (Eds.)

Logic Program Synthesis and Transformation,
Proceedings of LOPSTR 91, International Workshop on Logic Program Synthesis and Transformation, University of Manchester, 4–5 July 1991
T.P. Clement and K.-K. Lau (Eds.)

Declarative Programming, Sasbachwalden 1991
PHOENIX Seminar and Workshop on Declarative Programming, Sasbachwalden, Black Forest, Germany, 18–22 November 1991
John Darlington and Roland Dietrich (Eds.)

Building Interactive Systems: Architectures and Tools
Philip Gray and Roger Took (Eds.)

Object Orientation in Z
Susan Stepney, Rosalind Barden and David Cooper (Eds.)

continued on back page...

Robert Giegerich and Susan L. Graham (Eds.)

Code Generation – Concepts, Tools, Techniques

Proceedings of the International Workshop on Code Generation, Dagstuhl, Germany, 20–24 May 1991

Published in collaboration with the
British Computer Society

Springer-Verlag
London Berlin Heidelberg New York
Paris Tokyo Hong Kong
Barcelona Budapest

Robert Giegerich, Dr
Arbeitsgruppe Praktische Informatik
Universität Bielefeld, Technische Fakultät
Postfach 10 01 31, 4800 Bielefeld 1,
Germany

Susan Graham, PhD
Computer Science Division – EECS
University of California, Berkeley
571 Evans Hall, Berkeley, CA 94720
USA

ISBN 3-540-19757-5 Springer-Verlag Berlin Heidelberg New York
ISBN 0-387-19757-5 Springer-Verlag New York Berlin Heidelberg

British Library Cataloguing in Publication Data
Code Generation: Concepts, Tools, Techniques – Proceedings of the International Workshop on Code Generation, Dagstuhl, Germany, 20–24 May 1991. – (Workshops in Computing Series)
I. Giegerich, Robert II. Graham, Susan L. III. Series
005. 13
ISBN 3-540-19757-5

Library of Congress Cataloging-in-Publication Data
International Workshop on Code Generation (1991 : Dagstuhl, Wadern, Germany)
Code generation–concepts, tools, techniques : proceedings of the International Workshop on Code Generation, Dagstuhl, Germany, 20-24 May 1991 / Robert Giegerich and Susan L. Graham (eds.).
p. cm. – (Workshops in computing)
"Published in collaboration with the British Computer Society."
Includes bibliographical references and index.
ISBN 0-387-19757-5 (New York : alk. paper)
1. Code generators–Congresses. I. Giegerich, Robert, *1931–* . II. Graham, Susan L. III. British Computer Society. IV. Title. V. Series.
QA76.76.G46I58 1991 92-21735
005.4'5–dc20 CIP

Printed in Germany

34/3830-543210 Printed on acid-free paper

Preface

The goal of the international workshop "Code Generation – Concepts, Tools, Techniques" was to evaluate the state of the art, and to point out the main directions of code generation research in the coming years. The workshop had 36 participants, 20 from Europe and 16 from the USA.

Most of the papers presented at the workshop centered around four topics:

- Tools and techniques for code selection
- Code generation for parallel architectures
- Register allocation and phase ordering problems
- Formal models and validation

In addition, there were presentations on some new topics, including dynamic compilation and object-oriented methods for code generation.

This volume contains revised and expanded versions of 14 papers presented at the workshop, together with summaries of two discussion meetings. The papers were reviewed after the workshop, and were subsequently revised to address the concerns of the reviewers.

Tools and Techniques for Code Selection

It is widely agreed that tree pattern matching is the preferable technique for code selection. Much discussion was devoted to relating the BURS approach, tree parsing, and the new approach of "regular controlled rewriting". While the pure matching problem seems to have been solved satisfactorily, the big remaining problem is the integration of the pattern driven code selector with other code generation tasks. "Considerate code selection" allows the postponement of decisions in the code selection phase. By contrast, existing tools incorporate a specific time at which decisions are made.

An in-depth discussion on specification techniques led to the decision that a group of the participants would cooperate to make a pure BURS system available for public distribution. The resulting system, named

BURG, is now available. A summary of the discussion is included in this volume.

Code Generation for Parallel Architectures

Parallelism in computer architecture is found both at the coarse level of multiple processors or simultaneous access to multiple data, and at the fine-grained level of overlapping execution of operations.

Research in coarse grain parallelism is characterised by attempts to provide a high-level, architecture-independent model of parallelism to be used in programming or, alternatively, programming techniques and language features that expose the architecture to the programmer. The latter reduces compiler complexity, but also program portability. A summary of the discussion of this topic is included.

As for fine grain parallelism, while a general model of pipeline scheduling is still not available, some comparative results for different RISC architectures and different scheduling techniques are now available. It is an open research question to characterize the class of machines for which these results are valid. As expected, interaction between scheduler and register allocator is crucial.

Register Allocation and Phase Ordering

Register allocation interacts with all code generation tasks. Contributions treat techniques for code rearrangement and multi-level window models. A study of register allocation for a vector machine is included in the section on parallel architectures.

Formal Models and Validation

Formal methods try to enhance the reliability of code generators by providing a declarative meaning for code generator descriptions and formal proof techniques. A number of interesting approaches were presented. Some (parts of) simple code generators have been proved correct mechanically, some more realistic ones have been proved "by hand", but the effort is usually immense. Currently, no proof techniques are available for the code generation techniques used in practice. Both sides must advance – future tools should provide a declarative semantics, and validation methods must be geared to code generation techniques.

Additional Topics

Code generation and debugging are usually seen as incompatible, in the sense that debuggers tend to use interpreted rather than compiled code. "Dynamic compilation" provides a method for updates to compiled code that preserve the execution state during debugging.

The increased use of object-based programming has created challenging efficiency problems. An efficient back-end "object server" provides significant performance improvements for the execution of data-intensive operations on objects.

Acknowledgements

The workshop provided an excellent forum for the exchange of ideas, bringing together groups of experts who are unlikely to have the opportunity for extensive discussion at a more general conference. Strong participation from the USA was made possible by a travel grant from the US National Science Foundation.

The participants were delighted with the facilities and the hospitality of the Dagstuhl Institute. The charming surroundings and the relaxed, but highly professional management helped to make this workshop a pleasant and rewarding experience.

We gratefully acknowledge the help of H. Hogenkamp both with the workshop organisation and the preparation of these proceedings. His highly competent support was a major contribution to the workshop. The availability of electronic communication via the Internet was also of great help to us.

May 1992

R. Giegerich
Universität Bielefeld

S.L. Graham
University of California, Berkeley

Contents

Code Selection

Code Generation for Parallel Architectures

Register Allocation and Phase Ordering

Formal Methods

Additional Topics

Code Selection

Code Selection by Regularly Controlled Term Rewriting *

Helmut Emmelmann

email: emmel@karlsruhe.gmd.de

GMD Research Center at the University of Karlsruhe

Vincenz-Prießnitz-Str. 1, 7500 Karlsruhe, Germany

Abstract

Regularly controlled term rewriting allows the efficient implementation of a class of non-deterministic term rewriting systems by using regular tree automata to control rule applications. This makes it possible to describe code selectors using very high level specifications: The mapping from intermediate to target code is described by term rewriting rules or by equations. A tree grammar is used to specify the set of target terms and their costs. The paper presents an algorithm to generate efficient tree transducers that map intermediate code terms to cost minimal target terms. First practical experiences using the proposed algorithm are reported.

1 Introduction

Code generation is the task of translating programs from some intermediate representation to machine or assembler code. Classically code generation has two important subtasks: code selection and register allocation. This paper is only concerned with code selection.

Recent research has led to usable generators that produce efficient code selectors from declarative specifications. Development of those specifications is easier and cheaper than programming a code selector by hand. This paper introduces a different formalism that allows one to write much better, concise specifications, which are easier to read and to develop.

We assume that the intermediate code and the target code are represented as trees or terms. Our description formalism specifies the mapping from intermediate code to target code by term rewriting rules. This is a very natural way of specification, as simply algebraic properties of the intermediate and target operators have to be specified.

We allow the term rewriting system to be non-deterministic and non-confluent. So it becomes possible to write several rules for one intermediate operator and let the generator select the best one, depending on the context. More generally speaking, for one intermediate code term the term rewriting system allows the production of a lot of different target terms, each of them correct but with varying code quality.

It is the task of the code selector to apply the term rewriting rules the right way in order to transform the intermediate code term into a target term of minimal cost, according to a user defined cost measure.

*This work was partly carried out within the Esprit Project #5399 (COMPARE)

The central part of the paper describes a method to automatically derive code selectors from these specifications. Actually we do not generate the code selectors directly but we produce a tree pattern matching based code selector description as output. Then a code selector can be produced by well known techniques.

The rest of the paper is structured as follows: First, section 2 explains more precisely how code selectors are specified using our method. Section 3 explains the main algorithms we use. Finally section 4 gives practical results.

2 Code Selection as a Term Transformation Problem

Our code selector specifications consist of two parts. The first part is called *mapping specification* and is a set of term transformation rules. Provided all the rules are correct, applying rules onto a term t leading to s implies that t can be implemented by s. Terms that correspond to legal target code are called *legal target terms.* The second part of the specification, called *machine specification*, describes which terms are legal target terms, and it specifies a cost function for these legal target terms.

To select code for a given intermediate code term t we have to select a term s that fulfills the following properties: s can be derived from t using the rules of the mapping specification, and s is a legal target term of minimal cost according to the machine specification.

The machine specification is, in contrast to the mapping specification, independent of the intermediate code. It is therefore the right place to put in other information about the machine instructions, to generate register allocators, assemblers, or instruction schedulers.

2.1 Input and Output of the Code Generator

As input of the code generator we assume a tree oriented intermediate representation. It consists of a sequence of terms. Each of these terms is translated separately to target code. In addition to the mapping and machine specifications, a code generator generator needs a description of this intermediate code.

The example intermediate representation we use in this paper consists of the operators *plus, minus, mult, div, assign, cont, c, one, zero, sc,* and *bb*. The operators *c, one, zero* and *bb* represent constants of different value (range) *zero*:0, *one*:1, *sc*:2, 4, 8, and *c*:any other value. *cont* gets a value from a given memory address and *assign* assigns the value of the second operand to the memory address given by the first operand. Figure 1 contains an example intermediate code tree. It is sometimes convenient to share some operators between the intermediate representation and the target terms e.g. the *bb* and *c* operators in the example.

We also need a term representation for the target machine instructions: Target instructions, addressing modes, constants, dedicated registers etc. are represented as operators. Terms made up by these operators are called *target terms.* The result of code selection is still a term and not a sequence of target instructions, because register allocation has not been performed yet. A register

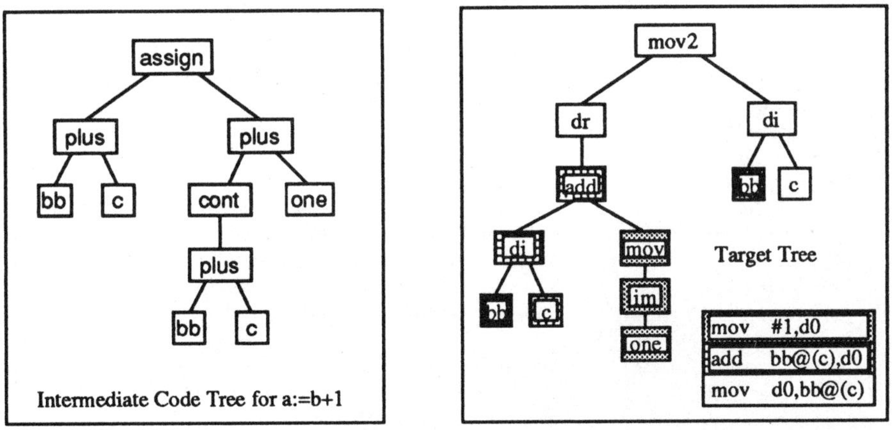

Figure 1: Intermediate and Target Terms

allocation algorithm has to be applied on the term, before the code can be produced by a bottom up tree walk.

One machine instruction is represented by one or more adjacent nodes of the target term. For example `add a1@(c),d0` is represented by $add(di(A, c), B)$. The operator *add* represents the `add` instruction, *di* the register indirect with displacement addressing mode, *c* a constant. A and B are subterms representing other instructions. Only the register allocator will determine where the results of A and B are placed e.g. in the `a1` and `d0` registers.

For some operations we need two operators depending on where the result should be stored. It can be stored either in a yet unknown register which will be determined by the register allocator or in a known memory[1] location. In our example the `mov` instruction is represented by the *mov* and *mov2* operators. The *mov* operator has only one operand and a result while the *mov2* has no result and two operands: source and address of the destination. It is also possible to use only one operator with two operands and leave the destination operand undefined if the location is still unknown.

Figure 1 shows the intermediate term, the target term and the final code produced for a statement $a := b+1$. a and b are supposed to be local variables, which are addressed by adding a constant to the block base register represented by the *bb* operator.

2.2 The Machine Specification

The machine specification describes for each machine instruction which addressing modes or register classes are allowed for the operands and for the result. It describes the syntactic form of the addressing modes and where which register

[1]Register variables, i.e. known register locations, are not supported in our example. For them another operator *movreg* is necessary, which tells the register allocator to use a previously assigned register as target.

```
Z   ::=mov2 (Ea, Mea)                                   Cost 4;
Ar  ::=mov (Ea) | lea (Mea) | add (Ea, Ar) | sub (Ea, Ar) Cost 4
Ar  ::=bb                                               Cost 0;
Dr  ::=mov (Ea) | add (Ea, Dr) | sub (Ea, Dr) |
       muls (Ea, Dr) | divs (Ea, Dr)                    Cost 4;

Ea  ::=im (C)              Immediate Addressing mode
Ea  ::=Mea                 Memory effective addresses are effective Addresses
Ea  ::=dr(Dr) | dr (Ar)    Register Direct Addressing mode
Mea::=di(Ar, C)            Address Register with Displacement Mode
Mea::=ir (Ar)              Register Indirect Addressing Mode
Mea::=in(Ar, C, Imul)      Indexed Addressing Mode
Imul::=inmul (Dr, Sc) |
       inmul (Ar, Sc)      Multiplication with 1, 2, 4, or 8
Sc  ::=sc | one            Constants one : 1, sc : 2,4,8
C   ::=c | zero | Sc       zero : 0, c : any other value
```

Figure 2: Machine Specification using a Regular Tree Grammar

classes or which constant ranges are allowed. Finally it defines a cost function on the target terms which is used to optimize the code quality.

A target term is said to be *legal* if it fulfills all these constraints. The machine specification defines the set of *legal target terms*. It is written in form of a regular tree grammar. All the terms produced by this grammar are defined to be legal.

The grammar rules are annotated with cost values. The cost of a derivation is defined as the sum of the cost of all rules applied. The cost of a legal target term is the cost of a minimal derivation in the grammar. This gives a cost measure for all the target terms. The code generator is supposed to optimize according to this cost measure.

The machine specification can be developed very easily, because it describes more or less only syntactic features of the machine language.

An example is given in Figure 2. It describes part of the 68k processor. Identifiers starting with capital letters are nonterminals, and Z is the start symbol. The target term given in figure 1 is legal according to this grammar. The nonterminals Sc and C describe constants of different value ranges. Ea stands for any legal addressing mode and Mea for addressing modes accessing memory. Ar and Dr denote address and data registers respectively. For rules with cost zero the cost value is omitted.

2.3 The Mapping Specification

The mapping specification describes the mapping from intermediate to target terms. This is done by a non-confluent term rewriting system. So the mapping specification does not define a function but a relation, which maps one intermediate code term into a set of legal target terms. Only the code generator selects according to the cost measure specified in the machine specification one of the cheapest legal target terms.

(1)	plus (A, B)	$\longrightarrow$	add (A, B)
(2)	minus(A, B)	$\longrightarrow$	sub (B, A)
(3)	mult (A, B)	$\longrightarrow$	muls (A, B)
(4)	div (A, B)	$\longrightarrow$	divs (B, A)
(5)	assign (adr(A), B)	$\longrightarrow$	mov2 (B, A)
(6)	A	$\longrightarrow$	dr (A)
(7)	cont(A)	$\longrightarrow$	ir (A)
(8)	A	$\longrightarrow$	im (A)
(9)	cont (plus (A, B))	$\longrightarrow$	di (A, B)
(10)	mult (A, B)	$\longrightarrow$	inmul (A, B)
(11)	cont (plus (B, plus(A, C)))	$\longrightarrow$	in (A, B, C)
(12)	A	$\longrightarrow$	adr (cont (A))
(13)	adr(A)	$\longrightarrow$	lea (A)
(14)	A	$\longrightarrow$	mov (A)
(15)	mult (A, B)	=	mult (B, A)
(16)	A	$\longrightarrow$	mult (A, one)
(17)	plus (A, B)	=	plus (B, A)
(18)	A	$\longrightarrow$	plus(A, zero)

Figure 3: Mapping Specification using Term Rewriting Rules

Figure 3 gives an example. Identifiers with capital letters denote variables. The equations are an abbreviation for two term rewriting rules one in each direction. To make our evaluation algorithm work, all the rules have to be linear. This means every variable occurring in the rule must occur exactly once on the right hand side and once on the left hand side.

Semantically most of the rules in the example can be read as equations. The transformation rules only make evaluation easier. The equations define an equivalence relation on the terms. If all the rules are correct the equivalence of two terms implies the semantic equivalence. Suppose we have a given input term t. From all the terms equivalent to t, the target machine can evaluate only those that are legal target terms. The minimizing transformation problem is nothing else but selecting from those legal target terms one of the cheapest. What happens to the target terms equivalent to t that are not legal ? For example the second operand of the *di* operator might not be constant. The code generator makes sure that these terms are not produced, because they can not be evaluated by the processor. Nevertheless these terms do have a semantics: *di* is simply an operator adding two addresses and getting the content of that memory location.

Let us have a closer look at some of the rules. Rule 14 correctly describes the *mov* instruction doing nothing. In fact *mov* does not change the value at all. Nevertheless the code selector is forced to use the *mov* instruction to find legal target terms. An example is figure 1. There the *mov* instruction must be used, because one operand of the add instruction has to be in a register. Rule 5 is a bit more tricky. The *mov2* instruction is described as an operator that assigns a value to the address of its destination operand. This is necessary, because the destination operand is an alterable addressing mode, for example *di*. These addressing modes have been described with a *cont* operator on top, which will be neutralized by the *adr* operator. Section 4.4 contains an example derivation.

The problem we solve using the *adr* operator is the following: An addressing mode, for example *di* works differently for the destination and the source operand of a *mov2* instruction. For the destination operand *di* means adding a register and constant, as source operand it means the content of the so addressed memory location. We cannot define the source operand of the *mov2* instruction to automatically perform a *cont* because the source operand may be an immediate or direct register addressing mode. So what we do is to define the operators representing addressing modes, e.g. *di* including the *cont*. Then we define the *mov2* operator to take the address of the destination operand using the *adr* operator. The problem of the *adr* operator is that there exist terms without well defined meaning, e.g. *adr*(*one*). Well defined means that all the *adr* operators occur immediately on top of a *cont*, *di* or *ir* operator. In these cases the meaning is clear: $adr(cont(A)) = A$, $adr(di(A, B)) = plus(A, B)$ and $adr(ir(A)) = A$. The description makes sure that only well defined terms can be rewritten into legal target terms. This can be checked by looking at the rules in backward direction. Hence in derivations from intermediate code to target code only well defined terms can occur.

2.4 Variations of the Description Technique

Our example description contains two kinds of rewritings, rewritings from intermediate code into target code and rewritings transforming the intermediate code into itself. The latter specify properties of the *intermediate code* which can be exploited to generate better code. Additionally it is possible to specify rewriting rules transforming *target code* into itself. Such transformations can be used to specify properties of the target code that can be used by the code generator. Because these rules are independent of the intermediate code they belong to the machine description.

If it is not desired to split the description into an intermediate code independent machine specification and a mapping specification our technique can be used differently: The regular tree grammar can be used just the way it is used in usual tree pattern matching based code selector specifications. This becomes possible because there is no restriction saying that intermediate operators may not occur in the tree grammar. The tree rewriting rules could be used to specify algebraic properties of the intermediate code. The descriptions we obtain this way are shorter and more natural than corresponding tree pattern matching based descriptions, because many things can be expressed easier using the term rewriting rules. However we prefer the other method, because there the code selection is expressed explicitly by term transformation rules.

2.5 Comparison to Code Selection based on Tree Pattern Matching

Comparing our kind of specifications to tree pattern matching based specifications [1, 2, 3, 4, 5, 6, 7, 8, 9, 10] one difference is obvious: Our descriptions are split into two parts, a machine specification and a mapping specification. This allows the machine specification to be written once for each machine. The properties of each machine instruction it currently describes are the addressing modes or register classes allowed for each operand and the result and the cost of the instruction. It is no problem to extend the description by all the information required to generate a register allocator, an assembler, or an instruction scheduler.

The rules used by the tree pattern matching approach reduce the input term finally to a single leaf operator. Output is produced by side effects of the rules. In our approach the term transformation rules really perform the desired transformation. This makes the description easier to read and write, because the concept of term rewriting is very well known. It also aids correctness proofs of the specifications. Using term rewriting rules has another very important advantage: The result of a rule can be further processed by other rules. Note that this is not possible with tree pattern matching. If a rule is taken then the code associated with the rule is emitted as a side effect and cannot be transformed by any other rule.

This feature of our technique makes descriptions much simpler. For example suppose we have a machine without a negate instruction but with a three address subtract instruction and a register that always contains zero. This can be handled by the rule: $negate(A) \rightarrow minus(zero, A)$. You might argue that it can easily be handled by some preprocessing of the intermediate language. However we think including the preprocessing into the description makes things much easier and more consistent. Suppose the machine contains a strange *neg* instruction that works only with some specific addressing modes, which makes it sometimes cheaper to use negate and sometimes cheaper to use subtract depending on the operand. Then preprocessing is no longer possible, because either decision, replacing the *negate* operator or not replacing it will produce suboptimal code under some circumstances. Our method can handle the problem simply by writing $negate(A) \rightarrow neg(A)$. The *neg* instruction has to be described in the machine specification as well as the addressing mode it can be used with.

As this example showed, it is possible to implement an intermediate operator not only by giving an appropriate machine instruction (or a sequence of instructions) but also by reduction to another intermediate term. Exploiting this opportunity, one can process a bigger class of intermediate languages, and it is easier to adapt the specification after changes of the IR. For example one can easily describe the operator *localvar*, which returns the address of a local variable, by $localvar(A) \rightarrow plus(bb, A)$.

It is also possible to use term transformation rules to specify possible transformations on intermediate code level. For example the commutativity of an operator can easily be expressed, or a rule like $not(not(A)) \rightarrow A$ can be specified. Another very important point is factoring out certain properties in order to get small descriptions: Instead of one rule $plus(A, zero) \rightarrow A$ tree pattern matching needs several rules $plus(Ar, zero) \rightarrow Ar$; $plus(Dr, zero) \rightarrow Dr$; ...One such rule is needed for every nonterminal. Very good examples for the power of our description techniques are the rules (16) and (18) of figure 3:

(16) A ⟶ mult(A,one)
(18) A ⟶ plus(A,zero)

At the first glance these rules look senseless, as they insert additional operations which usually make things worse. They are also not terminating but the code selector takes care of this and applies them only as often as necessary. One can just look at them as algebraic properties of plus and mult. Consider the following rules taken from the machine and mapping specifications of figures 2 and 3:

	Mea	::=	in(Ar,C,Imul)
	Imul	::=	inmul(Dr,Sc) | inmul(Ar,Sc)
(10)	mult(A,B)	$\longrightarrow$	inmul(A,B)
(11)	cont(plus(B,plus(A,C)))	$\longrightarrow$	in(A,B,C)

They describe the indirect indexed addressing mode. This addressing mode adds the content of a base register, an offset, and the content of an index register multiplied by a scale factor (which can be 1,2,4, or 8). Of course this addressing mode can be used also to add two registers by using zero for the displacement and scale factor one, or it can be used with displacement zero and an arbitrary scale factor, or it can be used to add two registers and a displacement by using scale factor one. All these possibilities follow from the two simple algebraic properties described by rule 16 and 18. For example suppose B is an expression which later goes into an address register and A goes into a data register then we can derive:

$$
\begin{array}{ll}
\text{cont (plus (B, A))} & \xrightarrow{18} \\
\text{cont (plus (plus(B, A), zero))} & \xrightarrow{17} \\
\text{cont (plus (zero, plus(B, A)))} & \xrightarrow{11} \\
\text{in (B, zero, A)} & \xrightarrow{16} \\
\text{in (B, zero, mult(A, one))} & \xrightarrow{10} \\
\text{in (B, zero, inmul(A, one))} &
\end{array}
$$

The result *in (B, zero, inmul(A, one))* is the legal representation of the indexed addressing mode of the 68k according to the machine specification [2]. Tree pattern matching based specifications would have to write rules for each of these cases:

Mea ::= cont(plus(C,plus(Ar,mult(Dr,Sc))))	emit in(Ar,C,inmul(Dr,Sc))
Mea ::= cont(plus(C,plus(Ar_1,mult(Ar_2,Sc))))	emit in(Ar_1,C,inmul(Ar_2,Sc))
Mea ::= cont(plus(C,plus(Ar,Dr)))	emit in(Ar,C,inmul(Dr,one))
Mea ::= cont(plus(C,plus(Ar_1,Ar_2)))	emit in(Ar_1,C,inmul(Ar_2,Sc))
Mea ::= cont(plus(Ar,mult(Dr,Sc)))	emit in(Ar,zero,inmul(Dr,Sc))
Mea ::= cont(plus(Ar_1,mult(Ar_2,Sc)))	emit in(Ar_1,zero,inmul(Ar_2,Sc))
Mea ::= cont(plus(Ar,Dr))	emit in(Ar,zero,inmul(Dr,one))
Mea ::= cont(plus(Ar_1,Ar_2))	emit in(Ar_1,zero,inmul(Ar_2,one))

Writing these rules we have ignored the fact that *plus* and *mult* are declared to be commutative, which would make rule numbers explode. However tree pattern matching based code generator systems usually have a way to handle this. Of course it is possible to use factoring to make the specification a bit smaller:

Mult	::=	mult(Dr, Sc)	emit inmul (Dr,Sc)
Mult	::=	mult(Ar, Sc)	emit inmul (Ar,Sc)
Mult	::=	Dr	emit inmul (Dr,one)
Mult	::=	Ar	emit inmul (Ar,one)
Mea	::=	cont(plus(C, plus(Ar, Mult)))	emit in (Ar,C,Mult)
Mea	::=	cont(plus(Ar, Mult))	emit in (Ar,zero,Mult)

[2]Note that this representation is more complex than necessary because the current implementation can not handle operators of arity bigger than three.

2.6 Other Related Work on Code Generation

The idea to describe code selection using tree pattern matching and term rewriting rules is quite old. In [11] Cattell describes these ideas and a system based on them. However Cattell uses the term rewriting rules only to express algebraic laws of the intermediate code, the code production itself is performed by the pattern matching rules. In contrast we propose to use the tree rewriting rules besides the specification of algebraic properties also to express the mapping from intermediate code to target code.

The main difference, however, is the evaluation algorithm. Cattell uses an heuristic search algorithm to apply the rules in a top down manner. It is not guaranteed that the algorithm always applies the rules the right way to produce the best possible code. For example only a small part of the input tree is used to decide which rule should be applied next. In contrast our method makes sure that the rules are always applied the best way. Finally the efficiency of the generated code generators is better with our approach, because Cattells generated code generator still performs the pattern matching at execution time and does not use the newst methods on tree pattern matching.

Compared to tree pattern matching an in some respects more powerful description method is the BURS theory, presented in [12]. It can handle a bigger class of rules, which for example allows commutativity. However BURS–specifications are still very similar to the common tree pattern matching based descriptions. As BURS can produce very efficient code generators [12, 13] it is well suited to finally implement the code selector descriptions our generator produces as output.

The way we use to describe code selection is partly derived from Robert Giegerich's approach [14, 15]. Like his descriptions our specifications consist of two parts. One part describes the target terms. We use a regular tree grammar, and he uses an order sorted type system. Both mechanisms are similar for this purpose. Giegerich uses a derivor to describe the mapping from machine code to intermediate code. Hence the inversed derivor does the desired mapping. Giegerich shows that a derivor can be inverted by using the usual pattern matching based systems. An inverted derivor however can be seen as a special restricted term rewriting system. So our method can be seen as an extension. The rules of an inverted derivor on the other hand are restricted so that the left hand side has only operators of the intermediate representation and the right hand side has only target operators So it is impossible that a target operator produced by a rule application can be transformed further by another rule application. Hence Giegerich's approach does not have all of the advantages presented in section 2.5. Giegerich's approach tackles some more problems besides code selection, for example register allocation.

3 The Generation Algorithm

The problem to generate a code selector from our kind of specification is hard. We will give a solution, which works, at least for small examples at the moment. First let us formulate the problem more precisely:

> A term rewriting system T and a *weighted* (i. e. rules are annotated with costs) regular tree grammar G are given. We use the term

> *transformation problem* for the task to transform an input tree t using the rules of T into an output tree s that is in the language of G. If we additionally require that s has minimal cost according to G we call the problem the *minimizing transformation problem.*
>
> The task of a code generator generator is to produce an efficient program that solves the *minimizing transformation problem.*

In our case the TRS T is the mapping specification. It has none of the nice properties like confluence or termination that are required to apply standard term rewriting techniques. Confluence is not desired at all, because there are always many possibilities to produce code for an input tree, and we want to be able to describe this. It should be the task of the code selector to select the best alternative. The mapping specification is also not terminating because we want to write equations, to specify commutativity, and to use rules with a variable as left hand side.

Many problems can occur with such a general term rewriting problem: Rewriting may stop at a dead end where no rule is applicable any more but the result is no legal target term. It may also happen that rewriting gets caught in an infinite loop never reaching a legal target term. Even if we have a strategy to apply rules to find a legal target term there is no guarantee that it is optimal. In extreme cases it is necessary to inspect the whole input tree before a decision which rule to apply next can be made.

In general it is even undecidable if the transformation problem is solvable for a given input term, because the problem is more general than the word problem.

3.1 Informal Overview

Our solution is a generator that produces an non–deterministic bottom up tree transducer, which performs the desired transformation. Such a tree transducer is a conventional pattern matching based code selector specification where the action parts of the rules are used to construct the output tree in a bottom up fashion. So our system can be seen as a preprocessor that generates conventional code generator specifications. All the techniques known how to build generators for them [2, 9, 12, 13, 16] can be reused. This makes sure that the final code selector is very efficient.

So the real hard problem has been shifted into the generator, which has to produce the tree transducer from the description. The central point of this paper is the theory and the algorithm used in the generator.

The algorithm first builds a bigger tree transducer that can rewrite all terms that can be rewritten into legal target terms. Afterwards the transducer is restricted to the terms representing intermediate code statements. The algorithm starts with a trivial tree transducer that can transform only legal target terms into legal target terms. So it is just the identity function on legal target terms. Then this tree transducer is successively extended to accept more terms: Suppose there exist terms t and s, t can be rewritten into s by one rule application of the term rewriting system but only s can be transformed into a legal target term by the tree transducer. Then we extend the tree transducer, so that it accepts t also. This process is iterated until no terms s and t with the properties required above exist any more. Then one can prove that the tree transducer can process all terms that can be rewritten into legal target terms. That means we have found a solution.

It may happen that the algorithm does not terminate, and this happens for quite a lot of complex term rewriting systems. However, it does terminate for a big class of systems that are used for code selection. When the algorithm has terminated, the tree transducer can be restricted to accept only terms of the intermediate language. This makes it smaller and easier to implement.

The algorithm described will produce a tree transducer that can generate code, but the code produced may not be optimal. However the algorithm can be extended to *weighted* tree languages that will then produce a *weighted* tree transducer that always finds the target term of minimal cost.

3.2 Theoretical Background

3.2.1 Terms

A term is a labeled directed tree. The labels are named operators and are taken from a finite alphabet Σ and have a fixed arity $\alpha(\theta)$ (for $\theta \in \Sigma$). Where Σ and α are obvious we simply write T for the set of all terms with alphabet $\langle \Sigma, \alpha \rangle$. For a set S disjunct from Σ let $T(S)$ denote the set of all terms with alphabet $\Sigma \cup S$. Operators of S have arity zero.

A term stub is a term of $T(\{X\})$ that contains X exactly once. X is a fixed symbol different from all other symbols in Σ. The set of all term stubs is denoted by T_X. The term $t \circ s$ with $t \in T_X$ denotes the term one gets by replacing the X in t by s. If s is in T then $t \circ s$ is also in T; otherwise if s is in T_X then $t \circ s$ is in T_X.

3.2.2 Term Rewriting

A *Term Rewriting System* (TRS) is a tuple $(\langle \Sigma, \alpha \rangle, \Xi, V)$ where V is a finite set of variables. Ξ is a finite set of rules $l \to r$ with $l, r \in T(V)$. The derivation relation $\xrightarrow{\Xi}$ and its transitive and reflexive closure $\xRightarrow{\Xi}$ are defined in the usual way: A rule $l \to r$ is applicable on a tree t if there exists a substitution σ and a term stub u with $t = u \circ \sigma l$. The result of the rule application is $s = u \circ \sigma r$.

A term $t \in T(V)$ is called linear if each variable occurs at most once in t. A rule is called left/right linear, if the left/right hand side is linear. It is called linear, if both sides are linear, and if every variable occurring on the left hand side also occurs on the right hand side and vice versa. A TRS is (left/right) linear if all rules are (left/right) linear. A TRS can also be weighted by assigning a cost to each rule.

3.2.3 Tree Semi–Thue–Systems

A tree Semi–Thue–System (STS) is a tuple $STS = (\langle \Sigma, \alpha \rangle, \Pi)$. $\langle \Sigma, \alpha \rangle$ is a finite alphabet and $\Pi \subset T \times T$ is a (possibly infinite) system of rules. A rule $(l, r) \in \Pi$ is usually written in the form $l \to r$ or sometimes $l ::= r$. STS defines a derivation relation $\xrightarrow{\Pi}$ in the following way: $s \xrightarrow{\Pi} t$ holds iff there exists a term stub u such that $s = u \circ l$, $t = u \circ r$, and $l \to r \in \Pi$ holds. $\xRightarrow{\Pi}$ denotes the reflexive and transitive closure of $\xrightarrow{\Pi}$.

3.2.4 *Regular Tree Languages*

A regular tree grammar $G = (\langle\Sigma,\alpha\rangle, N, \Pi, Z)$ consists of a finite set of non-terminals N with $N \cap \Sigma = \emptyset$, a start symbol $Z \in N$, and a finite system of rules $\Pi \subset N \times T(N)$. The rules look like $l ::= r$ with $l \in N$ and $r \in T(N)$. $(\langle\Sigma \cup N, \alpha'\rangle, \Pi)$ with $\alpha'(\theta) = \alpha(\theta)$ for $\theta \in \Sigma$ and $\alpha'(\theta) = 0$ for $\theta \in N$ is a tree semi–thue–system and defines the derivation relation $\stackrel{\Pi}{\rightarrow}$. G generates the tree language $L(G) = \{z \in T | Z \stackrel{\Pi}{\Rightarrow} z\}$. In contrast to a context free grammar, a regular tree grammar generates a set of terms rather than a set of strings.

The class of tree languages defined by regular tree grammars is named the set of regular tree languages. It has very pleasant properties, just like the regular string languages: It is closed under union, intersection, difference, and complementation, it contains all finite sets of terms, and it can be checked whether two elements are equal or subset of each other [17, 18].

3.2.5 *Bottom–Up Tree Automata*

An *non–deterministic tree automaton* (see [19]) $\mathcal{A} = (\langle\Sigma,\alpha\rangle, \mathcal{S}, \Pi, f)$ consists of a set of states $\mathcal{S}$, a system of rules Π and a final state $f \in \mathcal{S}$. Rules have the form $\theta s_1 \ldots s_{\alpha(\theta)} \rightarrow s_0$ or $s_1 \rightarrow s_0$ (Chain Rules) with $\theta \in \Sigma$, $s_i \in \mathcal{S}$. $(\langle\Sigma \cup \mathcal{S}, \alpha'\rangle, \Pi)$ with $\alpha'(\theta) = \alpha(\theta)$ for $\theta \in \Sigma$ and $\alpha'(\theta) = 0$ for $\theta \in N$ is a tree semi–thue–system and defines the derivation relation $\stackrel{\Pi}{\rightarrow}$. It accepts $L(\mathcal{A}) = \{t \in T | t \stackrel{\Pi}{\Rightarrow} f\}$. An non–deterministic tree automaton is called *finite* if $\mathcal{S}$ and therefore Π is finite.

A tree automaton is called *deterministic* if it has no chain rules and if from the equality of the left hand sides of two rules follows the equality of the rules. For each finite regular tree grammar a finite non–deterministic automaton can be build and vice versa. One can also produce a deterministic tree automaton from a finite non–deterministic one by using the subset construction.

The language $L(s)$ of a state $s \in \mathcal{S}$ is $L(s) = \{t \in T | t \stackrel{\Pi}{\Rightarrow} s\}$. The context $L_C(s)$ of a state $s \in \mathcal{S}$ is $L_C(s) = \{t \in T_X | t \circ s \stackrel{\Pi}{\Rightarrow} f\}$. For two states $g, h \in \mathcal{S}$ we define the relation "$\prec$" as follows:

$$g \prec h \text{ iff } L_C(g) \subset L_C(h) \tag{1}$$

Obviously $\prec$ is transitive and reflexive. The equivalence relation $g \sim h :\Longleftrightarrow g \prec h \wedge h \prec g$ is just the relation needed for minimization of the automaton [20]. It is possible to calculate $\prec$, however it is not easy and not very efficient. We will not go into details here.

For deterministic automata there exists at most one state a given term t can be derived to. So we can define the (partial) transition function $\phi : T(\mathcal{S}) \rightarrow \mathcal{S}$ with $\phi(t)$ is the $s \in \mathcal{S}$ with $t \stackrel{\Pi}{\Rightarrow} s$. ϕ can always be made a total function by adding an error state to $\mathcal{A}$. We will assume this in the rest of the paper.

An automaton $\mathcal{U} = (\langle\Sigma,\alpha\rangle, \mathcal{S}, \Pi, f)$ is called a *subautomaton* of $\mathcal{A} = (\langle\Sigma,\alpha\rangle, \mathcal{S}', \Pi', f)$ (written as $\mathcal{U} \subset \mathcal{A}$) if $\mathcal{S} \subset \mathcal{S}'$ and $\Pi \subset \Pi'$ holds. Then $L(\mathcal{U}) \subset L(\mathcal{A})$ holds for a (possibly infinite) automaton $\mathcal{A}$.

One can define weighted tree grammars and automata. They additionally have a cost value $\beta(\pi)$ associated with every rule π. The cost of a derivation is defined as the sum of the costs of all rule applications in that derivation. A weighted automaton defines a weighted tree language, that is a function

$M : T \rightarrow \mathbb{N} \cup \{\infty\}$. $M(t)$ is the cost of a minimal derivation or it is ∞ if no derivation exists. This can be seen as an extension to the unweighted tree languages because a language L can be seen as a function $T \rightarrow$ Bool, which assigns true to the terms in the language and false to the terms which are not in the language. For two weighted tree languages M and N we define $M \subset N$ as $M \subset N :\Longleftrightarrow \forall t \in T : N(t) \leq M(t)$. For a cost value $c \in \mathbb{N}$ and a weighted tree language M the tree language $N = M + c$ is defined by $\forall t \in T : N(t) = M(t) + c$.

The subset construction can be applied on finite weighted non-deterministic tree automata, however the number of states of the deterministic automaton can become infinite. Fortunately this usually does not happen when considering code selection [9]. Efficient tree parsers can be constructed by known code selector generation techniques, either by implementing the deterministic automaton dynamically [1, 3], as the dynamic programming algorithm for code selection does, or statically [9], which requires the deterministic automaton having a finite number of states.

3.3 Regular Languages Closed under a TRS

This section will present the most important subalgorithm needed for the main algorithm described in section 3.4.1. We present first non-weighted and then weighted systems.

3.3.1 The Non-Weighted Case

Definition 1 *A regular tree language L is* closed *under a TRS $(\langle\Sigma, \alpha\rangle, \Xi, V)$ iff for all $t \in L, s \in T : t \xrightarrow{\Xi} s$ implies $s \in L$. L is closed under a rule $\pi \in \Xi$ iff for all $t \in L, s \in T : t \xrightarrow{\pi} s$ implies $s \in L$.*

It is obvious that a tree language is closed under a TRS iff it is closed under all rules of this TRS. Induction leads to the following condition, which is equivalent to L being closed under TRS: for all $t \in L, s \in T : t \xrightarrow{\Xi}{}^{*} s$ implies $s \in L$.

This closure property is very important: When we have found a tree language L that is closed according to a TRS and if we know that all possible inputs of the TRS are in L then we know that all terms we can derive are also in L. We will now give an algorithm which checks the closure–property. The main algorithm of section 3.4 will use this algorithm, mainly to calculate counterexamples.

The closure–test algorithm we want to present here uses a deterministic finite tree automaton to represent the regular tree language. As the efficiency of the algorithm is highly dependent on the number of states of the automaton it is good to minimize the automaton first. There are also algorithms working on non–deterministic automata. They promise to be much faster, because non–deterministic automata have fewer states, but they are also much more complicated and have some restrictions like requiring linear right hand sides.

Let the deterministic finite tree automaton $\mathcal{A} = (\langle\Sigma, \alpha\rangle, \mathcal{S}, \Pi, f)$ define the tree language $L = L(\mathcal{A})$. We assume that $\mathcal{A}$ contains no unreachable states. That means for all $s \in \mathcal{S}$ the language $L(s)$ is not empty. Let ϕ be the transition function of $\mathcal{A}$ and let $\pi = l \rightarrow r$ be a term rewriting rule. It has to be tested if $L(\mathcal{A})$ is closed under π.

Let R be the set of substitutions σ that replace every variable in π by a state in $\mathcal{S}$. If π contains no variables then R contains only the identity. Obviously R is finite because π contains only a finite number of variables and $\mathcal{S}$ is also finite. $L(\mathcal{A})$ is closed under the rule $\pi = l \rightarrow r$ iff

$$\forall \sigma \in R \ : \ \phi(\sigma l) \prec \phi(\sigma r) \tag{2}$$

Proof that $L(\mathcal{A})$ is closed follows from (2):

Suppose we have a given term $t \in L(\mathcal{A})$ and $\pi = l \rightarrow r$ is applicable on t. Then t has the form $t = u \circ \sigma' l$. σ' is the ground substitution used when applying the rule. After applying the rule we get $s = u \circ \sigma' r$. We have to prove that s is in $L(\mathcal{A})$. Now we define the substitution $\sigma \in R$ as $\sigma v := \phi(\sigma' v)$ for all variables v contained in π. As $\mathcal{A}$ is deterministic $\phi(\sigma' l) = \phi(\sigma l)$ holds and $t = u \circ \sigma' l \in L(\mathcal{A})$ implies $u \in L_C(\phi(\sigma l))$. From (1) and (2) we know $L_C(\phi(\sigma l)) \subset L_C(\phi(\sigma r))$. So $u \in L_C(\phi(\sigma r))$ holds, which means $u \circ \sigma' r \in L(\mathcal{A})$.

The property (2) can be tested by enumerating all elements of R and checking the condition. This is the basic idea of the closure-test algorithm. If the test fails we get a substitution σ that tells us where it failed. This information can be used to build a counterexample: $s, t \in T, t \in L(\mathcal{A}), s \notin L(\mathcal{A}), t \overset{l \rightarrow r}{\rightarrow} s$.

3.3.2 The Weighted Case

The closure property can be extended to weighted tree automata and weighted term rewriting systems. Our closure–test algorithm requires a deterministic weighted automaton. So it works only if a deterministic automaton exists, which is not always the case for weighted automata. However it is usually the case when considering code selection. It is not clear if there exists always a closure–test algorithm.

Definition 2 *A weighted regular tree language M is* closed *under a rule $\pi \in \Xi$ of a weighted TRS $(\langle \Sigma, \alpha \rangle, \Xi, V, \beta)$ iff for all $t, s \in T : t \overset{\pi}{\rightarrow} s$ implies $M(s) \leq M(t) + \beta(\pi)$. The TRS is said to be closed iff all rules are closed.*

It follows by induction that for all $t, s \in T : t \overset{\Xi}{\Rightarrow} s$ with cost c implies $M(s) \leq M(t) + c$.

To intuitively understand this property look at non–weighted TRS, that means $\beta(\pi) = 0$ for all rules $\pi \in \Xi$. We interpret the weighted tree language M as a cost function on terms. Then being closed means that applying some rules cannot make costs worse, so costs will become better or stay the same.

The closure–test can be extended to weighted tree grammars, provided we have a finite deterministic automaton $\mathcal{A} = (\langle \Sigma, \alpha \rangle, \mathcal{S}, \Xi, f, \beta)$. For a deterministic weighted automaton we need besides the transition function ϕ a cost function $\overline{\phi} : T(S) \rightarrow \mathbb{N}$. $\overline{\phi}(s)$ returns the cost value needed to reduce an input term s to $\phi(s)$.

Then M_C is defined as a function mapping states of $\mathcal{S}$ to weighted regular tree languages. It corresponds to L_C in the non-weighted case. For $s \in \mathcal{S}$

$M_C(s)$ is a weighted regular tree language, which is a function assigning to each term $t \in T_X$ the cost of a minimal derivation $t \circ s \stackrel{\Xi}{\Rightarrow} f$.

M is closed under the rule $\pi = l \rightarrow r$ iff

$$\forall \sigma \in R : M_C(\sigma l) + \overline{\phi}(\sigma l) \sqsubset M_C(\sigma r) + \overline{\phi}(\sigma r) + \beta(\pi)$$

The calculation of the "$\sqsubset$" relation is even more difficult than the calculation of the $\prec$ relation in the non-weighted case.

3.4 The Transformation Problem

3.4.1 Term Rewriting Systems with Regular Output

A TRS with weighted regular output consists of a TRS $(\langle\Sigma, \alpha\rangle, \Xi, V)$ and a weighted finite tree automaton $\mathcal{A} = (\langle\Sigma, \alpha\rangle, \mathcal{S}, \Pi, f, \beta)$. Such a kind of system models the code selector specifications proposed in section 2. The weighted tree grammar of section 2 can easily be transformed into the non-deterministic automaton $\mathcal{A}$.

The minimal transformation problem is to find for a given input term $i \in T$ a result $t \in T$ with $i \stackrel{\Xi}{\Rightarrow} t$ and the cost $M_{\mathcal{A}}(t)$ is minimal or to prove that $M_{\mathcal{A}}(t) = \infty$ for all $i \stackrel{\Xi}{\Rightarrow} t$, $t \in T$. We want to produce a tree transducer that performs exactly this transformation.

3.4.2 Reduction to a Term Acception Problem

The first step is to reduce the term transformation problem we have so far to a term acception problem. By acception problem we mean the problem to reduce a given input term i to a single leaf operator f. As we will see, the derivation of the acception problem can be used to solve the transformation problem.

This construction works in the weighted case only for linear TRS. In the non-weighted case one can allow some kind of non-linearity on the right hand sides. We look at the term rewriting system *TRS'*$= (\langle\Sigma \cup \mathcal{S}, \alpha\rangle, \Pi \cup \Xi, V, \beta)$. The cost $\beta(\xi)$ is defined to be zero for $\xi \in \Xi$. Now we look for derivations $i \stackrel{\Pi\cup\Xi}{\Rightarrow} f$. Note that *TRS'* works in $T(\mathcal{S})$ rather than T.

If we have found a minimal derivation $i \stackrel{\Pi\cup\Xi}{\Rightarrow} f$ in *TRS'* we can construct a derivation $i \stackrel{\Xi}{\Rightarrow} v \stackrel{\Pi}{\Rightarrow} f$. v is the desired t. $v \in L(\mathcal{A})$ holds because $v \stackrel{\Pi}{\Rightarrow} f$. We will give the construction now and tackle the problem how to find the derivation $i \stackrel{\Pi\cup\Xi}{\Rightarrow} f$ in the next section.

Consider the following situation $u \stackrel{\pi}{\rightarrow} v \stackrel{\xi}{\rightarrow} w$ with $\pi \in \Pi$ and $\xi \in \Xi$. The right hand side of π is only a state. But states do not occur on the left hand side of ξ. And ξ is linear by definition. Hence we can swap the two rule applications and get $u \stackrel{\xi}{\rightarrow} v' \stackrel{\pi}{\rightarrow} w$.

Now suppose we have a derivation $i \stackrel{\Pi\cup\Xi}{\Rightarrow} f$ of minimal cost. We can apply the swapping until we get a derivation $i \stackrel{\Xi}{\rightarrow} v \stackrel{\Pi}{\rightarrow} f$. That is all we want to have: let $t := v$. Then $i \stackrel{\Xi}{\Rightarrow} t$ holds and $t \in L(\mathcal{A})$ because of $v \stackrel{\Pi}{\Rightarrow} f$. $M_{\mathcal{A}}(t)$ is also minimal, because the cost of a derivation does not change during swapping of rules.

$$
\begin{array}{rcl}
S & = & \{[t] \mid t \in T(\langle \Sigma, \alpha \rangle)\} \\
f & = & [z] \\
\Pi & = & \{\theta[t_1] \ldots [t_{\alpha(\theta)}] \to [\theta t_1 \ldots t_{\alpha(\theta)}] \mid t_i \in T(\langle \Sigma, \alpha \rangle), \theta \in \Sigma\} \\
 & \cup & \left\{[t] \to [s] \;\middle|\; t \overset{\Xi}{\to} s\right\} \\
\mathcal{B} & = & (\langle \Sigma, \alpha \rangle, S, \Pi, f)
\end{array}
$$

Figure 4: Infinite Automaton accepting Q

If we have a non-weighted automaton $\mathcal{A}$ this transformation can be generalized to non-right linear systems: During swapping it then might become necessary to copy the π rule application several times or to delete it.

3.5 Solving the Acception Problem

Until now we have considered the weighted and the non weighted case together. As the following things become more complicated only the non-weighted case will be presented in depth. Although for code selection we are interested only in the weighted case, it is easier to understand this way. Section 3.5.5 will then explain how the non-weighted case can be extended to the weighted case.

The problem we address in this section is the following: We have a (non-weighted for the moment) TRS $(\langle \Sigma, \alpha \rangle, \Xi, V)$ and a leaf operator $z \in \Sigma$. For a given input term we are looking for derivations $t \overset{\Xi}{\Rightarrow} z$. The set of all terms for which this is possible is named $Q = \{t \in T | t \overset{\Xi}{\Rightarrow} z\}$.

3.5.1 Using Infinite Automata

We can easily give an infinite tree automaton which accepts Q. Figure 4 gives one. The states are written $[t]$ where t is a term. So the set of states of $\mathcal{B}$ is isomorphic to the set of all terms and hence infinite. If we have a derivation in $\mathcal{B}$ accepting an input term t we can easily construct the desired derivation in the TRS. Intuitively this works by writing down the derivation in $\mathcal{B}$ and leaving out all square brackets.

So what we have to do is to parse a given input term using $\mathcal{B}$. Of course an infinite automaton can not be implemented. In general it is even undecidable if one state can be derived from another by a sequence of chain rules. But there are classes of TRS where it works out fine:

3.5.2 Finite Subautomata

Let us have a look on finite subautomata $\mathcal{U} \subset \mathcal{B}$. As $\mathcal{U}$ is a subautomaton we know $L(\mathcal{U}) \subset L(\mathcal{B}) = Q$. And because $\mathcal{U}$ is finite it can be implemented. That means for a given input term $t \in L(\mathcal{U})$ we can determine a derivation in $\mathcal{U}$. This derivation is also a derivation in $\mathcal{B}$, because the rules and states of $\mathcal{U}$ are just subsets of those in $\mathcal{B}$. Hence for each term $t \in L(\mathcal{U})$ the transformation problem can be solved.

If we can find a subautomaton $\mathcal{U}$ with $L(\mathcal{U}) = L(\mathcal{B})$ then we have solved our problem. There are of course many cases where such a subautomaton does not exist at all. In fact, its existence implies that Q is a regular tree language (because it is accepted by the finite tree automaton $\mathcal{U}$) which is a proper restriction. However it is still sufficient for code selection.

Let $\overleftarrow{\Xi}$ denote the set of rules one gets by swapping the left and right side of all rules in Ξ. Now let us deal with the problem how to check whether $L(\mathcal{U}) = L(\mathcal{B})$:

$$L(\mathcal{U}) = L(\mathcal{B}) \text{ iff } L(\mathcal{U}) \text{ is closed under } \overleftarrow{\Xi} \text{ and } z \in L(\mathcal{U}) \tag{3}$$

The proof is quite simple:

Suppose $L(\mathcal{U}) = L(\mathcal{B}) = Q = \{t \in T | t \overset{\Xi}{\Rightarrow} z\}$. Then $z \in L(\mathcal{U}) = Q$ is trivially true. And Q is closed under $\overleftarrow{\Xi}$ because taking $s \in Q$ and $s' \in T$ with $s \overset{\overleftarrow{\Xi}}{\rightarrow} s'$ means $s' \overset{\Xi}{\rightarrow} s \overset{\Xi}{\Rightarrow} z$ and therefore $s' \in Q$.

In the other direction we have to prove $L(\mathcal{U}) = L(\mathcal{B})$. Assume $t \in L(\mathcal{B}) = Q$. That means $t \overset{\Xi}{\Rightarrow} z$, which is equivalent to $z \overset{\overleftarrow{\Xi}}{\Rightarrow} t$. As $z \in L(\mathcal{U})$ and $L(\mathcal{U})$ is closed it follows $t \in L(\mathcal{U})$. Together with $\mathcal{U} \subset \mathcal{B}$ it follows $L(\mathcal{U}) = L(\mathcal{B})$.

The right hand side of (3) can be checked using the closure–test algorithm of section 3.3.1. We will call a subautomaton that satisfies $L(\mathcal{U}) = L(\mathcal{B})$ a *closed subautomaton*. Now we will treat the problem how to construct closed subautomata.

3.5.3 Construction of Closed Subautomata

Since we have an algorithm that tests if a subautomaton fulfills our requirements we can trivially give a completely unusable algorithm to determine such a subautomaton: enumerate all subautomata and test them. That can be done a bit more intelligently using the following fact: Suppose we have another subautomaton $\mathcal{V} \subset \mathcal{B}$ with $\mathcal{U} \subset \mathcal{V}$. Then $L(\mathcal{U}) \subset L(\mathcal{V}) \subset L(\mathcal{B})$ holds. Suppose $\mathcal{U}$ satisfies $L(\mathcal{U}) = L(\mathcal{B})$. Then $L(\mathcal{V}) = L(\mathcal{B})$ follows.

So when we are just looking for an algorithm to find one not necessarily minimal subautomaton $\mathcal{U}$ with $L(\mathcal{U}) = L(\mathcal{B})$ we do not need to enumerate all subautomata. It is enough if we give an infinite sequence of subautomata $\mathcal{V}_i$ for $i = 1, 2, \ldots$ with

$$\forall \mathcal{U} \subset \mathcal{B} \exists i \in \mathbb{N} : \mathcal{U} \subset \mathcal{V}_i \tag{4}$$

A *complete* subautomaton $\mathcal{U}$ of $\mathcal{B}$ with a given state set $\mathcal{S}$ contains all the rules of $\mathcal{B}$ that refer to only states of $\mathcal{S}$. Now we enumerate all terms in T: $t_1, t_2, t_3, \ldots$. We define $\mathcal{V}_j$ as the complete subautomaton with state set $\{[z], [t_1], \ldots, [t_j]\}$. This sequence satisfies (4). Hence we generate the $\mathcal{V}_j$ consecutively and test them. Condition (4) makes sure that the algorithm terminates iff there exists a closed subautomaton. The algorithm is therefore a semi-decision algorithm.

3.5.4 A More Efficient Algorithm

To sum up the algorithm we have so far: We start with the complete subautomaton $\mathcal{U}$ of $\mathcal{B}$ that contains only the state $[z]$. Then we successively add states until we reach a closed subautomaton. Now we intend to select the new states more carefully (see figure 5).

Therefore we use the output of the closure–test algorithm: an example for that $\mathcal{U}$ is not closed. Such a counterexample is given by two terms t and s with $t \in L(\mathcal{U}), s \in T$ but $s \notin L(\mathcal{U})$ and $t \overset{\overleftarrow{r \to l}}{\to} s$. Note that $r \to l$ is a rule of $\overleftarrow{\text{TRS}}$, so $l \to r$ is in TRS. We assume $r \to l$ to be linear. Because of the definition of rule application there is an $u \in T_X$ and a substitution σ with $t = u \circ \sigma r$ and $s = u \circ \sigma l$. As t is in $L(\mathcal{U})$ we can construct a corresponding derivation d in the finite non–deterministic automaton $\mathcal{U}$. d looks like $t = u \circ \sigma r \overset{\mathcal{U}}{\Rightarrow} [z]$. It first reduces the subterms of t that are bound to the variables. Let σ' be a substitution that replaces variables by states in a way such that d has the form $t = u \circ \sigma r \overset{\mathcal{U}}{\Rightarrow} u \circ \sigma' r \overset{\mathcal{U}}{\Rightarrow} [z]$. For all variables v in $l \to r$ $\sigma v \overset{\Pi}{\Rightarrow} \sigma' v$ and $\sigma' v \in \mathcal{S}$ holds. The derivation d reduces $\sigma' r$ to some state $[s_0]$. So we get finally the form $t = u \circ \sigma r \overset{\mathcal{U}}{\Rightarrow} u \circ \sigma' r \overset{\mathcal{U}}{\Rightarrow} u \circ [s_0] \overset{\mathcal{U}}{\Rightarrow} [z]$.

In that situation $\sigma' l \overset{\mathcal{U}}{\Rightarrow} [s_0]$ does not hold, because otherwise we would have the derivation $s = u \circ \sigma l \overset{\mathcal{U}}{\Rightarrow} u \circ \sigma' l \overset{\mathcal{U}}{\Rightarrow} u \circ [s_0] \overset{\mathcal{U}}{\Rightarrow} [z]$, which would mean $s \in L(\mathcal{U})$. Now we will give a derivation $\sigma' l \overset{\mathcal{B}}{\Rightarrow} [s_0]$ in $\mathcal{B}$ instead of $\mathcal{U}$. Let σ'' be a substitution with $\sigma'' v = w$ iff $\sigma' v = [w]$ for all variables v in $l \to r$. Then $\sigma' l \overset{\mathcal{B}}{\Rightarrow} [\sigma'' l]$ by using non-chain-rules of $\mathcal{B}$. On $\sigma'' l$ our rule $l \to r$ is applicable leading to $\sigma'' r$. From $\sigma' r \overset{\mathcal{B}}{\Rightarrow} [s_0]$ we can conclude $\sigma'' r \overset{TRS}{\Rightarrow} s_0$. So we have the derivation $s = u \circ \sigma l \overset{\mathcal{U}}{\Rightarrow} u \circ \sigma' l \overset{\mathcal{B}}{\Rightarrow} u \circ [\sigma'' l] \overset{\mathcal{B}}{\Rightarrow} u \circ [\sigma'' r] \overset{\mathcal{B}}{\Rightarrow} u \circ [s_0] \overset{\mathcal{U}}{\Rightarrow} [z]$.

Now we know that there is no derivation $\sigma' l \overset{\mathcal{U}}{\Rightarrow} [s_0]$ in $\mathcal{U}$ but there is one in $\mathcal{B}$. All we have to do is to add all the states occurring in that derivation including the corresponding transitions to $\mathcal{U}$ leading to $\mathcal{U}'$. Then we are sure that there is a derivation $\sigma' l \overset{\mathcal{U}'}{\Rightarrow} [s_0]$. Hence $s \in L(\mathcal{U}')$. So this powerful heuristic makes sure that in each step $L(\mathcal{U})$ becomes larger.

However the states it adds do not form an enumeration of all possible terms. Hence the arguments presented before do not hold, and it might happen that the algorithm does not find a finite closed subautomaton although there exists one. For example, consider a version of the algorithm applying the heuristic repeatedly on a rule, until it is closed. Then it might happen that the algorithm gets stuck at a rule that might produce some non regular part of Q and keeps adding states forever. Yet applying the heuristics on some other rules might lead to a closed subautomaton. There are a lot of possibilities how to apply the heuristics. The order in which rules are processed has to be selected. Also the order the closure–test algorithm delivers the counterexamples has to be determined.

3.5.5 Extension to the Weighted Case

For a given weighted TRS and an operator z we are now looking for minimal derivations to z. So instead of the set Q we now have a weighted tree language

```
Start with U as the complete subautomaton of B with state set {[z]}

WHILE L(U) is not closed DO
      get counterexample from closure-test and
      add states to U according to counterexample

      complete U by adding all rules connecting
      previously added states
END;

U is the result.
```

Figure 5: Principal Algorithm

Q (which is a function assigning costs to terms). As before we can give an infinite automaton $\mathcal{B}$ that accepts exactly Q. The only difference is that the chain rules of $\mathcal{B}$ get the cost value of the TRS rule they correspond to.

Then we look at finite subautomata $\mathcal{U}$ for which $M(\mathcal{U}) \subset M(\mathcal{B})$ holds. Note the definition of the "$\subset$"-relation for weighted tree languages given in section 3.2.5. The weighted closure-test can be used to decide $M(\mathcal{U}) = M(\mathcal{B})$. If not, it produces counterexamples, which can be processed exactly as in the non-weighted case.

3.5.6 The Final Generation Step

So far we have been interested in constructing a closed subautomaton $\mathcal{U}$. We have made clear that having $\mathcal{U}$ available principally solves our problem. Now we want to elaborate on this "principally": Suppose a given input term i can be parsed using $\mathcal{U}$. From the derivation in $\mathcal{U}$ we can easily deduce a derivation in the underlying term rewriting system TRS' (see section 3.5.1). This derivation can be transformed according to section 3.4.2 into a derivation in the original TRS. This derivation in turn can be used to rewrite the input i to the desired target term.

This works fine, and if one really needs the derivation that is the way to go. However, if we are only interested in the resulting target term, there is a better solution: Using the terminology of section 3.4.2 we can transform each derivation $i \overset{\Pi\cup\Xi}{\Rightarrow} f$ into one $i \overset{\Xi}{\Rightarrow} t \overset{\Pi}{\Rightarrow} f$, where i is the input term and t is the desired target term. Instead of rewriting $i \overset{\Xi}{\Rightarrow} t$ we use the derivation $t \overset{\Pi}{\Rightarrow} f$ backwards to rewrite f into t. This is much faster, because Π is the rule set of a tree automaton.

The usual tree parsing algorithms produce the derivation $i \overset{\Pi\cup\Xi}{\Rightarrow} f$ backwards, anyhow. So it finally turns out that performing the derivation $f \overset{\overleftarrow{\Pi}}{\Rightarrow} t$ can be done during the second pass of the tree parsing algorithms. That means we can add action parts to the rules of $\mathcal{U}$, which perform the derivation $f \overset{\overleftarrow{\Pi}}{\Rightarrow} t$ bottom up. The result is a kind of tree transducer. It can also be seen as a conventional tree pattern matching based code selector description, whose action parts build up the target tree.

Theoretically this description could be passed to a code generator generator implementing tree pattern matching. However the description produced by this method is rather big and contains unusually many chain rules. So it has to be optimized first.

The first thing we do to make $\mathcal{U}$ smaller is the following: $L(\mathcal{U})$ contains *all* terms that can be rewritten into legal target terms. Besides the terms representing intermediate code, these include the target terms themselves and all terms that occur as intermediate steps in a derivation. That was necessary to make the main algorithm work. Now, however we are only interested in processing the terms that can really occur as input for the code selector. So we can describe the intermediate code of the compiler by a tree grammar $\mathcal{G}$. Then we can construct an automaton $\mathcal{U}'$ accepting $L(\mathcal{G}) \cap L(\mathcal{U})$ and use $\mathcal{U}'$ instead of $\mathcal{U}$.

The resulting $\mathcal{U}'$ contains many chain rules and many nonterminals. A chain rule elimination algorithm is applied to get rid of these. Complete elimination of chain rules is possible, but makes the number of rules explode. So we do not eliminate all the chain rules but only those which can be eliminated without exploding rule numbers.

3.6 Related Research

In [17, 12] Eduardo Pelegri–Llopart presented a class of bottom up term rewriting systems for which a very efficient evaluator can be generated. His method is applicable to non–weighted and to weighted systems. He only solves the acception problem described in section 3.5.1. His descriptions are therefore similar to conventional pattern matching based code selector specifications, although he can process a larger class of rules e.g. to specify commutativity.

It is possible to use the transformation of section 3.4.2 to make this approach transform trees. However the class of finite BURS–term rewriting systems that Pelegri–Llopart can process does not include many systems our approach can handle. For example it does not include rules with the left hand side being only a variable. The example description in figure 3 shows that these rules are very desirable and that our approach can handle them.

The work of [8, 9] is especially useful for our approach. Robert Henry produces efficient evaluators for conventional tree-pattern-based code-selector-specifications. In our terminology he constructs deterministic weighted tree automata from non–deterministic ones. Besides the general algorithm he gives numerous improvements for the algorithm, which makes it applicable for large practical examples. We have not included many of these improvements into our prototype yet, but it certainly would be useful to do so.

Additionally [9] as well as [13, 17] are interesting to finally implement the tree transducers our generator produces as output.

4 Practical Results

The algorithm has been described above in a very abstract way. That makes it possible to understand what is going on in principle without too much detail. When implementing the algorithm, however, all the complexity we have abstracted out comes back again. So in fact an implementation becomes a rather big and complicated program. In many cases one can not use the simplest algorithm available but is forced to use complicated algorithms to gain efficiency.

The main complexity comes from the algorithms handling the tree automata and by the closure–test algorithm. We will discuss this below. First we will describe our prototype.

4.1 The Prototype

We have implemented an experimental prototype of currently 12000 lines of Modula–2 code. It implements the algorithm as described in the weighted as well as in the non–weighted case. The program calculates a closed subautomaton $\mathcal{U}$ and builds it up internally. For testing purposes a term can be parsed according to $\mathcal{U}$ and a derivation in terms of the original TRS can be printed out. Finally $\mathcal{U}$ can be processed according to section 3.5.6 and a tree pattern matching based code selector description can be produced.

We have not yet always used the best algorithms known nor even tried out several algorithms and carefully tuned them for the special application. However several optimizations were necessary to make the prototype process sensible examples, it is currently not possible to process very large specifications with our prototype.

4.2 Testing if $\mathcal{U}$ is closed

Before the closure–test algorithm can be applied a deterministic automaton for $\mathcal{U}$ has to be constructed. This is basically the subset construction algorithm. Although working on trees does not make any theoretical problems the run time complexity of the algorithm explodes with the maximal arity of an operator. The run time complexity is $O(ms^a)$ where m is the number of operators, s the number of states of the resulting deterministic automaton, and a the maximal arity of an operator. It is necessary to use improvements like those presented in [21] to achieve acceptable execution times. The number of states of the deterministic automaton can explode, although it usually does not. Therefore s is of $O(2^n)$.

In the weighted case it is even worse. s is not bound by 2^n. [9] handles this problem in depth. A lot of work has to be done in this area to achieve acceptable run time.

Afterwards the deterministic automaton has to be minimized. That is necessary because the closure–test algorithm is time critical and therefore needs to work on an automaton that is as small as possible. Then for the closure–test the "$\prec$"–relation has to be computed. This is not easy, in fact it is even more complicated and time consuming than minimization.

The closure–test itself is very time consuming, as it has to check all possible substitutions, which replace a variable of the rule by a state of the automaton. A similar improvement as in [21] can be used to reduce the size of the set of substitutions that actually have to be checked.

Data about the example description:	
Number of TRS-Rules	20
Number of rules of regular automaton	25
Data about the TRS produced according to section 3.4.2:	
Number of Rules	45
Number of Operators	33
Data about the closed subautomaton $\mathcal{U}$:	
Number of States	70
Number of Rules	145
Number of Chain Rules	83
Number of non Chain Rules	62
Data about the non-weighted deterministic automaton produced from $\mathcal{U}$	
Number of States:	21
Number of States of minimized automaton:	6
Data about the weighted deterministic automaton produced from $\mathcal{U}$	
Number of States:	96
Number of States of minimized automaton:	21

Table 1: Some statistics about the example description

4.3 Some Improvements

As we have seen above a lot of processing has to be applied to the non-deterministic automaton $\mathcal{U}$ before the closure–test actually can start: to build up and to minimize the deterministic automaton $\mathcal{D}$ with $L(\mathcal{D}) = L(\mathcal{U})$. When the closure–test fails more states and rules are added to $\mathcal{U}$. As $\mathcal{U}$ has been changed the complete processing has to start again. Of course it would be very interesting to find some incremental algorithm that allows us to change the old $\mathcal{D}$. We have not done so yet, because this turns out to be very difficult. So $\mathcal{D}$ is always built up from scratch.

We do something different: We get more than one counterexample from one application of the closure–test. Then we add the states for all these counterexamples. However the second counterexample might not be a counterexample any more after adding the states for the first one. So one might add too many states. A solution can be the following: First add the states for the first counterexample to $\mathcal{U}$ leading to $\mathcal{U}'$. Then parse the second counterexample using $\mathcal{U}'$ and check if it is a still a counterexample. Of course checking just one example is much cheaper than building up $\mathcal{D}$. If the second counterexample is still one it can be used and one has saved building up $\mathcal{D}$, otherwise one cannot use the counterexample and has lost the time to generate it and to check it.

4.4 Examples

The example code selector specification of figures 2 and 3 can be processed by our prototype. It takes about 250 seconds (Unix user time) on a DecStation 3100 to build up the closed subautomaton $\mathcal{U}$. Table 1 contains several figures about this example.

Derivation in TRS	Derivation in $\mathcal{U}$	
assign(plus(bb,c),plus(cont(plus(bb,c)),one))		
	assign(plus(bb,c),plus(cont(plus(bb,c)),one))	a
	assign(plus([bb] ,c),plus(cont(plus(bb,c)),one))	t
	assign(plus([Ar] ,c),plus(cont(plus(bb,c)),one))	a
	assign(plus([Ar] , [c]),plus(cont(plus(bb,c)),one))	t
	assign(plus([Ar] , [C]),plus(cont(plus(bb,c)),one))	a
	assign([plus(Ar,C)] ,plus(cont(plus(bb,c)),one))	12
assign(adr(cont(plus(bb,c))),plus(cont(plus(bb,c)),one))		
	assign([adr(cont(plus(Ar,C)))] ,...)	9
assign(adr(di(bb,c)),plus(cont(plus(bb,c)),one))		
	...	9
assign(adr(di(bb,c)),plus(di(bb,c),one))		
	...	8
assign(adr(di(bb,c)),plus(di(bb,c),im(one)))		
	...	14
assign(adr(di(bb,c)),plus(di(bb,c),mov(im(one))))		
	...	1
assign(adr(di(bb,c)),add(di(bb,c),mov(im(one))))		
	assign([adr(Mea)] , [add(Ea,Dr)])	t
	assign([adr(Mea)] , [Dr])	6
assign(adr(di(bb,c)),dr(add(di(bb,c),mov(im(one)))))		
	assign([adr(Mea)] , [dr(Dr)])	t
	assign([adr(Mea)] , [Ea])	t
	[assign(adr(Mea),Ea)]	t
	[mov2(Ea,Mea)]	5
mov2(dr(add(di(bb,c),mov(im(one)))),di(bb,c))		
	[Z]	

Figure 6: Example derivation

4.4.1 An Example Derivation

Figure 6 shows the test output of a derivation translating the example expression tree given in figure 1. The left column contains the derivation in terms of the term rewriting system *TRS* given in figure 2. The second column gives the derivation in the closed subautomaton $\mathcal{U}$, which is also a derivation in $\mathcal{B}$. The third column specifies which rule has been applied. An "a" marks an accepting rule of $\mathcal{B}$. All other rule applications are chain rule applications of $\mathcal{B}$. Each chain rule of $\mathcal{B}$ corresponds to a rule of *TRS'*, where *TRS'* is the term rewriting system constructed according to section 3.4.2 from the original *TRS*. A "t" in the last column marks the application of a rule of *TRS'* that originally stems from the target term specification in figure 2. A number marks the application of a rule of the *TRS* given in figure 3.

To construct the first column from the second the following has to be done: Leaving out the square brackets "[" and "]" in the second column one gets the derivation in *TRS'*. Then the transformation introduced in section 3.4.2 has to be applied. The derivation $i \overset{\Pi\cup\Xi}{\Rightarrow} f$ has to be transformed into $i \overset{\Xi}{\Rightarrow} t \overset{\Pi}{\Rightarrow} f$ by appropriate swapping of rules. However the part $t \overset{\Pi}{\Rightarrow} f$ is not needed, so in fact the derivation $i \overset{\Xi}{\Rightarrow} t$ can be derived from the derivation $t \overset{\Pi}{\Rightarrow} f$ just by leaving out rule applications. In our example all the rule applications marked by "t" have to be left out.

4.4.2 Final Output

Final output of our prototype is a tree pattern matching based code selector specification which performs the desired tree transformation. Figure 7 shows the output for the example of figures 2 and 3.

Each line of figure 7 contains one rule. It consists of a rewriting rule, a cost value, which is omitted if it is zero, and an action part. So it has just the form of a conventional tree pattern matching based code selector description. The action parts do some bottom up attribute calculations that build up the desired target tree. Every nonterminal N has one or more attributes associated with it, they are written N_n for $n \in \{1,2,3\}$. With R_n the n-th attribute of the result nonterminal is specified. The operators occurring in the action part simply build up the tree accordingly.

The code generator description of figure 7 has been produced using the methods of section 3.5.6. Starting from $\mathcal{U}$ with 70 states and 145 rules first $\mathcal{U}'$ which only accepts operators of the intermediate language has been constructed. The generator has been told that the intermediate representation contains only the operators *plus, minus, mult, div, assign, cont, c, one, zero, sc*, and *bb*. This corresponds to the grammar G of section 3.5.6, which describes the intermediate representation. In the current implementation this grammar is very restricted; one can specify just the operators that occur in the intermediate representation.

Afterwards $\mathcal{U}'$ has been optimized by removing redundant states and rules and by eliminating some chain rules. The final result is the code generator description of figure 7 with 11 nonterminals and 42 rules, 14 chain rules and 28 non-chain rules.

5 Conclusion

Within this paper we have presented a very powerful method to specify code selectors. Our descriptions are more concise, better readable, and easier to develop than the descriptions used so far. For specification we use a very ambitious class of non–deterministic term rewriting systems.

We have given a rather complicated algorithm that analyzes our specifications and translates them into tree pattern matching based code selector descriptions. These can be further processed by well known techniques, finally leading to efficient code selectors.

Our practical experience shows the big complexity which has to be traded against the great class of term rewriting systems, although the algorithms can be described easily on an abstract level. Our prototype shows that the algorithms work and can successfully process several code selector descriptions. However some work has to be done before it can process large specifications with reasonable generation times.

```
Z          <-assign(AdrMea Ea)    4  R1:=mov2(Ea1,AdrMea1);

Ar         <-AdrMea               4  R1:=lea(AdrMea1);
Ar         <-Ea                   4  R1:=mov(Ea1);
Ar         <-minus(Ar Ea)         4  R1:=sub(Ea1,Ar1);
Ar         <-plus(Ea Ar)          4  R1:=add(Ea1,Ar1);
Ar         <-plus(Ar Ea)          4  R1:=add(Ea1,Ar1);
Ar         <-bb()                    R1:=bb();

Sc         <-one()                   R1:=one();
Sc         <-sc()                    R1:=sc();

C          <-Sc                      R1:=Sc1;
C          <-zero()                  R1:=zero();
C          <-c()                     R1:=c();


Dr         <-Ea                   4  R1:=mov(Ea1);
Dr         <-div(Dr Ea)           4  R1:=divs(Ea1,Dr1);
Dr         <-mult(Ea Dr)          4  R1:=muls(Ea1,Dr1);
Dr         <-mult(Dr Ea)          4  R1:=muls(Ea1,Dr1);
Dr         <-minus(Dr Ea)         4  R1:=sub(Ea1,Dr1);
Dr         <-plus(Ea Dr)          4  R1:=add(Ea1,Dr1);
Dr         <-plus(Dr Ea)          4  R1:=add(Ea1,Dr1);

Imul       <-Dr                      R1:=inmul(Dr1,one());
Imul       <-Ar                      R1:=inmul(Ar1,one());
Imul       <-mult(Dr Sc)             R1:=inmul(Dr1,Sc1);
Imul       <-mult(Ar Sc)             R1:=inmul(Ar1,Sc1);
Imul       <-mult(Sc Dr)             R1:=inmul(Dr1,Sc1);
Imul       <-mult(Sc Ar)             R1:=inmul(Ar1,Sc1);

Ea         <-Dr                      R1:=dr(Dr1);
Ea         <-C                       R1:=im(C1);
Ea         <-Ar                      R1:=dr(Ar1);
Ea         <-cont(Ar)                R1:=ir(Ar1);
Ea         <-cont(PlArC)             R1:=di(PlArC1,PlArC2);
Ea         <-cont(PlCArImul)         R1:=in(PlCArImul2,PlCArImul1,
                                          PlCArImul3);

AdrMea     <-PlCArImul               R1:=in(PlCArImul2,PlCArImul1,
                                          PlCArImul3);
AdrMea     <-PlArC                   R1:=di(PlArC1,PlArC2);
AdrMea     <-Ar                      R1:=ir(Ar1);

PlArC      <-plus(Ar C)              R1:=Ar1; R2:=C1;
PlArC      <-plus(C Ar)              R1:=Ar1; R2:=C1;

PlCArImul<-PlArImul                  R1:=zero(); R2:=PlArImul1; R3:=PlArImul2;
PlCArImul<-plus(C PlArImul)          R1:=C1; R2:=PlArImul1; R3:=PlArImul2;
PlCArImul<-plus(PlArImul C)          R1:=C1; R2:=PlArImul1; R3:=PlArImul2;

PlArImul   <-Imul                 4  R1:=mov(im(zero())); R2:=Imul1;
PlArImul   <-plus(Ar Imul)           R1:=Ar1; R2:=Imul1;
PlArImul   <-plus(Imul Ar)           R1:=Ar1; R2:=Imul1;
```

Figure 7: Finally generated code generator description

6 Acknowledgement

I would like to thank my colleagues and the reviewers for carefully reading and commenting the manuscript. I would also like to thank Robert Giegerich and Christopher Fraser for their invaluable discussions and comments.

References

[1] A.V.Aho, M.Ganapathi, S.W. Tjiang, Code Generation Using Tree Matching and Dynamic Programming, Technical Report, Bell Laboratories, Murray Hill, NJ, January 1986

[2] A. Balachandran, D. M. Dhamdhere, S. Biswas, Efficient Retargetable Code Generation Using Bottom-up Tree Pattern Matching, Computer Languages, 15(3):127–140, 1990

[3] H.Emmelmann, F-W.Schröer, R.Landwehr, BEG – a Generator for Efficient Back Ends, Proc. of the Sigplan'89 Conference on Programming Language Design and Implementation, Sigplan Notices, Vol. 24, Number 7, July 1989

[4] M.Ganapathi, C.N.Fischer, J.L. Hennessy, Retargetable Compiler Code Generation, Computing Surveys Vol.14 No.4, Dec 82

[5] R.S.Glanville, S.L.Graham, A New Method for Compiler Code Generation, Proceedings 5th ACM Symposium on Principles of Programming Languages, pp.231-240, 1977

[6] P.J.Hatcher, T.W. Christopher, High–Quality Code Generation Via Bottom Up Tree Pattern Matching, Proceedings 13th ACM Symposium on Principles of Programming Languages pp. 119-130, 1986

[7] R. Henry, P.Damron, Performance of Table–Driven Code Generators Using Tree-Pattern Matching, Technical Report # 89-02-02 Computer Science Department, FR-35 University of Washington, Seattle, WA 98195 USA

[8] R. Henry, P.Damron, Algorithms for Table–Driven Code Generators Using Tree–Pattern Matching, Technical Report # 89-02-03 Computer Science Department, FR-35 University of Washington, Seattle, WA 98195 USA

[9] R. Henry, Encoding Optimal Pattern Selection in a Table–Driven Bottom–Up Tree–Pattern Matcher, Technical Report # 89-02-04 Computer Science Department, FR-35 University of Washington, Seattle, WA 98195 USA

[10] B.Weisgerber, R.Wilhelm, Two Tree Pattern Matchers for Code Selection (Including Targeting), Technical Report, Universität des Saarlandes, Saarbrücken, W.Germany, February 1986

[11] R.G.G.Cattell, Automatic Derivation of Code Generators from Machine Descriptions, ACM Transactions on Programming Languages and Systems, April 1980, Volume 2, Number 2, p. 173-190

[12] E. Pelegri-Llopart, S. Graham, Optimal Code Generation for Expression Trees: An Application of BURS Theory, Proc. of the 15th ACM Symposium on Principles of Programming Languages, 1988, p.294-308

[13] C.W. Fraser, R.R. Henry, Hard-coding Bottom-up Code Generation Tables to Save Time and Space, Software Practice & Experience, January 1991, Volume 21, No. 1

[14] R.Giegerich, Code Selection by Inversion of Order-Sorted Derivors, Theoretical Computer Science 73 (1990), p. 177-211

[15] R.Giegerich, On the Structure of Verifiable Code Generator Specifications, Proc. of the ACM SIGPLAN'90 Conference on Programming Language Design and Implementation, p.1-8, Sigplan Notices, Vol. 25, Number 6, June 1990

[16] C.Hoffmann, J.O'Donnell, Pattern Matching in Trees, Journal of the ACM Vol. 29, No. 1, January 1982, pp. 68-95

[17] E. Pelegri-Llopart, Rewrite Systems, Pattern Matching and Code Generation, Dissertation, EECS-Report, UC Berkeley, 1987

[18] J.R. Büchi, Finite Automata, Their Algebras and Grammars, Towards a Theory of Formal Expressions, Springer–Verlag, New York, 1989

[19] J.W.Thatcher, Tree Automata: An Informal Survey, Currents in the Theory of Computing, A.V. Aho (editor), Prentice Hall, Englewood CLiffs, NJ, 1973, 143-172

[20] W.S.Brainerd, Minimalization of Tree Automata, Information and Control 13(1968) p.484-491

[21] D.R.Chase, An Improvement to Bottom-up Tree Pattern Matching, POPL87, Munich, Germany, January 1987

Tree Automata for Code Selection

Christian Ferdinand*
Helmut Seidl†
Reinhard Wilhelm
FB 14 – Informatik, Universität des Saarlandes
Saarbrücken Germany

Abstract

We deal with the generation of code selectors. The fundamental concepts are systematically derived from the theory of regular tree grammars and finite tree automata. We use this general approach to construct algorithms that generalize and improve existing methods.

1 Introduction

A code generator for a compiler is applied to an intermediate representation *IR* of the input program which has been computed during preceding phases of compilation. This intermediate representation can be viewed as code for an ***abstract machine***. The task of code generation now is to translate this code into a efficient sequence of instructions for a concrete machine.

Besides register allocation and instruction scheduling (for processors with pipelined architectures), code selection, i.e., the selection of instructions, is one subtask of code generation. It is especially important for CISC (*C*omplex *I*nstruction *S*et *C*omputer) architectures where there are usually many possibilities to generate code for the same piece of program.

Example 1.1
Consider the simplest member of the MC680x0 family, namely the MC68000. The instruction

MOVE.B *dist*(A1, D1.W), D5

loads one byte into the lowest quarter of data register D5. The address of the operand is determined by adding the lower half of the contents of D1 together with the 8 bit constant *dist* to the contents of base register A1. This addressing mode is called "address register indirect with index and 8 bit displacement". If the costs of instructions are counted in terms of execution time, i.e., the number of necessary processor cycles, then this instruction has cost 14. An alternative code sequence without indexed addressing and displacement is:

*Funded by the ESPRIT Project #5399 (COMPARE)
†Funded by DFG SFB #124 VLSI-Design and Parallelism

ADD.W	#*dist*, A1	**costs: 16**
ADD.W	D1, A1	**costs: 8**
MOVE.B	(A1), D5	**costs: 8**
	with total costs 32	

Another possibility is:

ADD.W	D1, A1	**costs: 8**
MOVE.B	*dist*(A1), D5	**costs: 12**
	with total costs 20	

This example shows the necessity of an intelligent code selection algorithm for CISC architectures.

Note however, that the two alternative code sequences above are equivalent only with respect to the storage and to the result register D5. They are not equivalent with respect to the condition codes and register A1! The code selector has to guarantee that these alternatives are valid in a given context. □

The use of code selector *generators* significantly simplifies the development of code generators for new target architectures.

The input of a code selector generator is some kind of machine language description. One possibility to describe machine instructions is by rules of a regular tree grammar. The right hand side of a rule describes the "effect" of the instruction (in terms of *IR* operators). The terminals denote (sub-)operations which are executed by the instruction. Nonterminals denote locations or resource classes, e.g., different types of registers. The left hand side nonterminal of a rule describes where (i.e., in which resource class) the result of the instruction is stored.

Such a *machine grammar* allows to derive the *IR* trees of expressions. An derivation tree for an *IR* tree describes one possibility to generate code for the corresponding expression. In general (especially for CISC processors), the machine grammar is ambiguous. In this case several derivation trees may exist for the same expression corresponding to several possible instruction sequences. To allow for a selection of an efficient instruction sequence one annotates the rules of the grammar with costs that, e.g., give the number of machine cycles to execute the instruction. The goal is to pick the minimal cost derivation tree. This corresponds to a *locally optimal* instruction sequence. However, there are processors (e.g., Motorola 68020) for which the number of necessary machine cycles cannot precisely be predicted since the execution time depends on the runtime context. Here, we have to use approximations.

The number of combinations of instructions, addressing modes and word lengths of customary CISC processors is rather large. To avoid the introduction of distinct rules and costs for all combinations one introduces separate rules and costs for address modes and word lengths.

To enlarge the applicability of code selection one can allow jump or assignment operators at the root node of a tree. Jumps or assignments do not return a "result" in the above sense. Therefore, rules for such instructions contain a *dummy* nonterminal as left hand sides. This nonterminal does not occur in the right hand sides of any of the rules. It serves as a kind of initial nonterminal.

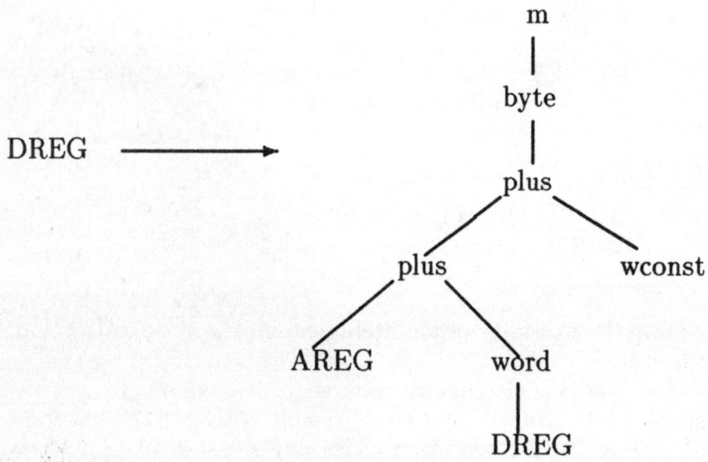

$$DREG \quad \rightarrow \quad m(byte(plus(plus(AREG, word(DREG)), wconst)))$$

Figure 1: Instruction of example 1.1

2 Comparison to Related Work

Ripken [25] was the first to suggest a machine description language for processor architectures from which a code generator should be generated. Since the necessary tree parsing algorithms were not available Glanville and Graham [11, 12] proposed a linearization of the intermediate language to apply LALR parser techniques to code selection. This idea was further developed and brought to applicability by Henry [14]. Other approaches combined efficient algorithms for pattern matching in trees [18, 17, 3, 21] with dynamic programming to determine locally optimal instruction sequences [1, 15, 26] or extended the tree pattern matchers to allow for a direct selection of locally optimal instruction sequences [24, 16].

In a sequence of publications Giegerich and Schmal [10, 9] try to develop a unified framework for the two different approaches of tree pattern matching and tree parsing. The problem of code selection is reduced to determining the inverse of a "derivor", i.e., a tree homomorphism from a target algebra to an IR-algebra.

Pelegri-Llopart [23] and Emmelmann [6] use (restricted versions of) term rewriting systems as specification tools for their generators. These systems allow for more convenient machine descriptions. E.g., commutativity of operators can be expressed easily.

Most of these works ignore the theoretically well known connections between algorithms for tree pattern matching and tree parsing on the one side and finite tree automata on the other. A good overview about the classical results on tree automata can be found, e.g., in [8]. Without explicitly referring to code selection Kron in [18] anticipates many of nowaday's techniques for tree pattern matching.

The present paper systematically presents the basic theory behind code selection. For simplicity, we restrict ourselves to machine descriptions by means of regular tree grammars. A compilation of ground term rewriting systems or other restricted classes of rewrite systems to tree automata is possible as well (see [23, 4, 6]). We exhibit the connections both of tree pattern matching and tree parsing algorithms to finite tree automata. We present general methods for the implementation of tree automata. Especially, we generalize the method of Kron to arbitrary tree automata. This allows to derive efficient generators of efficient code selectors.

Our results are also of interest for other areas. Both tree pattern matching and tree parsing are useful for checking the syntactical applicability of tree transformation rules [7, 22]. Especially tree pattern matching is used for the implementation of term rewriting systems [13].

3 Tree Pattern Matching

A *ranked alphabet* is a finite set Σ of operators[1] together with a ranking function $\rho : \Sigma \to \mathbb{N}_0$. We write Σ_k for $\{a \in \Sigma \mid \rho(a) = k\}$. The *homogeneous tree language* over Σ, T_Σ is the smallest set T such that

- $\Sigma_0 \subseteq T$;
- If $t_1, \ldots, t_n$ in T and $a \in \Sigma_n$ then $a(t_1, \ldots, t_n) \in T$.

As usual, *nodes* or *occurrences* in a tree are denoted by addresses in $\mathbb{N}^*$. The set $O(t)$ of nodes of a tree $t = a(t_1, \ldots, t_k)$ is inductively defined by: $O(t) := \{\epsilon\} \cup \bigcup_{j=1}^{k} j.O(t_j)$. The *subtree* t/n of t at node n is defined by $t/\epsilon := t$ and $t/n := t_j/n'$ if $t = a(t_1, \ldots, t_k)$ and $n = j.n'$.

Assume V is a set of variables of rank 0. A member of $T_\Sigma(V) := T_{\Sigma \cup V}$ is called *pattern* over Σ. A pattern is called *linear* if no variable in it occurs more than once.

Example 3.1 Let $\Sigma = \{a, cons, nil\}$ with $\rho(a) = \rho(nil) = 0$, $\rho(cons) = 2$. Trees over Σ are, e.g., a, $cons(nil, nil)$, $cons(cons(a, nil), nil)$.
Let $V = \{X\}$. Then, X, $cons(nil, X)$, and $cons(X, nil)$ are patterns over Σ. □

A *substitution* is a map $\Theta : V \to T_\Sigma(V)$. Θ is extended to a map $\Theta : T_\Sigma(V) \to T_\Sigma(V)$ by $t\Theta = x\Theta$ if $t = x \in V$ and $t\Theta = a(t_1\Theta, \ldots, t_k\Theta)$ if $t = a(t_1, \ldots, t_k)$.[2] We also write $t\Theta = t[t_1/x_1, \ldots, t_k/x_k]$ if the variables occurring in t are from $\{x_1, \ldots, x_k\}$ and $x_j\Theta = t_j$ for all j.

A pattern $\tau \in T_\Sigma(V)$ with variables from $\{x_1, \ldots, x_k\}$ *matches* a tree t if there are trees $t_1, \ldots, t_k$ in T_Σ such that $t = \tau[t_1/x_1, \ldots \ldots, t_k/x_k]$.

Definition 3.1 (The Tree Pattern Matching Problem)
An instance of the *tree pattern matching problem* consists of a finite set of patterns $T = \{\tau_1, \ldots, \tau_k\} \subset T_\Sigma(V)$ together with an input tree $t \in T_\Sigma$. The solution of the tree pattern matching problem for this instance is the set of all pairs (n, i) such that pattern τ_i matches t/n. An algorithm which for every

[1] in functional languages also called constructors

[2] Traditionally, the application of a substitution Θ to a pattern t is written $t\Theta$.

input tree $t \in T_\Sigma$ returns the solution of the tree pattern matching problem for (T, t) is called *tree pattern matcher* for T. An algorithm which on input of a pattern set T returns a tree pattern matcher for T is called *tree pattern matcher generator*. □

Example 3.2
Assume $\tau_1 = cons(X, nil)$ and $\tau_2 = cons(a, X)$ are patterns, and $t = cons(cons(a, nil), nil)$ is an input tree. The solution of the instance $(\{\tau_1, \tau_2\}, t)$ of the pattern matching problem is the set $\{(\varepsilon, 1), (1, 1), (1, 2)\}$. □

In fact, we are interested in constructing efficient tree pattern matcher generators. The pattern matchers generated by the following algorithms will only work for *linear* patterns. We have two possibilities to generate tree pattern matchers for sets of non-linear patterns. Either, we introduce tests for equality of subtrees whenever needed. This may not be efficient since the pattern matcher may have to visit the same subtree several times. The second alternative is to let the tree pattern matcher execute all possible equality tests in advance. This is achieved by representing the input tree as a directed acyclic graph which contains exactly one node for every occurring subtree. This *subtree graph* can be computed in linear time [5].

4 Tree Parsing

A *regular tree grammar* G is a triple (N, Σ, P) where

- N is a finite set of *nonterminals*,
- Σ is the ranked alphabet of *terminals* [3]
- P is a finite set of *rules* of the form $X \to s$ with $X \in N$ and $s \in T_{\Sigma \cup N}$.

Let $p : X \to s$ be a rule of P. p is called *chain rule*, if $s \in N$, and *non-chain rule* otherwise. p is of *type* $(X_1, \ldots, X_k) \to X$ if the j-th occurrence of a nonterminal in s is X_j. For a right side s, we define the pattern $\tilde{s}$ as the pattern in $T_\Sigma(\{x_1, \ldots, x_k\})$ which one obtains from s by replacing for all j the j-th occurrence of a nonterminal by the variable x_j.

A X*-derivation tree* for a tree $t \in T_{\Sigma \cup N}$ is a tree $\psi \in T_{P \cup N}$ satisfying the following conditions:

- If $\psi \in N$ then $\psi = X = t$.
- If $\psi \notin N$ then $\psi = p(\psi_1, \ldots, \psi_k)$ for some rule $p : X \to s \in P$ of type $(X_1, \ldots, X_k) \to X$ such that $t = \tilde{s}[t_1/x_1, \ldots, t_k/x_k]$ and ψ_j are X_j–derivation trees for the trees t_j.

Finally, we define the *derivation head*, $head(\psi)$, of a X–derivation tree ψ.

- If $\psi = X$ then $head(\psi) := X$.
- If $\psi = p(\psi_1, \ldots, \psi_k)$ and p is a non-chain rule then $head(\psi) := p$.

[3] The notion terminals was chosen in analogy to e.g., context free word grammars.

- If $\psi = p(\psi_1)$ and p is a chain rule then $\boldsymbol{head}(\psi) := p \cdot \boldsymbol{head}(\psi_1)$.

The derivation head of a X–derivation tree is also called X–derivation head.

Thus, the derivation head of ψ describes the "upper" part of ψ which consists of a sequence of applications of chain rules followed by the first non-chain rule or a nonterminal respectively.

For $X \in N$ we define the ***language*** of G relative to X as $L(G,X) := \{t \in T_\Sigma \mid \exists \psi \in T_{P \cup N} : \psi \text{ is } X\text{–derivation tree for } t\}$.

Example 4.1 Let G_1 be the regular tree grammar (N_1, Σ, P_1); $\Sigma = \{a, \mathit{cons}, \mathit{nil}\}$ with $\rho(a) = \rho(\mathit{nil}) = 0, \rho(\mathit{cons}) = 2$, $N_1 = \{E, S\}$ and

$$P_1 = \{ \begin{array}{lll} S & \rightarrow & \mathit{nil}, \\ S & \rightarrow & \mathit{cons}(E,S), \\ E & \rightarrow & a\} \end{array}$$

$L(G_1, S)$ is the set of linear lists of a's including the empty list, i.e., $L(G_1,S) = \{\mathit{nil}, \mathit{cons}(a,\mathit{nil}), \mathit{cons}(a, \mathit{cons}(a,\mathit{nil})), \ldots\}$.

□

Example 4.2 Let G_m be the regular tree grammar (N_m, Σ, P_m); $\Sigma = \{\mathit{const}, m, \mathit{plus}, \mathit{REG}\}$ with $\rho(\mathit{const}) = 0; \rho(m) = 1, \rho(\mathit{plus}) = 2$, $N_m = \{\mathit{REG}\}$ and

$$P_m = \{ \begin{array}{llll} \mathit{addmc}: & \mathit{REG} & \rightarrow & \mathit{plus}(m(\mathit{const}), \mathit{REG}), \\ \mathit{addm}: & \mathit{REG} & \rightarrow & \mathit{plus}(m(\mathit{REG}), \mathit{REG}), \\ \mathit{add}: & \mathit{REG} & \rightarrow & \mathit{plus}(\mathit{REG}, \mathit{REG}), \\ \mathit{ldmc}: & \mathit{REG} & \rightarrow & m(\mathit{const}), \\ \mathit{ldc}: & \mathit{REG} & \rightarrow & \mathit{const}, \\ \mathit{ld}: & \mathit{REG} & \rightarrow & \mathit{REG}\} \end{array}$$

P_m describes a subset of an instruction set of a simple processor. The rules are labeled with the names of the corresponding instructions.

The first three rules represent instructions for addition that add

- the contents of a storage cell whose address is given by a constant
- the contents of a storage cell whose address resides in a register
- the contents of a register itself

to the contents of a register and store the resulting value into a register.

The remaining three rules describe load instructions that load

- the contents of a storage cell whose address is given by a constant
- a constant
- the contents of a register

into a register. □

Definition 4.1 (The Tree Parsing Problem)
An instance of the ***tree parsing problem*** consists of a regular tree grammar G together with a nonterminal X and an input tree t. The solution of the tree parsing problem for this instance is (a representation of) the set of all X–derivation trees of G for t. A ***tree parser*** for G is an algorithm which for every tree t returns the solution of the instance (G,t) of the tree parsing problem. A ***tree parser generator*** is an algorithm which for every regular tree grammar G returns a tree parser for G. □

Similar to regular word languages, the family of languages generated by regular tree grammars (relative to some nonterminal) has particularly nice properties. For example, it is closed under intersection and complementation. Also, emptyness can be decided in polynomial time.

In the following we show how finite tree automata can be used to implement both tree pattern matchers and tree parsers.

5 Finite Tree Automata

A *finite tree automaton* A is a 4-tuple $A = (Q, \Sigma, \delta, Q_F)$ where

- Q is a finite set of *states*;
- $Q_F \subseteq Q$ is the set of *final* or *accepting* states;
- Σ is the finite ranked input alphabet; and
- $\delta \subseteq \bigcup_{j \geq 0} Q \times \Sigma_j \times Q^j$ is the set of *transitions*.

The automaton A is called *deterministic* if for every $a \in \Sigma_k$ and every sequence $q_1, \ldots, q_k$ of states there is at most one transition $(q, a, q_1 \ldots q_k) \in \delta$. In this case, δ can be written as partial function

- $\delta : \bigcup_{j \geq 0} \Sigma_j \times Q^j \to Q$

Given an input tree t the automaton A traverses t. At every visited node, A changes its state according to the transition from δ chosen at this node. If A is deterministic then there is at most one possible choice at every node, otherwise possibly several. Technically, we describe such a computation by an *annotation* of the input tree. For this, we introduce an extended alphabet $\Sigma \times Q$ whose operators now consist of *pairs* of operators from Σ and states of A.

So, let $\Sigma \times Q$ be the ranked alphabet $\{\langle a, q\rangle \mid a \in \Sigma, q \in Q\}$ where $\langle a, q\rangle$ has the same rank as a. A *q–computation* ϕ of the finite tree automaton A on the input tree $t = a(t_1, \ldots, t_m)$ is inductively defined as a tree $\phi = \langle a, q\rangle(\phi_1, \ldots, \phi_m) \in T_{\Sigma \times Q}$ where ϕ_j are q_j–computations for the subtrees t_j, $j = 1, \ldots, m$, for some states q_j such that $(q, a, q_1 \ldots q_m)$ is a transition from δ. ϕ is called *accepting*, if $q \in Q_F$. The language $L(A)$ accepted by A consists of all trees for which an accepting computation of A exists. A transition $\tau \in \delta$ is called *superfluous* if it does not occur in any computation of A. Clearly, superfluous transitions can be removed from δ without changing the "behavior" of A.

In the literature a distinction is sometimes made between bottom-up tree automata and top-down tree automata which in the nondeterministic case are equivalent [8]. According to our definition of a computation the direction is irrelevant. In informal descriptions we allow ourselves any of the two views to support intuition.

If A is deterministic then at most one computation exists for every input tree. We can extend the partial function δ to a partial function $\delta^* : T_\Sigma \to Q$ by: $\delta^*(t) = \delta(a, \delta^*(t_1) \ldots \delta^*(t_k))$ whenever $t = a(t_1, \ldots, t_k)$. For simplicity, we also denote δ^* by δ. Induction on the structure of t shows that $\delta^*(t)$ is defined and equals q if and only if a q–computation of A for t exists.

As a first application consider the tree pattern matching problem. Let τ be a linear pattern in $T_\Sigma(V)$. We want to construct a (possibly non-deterministic) finite tree automaton A_τ that detects whether or not τ matches the given input tree. Intuitively, A_τ works as follows. Outside of pattern τ, A_τ is in an unspecific state $\bot$; whereas inside of pattern τ the state memorizes the subpattern already traversed. Since we are not interested in the precise numbering of the variables we replace all variables by $\bot$ ("everything is matched by a variable"). Hence in the sequel, we assume that $\tau \in T_{\Sigma \cup \{\bot\}}$. Then we define $A_\tau := (Q_\tau, \Sigma, \delta_\tau, Q_{\tau,F})$ where $Q_\tau := \{s \mid s \text{ subpattern of } \tau\} \cup \{\bot\}$, $Q_{\tau,F} := \{\tau\}$, and δ_τ is defined as follows.

- $(\bot, a, \bot \ldots \bot) \in \delta$ for all $a \in \Sigma$;
- If $s \in Q_\tau$ and $s = a(s_1, \ldots, s_k)$ then $(s, a, s_1 \ldots s_k) \in \delta$.

Obviously, we have:

1. For every tree t there is a $\bot$–computation;
2. For a tree t there is a τ–computation if and only if τ matches t.

The example easily generalizes to the case of a set $T = \{\tau_1, \ldots, \tau_n\}$ of linear patterns of which we again w.l.o.g. assume that all occurrences of variables are replaced with $\bot$. As set of states for the finite tree automaton A_T we now choose $Q_T := \bigcup_{j=1}^{n} Q_{\tau_j}$ with $Q_{T,F} := T$. Textually, the definition of the set of transitions does not change.

If we want to determine which patterns of T match an input tree t we just have to compute the set of all final states of accepting computations of A_T for t. A method to determine this set can be obtained from A_T by means of the *subset construction* for finite tree automata.

Definition 5.1 (Subset Construction I)
Let $A = (Q, \Sigma, \delta, Q_F)$ be a finite tree automaton. The corresponding subset automaton is the deterministic finite tree automaton $P(A) = (Q_1, \Sigma, \delta_1, Q_{1,F})$ with

- $Q_1 := 2^Q$ is the power set of Q;
- $Q_{1,F} := \{B \subseteq Q \mid B \cap Q_F \neq \emptyset\}$;
- δ_1 is the (total) function with $\delta_1(a, B_1 \ldots B_k) = \{q \in Q \mid \exists q_1 \in B_1, \ldots, q_k \in B_k : (q, a, q_1 \ldots q_k) \in \delta\}$. □

By induction on the structure of an input tree one finds:

Lemma 5.1 *Let $t \in T_\Sigma$. Then $\delta_1(t)$ is the set of all states $q \in Q$ for which there is a q–computation of A for t. Especially, $L(A) = L(P(A))$.* □

The subset construction provides an algorithm to generate tree pattern matchers. The generation proceeds in two stages. Given pattern set T, we first construct the finite tree automaton A_T. Then we apply the subset construction to obtain $P(A_T) = (Q, \Sigma, \delta, Q_F)$. Whenever an input tree t is given, the set $\delta(t) \cap T$ consists precisely of all patterns from T that match t.

Example 5.1 *Let* $T = \{\tau_1, \tau_2\}$ *with*

$$\tau_1 = b(a(a(X_1, X_2), X_3), X_4) \text{ and } \tau_2 = b(X_1, c(X_2, c(X_3, X_4))).$$

Then, $A_T = (Q_T, \Sigma, \delta_T, Q_{T,F})$ *where*

$$\begin{array}{llll} Q_T = \{\bot, & a(\bot,\bot), & a(a(\bot,\bot),\bot), & b(a(a(\bot,\bot),\bot),\bot), \\ & c(\bot,\bot), & c(\bot,c(\bot,\bot)), & b(\bot,c(\bot,c(\bot,\bot)))\ \}. \end{array}$$

□

A_T needs 7 states. If we apply Construction I we find that for our example (as for most practical cases) this construction is hopelessly inefficient: the generated automaton for the given two small (!) patterns has already $2^7 = 128$ states. It can be shown that in the worst case exponentially many states are inevitable. However, often most of the states introduced by Construction I are superfluous. For instance in our example the set $\{a(\bot,\bot), b(\bot, c(\bot, c(\bot,\bot)))\}$ is generated which consists of "contradicting" patterns, i.e., patterns that cannot match the same tree. Therefore, we present a "cheaper" Construction II which from the beginning generates only such subsets of states which actually occur in computations of the subset automaton.

Definition 5.2 (Subset Construction II)
Let $A = (Q, \Sigma, \delta, Q_F)$ be a finite tree automaton. The corresponding (reduced) subset automaton is the deterministic finite tree automaton $P_r(A) = (Q_r, \Sigma, \delta_r, Q_{r,F})$ with $Q_{r,F} := \{B \in Q_r \mid B \cap Q_F \neq \emptyset\}$ whose sets of states and transitions are iteratively determined by $Q_r := \bigcup_{n\geq 0} Q_r^{(n)}$ and $\delta_r := \bigcup_{n\geq 0} \delta_r^{(n)}$ where

- $Q_r^{(0)} := \emptyset$;
- Assume $n > 0$. For $a \in \Sigma_k$ and $B_1, \ldots, B_k \in Q_r^{(n-1)}$ let $B := \{q \in Q \mid \exists q_1 \in B_1, \ldots, q_k \in B_k : (q, a, q_1 \ldots q_k) \in \delta\}$. If $B \neq \emptyset$ then $B \in Q_r^{(n)}$ and $(B, a, B_1 \ldots B_k) \in \delta_r^{(n)}$. □

Since for all n, $Q_r^{(n)} \subseteq Q_r^{(n+1)}$ and $\delta_r^{(n)} \subseteq \delta_r^{(n+1)}$ iteration can be terminated as soon as no new states are generated. Therefore, $Q_r = Q_r^{(n)}$ and $\delta_r = \delta_r^{(n)}$ for the first n with $Q_r^{(n)} = Q_r^{(n+1)}$. Consequently, the algorithm terminates after at most $2^{|Q|}$ iterations.

By induction on the structure of an input tree one finds:

Lemma 5.2

1. *For every* $t \in T_\Sigma$ *the following holds.*
   - *If* $\delta_r(t)$ *is undefined then no computation of* A *for* t *exists.*
   - *If* $\delta_r(t)$ *is defined then* $\delta_r(t)$ *is the set of all states* q *for which a* q*–computation of* A *for* t *exists.*
2. $L(A) = L(P_r(A))$.
3. *For every state* $B \in Q_r$*, a tree* t *exists such that* $\delta_r(t) = B$. □

Consider the finite tree automaton A_T. We find that no longer *all* subsets of subpatterns are generated as new states but only subsets which are *maximally compatible*. Here, a set $S \subseteq T$ of patterns is called *compatible* if a tree t exists which is matched by every pattern in S. S is called *maximally* compatible if there is a tree which is matched by all patterns from S and not matched by any of the patterns in $T \backslash S$.

The set of states Q_r of the reduced subset automaton for A_T consists exactly of the maximally compatible subsets S of subpatterns. Thus, we obtain for our example:

$$\begin{array}{llll} Q_r = \{ & \{\bot\}, & \{\bot, b(a(a(\bot,\bot),\bot),\bot), b(\bot, c(\bot, c(\bot,\bot)))\}, & \\ & \{\bot, a(\bot,\bot)\}, & \{\bot, a(\bot,\bot), a(a(\bot,\bot),\bot)\}, & \{\bot, b(a(a(\bot,\bot),\bot),\bot)\}, \\ & \{\bot, c(\bot,\bot)\}, & \{\bot, c(\bot,\bot), c(\bot, c(\bot,\bot))\}, & \{\bot, b(\bot, c(\bot, c(\bot,\bot)))\}\} \end{array}$$

The reduced subset automaton possesses eight states! Compared with 128 states according to Construction I a significant improvement.

6 How to Generate Tree Parsers

Let $G = (N, \Sigma, P)$ be a regular tree grammar and $X \in N$. To obtain a description of all possible X–derivation trees for a given input tree, we proceed as in the case of tree pattern matching. First, we construct a (possibly non-deterministic) finite tree automaton $A_{G,X}$ whose computations represent derivation trees of G. Then, we apply Subset Construction II to $A_{G,X}$. This automaton is the basis of our tree parser.

Intuitively, the finite tree automaton $A_{G,X}$ operates on input $t \notin N$ as follows. At the root, $A_{G,X}$ guesses an X–derivation head $p_1 \ldots p_k p$ of an X–derivation tree for t with $p : X' \to s$. Then, $A_{G,X}$ verifies that s in fact "fits" i.e., that $\tilde{s}$ matches t. If during verification, $A_{G,X}$ hits a node where the right hand side s contains a nonterminal X_j, then $A_{G,X}$ again guesses an X_j–derivation head and so on. Formally, we therefore define $A_{G,X} = (Q_G, \Sigma, \delta_G, \{X\})$ where $Q_G = N \cup \{s' \mid \exists X \to s \in P \text{ with } s' \text{ subpattern of } s\}$.

δ_G consists of two components: the first one is responsible for the verification of the right hand sides whereas the second one performs the guesses. We define:

$$\begin{array}{rl} \delta_G := & \{(X, s, \epsilon) \mid s \in \Sigma \text{ and } \exists X\text{–derivation tree for } s\} \ \cup \\ & \{(s, a, s_1 \ldots s_k) \mid s = a(s_1, \ldots, s_k) \in Q_G\} \ \cup \\ & \{(X, a, s_1 \ldots s_k) \mid \exists X' \to s \in P : \exists X\text{–derivation tree for } X' \\ & \text{and } s = a(s_1, \ldots, s_k)\} \end{array}$$

It can be shown that several of the tree parsers described in the literature can be obtained from $A_{G,X}$ as defined above by means of Subset Construction II. However, taking a closer look at the definition one finds that δ_G contains several superfluous transitions! The automaton also allows $(s, a, s_1 \ldots s_k)$ if s is a right hand side but itself is not a proper subpattern of another right hand side. Obviously, such transitions cannot be used by any X–computation. Therefore, we define instead:

$$\begin{aligned}\delta_G := \ & \{(X, s, \epsilon) \mid s \in \Sigma \text{ and } \exists X\text{-derivation tree for } s\} \ \cup \\ & \{(s, a, s_1 \dots s_k) \mid s = a(s_1, \dots, s_k) \text{ proper subpattern of a right hand side}\} \ \cup \\ & \{(X, a, s_1 \dots s_k) \mid \exists X' \to s \in P : \exists X\text{-derivation tree for } X' \\ & \ \text{and } s = a(s_1, \dots, s_k)\}\end{aligned}$$

Lemma 6.1 *Let G be a regular tree grammar and t an input tree.*

- *A X-derivation tree of G exists for t if and only if a X-computation of $A_{G,X}$ exists for t.*

  Especially, $L(G, X) = L(A_{G,X})$.

- *Let $A = (Q, \Sigma, \delta, Q_F)$ be the (reduced) subset automaton for $A_{G,X}$. Then $\delta(t) \cap N = \{X' \in N \mid \exists X'\text{-derivation tree for } t\}$.* □

It is easy to reconstruct the X–derivation trees of G for a given input tree t from the X–computations of $A_{G,X}$ for t.[4] Hence, the tree parsing problem for a regular tree grammar G can be reduced to the problem of determining all accepting computations of a finite tree automaton A for a given input tree.

Let $A = (Q, \Sigma, \delta, Q_F)$ be a finite tree automaton and $A_r = (Q_r, \Sigma, \delta_r, Q_{r,F})$ the corresponding (reduced) subset automaton. The following simple algorithm allows to enumerate the q–computations for a tree t on input of a B–computation of A_r for t.

Let $\tau = (B, a, B_1 \dots B_k) \in \delta_r$ and $q \in B$. Define

$$\Theta(\tau)_q := \{(q, a, q_1 \dots q_k) \in \delta \mid q_1 \in B_1, \dots, q_k \in B_k\}$$

$\Theta(\tau)_q$ denotes the set of transitions of A corresponding to τ with q as successor state.

Assume $\phi = \langle a, B\rangle(\phi_1, \dots, \phi_k)$ is the B–computation of A_r for t. The algorithm traverses ϕ in pre-order. Let τ be the transition chosen at the root of ϕ. The algorithm selects a transition $(q, a, q_1 \dots q_k) \in \Theta(\tau)_q$. Then, recursively q_j–computations ψ_j, $j = 1, \dots, k$, are determined from the B_j–computations ϕ_j. Finally, the algorithm returns $\langle a, q\rangle(\psi_1, \dots, \psi_k)$. Different choices of transitions correspond to different derivation trees. This algorithm allows to enumerate all derivation trees.

7 Application to Code Selection

We would like to apply our tree parser generator to the code selection problem. In this setting we have to select the "best" derivation tree from the possible huge set of all derivation trees. As for the generation of tree parsers we proceed in three steps. We assume that the rules of the grammar G are annotated with *cost functions* that describe the "costs" of the corresponding instruction. We translate these cost functions into cost functions for the transitions of the tree automaton $A_{G,X}$. Finally, we show how a cheapest computation of $A_{G,X}$ can be determined from the computation of the subset automaton for $A_{G,X}$.

[4] However, observe that the number of X–computations for t is always *finite* even if the number of X–derivation trees may be infinite. This is due to the fact that the set of derivation heads corresponding to a guessing transition may form an *infinite* regular set.

Hence, assume that for every rule p of type $(X_1, \ldots, X_k) \to X$ we are given a k-ary function $C(p) : \mathbb{N}_0{}^k \to \mathbb{N}_0$. C can be extended to a function which maps every derivation tree ψ to costs $C(\psi) \in \mathbb{N}_0$. If $\psi = X \in N$ then $C(\psi) := 0$. If $\psi = p(\psi_1, \ldots, \psi_k)$ then $C(\psi) := C(p)C(\psi_1)\ldots C(\psi_k)$, i.e., we apply the function $C(p)$ to the already computed values $C(\psi_1), \ldots, C(\psi_k)$.

Analogously, we can attach cost functions to transitions of finite tree automata and use them to compute the costs of computations.

A cost measure C is called ***monotone*** or ***additive*** if $C(p)$ is monotone or of the form $C(p) = c_p + x_1 + \cdots + x_k, c_p \in \mathbb{N}_0$, respectively, for all $p \in P$. Cost measures that are used in practice usually are additive. Examples are cost measures that compute the number of necessary processor cycles, the number of referenced memory cells, or the number of the operands of an instruction. A cost measure which is monotone but not additive is given by C_R which computes the minimal number of registers necessary to evaluate an expression. The advantage of additive cost measures (even if they approximate "reality" in complex processor architectures rather roughly) is that they are easy to implement and maintain.

A simple cost measure is $C_\|$ which maps every chain rule p to the cost function $C_\|(p) = x_1$ and every non-chain rule p of type $(X_1, \ldots, X_k) \to X$ to the cost function $C_\|(p) = 1 + x_1 + \cdots + x_k$. Then for every derivation tree ψ, $C_\|(\psi)$ evaluates to the number of occurrences of non-chain rules in ψ.

We now translate the cost annotation C of the grammar G into a cost annotation C^* of the corresponding tree automaton $A_{G,X}$ for some nonterminal X of G. The proposed constructions assume an additive cost measure. In this case, we can represent the cost function of every rule by a cost in $\mathbb{N}_0$. Hence in the sequel we consider C as a function from $P \to \mathbb{N}_0$. Then we define C^* as follows.

- If $\tau = (X, a, \epsilon)$ for $a \in \Sigma$ then $C^*(\tau)$ is the minimal cost of a X-derivation tree for a.
- If $\tau = (s, a, s_1 \ldots s_k)$ with $s = a(s_1, \ldots, s_k)$ then $C^*(\tau) := 0$.
- If $\tau = (X, a, s_1 \ldots s_k)$ then $C^*(\tau)$ is the minimum of the values $(\gamma + C(p))$ for rules $p : X' \to a(s_1, \ldots, s_k)$ and minimal cost γ of a X-derivation tree for X'.

By this definition, the cost $C^*(\phi)$ of a X-computation ϕ coincides with the minimal cost of a X-derivation tree represented by ϕ.

More generally, assume $A = (Q, \Sigma, \delta, Q_F)$ is a finite tree automaton and $C : \delta \to \mathbb{N}_0$ is an additive cost measure. Let $A_r = (Q_r, \Sigma, \delta_r, Q_{r,F})$ be the (reduced) subset automaton for A. We modify the above algorithm enumerating the computations of A to return a cheapest computation of A only. The idea is to provide every choice point of the algorithm with information about an optimal choice. Assume ϕ is a B-computation of the subset automaton A_r for some input tree t. To ϕ we attach two tuples $C(\phi) = \langle C(\phi)_q \rangle_{q \in B}$ and $D(\phi) = \langle D(\phi)_q \rangle_{q \in B}$ where $C(\phi)_q$ contains the cost of a cheapest q-computation for t and $D(\phi)_q$ the transition selected at the root of a q-computation with cost $C(\phi)_q$. The tuples $C(\phi/n)$ and $D(\phi/n)$ for all nodes n of ϕ can be computed during a post-order traversal of ϕ.

Now, the modified algorithm traverses the computation ϕ of A_r for t in pre-order. At every node n it selects the corresponding component from $D(\phi/n)$. Thus, it returns a q–computation of A for t with minimal costs.

Computing all the tuples of costs can be rather expensive. Therefore, Pelegri–Llopart tried to incorporate the cost computations into the state transitions themselves [23, 24]. He observed that for usual machine grammars $G_m = (N_m, \Sigma, P_m)$, the differences of the minimal costs of X–derivation trees and X'–derivation trees for the same tree t are bounded by some constant. This is due to the presence of MOVE instructions in most physical machines that introduce chain rules between (almost) all nonterminals [24]. This is the reason why it suffices to consider bounded *cost differences* instead of total costs, when constructing a cheapest computation of the non-deterministic automaton $A = (Q, \Sigma, \delta, Q_F)$ from the computation of the subset automaton.

The finitely many cost differences can be compiled into the states of the subset automaton. This results in the subset automaton $A_c = (Q_c, \Sigma, \delta_c, Q_{c,F})$. Assume $B \in Q_c$ is a state of A_c. Then B contains information about reached states q of A together with a cost difference d, i.e., $B \subseteq \{\langle q, d\rangle \mid q \in Q \text{ and } d \in \mathbb{N}_0\}$. For $\langle q, d\rangle \in B$, the cost difference d describes the difference between the cost of a cheapest q–computation of A and the cost of a cheapest computation at all.

Definition 7.1 (Subset Construction III)
Let $A = (Q, \Sigma, \delta, Q_F)$ be a finite tree automaton and $C : \delta \longrightarrow \mathbb{N}_0$ a cost function which maps every transition from δ to a cost in $\mathbb{N}_0$. The corresponding *(reduced) subset automaton with integrated costs* is the deterministic finite tree automaton $P_c(A) = (Q_c, \Sigma, \delta_c, Q_{c,F})$ with $Q_{c,F} := \{B \in Q_c \mid \langle q, d\rangle \in B \text{ and } q \in Q_F\}$ whose sets of states and transitions are iteratively given by $Q_c := \bigcup_{n\geq 0} Q_c^{(n)}$ and $\delta_c := \bigcup_{n\geq 0} \delta_c^{(n)}$ as follows.

- $Q_c^{(0)} := \emptyset$;
- Let $n > 0$. For $a \in \Sigma_k$ and $B_1, \ldots, B_k \in Q_c^{(n-1)}$ let
  $B := \{\langle q, d\rangle \mid \exists \langle q_1, d_1\rangle \in B_1, \ldots, \langle q_k, d_k\rangle \in B_k \text{ and } \tau = (q, a, q_1 \ldots q_k) \in \delta \text{ such that } d = C(\tau) + d_1 + \ldots + d_k \text{ is minimal}\}$.

  If $B \neq \emptyset$ then $norm(B) \in Q_c^{(n)}$ and $(norm(B), a, B_1 \ldots B_k) \in \delta_c^{(n)}$ with $norm(B) = \{\langle q, (d - \epsilon)\rangle \mid \langle q, d\rangle \in B \text{ and } \epsilon = min_{i=1}^{|B|}(d_i) \text{ with } \langle q_i, d_i\rangle \in B\}$ □

The algorithm to construct a q–computation of A from a computation of the subset automaton can be used to compute cheapest computations when given a computation of the (reduced) subset automaton with integrated costs $A_c = (Q_c, \Sigma, \delta_c, Q_{c,F})$ just by replacing the sets of transitions $\Theta(\tau)_q$ with $\Theta_c(\tau)_q$. Here, for a transition $\tau = (B, a, B_1 \ldots B_k) \in \delta_c$ and $\langle q, d\rangle \in B$, $\Theta_c(\tau)_q$ denotes the set of cheapest transitions of A contained in τ with q as successor state. Formally, it is defined by $\Theta_c(\tau)_q := \{\eta = (q, a, q_1 \ldots q_k) \in \delta \mid \langle q_1, d_1\rangle \in B_1, \ldots, \langle q_k, d_k\rangle \in B_k \text{ such that } C(\eta) + d_1 + \ldots + d_k \text{ minimal}\}$. Let $\phi = \langle a, B\rangle(\phi_1, \ldots, \phi_k)$ be the B–computation of A_c for some input tree t. The algorithm traverses ϕ in pre-order. Let τ be the transition at the root of ϕ. The algorithm chooses a transition $(q, a, q_1 \ldots q_k)$, now from $\Theta_c(\tau)_q$. Then, it recursively determines q_j–computations ψ_j, $j = 1, \ldots, k$ from ϕ_j. As the result it returns $\langle a, q\rangle(\psi_1, \ldots, \psi_k)$. All possible outputs are cheapest q–computations of A.

In general, the subset automata of Construction III are larger than the corresponding automata generated by Construction II without cost differences. Also, Construction III terminates only for finite tree automata with cost functions where the differences between cheapest computations for trees t are bounded by a constant. The advantage of subset automata with integrated costs is that they allow for a much faster construction of a cheapest computation of the original tree automaton.

The next section deals with efficient implementation techniques for tree automata. For simplicity, we will only consider subset constructions without integrated costs.

8 Implementation of Deterministic Finite Tree Automata

Assume $A = (Q, \Sigma, \delta, Q_F)$ is a deterministic tree automaton. As a first approach, we represent the set δ_a of transitions for an operator a of rank k as a k–dimensional array M_a. $M_a[q_1, \ldots, q_k] = \delta(a, q_1 \ldots q_k)$ whenever δ is defined for these arguments and $M_a[q_1, \ldots, q_k] = \bot$ otherwise, where $\bot$ is a special error symbol.

Assume that the input tree t is given as a node labeled ordered rooted tree in the sense of [20]. The state at a node n with label $a \in \Sigma_k$ is determined as $M_a[q_1, \ldots, q_k]$ where $q_1, \ldots, q_k$ are the states at the sons of n. The states are computed during a post-order traversal of t. Therefore, the computation time for such a "run" of the tree automaton consists of the time spent for the tree traversal which is proportional to the size of t together with an indexed array access for every node in t.

In most of the existing processors, the time for such an array access is proportional to the number of indices. Since every subtree of t takes part in indexed accesses only once the total time is linear in the size of t and independent of the ranks of operators.

Example 8.1 Example 4.2 continued
Let G_m be the grammar from example 4.2. The non-deterministic automaton $A = (Q, \Sigma, \delta, Q_F)$ for G_m has the set of states

$$Q = \{const, REG, m(const), m(REG)\}$$

and the set of transitions:

$$\begin{aligned}\delta = \{\ & (const, const, \epsilon)\\ & (REG, const, \epsilon)\\ & (REG, REG, \epsilon)\\ & (m(const), m, const)\\ & (REG, m, const)\\ & (m(REG), m, REG)\\ & (REG, plus, m(const)\ REG)\\ & (REG, plus, m(REG)\ REG)\\ & (REG, plus, REG\ REG)\}\end{aligned}$$

The reduced subset automaton $A_r = (Q_r, \Sigma, \delta_r, Q_{F,r})$ for A has the set of states

$$
\begin{aligned}
Q_r = \{\ q_1 &= \{REG\} \\
q_2 &= \{const, REG\} \\
q_3 &= \{m(REG)\} \\
q_4 &= \{m(const), REG, m(REG)\}\ \}
\end{aligned}
$$

and the set of transitions δ_r (represented as tables):

$\delta_{r,const} =$ q_2

$\delta_{r,REG} =$ q_1

$\delta_{r,m} =$

son			
q_1	q_2	q_3	q_4
q_3	q_4	$\perp$	q_3

$\delta_{r,plus} =$

left son	right son: q_1	q_2	q_3	q_4
q_1	q_1	q_1	$\perp$	q_1
q_2	q_1	q_1	$\perp$	q_1
q_3	q_1	q_1	$\perp$	q_1
q_4	q_1	q_1	$\perp$	q_1

The representation of δ as a set of arrays is usually rather storage space consuming because the size of an array M_a for an operator $a \in \Sigma_k$ is proportional to $|Q|^k$, i.e., exponential in the rank of a no matter how many (few) defined transitions the implemented automaton has for a. In most of the cases occurring in practice the necessary storage space can significantly be reduced by standard table compression methods.

An alternative method to represent the transition functions δ_a is provided by *decision trees*. Let Q and D be finite sets and $H : Q^k \to D$ a partial function. A *decision tree* for H is a leaf labeled tree of height k whose set of vertices V is given by $V = V_0 \cup \ldots \cup V_k$ where

$$V_j := \{q_1 \ldots q_j \mid \exists q_{j+1}, \ldots, q_k \in Q : H(q_1 \ldots q_j q_{j+1} \ldots q_k) \text{ is defined }\}.$$

Here, nodes $q_1 \ldots q_{j-1}$ and $q_1 \ldots q_{j-1} q'$ are connected by a directed edge (of level j) with label q'. Furthermore, the leaves $b = q_1 \ldots q_k$ are labeled with $H(q_1 \ldots q_k)$.

For an operator a of rank k, we can represent δ_a by the decision tree for the function H_a that is given by $H_a(q_1 \ldots q_k) := \delta(a, q_1 \ldots q_k)$. The nodes of the decision tree exactly represent the prefixes of state sequences occurring in δ_a. The state at a node n with label $a \in \Sigma_k$ in the input tree for whose sons we have already computed the states $q_1, \ldots, q_k$ is obtained by following the path in the decision tree for δ_a whose edges successively are labeled with $q_1, \ldots, q_k$. The label at the final node on this path yields the desired result.

In case of the above presented tree parser generator the generated deterministic finite tree automaton is of the form $P_r(A_{G,X})$ for some regular tree grammar G and some nonterminal X of G. Here, we are not only interested in the state (of the subset automaton) at some node n but also in the set of possible transitions of the tree automaton $A_{G,X}$ at n. Accordingly, we choose H_a "more informative", i.e., as

$$H_a(B_1 \dots B_k) := \langle \delta(a, B_1 \dots B_k), \Theta \rangle$$

where $\Theta := \{(q, a, q_1 \dots q_k) \in \delta_G \mid q_j \in B_j\}$.

If we represent the tree automaton by decision trees then the required storage space for the automaton is proportional to the size of δ. However, if the transition function δ of the deterministic finite tree automaton A is *total* (which is always the case for automata obtained by Subset Construction I) then the decision trees have the same size as the arrays.

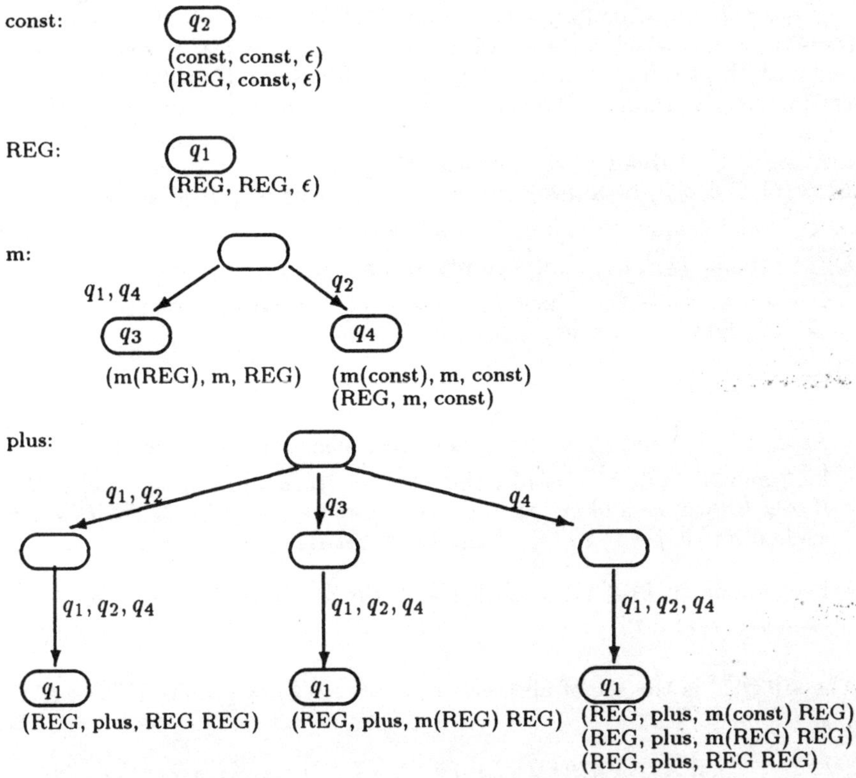

Figure 2: Compressed decision trees for the grammar of example 4.2

Decision trees can (possibly) more economically be represented by identifying isomorphic subtrees. Such a graph is called *compressed decision tree* or *decision graph*. Especially, we can represent a decision tree by its subtree graph. A (compressed) decision tree T_a again can be represented by a 2-dimensional array N_a whose first component is indexed with the inner nodes v of T_a and whose second component is indexed with labels q of edges. The entry $N_a[v, q]$ contains the successor node of v in T_a when following the edge labeled with q – if such a node exists and $\perp$ otherwise.

In the worst case, arrays N_a are up to a linear factor of the same sizes as arrays M_a. In practice however, arrays N_a are significantly smaller. Again, the arrays N_a can be subject to all kinds of further table compression methods. For example [2] consider various decision tree and table compression methods for tree automata.

Uncompressed decision trees often do not fit into main storage. Hence, one is interested to *directly* produce compressed decision trees during the generation phase. This leads to the Subset Construction IV.

Let $A = (Q, \Sigma, \delta, Q_F)$ be a (non-deterministic) finite tree automaton and $a \in \Sigma_k$. The idea of Subset Construction IV is to generate a decision graph for the set of transitions $(\delta_r)_a$ of the reduced subset automaton for a such that the nodes are sets of transitions of A tagged with the level of the node. The root is complete δ_a tagged 0. Edges are labeled with sets of states. An edge with label B leads from a node $(v, j-1)$ to a node (v', j) if and only if v' consists of all transitions of v which have a j-th argument $q \in B$. A leaf b is additionally labeled with the set of all states that occur as left sides in transitions in b. The generation of this graph can be combined with the Subset Construction II.

Definition 8.1 (Subset Construction IV)
Let $A = (Q, \Sigma, \delta, Q_F)$ be a finite tree automaton. For $n \geq 0$ we define a set of states $Q_s^{(n)}$ and graphs $T_a^{(n)}$, $a \in \Sigma$, as follows.

$Q_s^{(0)} := \emptyset$ and $T_a^{(0)}$, $a \in \Sigma$, are empty graphs.

Let $n > 0$ and $a \in \Sigma_k$. Then $T_a^{(n)}$ has a set of vertices $V = V_0 \cup \ldots \cup V_k$ and a set of edges E which are defined as follows.

- $V_0 := \{(\delta_a, 0)\}$.
- Assume $j > 0$ and V_{j-1} has already been defined. For every $(v, j-1) \in V_{j-1}$ and $B \in Q_s^{(n-1)}$ consider the set $v' := \{(q, a, q_1 \ldots q_k) \in v \mid q_j \in B\}$. If $v' \neq \emptyset$ then we add (v', j) to the set V_j and an edge to the set E which leads from $(v, j-1)$ to (v', j) and has label B.
- Every node $(v, k) \in V_k$ is labeled with the set $\{q \in Q \mid \exists q_1, \ldots q_k \in Q : (q, a, q_1 \ldots q_k) \in v\}$.

The set $Q_s^{(n)}$ is the set of all labels of leaves (b, k) of graphs $T_a^{(n)}$, $a \in \Sigma$. □

$T_a^{(n)}$ is a subgraph of $T_a^{(n+1)}$ and $T_a^{(n)} = T_a^{(n+1)}$ provided $Q_s^{(n)} = Q_s^{(n+1)}$. By induction over n one proves:

Lemma 8.1 *Assume $A = (Q, \Sigma, \delta, Q_F)$ is a finite tree automaton, and $Q_r^{(n)}$ and $\delta_r^{(n)}$ are the n-th approximations to the sets of states and transitions, respectively, of the reduced subset automaton according to Subset Construction II. Then for all $n \geq 0$:*

- $Q_s^{(n)} = Q_r^{(n)}$;
- *The graph obtained from $T_a^{(n)}$ by removing all nodes of which no labeled leaf can be reached is a decision graph for $(\delta_r^{(n)})_a$.* □

Therefore, define $T_a := T_a^{(n)}$ for the first n with $Q_s^{(n)} = Q_s^{(n+1)}$. Assume A itself has no superfluous transitions. It turns out that then T_a does not contain useless nodes, i.e., is a compressed decision tree for $(\delta_r)_a$.

For our generated tree parser every leaf should not only contain the state of the subset automaton but also the set of the transitions of A that correspond to the path to (b, k), namely b itself! Provided the finite tree automaton A did not contain superfluous transitions, the generated decision graph equipped with this extended labeling H_a is *minimal*.

Lemma 8.2 *Assume $A = (Q, \Sigma, \delta, Q_F)$ is a finite tree automaton without superfluous transitions. Then for all $a \in \Sigma$:*

- *T_a is a decision graph for δ_a;*
- *T_a is isomorphic to the subtree graph of the decision tree for H_a.*

Proof:

We only prove the second statement. Assume T_a were not isomorphic to the subtree graph of the decision tree for H_a. Then two nodes $(v, j) \neq (v', j)$ exist from which the same set of leaves are reachable. However, if every transition of A is used in some computation then the set of transitions of a node in T_a is precisely the union of the sets of transitions of the leaves reachable from it. Hence, $v = v'$ in contradiction to our assumption. □

Construction IV generalizes the method (implicitly) described in [18] which for the special case of tree pattern matchers directly generates compressed decision trees. [26] use a similar construction to derive tree parsers.

The Construction IV is optimal in that it returns decision graphs with a minimal number of nodes. However, Chase in [Ch87] observed that many states of the generated subset automaton are equivalent w.r.t. transitions. Again, let $A = (Q, \Sigma, \delta, Q_F)$ be a finite tree automaton and $a \in \Sigma_k$. For $j = 1, \ldots, k$ we define the set $Q_{a,j} := \{q_j \mid (q, a, q_1 \ldots q_k) \in \delta\}$. The (a, j)*-relevant part* of a set $B \subseteq Q$ is the set $B \cap Q_{a,j}$. Within the decision graph T_a of Construction IV, sets of states with identical (a, j)-relevant parts lead from the same nodes $(v, j-1)$ to the same nodes (v', j).

The fifth subset construction returns compressed decision trees T'_a whose sets of vertices coincide with those of the T_a, but whose edges of level j are only labeled with (a, j)-relevant parts. Thus, the decision graphs themselves can be represented much more succinctly. The price one has to pay is to maintain separate tables which, for all $a \in \Sigma_k$, $j \in \{1, \ldots, k\}$, and occurring sets of states B, contain the (a, j)-relevant parts of B. Determining the state at a node n with label $a \in \Sigma_k$ of the input tree is now done in two steps. First for the states $B_1, \ldots, B_k$ at the sons of n, we successively have to look up the (a, j)-relevant parts B'_j. Then, the path with edge labeling $B'_1, \ldots, B'_k$ in the decision graph for a yields the result.

As in Subset Construction IV, we construct the modified decision graphs by "need".

Definition 8.2 (Subset Construction V)
Let $A = (Q, \Sigma, \delta, Q_F)$ be a finite tree automaton. For $n \geq 0$ we define a set of

states $Q_s^{(n)}$ graphs $T_a^{'(n)}$, $a \in \Sigma_k$, together with sets $R_{a,j}^{(n)} = \{B \cap Q_{a,j} \mid B \in Q_s^{(n)}\} \backslash \{\emptyset\}$ for $1 \leq j \leq k$ as follows.

$Q_s^{(0)} := \emptyset$ and $T_a^{'(0)}$, $a \in \Sigma$ are empty graphs.

Let $n > 0$ and $a \in \Sigma_k$.

$T_a^{'(n)}$ has a set of vertices $V = V_0 \cup \ldots \cup V_k$ and a set of edges E which are defined as follows.

- $V_0 := \{(\delta_a, 0)\}$.
- Assume $j > 0$ and V_{j-1} has already been defined. For every $(v, j-1) \in V_{j-1}$ and $B \in R_{a,j}^{(n-1)}$ consider the set $v' := \{(q, a, q_1 \ldots q_k) \in v \mid q_j \in B\}$. If $v' \neq \emptyset$ then we add (v', j) to the set V_j and an edge to E which leads from $(v, j-1)$ to (v', j) and has label B.
- Every node $(v, k) \in V_k$ is labeled with the set $\{q \in Q \mid \exists q_1, \ldots q_k \in Q : (q, a, q_1 \ldots q_k) \in v\}$.

The set $Q_s^{(n)}$ is the set of all labels of leaves (b, k) in $T_a^{'(n)}$, $a \in \Sigma$. □

Chase uses the idea of an equivalence relation to generate compressed tables for pattern matching [3]. Our Construction V both generalizes his method an the method of Kron to arbitrary tree automata.

9 Practical Experience

Based on [26] a code selector generator was developed at the Universität des Saarlandes [19]. Given an annotated regular tree grammar it produces tables and a driver program that selects code for an *IR* tree. As an example, the processor NSC32000 was described by a grammar. This grammar has 763 rules with 54 nonterminals and 168 terminals. The generated tree parser has 970 states. The arrays M_a for this parser would consume about 180 Megabyte. The representation as compressed decision trees, i.e., as arrays N_a need about 1 Megabyte. Applying standard table compression methods like row displacement [2] we can further reduce the needed storage space to 14 Kilobytes.

Acknowledgements

We would like to thank Reinhold Heckmann for his helpful comments on this paper.

References

[1] Aho AV, Ganapathi M: Efficient Tree Pattern Matching: An Aid to Code Generation. In: Proc. of the 12th ACM Symp. on Principles of Programming Languages, 1985, pp 334-340

[2] Börstler J, Möncke U, Wilhelm R: Table Compression for Tree Automata. In: ACM Transactions on Programming Languages and Systems, Vol. 13, No. 3, July 1991, pp 295-314

[3] Chase DR: An improvement to bottom-up tree pattern matching. In: Proc. of 14th ACM Symposium on Principles of Programming Languages, 1987, pp 168-177

[4] Dauchet M, Deruyver A: Compilation of Ground Term Rewriting Systems and Applications. In Dershowitz (ed) Proceedings of the Conference: Rewriting Techniques and Applications, Springer, 1989, LNCS 355, pp 556-558

[5] Downey PJ, Sethi R, Tarjan ER: Variations on the common subexpression problem. In: JACM 27 , 1980, pp 758-771

[6] Emmelmann H: Code Selection by Regularly Controlled Term Rewriting. In: Proceedings of the Workshop: CODE'91 in Dagstuhl, 1991

[7] Ferdinand C: Pattern Matching in a Functional Transformation Language using Treeparsing. In: Deransart, Małuszyński (eds): Proceedings of the Workshop: Programming Language Implementation and Logic Programming 90, Springer, 1990, LNCS 456, pp 358-371

[8] Gecseg F, Steinby M: Tree Automata. Akademiai Kiado, Budapest, 1984

[9] Giegerich R: Code Selection by Inversion of Order-sorted Derivors. In: Theoretical Computer Science 73, 1990, pp 177-211

[10] Giegerich R, Schmal K: Code Selection Techniques: Pattern Matching, Tree Parsing, and Inversion of Derivors. In: Ganzinger (ed) Proc. ESOP 88, Springer, 1988, LNCS 300, pp 247-268

[11] Glanville RS: A Machine Independent Algorithm for Code Generation and its Use in Retargetable Compilers. Ph.D. Thesis, Univ. of California, Berkeley, 1977

[12] Glanville RS, Graham SL: A new Method for Compiler Code Generation. In: Proc. of the 5th ACM Symp. on Principles of Programming Languages, 1978, pp. 231-240

[13] Gräf A: Left-to-Right Tree Pattern Matching. In Book (ed) Proceedings of the Conference: Rewriting Techniques and Applications, Springer, 1991, LNCS 488, pp 323-334

[14] Henry RR: Graham–Glanville Code Generators. Ph.D. Thesis, Univ. of California, Berkeley, 1984

[15] Henry RR, Damron PC: Algorithms for Table-Driven Code Generators Using Tree-Pattern Matching. Technical Report # 89-02-03, University of Washington, Seattle, 1989

[16] Henry RR, Damron PC: Encoding Optimal Pattern Selection in a Table-Driven Bottom-Up Tree-Pattern Matcher. Technical Report # 89-02-04, University of Washington, Seattle, 1989

[17] Hoffmann DM, O'Donnell MJ: Pattern Matching in Trees. In: JACM 29,1, 1982, pp 68-95

[18] Kron H: Tree Templates and Subtree Transformational Grammars. Ph.D. Thesis, Univ. of California, Santa Cruz, 1975

[19] Mathis N: Weiterentwicklung eines Codeselektorgenerators und Anwendung auf den NSC32000. Diplomarbeit, Universität des Saarlandes, 1990

[20] Mehlhorn K: Datenstrukturen und Algorithmen. Teubner, 1986

[21] Möncke U: Simulating Automata for Weighted Tree Reductions. Technischer Bericht Nr. A10/87, Universität des Saarlandes, 1987

[22] Möncke U, Weisgerber B, Wilhelm R: Generative support for transformational programming. In: ESPRIT: Status Report of Continuing Work, Elsevier Sc., Brussels, 1986

[23] Pelegri-Llopart E: Rewrite Systems, Pattern Matching, and Code Selection. Ph.D. Thesis, Univ. of California, Berkeley, 1988

[24] Pelegri-Llopart E, Graham SL: Optimal Code Generation for Expression Trees: An Application of BURS Theory. In: Proc. of the 15th ACM Symposium on Principles of Programming Languages, 1988, San Diego, CA, pp 294-308

[25] Ripken K: Formale Beschreibungen von Maschinen, Implementierungen und optimierender Maschinencode–Erzeugung aus attributierten Programmgraphen. Dissertation, TU München, 1977

[26] Weisgerber B, Wilhelm R: Two tree pattern matchers for code selection. In: Hammer (ed) Proceedings of the Workshop: Compiler Compilers and High Speed Compilation, Springer, 1988, LNCS 371, pp 215-229

Considerate Code Selection

Robert Giegerich
Universität Bielefeld
Technische Fakultät
Postfach 10 01 31
W-4800 Bielefeld 1
Germany
robert@techfak.uni-bielefeld.de

Abstract

Considerate code selection is not another code selection technique. It is concerned with the integration of code selection with other subtasks of code generation, such as register allocation and scheduling. Considerate code selection allows to defer decisions between alternative encodings. This is achieved by means of a shared representation of the overall solution space. Subsequent phases are adapted to process all solutions simultaneously, again producing results in a shared representation. Decisions may be interspersed in this process whenever desired.

The paper introduces this technique in a framework where code selection in done by tree parsing, and later phases are described by attribute coupled grammars. Being a general technique rather than an algorithm, considerate code selection can be used with any of the current, pattern based approaches to code selection.

1 Motivation

The pattern matching approach to code selection, when implemented by bottom-up tree parsing, allows three ways to deal with the fact that there are many alternative encodings for a given source program:

- The *maximal-munch-heuristic* favours encodings with machine instructions that implement serveral source operators at a time. Precaution must be taken, as this strategy may lead into blind alleys. Also, the maximal size of munches does not strictly imply minimal target program costs.

- A cost driven heuristic such as *dynamic programming* tries to achieve good overall solutions composed from locally optimal subsolutions.

Both strategies have proved to be practical. Both, however, simplify code selection at the price of a negative effect on the modularity of the code generation problem as a whole: As alternative solutions are discarded at each stage, all other considerations such as register usage must be interleaved with the code selection process. In this paper, we propose a third approach:

- The set of all solutions is explicitly constructed. Later phases of code generation may apply register requirements analysis, instruction cost considerations and other criteria to successively reduce the solution set, eventually to a single target program. This approach will be called ***considerate code selection***, and the present paper is a first exploration of this idea. The name comes from the fact that for code selection proper, no heuristic is applied.

At the first glance, considerate code selection looks like a tantalizing idea. As the number of overall encodings for a given source program grows combinatorially with the number of encodings for its immediate subprograms, the set of all solutions is exponential in the size of the input. Hence, it should be excessively expensive to construct this solution set, as well as to process it further. At a second thought, however, we note the following:

- Since tree parsing can produce any encoding, it may as well produce all encodings without extra cost. In the pattern matching terminology, the bottom-up pattern matcher implicitly constructs all covers of the intermediate program tree in $\mathcal{O}(n)$, where n is the number of its nodes. What we need is a compact representation of this solution set of size $\mathcal{O}(2^n)$ in $\mathcal{O}(n)$ space, which can be achieved by an appropriate kind of sharing contexts.
- Later tasks of code generation can be described as analyses or transformations of a particular encoding. What we need is a mechanism to apply such operations to the compact representation of all solutions simultaneously, hopefully retaining the amount of sharing.

The data structure used for this purpose, introduced below, is called ***shared forest***. It is named after a related approach that has evolved independently in the area of natural language parsing [15]. Although intuitively, the problems to be solved and the data structures used are quite similar in that work and ours, the formalizations are different and their relationship has not been explored yet in any depth.

2 The Model of Code Generation

For the formal development of our approach, we need the following notations: A signature $\Sigma = (S, F)$ is given by a set of sorts S and a set of F of operators together with their arity. The set of Σ-Terms is denoted $T(\Sigma)$, while the set of Σ-terms of sort s is denoted $T(\Sigma) : s$. $T(\Sigma, X)$ denotes terms with variables from a variable set X. For $t \in T(\Sigma, X), var(t)$ denotes the set of variables occuring in t, $t\sigma$ denotes application of a substitution (of terms for variables) to t, yielding a term t' called an instance of t. Given a confluent and terminating term rewrite system $R, t\downarrow_R$ denotes the normal form of t with respect to R. For further terminology about term rewrite systems, see e.g. [3]. Following common usage, we will also use the words *trees* and *forests* for terms and sets of terms, respectively.

We use an algebraic model of code generation, as in [12, 8, 9]. Source and target programs are represented as terms of a source signature IL and a target signature *TL*. Target programs are further restricted by certain well-formedness predicates. These model target machine properties that cannot be expressed syntactically. The target is related to the source language by a *TL*-homomorphism, specified as a derivor (denoted m below). Code selection proper means inverting this derivor, i.e. constructing (one or all) t satisfying $m(t) = p$ for the given source program p. Code generation as a whole means furthermore to find a t' that satisfies all further well-formedness criteria (as well as $m(t') = p$).

For the presentation, consider the following trivial instance of a code selection problem: Let there be machine instructions $add(r,x,y)$, $addi(r,x,c)$ and $ld(r,c)$, denoting addition of two registers, add-immediate to a register, and load constant. The first argument within each instruction is the register number of the target register used. We want to generate code for source expressions p like $(1+2)+(3+4)$. The relation between target and source language is specified by the *TL*-homomorphism m in Example 2.1:

Example 2.1 :

> **signature** *TL* =
>
> **sorts** *R, C, Regno*
>
> **ops** *ld: Regno, C* $\rightarrow$ *R*
> *addi: Regno, R, C* $\rightarrow$ *R*
> *add: Regno, R, R* $\rightarrow$ *R*

$$
\begin{aligned}
m(ld(r,c)) &= c \\
m(addi(r,x,c)) &= m(x) + c \\
m(add(r,x,y)) &= m(x) + m(y)
\end{aligned}
$$

□

Code selection means solving the equation

$$m(z) = p \tag{1}$$

where z is a target program variable, and p a source program.

Here, the overall translation of a source program p depends on the root operator of p and choices of translations for certain subexpressions. In Example 2.1, the code selection problem $m(z) = p$ has four solutions for $p = (1+2)+(3+4)$, shown in Example 3.2 below. From them, we need to select one according to further constraints regarding register allocation and instruction costs.

3 Shared Forests

A Σ-forest of sort s is a subset of $T(\Sigma) : s$. A shared Σ-forest is a particular representation of a Σ-forest which exploits sharing of contexts and allows an (up to) logarithmic space reduction.

Definition 3.1 : Shared forests

1. *For a given* $\Sigma = (S, F)$, *and an S-sorted set of variables X let* $d\Sigma = (S \cup \{choices\}, F \cup \{\Box_s : s, choices, s \rightarrow s | s \in S\} \cup \{l :\rightarrow choices, r :\rightarrow choices\})$. *The operators* $\Box_s$ *are called choice operators.*
2. *Let* $V : choices$ *be a set of variables of sort choices.*
3. *The set of shared* Σ*-forests is* $T(d\Sigma, X \cup V)$.

□

Of course, we assume that the symbols added by the extension are not already present in Σ and X. Mostly, we shall omit the subscript s with $\Box$.

Example 3.2 : Shared forest solution *f_prog* **to** $m(z) = (a + b) + (c + d)$

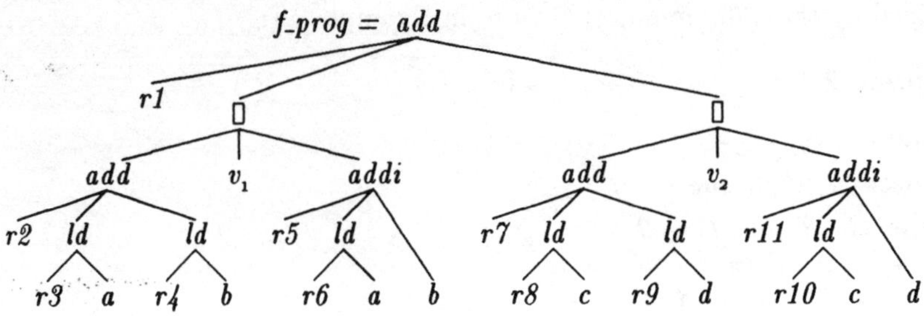

□

Two kinds of variables occur in the shared target forest of Example 3.2: $r1, r2, \cdots$ are variables for register numbers, yet to be instantiated. v_1 and v_2 are choice variables, whose purpose will become clear shortly.

A shared forest represents a forest in an obvious way:

Definition 3.3 : Semantics of shared forests

1. *Let A be the rewrite system given by* $\{\Box_s(x, l, y) \rightarrow x, \Box_s(x, r, y) \rightarrow y \mid s \in S\}$
2. *For all* $s \in S$, *the interpretation* $I : T(d\Sigma, V) : s \rightarrow 2^{T(\Sigma):s}$ *is given by* $I(w) = \{w\sigma\downarrow_A \mid \sigma$ *is a ground substitution for the choice variables in* $w\}$.

□

A shared Σ-forest w denotes a set of Σ-terms $I(w)$. Instantiating the choice variables in w by l or r and normalizing with A yields a particular element of $I(w)$. Note that we can represent neither empty nor infinite forests.

The sharing provided by shared forests is complementary to that provided by the dag-representation of trees. While dags share identical subterms within a term, shared forests share *identical contexts of different subterms*. Both kinds of sharing can be combined to a certain extent. For simplicity, we avoid dags in this paper.

The potential compactification in representing $I(w)$ by w is measured as follows:

Lemma 3.4 :

Let w be a shared forest containing n $\square$-operators.
Then we have $1 \leq |I(w)| \leq 2^n$, and this bound is sharp.

Proof:

To obtain $|I(W)|$, we can translate w into a term over $(N, +, *)$ by

$a \to 1$ for each constant $a \in F$

$x \to 1$ for each variable $x \in X$

$f(x_1, \cdots, x_n) \to *(x_1, \cdots, x_n)$
for each n-ary operator $f \in F, n \geq 1$

$\square(x_1, v, x_2) \to x_1 + x_2$

□

Evaluating the resulting expression yields an upper bound for $|I(w)|$. It is achieved when w is linear (i.e. no choice variable occurs more than once in w), all n $\square$-operators are independent, and when $\sigma \neq \sigma'$ implies $w\sigma \downarrow_A \neq w\sigma' \downarrow_A$. See Example 3.5.

Example 3.5 :

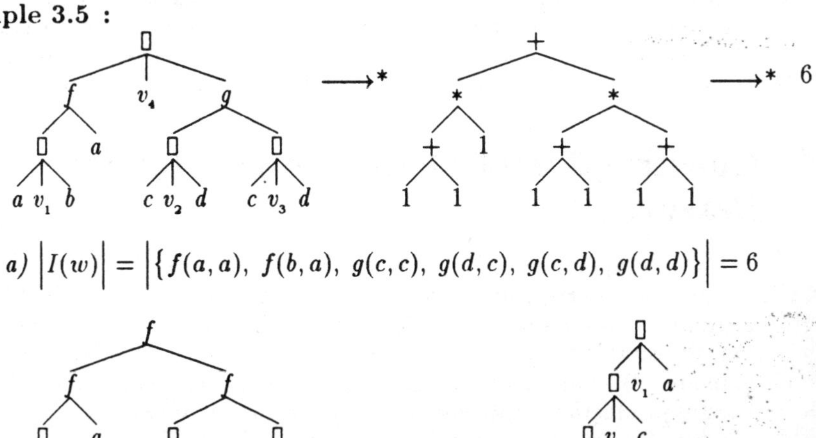

a) $\left|I(w)\right| = \left|\{f(a,a),\ f(b,a),\ g(c,c),\ g(d,c),\ g(c,d),\ g(d,d)\}\right| = 6$

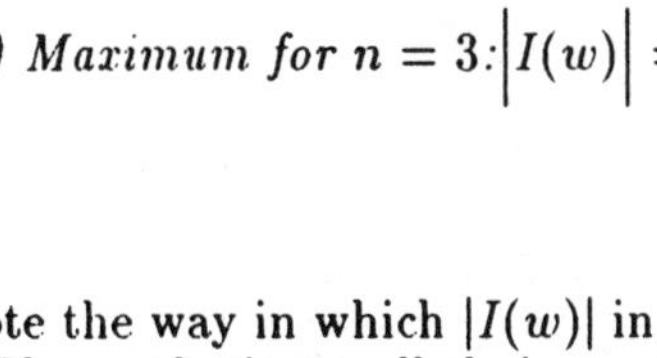

b.1) Maximum for $n = 3$: $\left|I(w)\right| = 8$ *b.2) Minimum for* $n = 3$: $\left|I(w)\right| = 1$

□

Note the way in which $|I(w)|$ in example 3.5b.1) depends on (non-)linearity of w. If we substitute all choice variables by the same variable v, $|I(w)| = 2$.

Considering space reduction, we must relate the $|w|$ (the size of w in terms of operators) to the sum over $|w\sigma|$ for all σ. This ratio depends on the amount of context sharing present in w.

The following axioms are consistent with the interpretation I:

Definition 3.6 : Condensation/Expansion Axioms

For all $s \in S$

1. $\square(x, v, x) = x$
2. $\square(f(x_1, \cdots, x_{i-1}, x, x_{i+1}, \cdots, x_n), v, f(x_1, \cdots, x_{i-1}, y, x_{i+1}, \cdots, x_n))$
$$= f(x_1, \cdots, x_{i-1}, \square(x, v, y), x_{i+1}, \cdots, x_n)$$
$$\forall f \in F \ \wedge \ 1 \leq i \leq n$$

□

The condensation rewrite rule system C is obtained by orienting these equations left-to-right. The expansion rewrite rule system E is obtained by orienting 2. right-to-left.

Each w has a condensed normal form $w\downarrow_c$. Clearly $I(w) = I(w\downarrow_c)$, but $w\downarrow_c$ is neither the smallest, nor a unique representation of $I(w)$, as we do not consider the commutative, associative and idempotent properties, which $\square$ has under the interpretation I.

Any $w \in T(d\Sigma, V)$ can be fully expanded by E, such that all $t \in I(w)$, including duplicates, show up separately under a root portion consisting of $\square$-operators only. Conversely, such a "shared" forest can be condensed by C. Pragmatically, neither of these should ever happen in a computation where w is a logarithmic reduction of $I(w)$! Our interest in shared forests arises from the fact that we know algorithms (e.g. for the code selection problem) that directly construct shared representations of the desired solution space.

4 Construction of Shared Forests by Tree Parsing

Let us recall the approach of [12] and [8]: The equation $m(t) = p$ is solved by first converting the derivor m into a regular tree grammar. The productions are labeled by the corresponding target operators. The grammar for our example is untypically simple, as our target signature is one-sorted (there is only one address mode, R). This leads to a grammar with a single nonterminal symbol R and three productions corresponding to the target operators *ld*, *addi* and *add*. The terminal symbol c matches arbitrary numeric constants

(*ld*)		$R \rightarrow c$
(*addi*)	(2)	$R \rightarrow R + c$
(*add*)	(3)	$R \rightarrow R + R$

For $m(t) = a + b$ (where a, b are constants), the tree parser detects parses

$R \rightarrow R + b \rightarrow a + b$, corresponding to $addi(r_{11}, ld(r_{12}, a), b)$, and

$R \rightarrow R + R \rightarrow R + b \rightarrow a + b$, corresponding to $add(r_{13}, ld(r_{14}, a), ld(r_{15}, b))$.

As both start from the same nonterminal, the corresponding target terms are of the same sort and can share contexts. Hence, the result is

$$t = \square(addi(r_{11}, ld(r_{12}, a), b), v_1, add(r_{13}, ld(r_{14}, a), ld(r_{15}, b)))$$

When reducing by production 2, its corresponding target operator $addi(r, x, c)$ is applied to arguments $ld(r_{12}, a)$ and b, while there is no argument corresponding to r. Thus, a free variable r_{11} is substituted, denoting a register number yet to be chosen. r_{11} must be unique in the overall target program forest constructed this way. Continuing this process for $p = (a + b) + (c + d)$, the shared forest of Example 3.2 is obtained.

This informal description of shared forests construction must suffice here. Technical details of the construction of a single target term from a single tree parse of the input can be found in [8], where also the possibilities of chain rules in the tree grammar and infinite derivations are considered. The latter lead to infinitely many target terms. According to recent results of [2], these can be represented finitely. A comprehensive treatment of derivor inversion by tree parsing is in preparation [11].

Shared forests that arise from tree parsing are linear in the choice variables. Later phases, as we shall see shortly, may well introduce non-linearities.

5 Translations of Shared Forests

In our approach to code generation, various subtasks are described as translations between appropriate representations. This class of representations and translations is given by the underlying specification technique. For the sake of modularity, it is wise to require that they form a category. Then, composition of specifications is possible where ever composition of translations is. We now show how a category of translations between terms gives rise to a category of translations between the corresponding shared forests. When H is a class of morphisms between term algebras $T(\Sigma)$ and $T(\Sigma')$, we want to derive for each $h \in H$ some morphism $dh : T(d\Sigma, V) \to T(d\Sigma', V)$ such that the following diagram commutes:

$$\begin{array}{ccc} 2^{T(\Sigma)} & \xrightarrow{h} & 2^{T(\Sigma')} \\ \uparrow I & & \uparrow I \\ T(d\Sigma, V) & \xrightarrow{dh} & T(d\Sigma', V) \end{array}$$

Whether and how this can be done depends on the way H is defined. We shall consider the class of morphisms defined by attribute coupled grammars [6].

Attribute coupled grammars are classical attribute grammars [14] where the underlying context free grammar is seen as an input signature $\Sigma = (S, F)$. Attributes are associated with the sorts s from S. Attribute values are terms of an output signature Σ'. "Semantic functions" are composite terms from $T(\Sigma', X)$. Attribute rules specify the values of attributes, depending on other attributes in the local context. Circular dependencies are forbidden. Thus, given $t \in T(\Sigma)$, the value of its designated root attribute is some $t' \in T(\Sigma')$, called the translation $h(t)$ of t. An attribute coupling is the translation from $T(\Sigma)$ to $T(\Sigma')$ specified in this way. Note that attributes are transient in this approach. A main appeal of this is that attribute couplings can be composed, thus supporting modularity. An example of an attribute coupling is given after Theorem 5.2.

Attribute coupled grammars are used here because they are a very general (and well-understood) scheme of inductive definition. They encompass standard structural induction as the special case of a single, synthesized attribute. It is straightforward to transfer the construction to more restricted forms of structural induction.

Definition 5.1 : Lifting of attribute couplings to shared forests

Given an attribute coupling $h : T(\Sigma) \rightarrow T(\Sigma')$, its "lifting" to shared forests is another attribute coupling $dh : T(d\Sigma, V) \rightarrow T(d\Sigma', V)$, obtained as follows:
Take over all attribute declarations and rules of h. Add the following rules for each choice operator:

$$t = \Box_s(x, v, y) : \left.\begin{array}{l} x.i = t.i \\ y.i = t.i \end{array}\right\} \quad \text{for each inherited attribute } i \text{ associated with } s$$

$$t.d = \Box_{s'}(x.d, v, y.d) \quad \text{for each synthesized attribute } d \text{ of sort } s' \text{ associated with } s$$

□

The clue in this (otherwise straightforward) construction is that the choice-variable v, associated with the input choice-operator $\Box_s$, is also associated with the output choice-operator $\Box_{s'}$. We must now show that this construction is consistent with our interpretation of shared forests.

Theorem 5.2 :

Let $w \in T(d\Sigma, V), h : T(\Sigma, X) \rightarrow T(\Sigma', X), dh : T(d\Sigma, X \cup V) \rightarrow T(d\Sigma', X \cup V)$ constructed according to Definition 5.1.
Then, $\{h(t) | t \in I(w)\} = I(dh(w))$.

Proof:

We show that for an arbitrary ground substitution σ that substitutes all the choice variables in w, $h(w\sigma\downarrow_A) = (dh(w))\sigma\downarrow_A$. Consider the following synchronized A-reduction step of $w\sigma$ and $(dh(w))\sigma$: Let $w\sigma \rightarrow_A w_1\sigma$ be a reduction of some choice operator $\Box_0(x_0, v\sigma, y_0)$.

Let s, the sort of $\Box_0$, have n synthesized attributes. According to the definition of dh, their values have the form

$$\Box_1(x_1, v\sigma, y_1), \cdots, \Box_n(x_n, v\sigma, y_n).$$

(Note that $\Box_0, \cdots \Box_n$ use the same choice variable).

Let $(dh(w)\sigma) \rightarrow^n_A q_1$ by n-fold reduction of these choice operators in $(dh(w))\sigma$. Since the choice is consistently x_i or y_i in all cases $(0 \le i \le n)$, and the inherited attributes of x_0 and y_0 are copied from $\Box_0$, we have $q_1 = dh(w_1)\sigma$. Iterating this step until all choice operators are eliminated, we obtain some w_k, q_k with $q_k = (dh(w_k))\sigma\downarrow_A = dh\ w_k = h\ w_k$, since dh and h coincide on terms without choice operators. Remembering that $w_k = w\sigma\downarrow_A$ and $q_k = (dh(w))\sigma\downarrow_A$, we have established $h(w\sigma\downarrow_A) = (dh(w))\sigma = \downarrow_A$, q.e.d.

□

Even when w is in C-normal form, $dh(w)$ need not be so. One may include a condensation step by reformulating the equation for synthesized attributes to

$$t.d = \textbf{ if } x.d = y.d \textbf{ then } x.d \textbf{ else } \Box_{s'}(x.d, v, y.d).$$

However, $x.d$ and $y.d$ may be rather large terms from $T(d\Sigma', V)$, which must be compared to achieve the condensation. It is a pragmatic question whether this step should be included.

As an example, we describe the linearization of target programs into schedules. The variables created for register numbers during construction of the shared forest now act as symbolic register names. The signature of schedules is obtained from *TL* by adding a sequencing operator (++) and an empty sequence [ ]. We assume that the processor architecture suggests to schedule all load-instructions before any arithmetic instructions. We specify this by an attribute coupling that should be largely self-explanatory. The purpose of the attributes[1] involved is:

il, sl: inherited/synthesized attribute pair containing a sequence of load instructions,
ic, sc: attributes containing final schedule,
n: number of register that holds result of a subtree, (this may be a variable from X : ***Regno***).

t = ld (children: r a)
t.n = r
t.sl = t.il ++ ld(r,a)
t.sc = t.ic

t = addi (children: r x a)
t.n = r
t.sl = x.sl
t.sc = x.sc ++ addi(r, x.n, a)
x.il = t.il
x.ic = t.ic

t = add (children: r x y)
t.n = r
t.sl = y.sl
t.sc = y.sc ++ add(r, x.n, y.n)
x.il = t.il
x.ic = t.ic
y.il = x.sl
y.ic = x.sc

t = prog (child: x)
t.code = x.sc
x.il = [ ]
x.ic = x.sl

According to Definition 5.1, this attribute coupling can be lifted to shared forests. Applied to the shared forest of Example 3.2, we obtain the following shared forest of schedules:

[1] An equivalent attribute coupling using synthesized attributes only may appear even simpler. This example was chosen to illustrate the role of choice variables in the presence of inherited attributes.

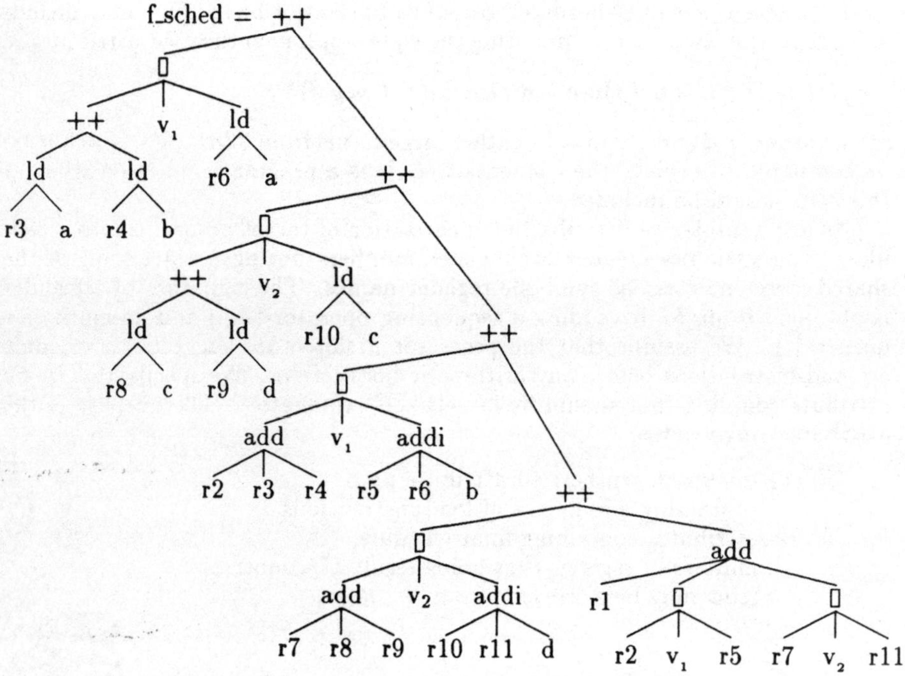

Note how the multiple occurences of the choice variables now control the effects of possible choices in quite different parts of the schedule, while retaining the sharing.

Another phase might measure schedules by (say) machine cycles. Again this measure could be described as an attribute coupling translating a single schedule into its cost. Let us say an *ld*-instruction takes 3, *addi* takes 2, and *add* takes 1 unit cost. The corresponding translation can be lifted to shared forests of schedules, and produces the following answer, a shared forest of costs:

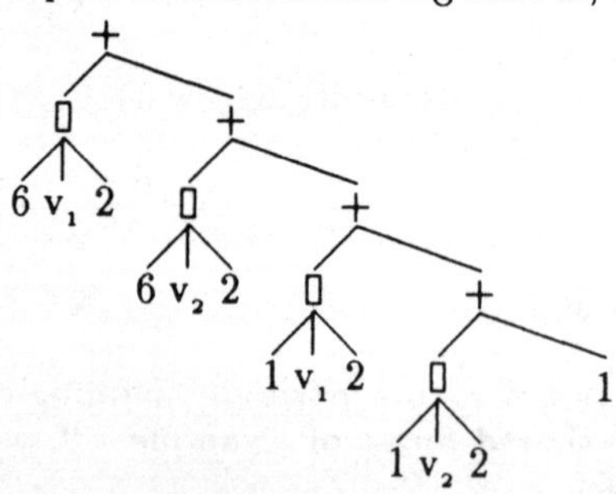

Using associative-commutative properties of $+$ and distributive laws like $\square(a, v, b) + \square(c, v, d) = \square(a + c, v, b + d)$, we obtain the shared cost forest:

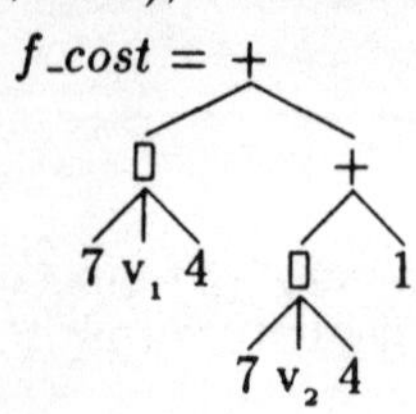

6 Selections from Shared Forests

Solution sets of potentially exponential size are likely to be intermediate results of a particular computation, while the final solution set often is of linear size, or even unitary. So we must provide ways to restrict the solution set represented by a shared forest. Even considerate code selection must make selections at some point.

One possibility is to adopt a general, nondeterministic method that (lazily) enumerates solutions from the shared representation. This approach retains the transparency of our implementation technique for the writer of a specification. A second possibility is to give up this transparency and allow an explicit handling of choice operators, to be provided by the specification writer. The first approach views each solution independently, the second approach, while more ad-hoc, allows for explicitly relating different sub-solutions and making choice based on a preference relation. We will sketch both approaches here.

From the shared cost forest *f_cost* obtained above, it is straightforward[2] to determine that the substitution $\sigma = [v_1 \leftarrow r, v_2 \leftarrow r]$ yields the minimal cost of 9 units. Now we finally do code selection: $(f\_sched)\sigma{\downarrow}_A$ is the minimal-cost schedule, $(f\_prog)\sigma{\downarrow}_A$ is the minimal-cost target program t with $m(t) = p$.

There is one thing ad-hoc with this way of selection (but we do not see a chance to avoid it altogether): Determining $min\ I(f\_cost)$ needs to relate different alternatives. Hence the specifier must make explicit reference to choice operators.

We now study a different way to restrict the solution space. Reconsider the setting of Example 1. Machine programs are related to source expressions by the morphism m. While m associates machine instructions with source operators, it does not care for register requirements. The equation system in Example 6.1 defines a predicate *alloc*, which checks if register numbers in a target program are assigned in the stack-like fashion typical for non-pipelined architectures. Thus, the first argument to *alloc* is a target program, the second is a list of registers (i.e. register numbers) available for allocation within the first argument. We borrow Prolog list notation in Example 6.1.

Example 6.1 :

$$\begin{aligned}
&alloc(add(i,x,y),[i|u]) = alloc(x,[i|u]) \wedge alloc(y,u)\\
&alloc(add(i,x,y),[\,]) = false\\
&alloc(addi(i,x,c),[i|u]) = alloc(x,[i|u])\\
&alloc(addi(i,x,c),[\,]) = false\\
&alloc(load(i,c),[i|u]) = true\\
&alloc(load(i,c),[\,]) = false
\end{aligned}$$

□

Note that the equations in Example 6.1, when oriented left-to-right, form a canonical rewrite system.

Given a source program p and a list *regs* of register numbers, the problem at hand is to generate well-allocated target programs. We have to solve

[2] In general, this is by no means straightforward. It may still involve minimalisation over an exponential solution space. Shared forests only defer combinatorial explosion, they do not avoid it. Their advantage is that heuristics may be applied after translation to a more suitable data structure.

1. $m(z) = p$

2. $alloc(z, regs) = true$

Given a canonical rewrite system for m, $alloc$, etc, we can solve both equations simultaneously using a narrowing procedure [13]. However, this only works in principle, due to the large solution space.

More efficiently than applying narrowing to (1) and (2), we may first solve (1) by pattern matching according to Section 4, obtaining a shared forest w representing the solution space $I(w)$ (w contains variables $r_1, r_2, \cdots$ for the register numbers yet to be assigned). A narrowing derivation from $alloc(t, regs) = true$, separately for each $t \in I(w)$, will either construct a register assignment (i.e. a ground substitution for $i_1, i_2, \cdots$), if t can be evaluated with the given list $regs$ of registers, or else it will fail.

But by combining the selection axioms A with the rules for $alloc$, we obtain a canonical rewrite system again. Hence, the narrowing procedure applies to shared forests w as well as to individual members $t \in I(w)$. The narrowing tree issuing from $alloc(w, regs) = true$ now shares prefixes of paths for different $t \in I(w)$. The calculated substitution of a successful narrowing derivation not only instantiates register variables, but also the choice variables, and hence indicates the selected element from $I(w)$.

Solving $alloc(f\_prog, [1, 2]) = true$ rejects the solutions that load d into a register, and returns calculated substitutions $\sigma_1 = [v_1 \leftarrow l, v_2 \leftarrow r]$ and $\sigma_2 = [v_1 \leftarrow r, v_2 \leftarrow r]$ with

1. $w\sigma_1\downarrow_A = add(1, add(1, ld(1, a), ld(2, b)), addi(2, ld(2, c), d))$, and

2. $w\sigma_2\downarrow_A = add(1, addi(1, ld(1, a), b), addi(2, ld(2, c), d))$.

Note that under both substitutions, $v_2 = r$. Hence we may form $f\_prog2 := f\_prog[v_2 \leftarrow r]\downarrow_A$, thus restricting the solution space to all encodings that do not need more than 2 registers. Now the scheduling and cost phases can just as well be applied to f_prog2, yielding a reduced f_sched2 and f_cost2. Of course, these are identical to $f\_sched[v_2 \leftarrow r]\downarrow_A$ and $f\_cost[v_2 \leftarrow r]\downarrow_A$.

7 Conclusion

7.1 Relation to other work

State-of-the-art techniques for retargetable code generation, based on tree parsing [1], [5], "BURS-theory" [16], or regularly controlled rewriting [4] combine pattern matching and cost analysis. A maximum of efficiency is achieved by encoding cost information into the states of the generated pattern matcher. These approaches provide no formalism to deal with further machine specific aspects of code generation, such as pipeline optimization, register allocation, machine data type coercions, peephole optimization, and maybe others. But these approaches can easily be extended to produce code as terms over some target program signature.

Given this extension, the pure tree parsing approach of [1], [5] is an implementation of our approach when we restrict it to perform cost analysis immediately subsequent to code selection. Since the two phases both work bottom-up, the y can be interleaved, and no shared forests of target programs need to be constructed in this case. The approach of [16] and that of [4] are more flexible and can detect even more encodings, as they are able to perform rewriting on the intermediate or target term. Cost considerations are built into the pattern matcher. If certain decisions were to be delayed, shared forests could be used to represent the result.

The specific virtue of the approach presented here is the gain in modularity of code generation, in particular on the specification level. While the overall specification adheres to the structure recommended in [9] for verifiabiliy, different ways of implementing overall code generation may be studied. As was indicated with scheduling, cost analysis and register allocation above, once a shared forest of target programs has been constructed, several subtasks may be applied independently, and even in parallel.

7.2 Implementation Status

The lifting operation on signatures and attribute couplings has been integrated into the compiler-writing system MARVIN [7] by M. Reinold [17]. While the essential construction is straight-forward to implement, there is a severe complication. Translations by attribute couplings according to [6] as well as in MARVIN involve a "semantic" subsignature Σ'_0 of Σ' where in terms are evaluated in a particular Σ'_0-algebra. Evaluation in the corresponding $d\Sigma'_0$-algebra must be incorporated. Evaluation of $1 + \square(2, v, 3)$ to $\square(3, v, 4)$ is an example. This extension is nontrivial, as this Σ'_0-algebra is implemented by the compiler writer. Although this implementation is operational, the techniques described here have not yet been applied to a realistic code generator specification.

The MARVIN system was used for the implementation of transformations on shared forests, mainly because it implements attribute couplings, which describe a rather general class of tree transformations. The construction used in the Definition 5.1, however, may as well be implemented in other tree transformation systems. The key is the proper handling of choice variables. Shared forests are a general programming language technique that is well-suited for functional or logic programming.

7.3 Future Work

While it is conceptually pleasing to represent the complete solution space in order to select from it considerately, the pragmatics of this aproach present problems that so far have only been dealt with in an ad-hoc way:

Some machine architectures require MOVEs between temporary registers. As temporaries are not represented in the intermediate language, they lead to derivor equations such as

$$m(tmove\ \ r) = m(r), \tag{2}$$

and hence to chain productions in the tree grammar like

$$R \rightarrow R. \tag{3}$$

This means that the grammar allows circular derivations, which correspond, on the target side, to circulating an intermediate result through temporary registers (maybe of different register classes). The tree parser can be modified to cut off such circular derivations, allowing only a finite number of such moves (usually at most 1 or 2). They are actually needed in and sufficient for rare situations like achieving a register pair or inserting sign extensions. But theoretically, they are always possible, and hence blow up the solution space, even in a shared representation. A solution to this is given in [11].

On the conceptual side, there are several open questions. One is the following: Applying narrowing as explained in section 6 yields an explicit enumeration of the remaining solution set. It should be possible to modify the narrowing procedure such that these solutions are again represented as a shared forest.

Furthermore, shared forests may have applications outside code generation as well.

Acknowledgements

Thanks go to H. Hogenkamp for discussing these ideas, to M. Reinold who extended the MARVIN system to shared forests, and to A. Bodzin for preparing the manuscript.

References

[1] Balachandran A, Dhamdhere DM, Biswas S. Efficient Retargetable Code Generation Using Bottom-Up Tree Pattern Matching. Computer Languages, 15(3):127–140, 1990.

[2] Chen H, Hsiang J. Logic Programming with Recurrence Domains. In Proceedings 18th International Colloquium on Automata, Languages and Programming, vol 510 of Lecture Notes in Computer Science (LNCS), pp 20–34. Springer, 1991.

[3] Dershowitz N, Jouannaud JP. Rewrite Systems, vol B of Handbook of Theoretical Computer Science, chapter 15. North Holland, 1990.

[4] Emmelmann H. Code Selection by Regularly Controlled Rewriting. In [10], 1992.

[5] Ferdinand C, Seidl H, Wilhelm R. Tree Automata for Code Selection. In [10], 1992.

[6] Ganzinger H, Giegerich R. Attribute Coupled Grammars. In Proceedings of the International Symposium on Compiler Construction, pp 70–80. Association for Computing Machinery (ACM), 1984. Issue 19(6),1984 of SIGPLAN NOTICES.

[7] Ganzinger H, Giegerich R, Vach M. MARVIN – A Tool for Applicative and Modular Compiler Specifications. Technical Report 220, University Dortmund, 1986.

[8] Giegerich R. Code Selection by Inversion of Order-Sorted Derivors. TCS, 73:177–211, 1990.

[9] Giegerich R. On the Structure of Verifiable Code Generator Specifications. In Proceedings SIGPLAN '90 Conference on Programming Language Design and Implementation, pp 1–8, 1990. Issue 25(6),1990 of SIGPLAN NOTICES.

[10] Giegerich R, Graham SL (eds). Code Generation – Concepts, Tools, Techniques. This vol of Workshops in Computing (WICS). Springer Verlag, 1992.

[11] Giegerich R, Hogenkamp H. Semi-Formal Validation in Code Generator Development. Submitted, 1992.

[12] Giegerich R, Schmal K. Code Selection Techniques: Pattern Matching, Tree Parsing and Inversion of Derivors. In Proceedings of the European Symposium on Programming 1988, vol 300 of Lecture Notes in Computer Science (LNCS), pp 247–268. Springer, 1988.

[13] Hullot JM. Canonical Forms and Unification. In Proceedings of the 5th Conference on Automated Deduction, vol 87 of Lecture Notes in Computer Science (LNCS), pp 318–334. Springer, 1980.

[14] Knuth DE. Semantics of Context-free Languages. Mathematical Systems Theory 2, pp 127–145, 1968.

[15] Lang B. Towards a Uniform Framework for Parsing. In Tomita M (ed), Current issues in parsing technologies. Kluver Academic Press, 1990.

[16] Pelegri-Llopart E. Rewrite Systems, Pattern Matching and Code Generation. PhD thesis, UC Berkeley, 1987. EECS-Report.

[17] Reinold M. Transformations in Shared Forests. Master's thesis, Universität Dortmund, 1991. in German.

Discussion: Code Generator Specification Techniques

Led by Chris Fraser
Summarized by John Boyland and Helmut Emmelmann

Major participants:

John Boyland, Helmut Emmelmann, Robert Giegerich, Susan Graham, Robert Henry, Uwe Kastens, Bill Waite, David Wall

Code generator specifications

The discussion started with some more questions on Chris Fraser's talk: Robert Giegerich suggested specifying code selection using a description (in the spirit of the system proposed by Helmut Emmelmann in his presentation) to separate rules about the machine description from code transformation rules. A code generator description would perhaps be split into the following parts:

- machine description
- IL description
- term rewriting rules
- optimizations

Chris Fraser felt that this may lead to overly verbose descriptions, and in particular, the IL description should not be part of code generator description. It was agreed that this topic is still research.

Chris Fraser continued the discussion by asking for suggestions for a common BURS tool. He mentioned that several research groups had already started to develop their own. In order to reduce redundant work, it would therefore be desirable to have one freely available BURS tool. Chris Fraser could develop such a tool, but then AT&T would own it. Robert Henry has a BURS tool (altogether about 25000 lines of code) but no time to adapt it for general distribution. However it is not time critical to finish the common BURS tool, because for experiments and for debugging of specifications, a implementation based on the Aho/Johnson dynamic programming algorithm (DP) can be used. Only for a production compiler would the BURS tool be necessary to make it run fast. Even with the BURS tool available, it would be desirable to continue to distribute the DP tool for debugging purposes.

Discussion then centered on defining a standard input format and in particular on the method for specifying actions and costs for each BURS rule, so that development of BURS code generators can go forward. Bill Waite observed that BURS technology could be useful for applications other than code generation, for example, operator identification; and thus the input format, and in particular the action clause, should not be code generation specific. Uwe Kastens raised the issue of specifying other types of costs, such as pipeline costs, but Susan Graham remarked that BURS can only handle integer cost values which combine additively; otherwise compile time dynamic programming becomes necessary. Rather than preclude other applications, therefore, and in order to avoid handling notational convenience (as discussed below), the group agreed on a simple low-level input format with integer costs and integer action numbers. Compiler writers would then be free to develop extended BURS (EBURS) processors that would use the low-level BURS tool to do the sophisticated work and that would implement a customized version of the input language. There was no discussion on a standard output format for the low-level BURS translator.

Extending BURS

After a short break, Chris Fraser raised the following issues he had noticed when he was writing BURS specifications:

1. how could factoring be handled in an extended BURS (EBURS) ?
2. how could DAGs be handled ?
3. how could scheduling be handled ?
4. how should one split code generator specifications into a machine description and rewrite rules ?

Factoring of BURS descriptions

Chris Fraser asked how factoring could be expressed in a EBURS–language. The following example of problem (which is part of the Chris Fraser's Vax description) shows that factoring (here, factoring on binary operators) is desirable:

```
expd: (BIN,D,xd,xd)
```

Factoring should also simplify certain recurring patterns, here demonstrated with the assignment operator:

```
stmt: (ASGN,D,inx8,expd)
stmt: (ASGN,F,inx4,expf)
stmt: (ASGN,I,inx4,expl)
stmt: (ASGN,S,inx2,expw)
stmt: (ASGN,C,inx1,expb)
```

similarly for ARG, LOAD, ... (in the place of ASGN)

The Vax description became about 40% shorter with factoring using ad-hoc regular-expression-like patterns. Robert Henry proposed using some textual macroprocessing mechanism. Chris Fraser said he would prefer something more powerful and cleaner, but will use macroprocessing if nothing else is found. Bill Waite asked if it would be enough that the system allow the programmer to specify the correspondences D/inx8/expd, F/inx4/expf, etc., to be used in rules for ASGN, ARG and LOAD. No agreement on a standard factoring method was reached.

Application of BURS to intermediate code in DAG form

The problem faced here was code generation for a DAG where shared nodes represent common subexpressions. One does not always want to allocate a register for common subexpressions: even ignoring the issues of register pressure, the code may end up longer! For example on the VAX, most addressing modes provide free computation of register + constant and immediate data (32 bits); these free quantities should not be assigned to registers. Other machines have different free operands: on MIPS, only 16 bit signed constants are free and only in certain situations (as right operands of ADD etc).

The bottom-up phase of a BURS automaton works with DAGs. The code emitter, working top-down, could count visits and for each node do one of the following things:

- generate the code as normal BURS does
- evaluate the shared subtree into a register and remember the register assigned
- not produce code for the shared subtree, but instead reuse the value stored in a register before

The second and third alternative however require that BURS has decided to place the result of the subtree into a register.

Chris Fraser identified two problems when producing code for DAGs using a BURS code selector:

- how to find out or how to specify which expressions are free (and should therefore not be placed into a register)
- how to force the code selector to put something into a register

For the first problem John Boyland proposed to just use the cost values in the description, addressing modes would have zero costs. Robert Henry remarked that we had to be careful: costs not always assigned in the right places in a description.

Then Bill Waite proposed to add new rules for free productions:

Before:

X : ⟨ free1⟩
X : ⟨ free2⟩
Y : use(X) (free)
Z : use(X) (costs)

After:

Xf :⟨ free1⟩
Xf :⟨ free2⟩
X : Xf
Y : use(Xf)
Z : use(X)

For the second problem, how to get copy into a register, Robert Henry proposed to insert a copy to a register in the DAG on the bottom-up pass, if we notice we need to put it in register. Bill Waite proposed to do it on the top-down pass (when we emit code); if a subtree doesn't have zero cost we calculate it into a register and then use the register at the node. However David Wall remarked that this would not work because a pattern may match over the DAG join.

Then Helmut Emmelmann proposed to add a DAG operator into the intermediate language and to put in rules which force the subtree below the DAG operator to be evaluated into a register. Robert Henry proposed the following rules for DAG:

```
reg : DAG(X)   1  ⟵ cost
Xf :  DAG(Xf)  0
```

Finally the group came up with a better solution:

```
reg : DAG(reg)  0
Xf :  DAG(Xf)   0
```

These two rules force everything below DAG into a register (first rule) unless it is free (second rule).

Problem 3 and 4 were not handled in the discussion, as they were considered still research topics.

Editorial remark

Several months after this discussion, in **comp.compilers** the following notice was posted:

> We write to announce the availability of BURG, a program that generates a fast tree parser using BURS (Bottom-Up Rewrite System) technology. It accepts a cost-augmented tree grammar and emits a C program that discovers in linear time an optimal parse of trees in the language described by the grammar. BURG has been used to construct fast optimal instruction selectors for use in code generation. BURG addresses many of the problems addressed by Twig, but it is somewhat less flexible and much faster. BURG and its documentation are available via anonymous ftp from **kaese.cs.wisc.edu.(128.105.2.38)**. The compressed shar file **pub/burg.shar.Z** holds the complete distribution.
>
> Christopher W. Fraser, AT&T Bell Lab., **cwf@research.att.com**
> Robert R. Henry, Tera Computer, **rrh@tera.com**
> Todd A. Proebsting, University of Wisconsin, **todd@cs.wisc.edu**

For further reference see

Christopher W. Fraser, Robert R. Henry, and Todd A. Proebsting.
BURG — Fast Optimal Instruction Selection and Tree Parsing.
SIGPLAN Notices, 27(4):68-76, April 1992.

Code Generation for Parallel Architectures

Scheduling Vector Straight Line Code on Vector Processors

C. W. Keßler*
Graduiertenkolleg Informatik der Universität Saarbrücken
Saarbrücken, Germany

W. J. Paul, T. Rauber†
Computer Science Department, University Saarbrücken
Saarbrücken, Germany

Abstract

We present an algorithm to schedule basic blocks of vector three-address-instructions. This algorithm is suited for a special class of vector processors containing a buffer (register file) which may be partitioned arbitrarily into vector registers by the user. The algorithm computes the best ratio of vector register spilling to strip mining, taking the vector length and the buffer size into consideration, as well as several machine parameters of the target architecture. We apply the algorithm to groups of vector instructions within a basic block that are quasiscalar, i.e. all vectors occurring in the group must have one fixed length L.

1 Introduction

For scalar processors register allocation is widely accepted as one of the most important optimizations in compiler construction. In [1] Allen and Kennedy claim that register allocation is even more important on vector processors with vector registers. They argue that by an effective use of the vector registers, the system performance can be enhanced by a factor of three[1], so vector register allocation is the single most important optimization. This justifies a great effort in improving the use of the vector registers. Allen and Kennedy claim that strategies for scalar register allocation are of little use in vector register allocation because they do not take into consideration that the vectors may not fit into the vector registers. This argument is true, but we think that when considering basic blocks a scalar strategy (e.g. the one described in [7]) is useful provided that it is followed by an adaption algorithm which is presented in this paper.

We first give some basic definitions:

In general the front end of a compiler generates an intermediate code representation of the source program, often in the form of *three-address-instructions*,

---

*research partially funded by the Leibniz program of the DFG

†research partially funded by DFG, SFB 124

[1] This can be explained by saving Load and Store operations when holding intermediate results and operands in vector registers.

to which code optimization can be applied. A sequence of three-address-instructions which can only be entered via the first and only be left via the last statement is called a *basic block*. The data dependencies in a basic block can be described by a *directed acyclic graph (DAG)*. Evaluating this DAG means ordering the nodes v of the DAG such that each node appears after all its sons in the evaluation, i.e. an *evaluation* is a topological order of the DAG.

A mapping *reg* from the set V of the DAG nodes to the set of registers is called a (consistent) *register allocation* for a given evaluation A if for all nodes $u, v, w \in V$ the following holds: If u is a son of w, and v appears in A between u and w, then $reg(u) \neq reg(v)$.

Each evaluation A requires a certain number $m(A)$ of registers. We call

$$m(A) = \min_{reg \text{ is reg. alloc. for } A} \{ \max_{v \text{ appears in } A} \{reg(v) + 1\}\}$$

the *register need* of the evaluation A. The problem of finding an *optimal* evaluation A_{opt} with minimal register need

$$m_{opt} = m(A_{opt}) = \min_A m(A)$$

is NP-complete (see [16]). A heuristic which produces fairly good evaluations with little register need for a scalar DAG in linear time has been presented in [7]. An improved complete search algorithm will be given in a later paper (see [8]).

In general it is advisable to minimize the register need m while maximizing register usage for registers $1, ..., m$ in order to get a good register allocation. For our considerations, however, it is much better to keep register usage as *uneven* as possible, as suggested in [7, 8]. This yields the same register need as an allocation with even register usage, but now registers with low usage will be very good spilling candidates. That will be utilized by the optimization algorithm described in this paper.

Here we adjust a given evaluation A for a vector basic block to a special class of vector processors by taking into account some important machine constraints and architecture parameters. We present the target processor in section 2. The third section gives two different strategies and a combination of them which map the symbolic registers to the limited buffer of the processor. By applying the combination to an example DAG we find an interesting tradeoff-effect in section 4. Finally we generalize this in the fifth section and close with a look to the applicability of our results to real vector processors.

2 An abstract machine model of a vector processor

In order to maintain generality we do not consider any special vector processor but an abstract model $\mathcal{MV}$ (see Fig. 1) representing a wide class of real vector processors. A typical representative of this class is the SPARK 2.0 (see [2, 3, 15, 11, 4]) developed at university Saarbrücken. Since this is the only real vector processor we know all the exact machine parameters about that are essential for our optimizations, we will carry out the example computations in this paper for this processor. Nevertheless, the results are still valid for several other vector processors, as indicated in section 6.

Omitting control logic and adressing units we describe here only the main architecture components of $\mathcal{MV}$ which are relevant for our optimization ideas:

- The vector floating-point unit (**VFPU**) of the processor which is divided into d pipeline stages executes the arithmetical operations (e. g. addition, subtraction, multiplication). We suppose the execution of 1 stage to take 1 machine cycle. So a scalar operation needs $d + 1$ machine cycles from filling in the operands up to the result being available. A vector instruction of length L needs exactly

$$t_{COMP}(L) \;=\; L + d$$

machine cycles. d is called ***pipeline depth***; typical values for d are between 3 and 10 (cf. [14]).

- The floating-point memory (**FM**) is a very fast buffer (usually realized by a static RAM register file) for M floating-point words; the FM may be arbitrarily partitioned into ***vector registers***. Because of the high cost, the FM is not very large, e. g. $M = 4096$ for the SPARK 2.0 or $M = 512$ for the *INTEL Hypercube VX* (see [5]). The data which do not fit into the FM must reside in the main memory (MM).

- **processor bus:** We require the bandwidth of the connection between VFPU and FM being large enough to ensure that two operands and one result can be transported from FM to VFPU (respectively vice versa), i.e. in one machine cycle the following operations may be executed:
  - computation of 1 result element in the VFPU
  - transport of 2 values stored in the FM to the VFPU as operands
  - transport of 1 result value from the VFPU to the FM.

- The main memory (**MM**) is slower than the FM in general, but large enough to store all data occurring in the source program. It is connected to the FM via the

- **memory bus:** The data transmission rate of this connection is dominated by the access time of the slower MM. We express this by the inverse

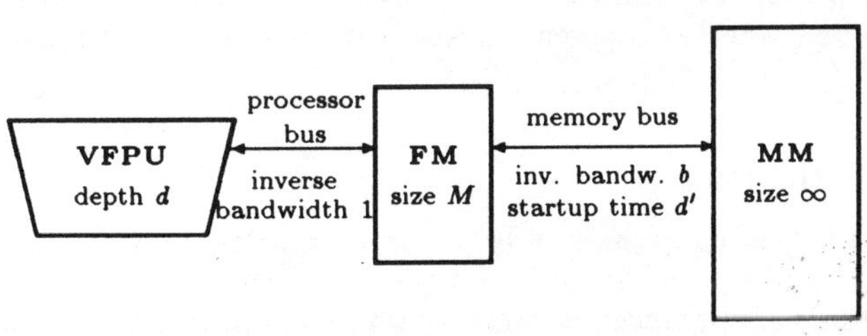

Figure 1: Block diagram of the abstract vector processor $\mathcal{MV}$: floating-point data paths

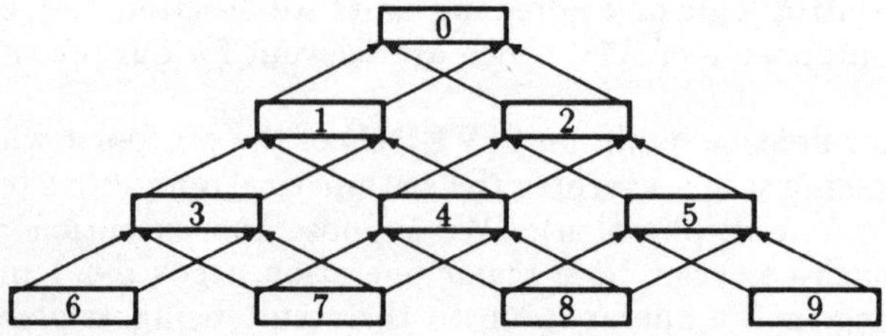

Figure 2: A (quasiscalar) 4–pyramid (4 leaves)

bandwidth[2] b of the memory bus. Furthermore each vector move needs some *startup time* d'. In general the time needed for moving a vector of length L from FM to MM or vice versa is

$$t_{MOVE}(L) = t_{LOAD}(L) \;=\; t_{STORE}(L) = L \cdot b \;+\; d'.$$

Typical values for b are e.g. 1 (SPARK 2.0) and e.g. 3 for d' (SPARK 2.0). Moving a vector a from MM to FM is denoted by `Load`(a), from FM to MM by `Store`(a).

3 Evaluating quasiscalar vector DAGs

Definition: Let (V, E) be a DAG and $\Lambda = (L_1, \ldots, L_{|V|})$ be a list of positive integer values that associates a length L_v to each node $v \in V$. We call $G = (V, E, \Lambda)$ a vector DAG (short: *VDAG*). The VDAG G is called ***quasiscalar*** if all nodes have equal length L and if the VDAG has only one root. To make things not too complicated we first consider only basic blocks in which the operands of each instruction are addressed successively. The generalization to the case that the operands are addressed by constant stride > 1 is handled in section 7.

If we have an arbitrarily large register file we can evaluate quasiscalar VDAGs in the same way as scalar DAGs.

We can imagine a quasiscalar VDAG as a stack of L equally structured scalar DAGs which represent the data dependencies of the respective vector components. From the definition of a quasiscalar VDAG we easily obtain an algorithm to test whether a given VDAG G with n nodes is quasiscalar in time $O(n)$.

3.1 Strip mining

Quasiscalar VDAGs have the handy property that the evaluation of a certain (e.g. the i–th) component of the root only depends on the i–th component of the other nodes, i.e. it does not matter which components are combined and in which order the component–DAGs are evaluated.

[2]The inverse bandwidth is the number of machine cycles needed to transport a value from MM to FM or vice versa.

node	6	7	3	8	4	1	9	5	2	0
in reg.	0	1	2	0	3	1	2	4	0	3

Table 1: An evaluation for the 4–pyramid

In the following we will see that sometimes it is necessary or appropriate to evaluate a quasiscalar VDAG not by a single phase (handle whole vectors) but to split the evaluation in T phases. Each phase consists of an evaluation of a strip of the DAG with the ***strip length***

$$str = \left\lceil \frac{L}{T} \right\rceil .$$

In the jth phase $(1 \leq j < T)$ for all nodes only the interval $[(j-1) \cdot str + 1 \; : \; j \cdot str]$ is evaluated. In the Tth phase the rest interval $[(T-1) \cdot str + 1 \; : \; L]$ is evaluated; we call

$$lstr = L - (T-1)str$$

the ***strip rest length.***

This strategy known as ***strip mining*** (see [1]) is important if the required buffer size $m \cdot L$ of an evaluation (we need m vector registers of length L each) exceeds the number M of available registers. Then it seems advisable to use

$$T = \left\lceil \frac{m \cdot L}{M} \right\rceil \quad \text{strips.}$$

Example: Consider the 4–pyramid in Fig. 2. Let the node length be $L = 2000$. We need five vector registers of length 2000 to evaluate the DAG, thus 10000 floating–point words altogether. If we have e.g. only a FM size of $M = 4096$, we must divide the evaluation in two strips of length $str = 667$ and one of length $lstr = 666$, such that the evaluation of one strip requires at most $667 \cdot 5 = 3335 \leq 4096$ memory words. Inserting the remaining target machine parameters $d = 6$, $b = 1$ and $d' = 3$, we obtain for the SPARK 2.0 exactly 20144 machine cycles to evaluate the three strips. Additionally we must take into account some time (SPARK 2.0: 4 cycles) to handle the strip counter, thus 20148 cycles altogether, including an overhead of 148 cycles.

3.2 Spilling

For simplicity in this section we consider scalar DAGs. However, the considerations can also be applied to quasiscalar VDAGs.

Let $G = (V, E)$ be a DAG. *Spilling* a node $v \in V$ means to hold its value not in a register but in the main memory. As a consequence, before each occurrence of v as an operand in an evaluation A of G, the current value of v must be loaded into a free register (recall that the target machine can handle only operands residing in registers, not in the main memory), and after the occurrence of v in A as a result, we must store the value into the main memory. For scalar evaluations spilling becomes unavoidable if the target machine has less registers than required. However it is a difficult problem which nodes should be spilled and which ones should not.

We will present a simple algorithm to decide which nodes to spill in section 4. Before presenting the algorithm we look at a special case of spilling, the splitting of the DAG into several subDAGs. This special case is well suited to demonstrate how strip mining and spilling may be combined.

3.3 DAG splitting

For certain DAGs with very simple geometric structure, e.g. for the k–pyramid, it might be advisable to determine the spill nodes by splitting the given DAG G into several subDAGs S_i.

Instead of generating an evaluation A for G we compute an evaluation A_i for each S_i and put the pieces together to obtain an evaluation A' for G. By doing this we hope that

- the maximal register need $\max_i \{m(A_i)\}$ of the A_i is considerably smaller than the register need $m(A)$ of the original evaluation A, and that
- the additional **Load** and **Store** instructions required when concatenating the A_i in order to get A' do not become too numerous.

Here we consider *canonical segmentations* which are defined as follows:

Definition: A segmentation $\{S_1, \ldots, S_y\}$ of a scalar DAG $G = (V, E)$ into y segments $S_1 = (V_1, E_1)$, $\ldots$ $, S_y = (V_y, E_y)$ is called *canonical*, if:

1. $V_i \subset V$, $E_i \subset E \cap (V_i \times V_i)$ for all i, $1 \le i \le y$.
2. the S_i are edge–disjoint, i. e. $E_i \cap E_j = \emptyset$ for $i \neq j$, $1 \le i, j \le y$.
3. S_i has only one root w_i for all i, $1 \le i \le y$.
4. S_i is a weakly connected component[3] for all i, $1 \le i \le y$; in particular there exists a path in E_i from each node $v \in V_i$ to w_i.
5. There is no path $u, \ldots, v, \ldots, w$ in E such that $u, w \in V_i$ and $v \in V_j - V_i$ for $i \neq j$, $i, j \in \{1, ..., y\}$.
6. There exists a permutation $\pi : \{1, ..., y\} \rightarrow \{1, ..., y\}$, such that a path $(w_{\pi(i)}, \ldots, w_{\pi(j)})$ exists in E for all $i < j$.

Example: The segmentation $\{S_1, S_2\}$ in Fig. 3 is canonical (with $\pi(1) = 2$, $\pi(2) = 1$), the segmentation in Fig. 4 too (there π is the identity on $\{1, ..., 5\}$).

By construction the V_i are not disjoint for $y > 1$, i. e. there are nodes belonging to several (at least two) segments which are evaluated in exactly one segment S_i and used in the others. We call such a node a *bridge* of S_i.

Example: Consider Fig. 3. Nodes 5 and 8 are bridges since they are defined in S_2 and used in S_1. In S_1 they are leaves. Evaluating the segmented

[3] A weakly connected component of a directed graph G is a subgraph $G' = (V', E')$ of G where every two vertices are joined by a path in which the direction of each edge is ignored.

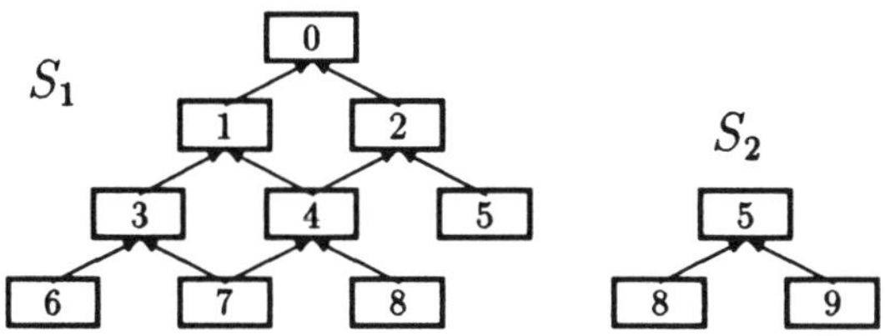

Figure 3: A 4–pyramid, canonically segmented into two segments

DAG $G = S_1 \cup S_2$ means: load nodes 8 and 9, compute node 5 and store it (node 8 needs not be stored again since it is already in the memory). In order to evaluate S_1 node 8 must be loaded again, and also node 5 (see Tab. 2). The evaluation in two segments requires only four registers; without the segmentation five registers would have been needed (cf. Tab. 1). Provided a FM size of $M = 4096$ and vectors of length $L = 2000$, this means that the DAG can be evaluated in 2 strips of length 1000. For the SPARK 2.0 this yields a run time of 26117 machine cycles.

We make the following observations:

- Since segmentation can be considered as a special form of spilling, the bridges can be considered as spilled nodes.
- Let S_j be a segment in which a bridge v is not evaluated but used as operand. Then v is a leaf in S_j.
- If a bridge is not the root of a segment, then its outdegree in S is at least 2. So we have to introduce at least one additional **Load** instruction for each bridge.
- The root w of the DAG G is also the root $w_{\pi(y)}$ of the topmost segment $S_{\pi(y)}$.

We get the **evaluation** A' of a canonically segmented DAG G by generating evaluations A_i for the segments S_i and then adding new **Load** and **Store** instructions to the sequence $A'' = (A_{\pi(1)}, \ldots, A_{\pi(y)})$: We insert a **Store**($v$) after the first occurrence of an inner bridge v in A'' (called definition point) and we insert a **Load**(v) before each occurrence of a bridge v as operand in A'' (called use point). As result we obtain A'.

Remarks: Because of points 5 and 6 in the definition of a canonical segmentation, the definition point for a bridge v in A'' appears before its use points, thus A'' is consistent and so is A' too. — Since a bridge does not need to reside in the same register all the time, it gets a register number in each A_i it is occurring in; thus the A_i are mutually independent and register allocation can start new from register no. 0 in each A_i.

Let us have another look at Tab. 2. We observe that register usage is suboptimal here: Reloading node 8 may be avoided since segment S_2 has only register need 3 while S_1 has register need 4, thus one register remains unused during the first part of the evaluation and could be used to hold the value of

node	8	9	5	Store 5	6	7	3	Load 8	4	1	Load 5	2	0
in reg.	0	1	2	—	0	1	2	0	3	1	2	0	3

Table 2: Evaluation of the segmented 4–pyramid

node 8. In general it may be possible to eliminate some **Loads** and **Stores** by first assigning *relative* register names separately for each segment (e. g. pairs $\langle segment - name,\ reg. - name \rangle$) and then deciding which bridge nodes may be held in the remaining free registers of a segment (i. e. which pairs $\langle S_i, r \rangle$ and $\langle S_{i+1}, r' \rangle$ should be coalesced). After that, the pairs are rearranged and mapped onto the real register names. — However, VDAGs with such a regular structure really do not occur in real programs. Furthermore, the optimization idea sketched above refers only to those segments that have lower register need than the maximal one. Even for the k–pyramid this situation occurs only at the last segment (if at all). Thus we omit these optimizations for simplicity and because of the little significance in practice. On the other hand, the simple optimization of spill code mentioned at the end of section 5 is much more useful instead.

3.4 Combination of strip mining and DAG splitting for the k–pyramid

Now we will combine strip mining with DAG splitting, at first for the example of the k–pyramid. Each of the $n = k(k+1)/2$ nodes of the k–pyramid should be evaluated exactly once.

For this special DAG e. g. a *left first* evaluation (see [6]) yields the minimal register need of $k+1$ vector registers.

Now, if $m \cdot L = (k+1)L > M$, i.e. the number m of the required vector registers is higher than the number of available vector registers, we must either spill some of the registers or virtually increase the number of vector registers by strip mining with several strips.

In order to get the optimal ratio of strip length to spilling rate which minimizes the run time of the evaluation on the target machine, we construct an algorithm which combines both possibilities:

Imagine we apply strip mining in order to obtain x vector registers ($3 \leq x < m$) each having a length of $str := \lfloor M/x \rfloor$ words. With x vector registers we can evaluate a $(x-1)$–pyramid or segments[4] of a greater pyramid of width $x-1$, as given in Fig. 4; there we have $k = 14$ and $x = 5$. The number of segments is $\lceil (k-1)/(x-2) \rceil$, the number of strips is $T := \lceil L/str \rceil$.

Here we suppose that the segmentation of the k–pyramid is given; the segmentation in Fig. 4 is canonical and seems to be the most favorable with respect to the number Br of bridges and to the number A_{Br} of "bridge chains"[5]:

$$A_{Br} := \left\lceil \frac{k-1}{x-2} \right\rceil - 1$$

[4] We obtain these segments by an appropriate canonical segmentation of the k–pyramid.
[5] A bridge chain is a chain of bridges that separates two segments.

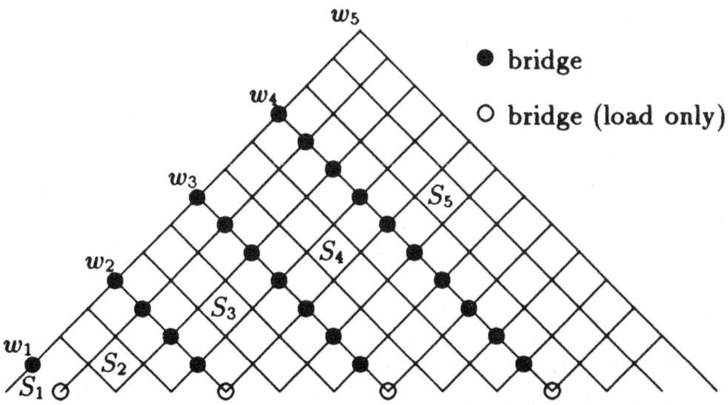

Figure 4: A 14–pyramid, splitted in segments of width $x - 1 = 4$

$$Br := \sum_{i=1}^{A_{Br}} (k - i(x - 2))$$

A_{Br} bridges are leaves. Leaf values need not be stored because they are already present in the main memory. So we need Br additional **Loads** and $Br - A_{Br}$ additional **Stores** in order to handle the bridge values in the main memory.

Thus we obtain the following procedure:

---

program *pyramid*
Input: k–pyramid, number x of vector registers
Output: an evaluation of the k–pyramid
Method:
(1) {divide the k–pyramid canonically into segments
 $S_1, S_2, \ldots$ and determine *str*, T, A_{Br}, Br}
(2) **for** *strip* **from** 1 **to** T
(3) **do for** i **from** 1 **to** $A_{Br} + 1$
(4) **do** {generate evaluation A_i for segment S_i}
(5)   {let π be the permutation
   to the canonical segmentation}
(6) $A'' = (A_{\pi(1)}, \ldots, A_{\pi(A_{Br}+1)})$;
(7)   {insert a **Load** instruction before each
   use point of a bridge in A''}
(8)   {insert a **Store** instruction after each
   definition point of a bridge in A''}
(9)   {return the resulting evaluation}
  od
od

We now want to compute the run time t of the evaluation generated by *pyramid* which depends on the strip length *str*, the strip rest length *lstr*, the number of strips T and the number of additional move instructions *moves*. We have to evaluate $T - 1$ strips of length *str*, each strip having computation cost $t_{COMP}(str)$ per compute operation and move cost $t_{MOVE}(str)$ per move operation. Then we have to evaluate the rest strip of length *lstr*. $comps = k(k-1)/2$ is the number of compute instructions (i.e. the number of inner nodes which is constant for fixed k) and $moves = k + 2Br - A_{Br}$ is the number of **Load** and **Store** instructions. Let $t_{loop}(T)$ denote the cost for handling the strip loop[6] which depends on the number of strips.

By substituting the values for *str*, *lstr*, T, *moves*, *comps*, t_{COMP} and t_{MOVE}, we see that t only depends on the pyramid size k, the vector length L, the number x of vector registers and on the machine parameters M, d, b and d':

$$\begin{aligned} t &= t(str, lstr, T, moves, comps) \\ &= (T-1)\cdot[comps\cdot t_{COMP}(str) \\ &\qquad\qquad + moves\cdot t_{MOVE}(str)] \\ &\quad + comps\cdot t_{COMP}(lstr) \\ &\quad + moves\cdot t_{MOVE}(lstr) \\ &\quad + t_{loop}(T) \\ &= t(x,k,L,M,d,b,d'). \end{aligned} \tag{1}$$

In the following we suppose k, L and the target machine parameters to be constant, so the evaluation A generated by *pyramid* depends only on x and so does t.

Now we must only determine the number $x = x_{opt}$ of registers that minimizes the run time $t(x)$ of $A(x)$. The next section describes how this can be done.

4 The Tradeoff–Effect for the k–pyramid

At this time we take the architecture parameters of the target machine into consideration.

Function $t(x)$ is not very handy because of the ceil and floor operations. Furthermore t is not differentiable. Therefore we simplify $t(x)$ such that it can be differentiated; we set

$$str \approx lstr \approx M/x, \quad T \approx L/str \approx Lx/M,$$

$$A_{Br} \approx \frac{k-1}{x-2} - 1$$

$$Br = A_{Br}k - (x-2)\sum_{i=1}^{A_{Br}} i \approx \frac{k^2 - kx + 2k - x + 1}{2(x-2)}$$

i. e. we neglect the ceil and floor operations. We obtain

$$moves = k + 2Br - A_{Br} \approx \frac{k^2 - k}{x-2}$$

[6] In the following we choose $t_{loop}(T) = T + 1$; that corresponds to the loop costs for the SPARK 2.0.

and the approximate run time t becomes

$$t(x) \approx \overbrace{\frac{Lx}{M}}^{\approx T} \left[\overbrace{\frac{k(k-1)}{2}}^{=comps} \left(\frac{M}{x} + d\right) + \overbrace{\frac{k^2-k}{x-2}}^{\approx moves} \left(b\frac{M}{x} + d'\right) \right]$$

neglecting the loop costs $t_{loop}(T)$ for simplification. Thus

$$t(x) \approx Lk(k-1)\left[\frac{1}{2} + \frac{d \cdot x}{2M} + \frac{b}{x-2} + \frac{d'}{M}\frac{x}{x-2}\right].$$

We differentiate this approximation of t with respect to x and obtain

$$\frac{dt(x)}{dx} \approx Lk(k-1)\left[\frac{d}{M} - \frac{b}{(x-2)^2} - \frac{d'}{M}\frac{2}{(x-2)^2}\right].$$

The necessary condition for a minimum is $dt(x)/dx = 0$, i. e.

$$(x-2)^2 - \frac{bM}{d} - 2\frac{d'}{d} = 0.$$

That yields

$$\boxed{x_{opt} \approx 2 \pm \sqrt{\frac{bM + 2d'}{d}}} \qquad (2)$$

For control we form the second derivation:

$$\frac{d^2t(x)}{(dx)^2} \approx 2Lk(k-1)\frac{b + 2d'/M}{(x-2)^3}.$$

By inserting the values for x_{opt} we see that the approximation of the function $t(x)$ is convex at the position $x_{opt,1} = 2 + \sqrt{\frac{bM+2d'}{d}}$, so $x_{opt,1}$ is a minimum position whereas $x_{opt,2} = 2 - \sqrt{\frac{bM+2d'}{d}}$ is a maximum position.

From formula 2 we conclude the following:

1. x_{opt} is independent of the vector length L (the small term depending on L got lost by neglecting $t_{loop}(T)$) and the size k of the pyramid.[7]
2. The smaller the buffer size M, the more registers will be spilled (x_{opt} moves towards the origin).
3. The greater the pipeline depth d, the smaller becomes x_{opt}, the more registers will be spilled.
4. The greater the inverse bandwidth b, the greater x_{opt} (less spillings).
5. d' is in practice not significant for x_{opt} because for existing vector processors (see section 6) the term $2d'$ is too small compared with the term bM.

[7] The value of t at position x_{opt} depends on the ratio of k to M.

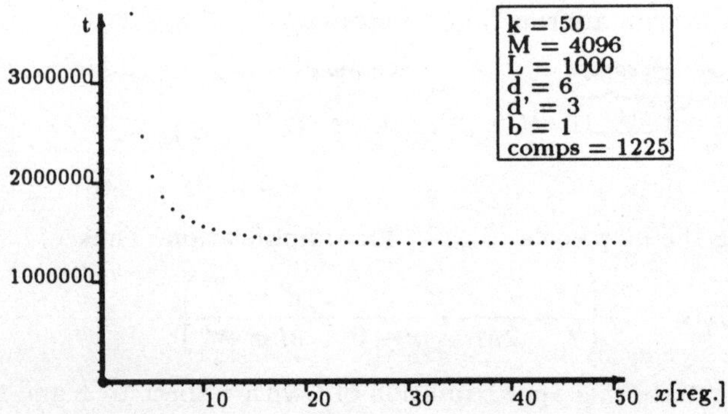

Figure 5: For the SPARK 2.0 with the whole FM available we have no clear minimum since M is large enough. The rapidly growing curve for very small values of x is caused by the immense bridge number and the communication overhead involved. For $x = 3$ all nodes are bridges, for $x = 4$ still nearly half of them. The net amount of the run time is $nL = (comps + k)L = 1275000$ cycles, the rest are startup times, loop- and communication costs.

These considerations are confirmed by the diagrams of Fig. 5 and Fig. 6. We call the existence of a local minimum of $t(x)$ *tradeoff-effect*, because strip length and spilling rate are traded off against each other in order to minimize the run time of the evaluation.

5 How to take advantage of the Tradeoff–Effect

We have computed the run time t (in machine cycles) of program *pyramid* for a 50-pyramid according to formula 1 and have varied all machine parameters. This results in a lot of $x/t(x)$-diagrams. Two of them are printed in Fig. 5 and 6. We make the following observations:

- The tradeoff-effect is most remarkable for a great pipeline depth d, cheap communication (especially a small b) and in particular for a small buffer size M with respect to the pyramid size k.
- If the register file is large enough even a deep pipeline does not make a difference; we have no clear minimum.
- A higher inverse bandwidth b attenuates the tradeoff-effect.
- The vector length L is unimportant and will be resolved cheaply by strip mining.
- The move startup time d' is unimportant.
- The curves are not smooth, several local minima are possible. A strict minimum search via (iterative) zero point determination of t' is not possible. So there remains *linear search* as it is done by the postprocessor algorithm described in the next section.

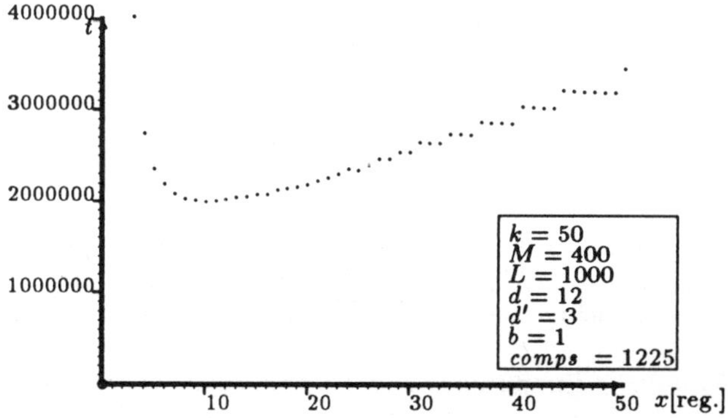

Figure 6: A deep pipeline increases the computation costs; the communication is cheap. If we suppose a small FM we get a remarkable tradeoff–effect: When using $x_{opt} = 10$ vector registers of length $\lfloor M/x_{opt} \rfloor = 40$ instead of $m = 51$ vector registers of length 7 we save about 43% of the run time.

So far we have used the k–pyramid as an example VDAG because of its regular structure which in particular enables splitting the DAG easily into segments of equal register need and minimizing the run time function analytically. This shows the existence of a minimum in many cases. However, real VDAGs do generally not have such a regular structure and thus DAG splitting cannot be applied. In this case we replace DAG splitting by the more general spilling method of subsection 3.2. This results in a new algorithm described in the following subsection.

5.1 The Postprocessor algorithm

For a given evaluation A with a register need of m symbolic vector registers of length L each, the following algorithm computes the best ratio of strip length str to the number x of registers used.

In opposition to the spilling decisions in the last section we now do not spill *single nodes* but *whole (vector) register contents* (i. e. in general several nodes at one time). The ideal spilling candidates are those (vector) registers which are referenced least.

The nodes to spill are determined by an algorithm which runs after the generation of the evaluation A (therefore we name it "postprocessor").

When spilling registers we get the following problem: For the registers to be spilled the evaluation generator allocated symbolic registers that now do no longer correspond to any physical register but to a main memory location. Since spilling was not provided in the original evaluation we must introduce $E \leq 2$ *communication registers* with the same size as the other vector registers. These are required because both operands used by an operation might be spilled. Two additional vector registers are sufficient since we need the value of a spilled node only for the time of one compute operation such that the result — if it is spilled too — can also be computed into one of the communication registers; because the VDAG is quasiscalar, there are no data dependency problems.

Furthermore, given an evaluation A, we compute for each register $i = 1, \ldots, m$ two lists of pointers to three-address-instructions in A:

$$\forall i = 1, \ldots, m: \quad Def_i = \{d_{i,1}, \ldots, d_{i,\theta_i}\}$$

$$\forall i = 1, \ldots, m: \quad Use_i = \{u_{i,1}, \ldots, u_{i,\mu_i}\}$$

where the $d_{i,j}$ point to three-address-instructions that compute a value into register i (i.e. $d_{i,j}$ is a definition point for register i) and the $u_{i,j}$ point to three-address-instructions using the contents of register i (i.e. $u_{i,j}$ is a use point of register i).

$move_i = \theta_i + \mu_i$ is the number of read and write accesses to the symbolic register i.

Moreover, for a three-address-instruction z let $node(z)$ denote the DAG node which is evaluated by z. Let $spilled[1...m]$ be a boolean array.

The postprocessor starts with building a sorted list $sortedreg[1 \ldots m]$ which contains the symbolic registers $1, \ldots, m$ in ascending order of $move_i$.

Next we determine the point x_0 up to which *one* communication register suffices, and after which we really need two, when spilling the registers in the order given by $sortedreg[1, ..., m]$. This is done by the following function in linear time:

```
(1) function last_point_one_extra_reg: integer;
(2) for i from 1 to m do spilled[i] = FALSE od;
(3) for z from 1 to m
(4) do i = sortedreg[z];
(5)     for all d_{i,j} ∈ Def_i
(6)     do spilled[reg(node(d_{i,j}))] = TRUE od;
(7)     for all u_{i,j} ∈ Use_i
(8)     do if spilled[reg(lson(node(u_{i,j})))]
              and spilled[reg(rson(node(u_{i,j})))]
(9)        then return m - z + 1 fi
        od
    od
    end last_point_one_extra_reg;
```

Then the following program fragment is executed which simulates the successive spilling of the symbolic registers in the order given by *sortedreg*. After each spill we compute the run time of the resulting computation with formula (1).

```
(1a) m_opt = m; moves = number of leaves;
(1b) t_opt = t(str, lstr, T, moves, comps);
(1c) x_0 = last_point_one_extra_reg;
(2)  for x from m - 1 downto ⌊M/L⌋
(3)  do i = sortedreg[m - x];
(4a)     moves = moves + move_i;
(4b)     if x ≥ x_0 then E = 1 else E = 2 fi;
(5)      if ⌊M/(x + E)⌋ > ⌊M/(x + E + 1)⌋
```

```
(6)       (* found candidate for local minimum: *)
(7a)      then str = ⌊M/(x + E)⌋;
(7b)           T = ⌊L/str⌋;
(7c)           lstr = L − (T − 1)str;
(8)            t_new = t(str, lstr, T, moves, comps);
(9a)           if t_new < t_opt
(9b)           then t_opt = t_new; m_opt = x fi
          fi
     od
     (* now spill reg. sortedreg[1, ..., m − m_opt]: *)
(10) for z from 1 to m − m_opt
(11) do i = sortedreg[z];
(12)      for all d_{i,j} ∈ Def_i
(13)      do {insert a Store after instruction d_{i,j}} od
(14)      for all u_{i,j} ∈ Use_i
(15)      do {insert a Load before instruction u_{i,j}} od
     od
(16) {renumber the remaining registers
      from 1 to m_opt and use the new
      register numbers in the modified evaluation}
```

---

moves contains the number of vector move instructions required. *moves* is initialized with the number of leaves in the DAG because we need a `Load` instruction for every leaf. t_{opt} contains the best run time found so far, m_{opt} contains the corresponding number of vector registers.

In lines (2) to (9) the spilling of the registers in the order given by *sortedreg* is simulated in order to find the number m_{opt} of vector registers which yields minimal cost t.

The condition in (5) prevents unnecessary computations since increasing *moves* in (4) without a gain in strip length can never lower the cost t.

By adding E extra registers to x respective $x+1$ in lines (5) and (7a) the communication registers are taken into account.

According to (9) m_{opt} is the number of registers giving the cost minimum t_{opt}. The actual spilling with inserting the `Load` and `Store` instructions into the evaluation is done in lines (10) to (15). In line (16) a consecutive numbering of the remaining registers is rearranged. The final number of registers used is $m_{opt} + E$.

Let us consider the run time of the postprocessor algorithm: Generating the lists Def_i and Use_i takes time $O(n)$ altogether since the original evaluation A has exactly n instructions. Since the register need can never be greater than n, there exist at most $2n$ of these lists. The total length of all lists Def_i and Use_i, $i = 1, ..., m$, cannot exceed $3n$ since each instruction in A has at most two operands and one result, thus at most two `Load`s and one `Store` have to be additionally generated for each instruction in A. It follows that the $move_i = \theta_i + \mu_i$ are natural numbers within $\{1, \ldots, 3n\}$. Thus we can apply *bucket sort* in order to sort the symbolic registers according to $move_i$ for which linear time suffices.

The body of the first loop (lines (3) to (9)) is executed in constant time; the loop (lines (2) to (9)) is executed less than m times. In line (2) x only needs to decrease down to $\lfloor M/L \rfloor$ since each further spilling can not lower the cost any more because the strip length *str* has already reached the whole vector length L.

The second loop (lines (10) to (15)) also runs in linear time because at most $3n$ move instructions are inserted. The same fact implies that renumbering the modified evaluation containing now at most $4n$ instructions can be done in linear time. We conclude that the whole postprocessor has run time $O(n)$.

5.2 Application in practical use

We have included the postprocessor in an optimizing vector PASCAL compiler for the SPARK 2.0 processor. We observe that with the whole FM with $M = 4096$ floating-point words available even for DAGs with rather high register need (ca. 30) no register was spilled. That corresponds to our observations at the example of the k-pyramid.

The tradeoff-effect becomes remarkable if only a small part of the FM is available for the evaluation of the DAG. This often occurs in practice because other vectors not used in the DAG may be stored in the FM too.

The implementation of the basic block optimizer of the vector PASCAL compiler developed at our institute consists of four parts:

1. a transformer which tests a given vector DAG constructed in a previous stage from a basic block (see [10]) on being quasiscalar. If the test is successful, the transformer translates the VDAG into a simple scalar DAG. If the test fails, the basic block is passed unchanged to the code generator.

2. a randomized heuristic evaluation generator for scalar DAGs (see [7])

3. the postprocessor

4. another transformer reconstructing a basic block from the modified evaluation to be passed to the code generator.

Some of the `Load` and `Store` instructions inserted by the postprocessor may be redundant in the final evaluation.[8] But these are filtered out by a simple peephole optimizer in linear time.

6 Real Vector Processors

Not all vector processors occurring in practice fulfill the preconditions given by $\mathcal{MV}$. For example, the CRAY-2 does not fit into our model since it has vector registers of a fixed length (64), i. e. the vector memory is prepartitioned such that the postprocessor could not vary the strip length at all.

The INTEL $i860$ has no real FM but only 32 scalar registers (32 bit wide) that can be combined to hold $M = 16$ 64-bit words.[9]

[8] E.g. if an inner node u and its father v are spilled and v is computed immediately after u then one operand Load of v can be saved because the value of u is still in a register.

[9] The hardware cache of the $i860$ is not accessible to the user.

In spite of these, the vector extension *VX* of the *INTEL Hypercube* (see [5]) fulfills our constraints: From the 16 Kbyte FM[10] 4 Kbyte ($\Rightarrow M = 512$ words) are available for the user. The inverse bandwidth b is 1 (cycle time 300 ns per addition or single precision multiplication). Unfortunately the values of d and d' are not available.

The postprocessor is also applicable to the vector node of the SUPRENUM (see [9]): The vector start addresses[11] of the vector registers are realized by pointers into the FM which contains up to $M = 8192$ words. — Another $\mathcal{MV}$-like vector processor is the Fujitsu VP–200 with the same FM size. — Furthermore, according to recent announcements, the vector node of the new CM–5 (see [17]) seems to be another good representative of $\mathcal{MV}$.

Unfortunately we do not have available all the required exact parameter values of all these machines. That is why we preferred our SPARK 2.0 processor for the example computations in this paper.

7 General VDAGs

The postprocessor can easily be adjusted to VDAGs which contain vectors addressed by a constant stride $s > 1$ provided that the single components do not interdepend and the effective vector length[12] is the same for all DAG nodes.

However some constructs of a vector programming language cause the resulting VDAG to be not quasiscalar, i.e. there are data dependencies between the single component DAGs. Such constructs are e.g. vectors addressed by index vectors, reduction operations with vector operands and scalar result (e.g. scalar product) or vector operations that use several VDAG nodes as a single operand.

This more general case seems to be rather hard to handle; a simple heuristic (but far from optimal) algorithm to generate evaluations for general VDAGs is given in [6]. However if the (not quasiscalar) VDAG is a tree then the algorithm in [12] computes an optimal evaluation of the tree in time $O(n \log n)$. Further research should yield sufficiently good heuristics which modify these evaluations too for the case that the required register space does exceed the buffer size M.

8 Acknowledgement

We thank Robert Giegerich for his comments on this paper.

References

[1] J.R. Allen, K. Kennedy: *Vector Register Allocation.* Rep. COMP TR 86-?, Rice University, April 1986.

[10] The FM of the Hypercube VX is realized by SRAMs with an access time of 100 ns; it can store 2048 words of 64 bit each.

[11] Of these there exist indeed only 8, but by holding addresses in the local memory of the node (while taking into account an additional memory access) we can simulate an arbitrarily great number of vector registers.

[12] The effective vector length of a vector of length L addressed by constant stride s is $\lfloor L/s \rfloor$.

[2] D. Auerbach, W.J. Paul, A. Bakker, C. Lutz, W. Rudge, F. Abraham: *A Special Purpose Parallel Computer for Molecular Dynamics.* Journal of Physical Chemistry, 1987, 91, 4881.

[3] A. Formella: *Entwurf, Bau und Test eines Vektorprozessors mit parallel arbeitenden Operationseinheiten, Teil 1.* Master thesis, 1989, Universität Saarbrücken.

[4] A. Formella, A. Obé, W.J. Paul, T. Rauber, D. Schmidt: *The SPARK 2.0 System — a Special Purpose Vector Processor with a VectorPASCAL Compiler.* Proceedings of the Twenty-fifth Annual Hawaii International Conference on System Sciences (HICSS-25) 1992.

[5] INTEL Corp.: *A Technical Summary of the iPSC/2 concurrent supercomputer.* Proc. of the Third Hypercube Conference, ACM 88.

[6] C.W. Keßler: *Code-Optimierung quasiskalarer vektorieller Grundblöcke für Vektorrechner.* Master thesis, 1990, Universität Saarbrücken.

[7] C.W. Keßler, W.J. Paul, T. Rauber: *A Randomized Heuristic Approach to Register Allocation.* Proceedings of PLILP91 Third symposium of programming Language Implementation and Logic Programming 1991, Passau (Germany), Springer LNCS Vol. 528, 195–206.

[8] C.W. Keßler, T. Rauber: *On the Complexity of Contiguous Evaluations.* Submitted (1992).

[9] H. Kammer: *The SUPRENUM Vector Floating Point Unit.* Proceedings 2nd International SUPRENUM Workshop, 1988.

[10] J. Lillig: *Konstruktion vektorieller DAGs für einen Vektorpascal-Compiler.* Program manual 1989, unpublished, Universität Saarbrücken.

[11] A. Obé: *Entwurf, Bau und Test eines Vektorprozessors mit parallel arbeitenden Operationseinheiten, Teil 3.* Master thesis, 1989, Universität Saarbrücken.

[12] T. Rauber: *Ein Compiler für Vektorrechner mit optimaler Auswertung von vektoriellen Ausdrucksbäumen.* Ph. D. thesis, 1990, Universität Saarbrücken.

[13] T. Rauber: *An Optimizing Compiler for Vector Processors.* Proc. ISMM International Conference Parallel and Distributed Computing and Systems, New York 1990, Acta press, 97–103.

[14] U. Reeder: *Die Vorhersage der Leistung von Vektorrechnern.* Master thesis, 1988, Universität Saarbrücken.

[15] D. Schmidt: *Entwurf, Bau und Test eines Vektorprozessors mit parallel arbeitenden Operationseinheiten, Teil 2.* Master thesis, 1989, Universität Saarbrücken.

[16] R. Sethi: *Complete register allocation problems.* SIAM J. Comput. **4**, 1975, 226–248.

[17] *The Connection Machine CM–5 Technical Summary*, Thinking Machines Corporation, Cambridge, Massachusetts, 1991.

Compiling for Massively Parallel Machines

Michael Philippsen
Walter F. Tichy
Department of Informatics, University of Karlsruhe
Karlsruhe, Germany

Abstract

This article discusses techniques for compiling high-level, explicitly-parallel languages for massively parallel machines.

We present mechanisms for translating asynchronous as well as synchronous parallelism for both SIMD and MIMD machines. We show how the parallelism specified in a program is mapped onto the available processors and discuss an effective optimization that eliminates redundant synchronization points. Approaches for improving scheduling, load balancing, and co-location of data and processes are also presented. We conclude with important architectural principles required of parallel computers to support efficient, compiled programs.

Our discussion is based on the language Modula-2*, an extension of Modula-2 for writing highly parallel programs in a machine-independent, problem-oriented way. The novel attributes of Modula-2* are that programs are independent of the number of processors, independent of whether memory is shared or distributed, and independent of the control mode (SIMD or MIMD) of a parallel machine. Similar extensions could easily be included in other languages.

1 Introduction

While the area of parallel algorithms is quite well developed (see for instance, textbooks [1, 7]), the state-of-the-art in compiler technology for translating parallel programs for highly parallel computers is unsatisfactory. This paper describes some of the problems that compilers for problem-oriented parallel programming languages must solve, and suggests possible solutions. It also identifies a set of architectural criteria that parallel machines must possess to allow for compiling high-level programs into efficient machine code.

We base our discussion on Modula-2* (pronounced Modula-2-star), an extension of Modula-2, for the formulation of explicitly parallel programs. The extensions are small and easy to learn, but provide a programming model that is far more general and machine independent than other proposals. Section 2 summarizes these extensions and gives a brief survey of related language proposals. Next, we discuss compilation techniques for targeting MIMD and SIMD machines and report on experience with our first Modula-2* compiler for the Connection Machine CM-2. Section 4 discusses optimization techniques. We conclude with the architectural criteria that would make the compilation of problem-oriented, parallel programs more effective.

2 The Language Modula-2*

2.1 Related Work

Most current programming languages for parallel and highly parallel machines, including *LISP, C*, MPL, VAL, Sisal, Occam, Ada, Fortran 90, Fortran D, Blaze, Dino, and Kali [16, 15, 21, 29, 2, 18, 5, 17, 23, 12] suffer from some or all of the following problems:

- Whereas the number of processors of a parallel machine is fixed, the problem size is not. Because most of the known parallel languages do not support the virtual processor concept, the programmer has to write explicit mappings for adapting the process structure of each program to the available processors. This is not only a tedious and repetitive task, but also one that makes programs non-portable.

- Co-locating data with the processors that operate upon the data is critical for the performance of distributed memory machines. Poor co-location results in high communication costs and poor performance. Good co-location is highly dependent on the topology of the communication network and must, at present, be programmed by hand. It is a primary source of machine dependence.

- All parallel machines provide facilities for inter-process communication; most of them by means of a message passing system. Nearly all parallel languages support only low level *send* and *get* communication commands. Programming communication with these primitives, especially if only nearest neighbor communication is available, is a time consuming and error prone task.

- There are several control modes for parallel machines, including MIMD, SIMD, data-flow, and systolic modes. Any extant, parallel language targets exactly one of those control modes. Whatever the choice, it severely limits portability as well as the space of solutions.

Modula-2* provides solutions to the basic problems mentioned above. The language abstracts from the memory organization and from the number of physical processors. Mapping of data to processors is performed by the compiler, optionally supported by high-level directives provided by the programmer. Communication is not directly visible. Instead, reading and writing in a (virtually) shared address space subsumes communication. A shared memory, however, is not required. Parallelism is explicit, and the programmer can choose among synchronous and asynchronous execution mode at any level of granularity. Thus, programs can use SIMD-mode for a synchronous algorithm, or use MIMD-mode where asynchronous concurrency is more appropriate. The two modes can even be intermixed freely.

The data-parallel approach, discussed in [9] and exemplified in languages such as *LISP, C*, and MPL is currently quite successful, because it has reduced machine dependence of parallel programs. Data-parallelism extends a synchronous, SIMD model with a global name space, which obviates the need for explicit message passing between processing elements. It also makes the number of (virtual) processing elements a function of the problem size, rather than a function of the target machine.

The data-parallel approach has three major advantages: (1) It is a natural extension of sequential programming. The only parallel instruction, a synchronous **forall** statement, is a simple extension of the well known **for** statement and is easy to understand. (2) Debugging data-parallel programs is not much more difficult than debugging sequential programs. The reason is that there is only a single locus of control, which dramatically simplifies the state space of a program compared to that of an MIMD program with thousands of independent loci of control. (3) There is a wide range of data-parallel algorithms. Most parallel algorithms in textbooks are data-parallel (compare for instance [1, 7]). According to Fox [6], more than 80% of the 84 existing, parallel applications he examined fall in the class of synchronous, data-parallel programs. Furthermore, systolic algorithms as well as vector-algorithms are special cases of data-parallel algorithms.

But data-parallelism, at least as defined by current languages, has some drawbacks [28]: (1) It is a synchronous model. Even if the problem is not amenable to a synchronous solution, there is no escape. In particular, parallel programs that interact with stochastic events are awkward to write and run inefficiently. (2) There is no nested parallelism. This means that once a parallel activity has started, the involved processes cannot start up additional, parallel activity. A parallel operation simply cannot expand itself and involve more processes. This property seriously limits parallel searches in irregular search spaces, for example. The effect is that data-parallel programs are strictly bimodal: They alternate between a sequential and a parallel mode, where the maximal degree of parallelism is fixed once the parallel mode is entered. To change the degree of parallelism, the program first has to stop all parallel activity and return to the sequential mode. (3) The use of procedures to structure a parallel program in a top-down fashion is severely limited. The problem here is that it is not possible to call a procedure in parallel mode, when the procedure itself invokes parallel operations (this is a consequence of (2)). Procedures cannot allocate local data and spawn data parallel operations on it, unless they are called from a sequential program. Thus, procedures can only be used in about half of the cases where they would be desirable. They also force the use of global data structures on the programmer.

When designing Modula-2* [27], we wanted to preserve the main advantages of data-parallel languages while avoiding the above drawbacks. The following list contains the main advances of Modula-2* over data-parallel languages.

- The programming model of Modula-2* is a strict superset of data-parallelism. It allows both synchronous and asynchronous parallel programs.
- Modula-2* is problem-oriented in the sense that the programmer can choose the degree of parallelism and mix the control mode (SIMD-like or MIMD-like) as needed by the intended algorithm.
- Parallelism may be nested at any level.
- Procedures may be called from sequential or parallel contexts and can generate parallel activity without any restrictions.
- Modula-2* is translatable for both SIMD and MIMD architectures.

Modula-2 has been chosen as a base for a parallel language because of its simplicity. There are no reasons why similar extensions could not be added to other imperative languages such as Fortran or ADA. The necessary extensions were surprisingly small. They consist of synchronous and asynchronous versions of a **forall** statement, plus simple, optional declarations for mapping array data onto processors in a machine independent fashion. An interconnection network is not directly visible in the language. We assume a shared address space among all processors, though not necessarily shared memory. There are no explicit message passing instructions; instead, reading and writing locations in shared address space subsume message passing. This approach simplifies programming dramatically and assures network independence of programs. The burden of distinguishing between local and non-local references, and substituting explicit message passing code for the latter, is placed on an (optimizing) compiler. The programmer can influence the distribution of data with a few, simple declarations, but these are only hints to the compiler with no effect on the semantics of the program whatsoever.

2.2 Overview of the forall statement

The **forall** statement creates a set of processes that execute in parallel. In the asynchronous form, the individual processes operate concurrently, and are joined at the end of the **forall** statement. The asynchronous **forall** simply terminates when the last of the created processes terminates. In the synchronous form, the processes created by the **forall** operate in unison until they reach a branch point, such as an **if** or **case** statement. At branch points, the set of processes partitions into two or more subsets. Processes within a single subset continue to operate in unison, but the subsets are not synchronized with respect to each other. Thus, the union of the subsets operate in MSIMD[1] mode. A statement causing a partition into subsets terminates when all its subsets terminate, at which point the subsets rejoin to continue with the following statement.

Variants of both the synchronous and asynchronous form of the **forall** statement have been introduced by previously proposed languages, such as Blaze, C*, Occam, Sisal, VAL, *LISP [17, 26, 21, 15, 16, 25] and others [3]. Note also that vector instructions are simple instances of the synchronous **forall**.

None of the languages mentioned above include *both* forms of the **forall** statement, even though both are necessary for writing readable and portable parallel programs. The synchronous form is often easier to handle than the asynchronous form, because it avoids synchronization hazards. However, the synchronous form may be overly constraining and may lead to poor machine utilization. The combination of synchronous and asynchronous forms in Modula-2* actually permits the full range of parallel programming styles between SIMD and MIMD.

The syntax of the **forall** is as follows.[2]

---

[1] MSIMD: Multiple SIMD. Few but more than one instruction streams operate on many data streams. A compromise between SIMD and MIMD.

[2] We use the EBNF syntax notation of the Modula-2 language definition, with keywords in upper case, | denoting alternation, [...] optionality, and (...) grouping of the enclosed sentential forms.

ForallStatement = FORALL ident ":" SimpleType IN (PARALLEL | SYNC)
StatementSequence
END.

The identifier introduced by the forall statement is local to the statement and serves as a run-time constant for every process created by the **forall**. *SimpleType* is an enumeration or a (sub-)range. The **forall** creates as many processes as there are elements in *SimpleType* and initializes the run-time constant of each process to a unique value in *SimpleType*. The created processes all execute the statements in *StatementSequence*.

2.3 The asynchronous forall

The created processes execute *StatementSequence* concurrently, without any implicit, intermediate synchronization. The execution of the **forall** terminates when all created processes have finished. Thus, the asynchronous **forall** contains only one synchronization point at the end. Any additional synchronization must be programmed explicitly with semaphores and the operations *WAIT* and *SIGNAL*.

In the following example, an asynchronous **forall** statement implements a vector addition.

```
FORALL i:[0..N-1] IN PARALLEL
  z[i] := x[i] + y[i]
END
```

Since no two processes created by the **forall** access the same vector element, no temporal ordering of the processes is necessary. The N processes may execute at whatever speed. The **forall** terminates when all processes created by it have terminated.

A more complicated example, illustrating recursive process creation, is the following. Procedure *ParSearch* searches a directed, possibly cyclic graph in parallel fashion. It can best be understood by comparing it with depth-first-search, except that *ParSearch* runs in parallel. It starts with a root of the graph and visits nodes in the graph in a parallel (and largely unpredictable) fashion.

```
PROCEDURE ParSearch( v: NodePtr );
BEGIN
  IF Marked( v ) THEN RETURN END;
  FORALL s:[0..v^.successors-1] IN PARALLEL
    ParSearch( succ(v, s) )
  END;
  visit( v );
END ParSearch;
```

The procedure *ParSearch* simply creates as many processes as a given node has successors, and starts each process with an instance of *ParSearch*. Before visiting a node, *ParSearch* has to test whether the node has already been visited and marked. Since multiple processes may reach the same node simultaneously, testing and setting the mark is done in a critical section (implemented with a semaphore associated with each node) by the procedure *Marked*. If the graph is a tree, no marking is necessary.

2.4 The synchronous forall

The processes created by a synchronous **forall** execute every single statement of *StatementSequence* in unison. To illustrate this mode, its semantics for selected statements is described in some detail below:

- A statement sequence is executed in unison by executing all its statements in order and in unison.

- In the case of branching statements such as `IF C THEN SS1 ELSE SS2 END`, the set of participating processes divides into *disjoint* and *independently operating* subsets, each of which executes one of the branches (`SS1` and `SS2` in the example) in unison. Note that in contrast to other data-parallel languages, *no* assumption about the relative speeds or relative order of the branches may be made. The execution of the entire statement terminates when all processes of all subsets have finished.

- In the case of loop statements such as `WHILE C DO SS END`, the set of processes for any iteration divides into two disjoint subsets, namely the *active* and the *inactive* ones (with respect to the loop statement). Initially, all processes entering the loop are active. Every iteration starts with the synchronous evaluation of the loop condition `C` by all active processes. The processes for which `C` evaluates to `FALSE` become inactive. The rest forms the active subset which executes statement sequence `SS` in unison. The execution of the whole loop statement terminates when the subset of active processes becomes empty.

Hence, synchronous parallel operation closely resembles the lock-step operation of SIMD machines with an important generalization for parallel branches.

As an example, consider the computation of all postfix sums of a vector V of length N. The program should place into $V[i]$ the sum of all elements $V[i] \dots V[N-1]$. A recursive doubling technique as in reference [9] computes all postfix sums in $O(\log N)$ time, where N is the length of the vector.

```
VAR V : ARRAY[0 .. N-1] OF REAL;
VAR s : CARDINAL;
BEGIN
   s := 1;
   WHILE s < N DO
      FORALL i:[0..N-1] IN SYNC
         IF (i+s)<N THEN
            V[i]:= V[i]+V[i+s]
         END
      END;
      s := s * 2
   END
END
```

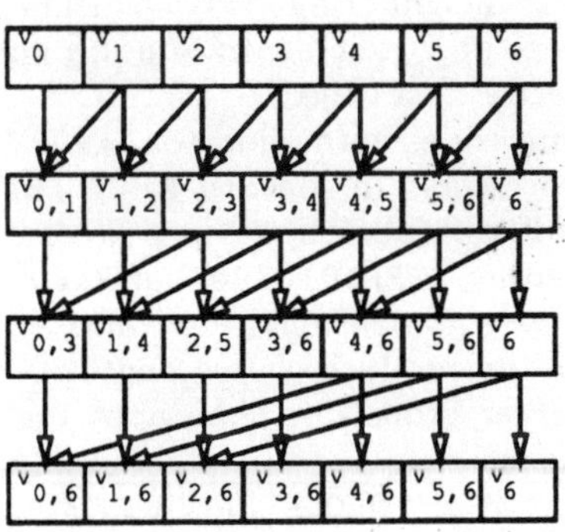

Figure 1: Computing postfix sums of a vector

Figure 1 illustrates the process. The program operates by computing partial sums of length $s = 2^j$, where j counts the iterations. The inner **forall** creates N processes. Note that there is a one-to-one mapping between process numbers and elements of the vector. In each iteration, the length of the partial sums is doubled by parallel summation of neighboring sums. The **if** statement inside the **forall** disables all processes that must not participate in the computation during a given iteration.

2.5 Allocation of array data

Co-location of data with the processors that access the data is important for parallel machines without uniform access time to memory locations. Poor alignment of data and processors may cause excessive communication overhead. We therefore provide a simple, machine-independent construct for controlling the allocation of array data. This construct is optional and does not change the meaning of a program; it affects only performance. A compiler for a machine with uniform memory access time may ignore the construct.

The allocation of array data to processors is controlled with one allocator per dimension. The modified declaration syntax for arrays is as follows:

```
ArrayType = ARRAY SimpleType [allocator]
                  {"," SimpleType [allocator]} OF type.
allocator = LOCAL | SPREAD | CYCLE | RANDOM | SBLOCK | CBLOCK.
```

Array elements whose indices differ only in dimensions that are marked `LOCAL` are associated with the same processor. This facility is used to avoid distribution of data in a given dimension.

Dimensions with allocator `SPREAD` are divided into segments, one for each of the available processors. A vector with n elements is assigned to P processors by allocating a segment of length $\lceil n/P \rceil$ to each processor. While utilizing all available processors, it minimizes the cost of nearest-neighbor communication.

Dimensions with allocator `CYCLE` are distributed in a round-robin fashion over the available processors. Given P processors, the elements of a vector whose indices are identical modulo P are associated with the same processor. In contrast to `SPREAD`, `CYCLE` maximizes the cost of nearest-neighbor communication: neighboring array elements are always in different processors, leading to better processor utilization if a parallel algorithm operates on subsegments of a vector at a time.

Dimensions with allocator `RANDOM` are distributed randomly over the available processors. In contrast to `CYCLE`, `RANDOM` leads to a better processor utilization if a parallel algorithms accesses the dimension in a random pattern.

If either `SPREAD`, `CYCLE`, or `RANDOM` apply to several successive dimensions, then these dimensions are "unrolled" into one pseudo-vector with a length that is the product of the lengths of the individual dimensions. This scheme idles fewer processors than applying `SPREAD`, `CYCLE`, or `RANDOM` to individual dimensions.

Allocators `SBLOCK` and `CBLOCK` apply `SPREAD` and `CYCLE` resp. to each dimension individually. For two successive dimensions, `SBLOCK` has the effect of creating rectangular subarrays and assigning those to the available processors. With this arrangement, nearest-neighbor communication in all dimensions is best supported when the interconnection network can be configured into the same number of dimensions as the arrays.

CBLOCK for two dimensions also creates two-dimensional subarrays, but the rows and columns of these subarrays are then distributed independently in a round-robin fashion over the processor grid. Again, SBLOCK minimizes nearest-neighbor communication, while CBLOCK allows high processor utilization if smaller subarrays are processed in parallel.

3 Implementing forall Statements

The main language constructs to be discussed are the two versions of the **forall**. We first present the more difficult case of compiling for MIMD, and then introduce the simplifications for SIMD.

3.1 Asynchronous forall

3.1.1 Asynchronous forall, *MIMD implementation*

A straightforward approach to implementing the **forall** on a MIMD machine is to create the required number of lightweight processes, or *threads*. In practice, we avoid the overhead of doing frequent context switches by having a single process per processor simulating the assigned (conceptual) threads. This is possible, since all the threads of a **forall** share the same program (the enclosed statement sequence), but have their own stacks. Furthermore, on a distributed memory machine, it pays to replicate the entire program to all processors. Code replication can be accomplished quickly during startup, either using a broadcast facility or recursive doubling. To ease understanding, we first omit the detailed description of the simulation and present the implementation of the asynchronous **forall** in terms of individually scheduled threads before giving some notes on a realistic MIMD implementation.

The main problems when compiling **forall** statements are thread creation, thread termination, and load balancing. All of these problems must be solved in a parallel fashion. Sequential implementations would cause a serious bottleneck, and, for algorithms with fine granularity, result in essentially sequential programs. Note also that **foralls** may be nested, so there may be several new sets of threads being created simultaneously.

The process reaching a **forall**, called the *spawner*, must -conceptually- create the set of threads prescribed by the **forall**. The spawner actually creates only the initial thread of the **forall**, called the *leader*. (A simple optimization is to let the spawner take on the role of the leader.) The leader then replicates itself. All threads created keep replicating themselves again and again, until the required number is obtained. This method is another variant of recursive doubling. In an implementation on current MIMD hardware only as many processes are spawned as there are processors available. Each of these processes simulates the necessary number of threads. After creation the (conceptual) threads begin execution of the **forall**'s code sequence – in practice by a process looping over the threads it manages.

Synchronization and thread termination at the **forall**'s end follow the same pattern. Each thread has a semaphore for receiving termination signals from other threads. A thread that reaches the end of its **forall** first waits for termination signals from all the threads it spawned during the replication process, then signals its creating thread, and destroys itself. If all n threads of a **forall** terminate at about the same time, then the leader learns about the combined termination in time proportional to $O(\log n)$, signals the spawner, and kills itself (or simply resumes the role of the spawner). In practice, synchronization is done on the processor level instead of the thread level, thus reducing the overhead.

The problem of load balancing is to distribute threads over the available processors so that (1) the load on the processors is equalized, (2) the threads are co-located with their data, and (3) co-scheduling of threads within the same **forall**-instance becomes possible. Again, a centralized solution must be avoided. We are exploring the following technique. All processors keep a running total of ready threads and the overall average. The overall average must be updated periodically (say at the end of a time-slice) by a recursive doubling technique in which all processors participate. Newly created threads are moved between neighboring processors depending on the current load in comparison to the average. Under certain circumstances, migrating a long-running thread (including its data) to another processor may be advantageous. In addition, static compiler analysis can indicate preferred processors for co-locating data and threads.

Co-scheduling of threads in the same **forall** is necessary to avoid delays inherent in context swaps when the threads communicate. Without co-scheduling, communicating threads may enter a situation where they execute alternatingly or in co-routine fashion instead of in parallel [19]. Co-scheduling can be accomplished by increasing the thread priority with the nesting depth of **foralls**, or by providing special mechanisms for "task forces", i.e., for scheduling groups of threads simultaneously.

Obviously, thread creation, termination, and load balancing must be as fast as possible. Various optimizations for bulk thread generation are feasible, but will not be discussed here for lack of space.

The above techniques have not been implemented in our first compiler, since its target, the CM-2, is a SIMD machine. However, work has started on a Modula-2* compiler targeting a Transputer cluster, where the techniques will be used.

3.1.2 Asynchronous forall, *SIMD implementation*

The synchronous nature of a SIMD machine, coupled with the broadcast bus from the front-end, makes all three of thread creation, termination, and load balancing operate in constant time or nearly constant time. For generality, assume nested **foralls**: m threads each execute a **forall** statement, each creating n new threads. Thus, the number of threads to be created is $t = nm$. If n is not uniform for all the m spawners, then a $O(\log m)$-time summation instead of (constant-time) multiplication must be performed to compute t.

Once t is known, t stacks are created by assigning to each of p processors a segment of $\lceil t \div p \rceil$ stacks. This operations takes constant time and balances the load perfectly. Process termination also takes constant time, since there is no synchronization overhead. However, it may be necessary to provide each thread with some initial data (such as its number) during creation. Spreading this information takes again logarithmic time, but as demonstrated by the Connection Machine CM-2, special instructions for spreading data are so fast that, in practice, they can be regarded as constant.

What remains to be discussed is the scheduling of instructions. Since the asynchronous **forall** prescribes no scheduling of the threads at all, the compiler writer can choose one that works well on a given SIMD or MSIMD machine. We describe briefly the implementation we chose for the Connection Machine CM-2 [13]. We assume initially, that the number of available processors equals the number of threads.

Activity Bits. The central idea of control flow on SIMD computers is deactivation and reactivation of processors, controlled by an activity bit associated with each processor. When the activity bit is off, the processor does not execute the instructions issued by the front-end. This facility is sufficient for simulating the usual control flow constructs in a parallel context. All that is needed is a stack of activity bits for each thread. The top of each activity stack is stored into the activity bit of a processor. Suitable manipulation of the activity bits turns threads on and off, as required by the instruction stream issuing from the front-end.

There are two small extensions of the usual control flow mechanism for SIMD machines. They are needed for recursion and for **exit** and **return** statements. First, consider parallel loops (i.e., loops within a **forall**). On a SIMD-machine, the front-end repeatedly issues the instructions for the loop body, until the termination conditions of all threads executing the loop are met. The usual technique is to evaluate a thread's termination condition directly into its activity bit. Before each iteration, the front-end tests whether there are any positive activity bits left. If not, the loop terminates. An **exit** statement may also terminate a loop, by turning off the activity bit of the corresponding thread. However, since an **exit** statement may be nested several levels deep within a loop, it must not only set the topmost activity bit to false, but all those that have been stacked since the last loop was entered. Similar considerations apply to the **return** statement. Consider the following example.

```
FORALL i:[0..N-1] IN PARALLEL
    LOOP
        IF ODD(i) THEN EXIT END;
        SS
    END
END
```

When control flow reaches the **exit**, then two activity bits have been stacked for each thread: one for the **loop**, and one for the **if** statement. To prevent a thread that has already executed the **exit** from being reactivated after the **if**, its top *two* activity bits must be set to **FALSE**.

Recursion termination is similar to loop termination. If a recursive call occurs inside a parallel **if** or **case**, then the front-end must sense whether there is any active thread left in a branch. If not, then the branch terminates. Without this provision, unbounded recursion would ensue.

Parallel Procedure Call. Because procedures can be called from both sequential and parallel contexts, each procedure must be compiled twice: Once for executing entirely on the front-end in sequential mode and a second time for executing within a **forall** statement. The difference is that in the parallel version, the procedure call and return instructions are executed only on the front-end. Thus, we need two types of stacks: On the front-end, we stack return addresses. On the stacks associated with the parallel threads, we store parameters and local data. This division is a direct consequence of SIMD and would even occur if front-end and parallel processors had the same instruction set. On the CM-2, the instruction sets differ, and so the sequential and parallel versions are completely different.

Our compiler relies on a minor language restriction: Procedures may not be nested within each other. The reason is that up-level addressing is quite expensive. Since it is in general unpredictable in what context a procedure is called, each memory access would have to distinguish at run-time whether its up-level addressing references data on the front-end or the parallel processors. This problem is avoided by disallowing procedure nesting and compiling each procedure twice.

Processor Virtualization. Simulating more threads than there are processors available is called *processor virtualization.* In SIMD mode, it is not possible to simply create new processes on demand and let the operating system schedule them. Instead, the front-end has to issue the instructions implementing the body of a **forall** in a loop. The number of iterations of this loop is given by the ratio of threads to available processors.

The PARIS instruction set of the CM-2 provides automatic processor virtualization. This means that processor virtualization is transparent to the programmer. The firmware simulates as many threads as required. The maximum number of threads is only limited by the available memory, because the local memory of each processor must be shared out among the assigned threads.

Our Modula-2* compiler uses the automatic processor virtualization. However, this virtualization is quite expensive. The main reason is that the virtualization actually implements synchronous virtualization, which requires many temporary variables. In essence, this virtualization wraps every single instruction into a virtualizing loop, even though a loop around the entire body of a **forall** would suffice (since the asynchronous **forall** prescribes no scheduling of threads). The latter simulation would be obviously much more efficient.

3.2 Synchronous forall

3.2.1 Synchronous forall*, MIMD implementation*

The synchronous **forall** requires many more synchronization points than the asynchronous form. There must be a synchronization point between every two statements inside a **forall**, and in the case of the assignment, even within a single statement. A parallel assignment of the from `L := R` means that the value of `R` is evaluated synchronously and stored in a temporary. Similarly, the address represented by `L` is evaluated synchronously and stored in a temporary. Only after both of these parallel evaluations have completed can the assignment be made. Otherwise, interference is possible, as in the assignment `A[i] := A[i+1]`.

A synchronization point is implemented with a scheme similar to the one used to terminate an asynchronous **forall**, except that now the threads do not terminate, but wait for a signal to proceed. First, a logarithmic reduction informs the leader that all threads in the process have reached the synchronization point. Then a logarithmic doubling process sends signals back out to the threads to continue.

Clearly, synchronization points are expensive. We are currently investigating methods to eliminate them where possible. For instance, the synchronization point inside an assignment is not necessary if the left and right hand sides do not interfere. Furthermore, by scheduling processes in a certain fashion, the overlaps may be reduced greatly. Even synchronization points between statements can be eliminated if there are no dependencies. Much of the dependency analysis developed for parallelizing compilers applies here. An example is shown in the next section.

3.2.2 Synchronous forall, *SIMD implementation*

The SIMD implementation of the synchronous **forall** was simple on the CM-2: the built-in virtualization does the job. However, this virtualization cannot take advantage of the optimizations described above. Instead, it must make conservative assumptions. The resulting virtualization is far from efficient. An optimizing compiler could produce a much faster virtualization in the majority of cases. Consider the following example.

```
FORALL i: [0..N-1] IN SYNC
    A[i] := (A[i] + 1) / 2
END
```

Below are two possible virtualizations on p processors, expressed in Modula-2*.

```
s := CEILING(N, p)
FORALL j : [0 .. p-1] IN PARALLEL
    FOR i:= j*s TO MIN((j+1)*s,N)-1
    DO
        TMP[i] := A[i] + 1;
        TMP[i] := TMP[i] / 2
    END
END
FORALL j : [0 .. p-1] IN PARALLEL
    FOR i:= j*s TO MIN((j+1)*s,N)-1
    DO
        A[i]   := TMP[i]
    END
END
```

```
s := CEILING(N, p)
FORALL j : [0 .. p-1] IN PARALLEL
    FOR i:= j*s TO MIN((j+1)*s,N)-1
    DO
        reg := A[i];
        reg := reg + 1;
        reg := reg / 2;
        A[i]:= reg
    END
END
```

The program on the left shows the conservative virtualization, as performed by PARIS. The optimized version on the right hand side exploits the fact that only one temporary location is required. By using a single register for it on every processor, the number of writes to memory are reduced to one third of the unoptimized version. Furthermore, no synchronization is necessary. On a SIMD machine, this means that the two loops can be merged; on a MIMD machine, we save the synchronization point. Furthermore, if the individual processors have a vector capability, the computation in each processor can even be interleaved [30].

While implementing the synchronous **forall** for the CM-2 we have identified the main sources of optimization in compiling for massively parallel machines.

We have started to include these optimizations in the next compilers for MasPar, CM-5, and Transputer, including the necessary data-dependence analysis [8, 14].

4 Optimizations

In the previous section, we presented the basic translation schemes. These straightforward schemes often result in poor performance of the generated code, when compared to hand-tuned versions. In this section, we briefly discuss some optimization techniques identified so far.

4.1 Eliminating Synchronization Events

The necessity to eliminate synchronization events in compiling for both MIMD and SIMD machines has been illustrated before. In this section we give a simple example which illustrates the strength of our approach.

```
FORALL i: [1..N] IN SYNC
    A[2*i-1] := A[2*i];
    A[2*i+1] := B[i];
    A[i]     := A[i]/2;
END
```

The given code fragment is chosen arbitrarily. Due to the semantics of Modula-2*, the evaluation of the right hand side of the assignment statements and the store operation to the left side address is separated by a synchronization. Furthermore, since there is a synchronization point in the language between every two statements, a straightforward implementation (on a MIMD machine) must contain a total of 5 synchronization events.

Synchronization points are necessary to preserve the semantics of the program if (1) some of the N threads use a common data element and (2) the usage pattern is critical, i.e., there are definition-use dependencies.

For example, consider the third assignment in the above code fragment. Since each thread i accesses only the data element $A[i]$, for two threads i and j with $i \neq j$, there is no common data element used. The same is true for the first assignment. In every process, only those elements of A with an even subscript $(2j)$ are read, whereas those with an odd subscript $(2i-1)$ are written. There is no conflict, since the equation derived from the subscript expressions in the statement

$$2i - 1 = 2j \wedge 1 \leq i, j \leq N \wedge i \neq j$$

has no integer solution. By trying to solve analogous equations for all pairs of data accesses, the compiler discovers the data-dependencies, which really require a synchronization event. For dealing with these equations there is a well developed theory [4] [31] [20] which was originally applied for finding potential parallelism in sequential Fortran loops.

Figure 2 shows on the left hand side the dependencies, found by the compiler. It is easy to see that at least two synchronization events, shown as dashed lines, are necessary to preserve the program's semantics, i.e., to cut all the dependence arcs. Different positions for the dashed lines are possible. We have found an algorithm to find a minimal set of barrier synchronization events for a given statement sequence. For loops and branching statements further investigations are in progress.

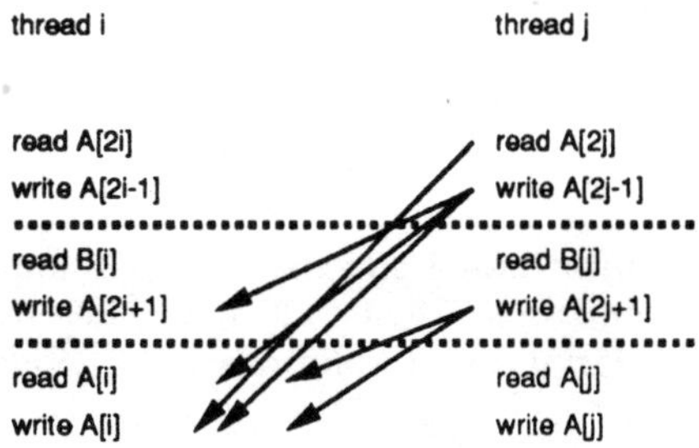


```
FORALL i: [1..N] IN PARALLEL
    A[2*i-1] := A[2*i];
END;

FORALL i: [1..N] IN PARALLEL
    A[2*i+1] := B[i];
END;

FORALL i: [1..N] IN PARALLEL
    A[i]     := A[i]/2;
END
```

Figure 2: Data-Dependencies

Thus, the given program can be transformed into the version on the right hand side of figure 2. Although our compiler uses an intermediate representation, we present the result in a Modula-2* formulation to ease understanding. The net effect is that there are only two synchronization events left.

Whereas for usage in parallelizing Fortran compilers, it is only necessary to find out whether there exists an integer solution for a given set of equations, for Modula-2* further transformations are possible by solving the equations exactly, which is easy in many standard situations.

By considering the example more closely, the reader and the compiler can figure out, that only $A[1]$ will survive the write access of the second assignment, since for the equation

$$2j - 1 = 2i + 1 \wedge 1 \leq i, j \leq N \wedge i \neq j$$

the set of solutions $\{(i,j) | j = i + 1 \wedge 1 \leq i, j \leq N\}$ does not contain a tuple $(1, j)$, i.e., $A[1]$ is written only once. Therefore, the compiler can take `A[1] := A[2]` out of the **forall**.

By studying the relationship between the second and the third assignment, the compiler finds integer solutions for

$$2j + 1 = i \wedge 1 \leq i, j \leq N \wedge i \neq j$$

and can figure out that there is no solution for $2i \geq N$; only the elements of A with an odd number (≥ 3) remain a source of conflict. If the compiler can find an inverse function for the subscript expression, this inverse can be used to eliminate a data-dependence. In the given example the compiler can apply the following transformation.

```
IF 2*i < N THEN                          IF odd(i) AND i >= 3 THEN
   A[2*i+1] := B[i]          =>             A[i] := B[(i-1)/2]
END                                      END
```

After all those elementary transformations the resulting program does not require a single synchronization event.

```
A[1] := A[2];
FORALL i: [1..N] IN PARALLEL
  IF 2*i >= N THEN
     A[2*i+1] := B[i]
  ELSE
     IF odd(i) AND i>=3 THEN
        A[i] := B[(i-1)/2]
     END;
     A[i] := A[i]/2
  END
END
```

Currently we apply data-dependence analysis based on existence tests and the Power test [32]. The number of synchronization events which can be eliminated so far is significant. Work on exploring exact solutions for finding program transformations has started.

4.2 Scheduling on SIMD

The central idea of control flow on SIMD computers is deactivation and reactivation of processors, which has been explained above. This basic technique, however, results in a poor utilization of the SIMD hardware, if the number of branches is high. While the front-end issues instructions for one group of processes, the rest idles.

Utilization can be increased by partially combining several branches. Consider the example of an **if**-statement with two arms. In each arm, there is an invocation of the same procedure. The two branches can be scheduled as follows: First, the front-end issues instructions for the **then** part, including stack operations to provide the procedure with its parameters. Then the context is switched. The **else** part is also executed up the point immediately before the procedure invocation. Then the procedure is invoked for both branches simultaneously, reducing the number of idling processors. When control flow returns from the procedure, both arms are separated again.

The compiler's task is to identify common sections of code in separate, but potentially simultaneously executing branches. These sections can be found with algorithms for computing longest common subsequences [24]. Of course, the common segments must be long enough to offset the cost caused by switching the activities of processors around.

Another possible optimization is to consider operations on semaphores in asynchronous **foralls**. Every **wait** operation may block a set of processes. When a **signal** operation is issued, some processes may become unblocked, but they are not on the branch of instructions that are presently being issued by the front-end of the SIMD machine. Thus, each **send** may increase the number of branches which must be issued by the front-end individually.

Again, the compiler must try to join different branches. A simple approach is the following: After a **send**, the front-end issues instructions for the unblocked processes, hoping that these would catch up with their partners that already passed the corresponding **wait** earlier.

Better strategies are possible. For example, consider a **wait** statement inside of a loop. Instead of having reactivated processes trying to catch up with the majority, a better hardware utilization can be reached by executing the majority first. In the next iteration, control flow automatically passes the waiting process at which point it can join the majority. Further research in this area is necessary.

Besides the above branch-level scheduling problems, techniques must be found for fine-grain load balancing. Load balancing may significantly increase the execution speed. Consider a situation where the load of active processes per processor is uneven: Some processors have lots of work to do, while others remain idle. Processes must be migrated by means of a distributed protocol.

Migration is easy if the hardware offers a (virtually) shared address space, since migrating a process does not require any changes in the code for referencing data elements. However, current SIMD hardware does not provide shared address spaces. Therefore, the front-end has to issue different code for the untouched and for the migrated processes: Access to local data elements must be replaced by explicit communication commands. Thus, simple migration does not result in increased parallelism, because the front-end must serve both groups individually. Again, the compiler must try to join different branches. One approach is to partition a branch into three phases by reordering the elementary commands of a branch. These phases are: (a) fetch necessary data, (b) execute statements, and (c) store changed data. For migrating jobs, a highly loaded processor first fetches the necessary data before migrating both process and data to a neighbor with low load. Depending on the addressing facilities of the hardware, phase (c) must again be executed by the original processor. Further research must identify a cost function to help decide when to migrate, plus a distributed migration algorithm.

4.3 Co-location of Data and Activity

Communication costs can be significantly reduced by co-locating each process with its data on one processor. Good co-location results in a high ratio of local to non-local accesses. There are basically two approaches: the data-oriented approach takes the layout of data as given and schedules processes where the data resides. The process-oriented approach first schedules the processes and then moves the data to them.

In some languages for parallel machines, such as C* [26] and Blaze [17], the burden of co-locating data and processes is placed entirely on the programmer. In high-level languages, the task is shared among programmer and compiler. The simple vector operations in Fortran 90 [18], for example, allow both approaches. The Fortran 90 compiler described by Knobe [10, 11] carefully analyzes the access patterns and then lays out the data accordingly.

In the data-oriented approach, the compiler's task of finding a good co-location is directed by the programmer who specifies how to map data elements onto the processors. The programmer, foreseeing the behavior of the intended algorithm, organizes the data in a way that allows good utilization of the hardware. Reference [22] addresses compiling for locality of reference, based on explicit mappings of data to processors.

Modula-2* supports the data-oriented approach, since it provides specific directives for data layout. Inside of a **forall** statement, the compiler assigns processes to those processors which actually store the required data. Rescheduling of processes may take place between every pair of statements or even inside individual statements.

For efficient, data-driven co-location of activity and data elements, a cost model is necessary. Based upon this model, the compiler can try to find a good, low-level schedule by trading off communication and computation costs. Further research is necessary to find appropriate cost models for parallel hardware.

5 Recommendations for Parallel Machine Architectures

The following list itemizes some broad requirements that parallel machine architectures should fulfill to allow for efficient, compiled programs. These requirements are likely to be encountered when designing the translation schemes for parallel, imperative languages.

- Hardware support for fast process creation, synchronization, and context switching.
- Shared address space.[3] All processors should be able to generate addresses for the entire memory on the system. Even the front-end's memory should be part of that address space.

  For pointers, system wide addresses are important, because otherwise they would have to be simulated quite inefficiently in software.
- Uniform memory access instructions. Most parallel machines today provide a set of instructions for accessing local memory, a second one for accessing memory in neighbors, and a third set for accessing distant memory units. The differences in speed are significant and therefore require that the compiler detects the faster cases. However, it is often impossible to know statically for which case to optimize. For instance, we found that in many cases it was impossible to determine in the compiler whether a procedure would access local or non-local memory. The generated code thus has to check all three cases at run-time. Such a simple and frequently repeated case analysis could be done much more efficiently in hardware.
- Simulating shared memory. A shared memory in which all memory units can be accessed in the same time would simplify programming and optimizing compilers greatly. Latency hiding and randomization techniques could help achieve a reasonable approximation of true shared memory. Latency hiding means that each processor can initiate several memory references before receiving a response. Thus, the network serves each processor's request in a pipelined fashion. The total network bandwidth of the network must be high enough to accept and serve memory accesses for all processors at rate that is comparable with accesses to local memory.
- Autonomous addressing capability. An autonomous addressing capability means that each processor can generate its own addresses for accessing memory. The Connection Machine CM-2, for example, does not have such a facility – each processor must use the same address into its own,

[3] A shared address space does not imply shared memory.

local memory for each parallel instruction. The lack of autonomous addressing not only makes many applications awkward to write, especially if they use pointers, but also precludes certain optimizations in processor virtualization.

- Single instruction set. SIMD machines today typically have different instruction sets for front-end and parallel processors. This property implies that the code generator of the compiler has to be written twice. Also, each procedure has to be translated twice, doubling code size. A single instruction set would simplify this aspect.

- Small instruction set. The Connection Machine CM-2, for example, offers about 400 instructions. As in sequential compilers, only a few dozens of these instructions can actually be generated. Clearly, a detailed study determining the most frequently used instructions in parallel programs is desperately needed.

6 Conclusion

Ease of programming as well as portability of programs will be of overwhelming importance for the acceptance of highly parallel machines. Modula-2* supports both: few extensions of a sequential programming language suffice for writing highly parallel, problem-oriented programs, and compilers that can generate efficient code for a wide range of parallel machines appear feasible. Improvements in hardware architecture, operating systems, programming languages and compiler technology should eventually render the current practice of machine dependent, parallel programming as obsolete as machine dependent, sequential programming.

References

[1] Akl SG. The Design and Analysis of Parallel Algorithms. Prentice Hall, Englewood Cliffs, New Jersey, 1989.

[2] American National Standards Institute, Inc., Washington, D.C. ANSI, Programming Language Fortran (Fortran90), Draft S8, Version 114 (X3.9-1990), 1990.

[3] Bal HE, Steiner JS, Tanenbaum AS. Programming languages for distributed computing systems. ACM Computing Surveys, 21(3):261–322, 1989.

[4] Banerjee U. Dependence Analysis for Supercomputing. Kluwer Academic Publishers, Boston, Dordrecht, London, 1988.

[5] Fox G, Hiranandani S, Kennedy K, Koelbel C, Kremer U, Tseng CW, Wu MY. Fortran D language specification. Technical Report CRPC-TR90079, Center for Research on Parallel Computation, Rice University, 1990.

[6] Fox GC. What have we learnt from using real parallel machines to solve real problems. In Proc. of the Third Conf. on Hypercube Concurrent Computers and Applications, vol 2, pp 897–955, Pasadena, CA, 1988. ACM Press, New York.

[7] Gibbons A, Rytter W. Efficient Parallel Algorithms. Cambridge University Press, 1988.

[8] Heinz EA. Automatische Elimination von Synchronisationsbarrieren in synchronen FORALLs. Master's thesis, University of Karlsruhe, Department of Informatics, 1991.

[9] Hillis WD, Steele GL. Data parallel algorithms. Communications of the ACM, 29(12):1170–1183, 1986.

[10] Knobe K, Lukas JD, Steele GL. Data optimization: Allocation of arrays to reduce communication on SIMD machines. Journal of Parallel and Distributed Computing, 8(2):102–118, 1990.

[11] Knobe K, Natarajan V. Data optimization: Minimizing residual interprocessor data motion on SIMD machines. In Frontiers '90:The Third Symposium on the Frontiers of Massively Parallel Computation, College Park, University of Maryland, 1990.

[12] Koelbel C, Mehrotra P. Supporting shared data structures and distributed memory architectures. In Proc. of the 2nd ACM SIGPLAN Symposium on Principles and Practice of Parallel Programming, pp 177–186, 1990.

[13] Kretzschmar R. Ein Modula-2*-Compiler für die Connection Machine CM-2. Master's thesis, University of Karlsruhe, Department of Informatics, 1991.

[14] Lukowicz P. Code-Erzeugung für Modula-2* für verschiedene Maschinenarchitekturen. Master's thesis, University of Karlsruhe, Department of Informatics, 1992.

[15] McGraw J, Skedzielewski S, Allan S, Oldehoeft R, Glauert J, Kirkham C, Noyce B, Thomas R. SISAL Language Reference Manual. Lawrence Livermore National Laboratory, 1985.

[16] McGraw JR. The VAL language: Description and analysis. ACM Transactions on Programming Languages and Systems, 4(1):44–82, 1982.

[17] Mehrotra P, Rosendale JV. The BLAZE language: A parallel language for scientific programming. Parallel Computing, 5:339–361, 1987.

[18] Metcalf M, Reid J. Fortran 90 Explained. Oxford Science Publications, 1990.

[19] Ousterhout JK, Scelza DA, Sindhu PS. Medusa: An experiment in distributed operating system structure. Communications of the ACM, 23(2):92–205, 1980.

[20] Polychronopoulos CD. Parallel Programming and Compilers. Kluwer Academic Publishers, Boston, Dordrecht, London, 1989.

[21] Prentice Hall, Englewood Cliffs, New Jersey. INMOS Limited: Occam Programming Manual, 1984.

[22] Rogers AM. Compiling for locality of reference. Technical Report TR 91-1195, Department of Computer Science, Cornell University, 1991.

[23] Rosing M, Schnabel R, Weaver R. DINO: Summary and example. In Proc. of the Third Conf. on Hypercube Concurrent Computers and Applications, pp 472–481, Pasadena, CA, 1988. ACM Press, New York.

[24] Sankoff D, (eds) JBK. Time Warps, String Edits, and Macromolecules: The Theory and Practice of Sequence Comparison. Addison-Wesley, Reading, Mass., 1983.

[25] Thinking Machines Corporation, Cambridge, Massachusetts. *Lisp Reference Manual, Version 5.0, 1988.

[26] Thinking Machines Corporation, Cambridge, Massachusetts. C* Programming Guide, Version 6.0, 1990.

[27] Tichy WF, Herter CG. Modula-2*: An extension of Modula-2 for highly parallel, portable programs. Technical Report No. 4/90, University of Karlsruhe, Department of Informatics, 1990.

[28] Tichy WF, Philippsen M, Hatcher P. A critique of the programming language C*. Technical Report No. 17/91, University of Karlsruhe, Department of Informatics, 1991.

[29] U.S. Government, Ada Joint Program Office. ANSI/MIL-Std 1815 A, Reference Manual for the Ada Programming Language, 1983.

[30] Weiss M. Strip mining on SIMD architectures. In 1991 ACM International Conference on Supercomputing, pp 234–243, Cologne, Germany, 1991.

[31] Wolfe M. Optimizing Supercompilers for Supercomputers. Research Monographs in Parallel and Distributed Computing. Pitman, London, 1989.

[32] Wolfe MJ, Tseng CW. The power test for data dependence. Technical Report CSE 90-015, Oregon Graduate Institute, 1990.

Discussion: Parallelism

Led by Walter F. Tichy
Summarized by Michael Philippsen
Department of Informatics, University of Karlsruhe
Karlsruhe, Germany

Parallel Machine Architecture and Parallel Programming

Today's sequential processors are not designed in a vacuum. Instead, they are built to fulfill the needs of extensive sets of benchmark programs and at the same time take into account the capabilities of compilers. A comparable level of maturity has not been reached in the design of parallel computers. The semantic gap between parallel hardware and high-level, parallel languages is substantial at present, and far too large to be bridged effectively by a compiler. The result is that programmers must code at a low, machine-oriented level and that parallel programs are largely non-portable. This poor state of affairs is not surprising, given that many of the variables involved in parallel system design are unknown and in a state of flux. These variables include the capabilities that parallel machines can offer, the translation and optimization techniques of compilers for parallel machines, and the appropriate high-level constructs in parallel programming languages. In addition, parallel system architecture allows many more degrees of freedom than sequential systems. In the long run, however, the practice of rewriting parallel programs for every new machine architecture is economically intolerable.

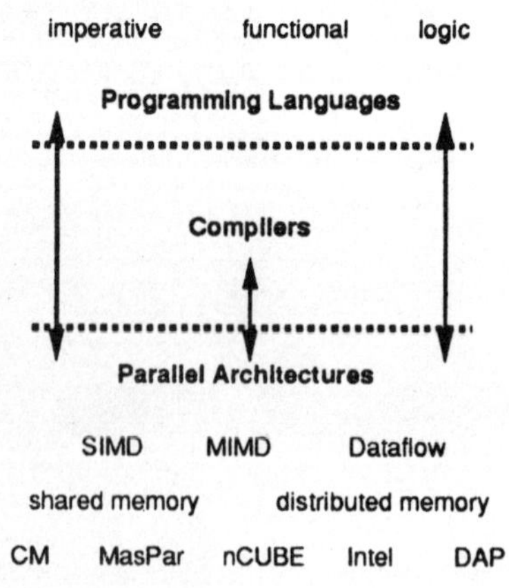

Figure 1: Interaction between Languages, Compilers, Architectures

A major challenge is hence the harmonization of parallel machine architectures, compilers, and programming languages, with the goal of allowing programs to be written in high-level, problem-oriented languages, while developing compilers that translate the programs into efficient target code for a wide variety of parallel architectures. Success will be measured by how well real, machine-independent application programs will execute on real, parallel computers. Since highly parallel machines with thousands and tens of thousands of processors are already being manufactured and used commercially, this challenge requires a solution urgently.

The purpose of the discussion was to approach this challenge from the language and compiler designer's viewpoint. The questions put to the audience were as follows:

- What are the needs of the programmers?
- What features of parallel computers are germane and must be reflected in the programming languages?
- What features of parallel computers are accidental or irrelevant for machine-independent programs?
- What are the major questions faced by compiler writers?
- What properties should parallel hardware possess to allow for efficient, compiled programs?

A view shared by many in the audience was that the approach of automatically parallelizing existing, sequential code should not be followed intensively. Although there is overwhelming economic justification for this approach, it will meet with only limited success in the short to medium term. The goal of automatically producing parallel programs can only, if ever, be achieved by program transformation systems that start with problem specifications and not with sequential implementations. In a sequential program, too many opportunities for parallelism have been hidden or eliminated.

A long term goal could be to develop *interactive* program transformation systems that assist programmers in parallelizing programs and provide feedback and guidance. The problem with this idea is that the approach of semiautomatic program transformations is still an object of active research, even for sequential programs. In the medium term, a production-quality transformer for deriving realistic, parallel programs is unlikely to appear. The traditional method of teaching algorithms and formulating them in programming languages with explicit parallelism is likely to be more successful, especially since the body of known parallel algorithms is large and growing rapidly. Initial indications seem to be that writing parallel software is not significantly harder than writing sequential software, provided the languages and support tools are adequate.

Concerns of the Programmer

The following is a general list of requirements on programming languages and support tools. The requirements are not new; they are borrowed from the world of sequential programs, but apply equally well to parallel programs.

- The programming language should permit clear expression of algorithms and systems architecture, to ease the writing, reading, verification, understanding, modification, and reuse of software systems.
- Programs should be portable to a wide range of hardware architectures.
- Programs should run (after compilation) with satisfactory efficiency and with effective utilization of the available hardware resources.
- Support tools for debugging, testing, and measuring of parallel programs should be available.

Current practice is quite different: Existing parallel programming languages do not allow clear expression of algorithms, parallel programs are not portable, and support tools are often poor. The goal of satisfactory efficiency can often be met only by writing low-level, machine-dependent code.

But what are properties of parallel architectures that should be visible in parallel programs? Should the number of processors be visible? Is it necessary for the programmer to know about the organization of memory or the layout of the data? Are explicit communication protocols necessary, or will the compiler be able to insert them into the generated code by analyzing the data usage patterns? Should the control mode be visible, i.e., should there be different programming languages specialized for SIMD, MIMD, Dataflow or systolic computers?

PRAM.

The PRAM is clearly the best studied approach to parallel programming today. Most algorithms are formulated for the PRAM model. The shared memory of this model makes programs much easier to understand than for models with distributed memory and explicit message passing.

During the discussion we could not agree on the performance losses involved in mapping the abstract PRAM model onto a real machine. If this mapping is possible without adding asymptotic complexity, the PRAM is likely to be broadly accepted. But this will be difficult to achieve, since the PRAM completely ignores the memory hierarchies of today's machines.

Due to the lack of high-level parallel languages, an adequate approach to parallel programming is still to develop a PRAM algorithm first and then to translate it (by hand or compiler) to fit the target machine.

Modula-2.*

One approach to the above questions is Modula-2*, which is presented in a separate article in this volume. Modula-2*, an extension of Modula-2, is problem-oriented in the sense that the programmer can choose and mix the degree of parallelism, i.e., the number of processors, and the control mode (SIMD-like or MIMD-like), as needed by the intended algorithm. An interconnection network is not directly visible in the language. A shared address space among all processors is assumed, though not the necessarily shared memory. There are no explicit message passing instructions; instead, reading and writing locations in shared address space subsume message passing. Special data allocation constructs help control the access times in distributed memory.

On the features of parallel machines that should be visible in programming languages we noted the following. The number of processors needs to be available (as a constant or variable), since algorithms that adapt to the number of processors often perform superior compared to those that don't. However, there are many algorithms for which simple, system-provided multiplexing of processors ("processor virtualization") is sufficient. In those cases, programmers should not be forced to program virtualization explicitly.

We do not think that programmers should be forced to specify much detail concerning data layout and network structure, since both of these tend to be major sources of machine dependence. Instead, we should develop tools that automatically or semi-automatically embed the data and access patterns into given hardware structures. Explicit message passing should also be avoided in high-level programming languages, because it is tedious and error-prone to program massively parallel message passing, and also because message passing instructions are intimately tied to the way a problem has been mapped onto a given architecture. Thus, message passing tends to cause machine dependence that is difficult to remove and scale.

Whereas in Modula-2* the organization of the memory is invisible, Knobe spoke out in defense of the visibility of local address spaces. If locality is present at the language level, it simplifies dependence analysis and enhances the efficiency of the generated code.

Recommendations for Parallel Architectures

The last part of the discussion centered on recommendations for parallel hardware. The starting point was a list of recommendations which were collected during the work on the compiler for Modula-2* by Philippsen and Tichy (see section 5 of *Compiling for Massively Parallel Machines* in this volume).

Register Allocation and Phase Ordering

A Quantitative Algorithm for Data Locality Optimization

François Bodin, William Jalby, Daniel Windheiser
IRISA, University of Rennes
Rennes, FRANCE

Christine Eisenbeis
INRIA
Rocquencourt, FRANCE

Abstract

In this paper, we consider the problem of optimizing register allocation and cache behavior for loop array references. We exploit techniques developed initially for data locality estimation and improvement. First we review the concept of "reference window" that serves as our basic tool for both data locality evaluation and management. Then we study how some loop restructuring techniques (interchanging, tiling,...) can help to improve data locality. We describe a register allocation algorithm and a cache usage optimization algorithm based on the window concept which can be effectively implemented in a compiler system. Experimental speedup measurements on a RISC processor, the IBM RS/6000, give evidence of the efficiency of our technique.

1 Introduction

Conventional compilers usually fail in allocating the elements of array variables into registers or to exploit the memory cache. New register allocation techniques need to be designed in order to take advantage of this improvement. Accesses to array variables give the opportunity to improve performance by allocating frequently used array elements to registers or to make efficient use of the cache. The problem is twofold: first we must be able to detect the array elements that are going to be reused, then we must be able to generate code exploiting this "locality". For a given iteration, the window is defined as the set of array elements that have been accessed at least once in the past and will be reused later in the loop execution. In this paper we present an original approach, based on the window idea [7], for improving register allocation of subscripted variables occurring in Fortran Do loops. We also present how the algorithms presented in this paper apply to cache.

Figure 1 illustrates our algorithms on the matrix-matrix multiply example (shown on Figure 2). The performance improvement is obtained from blocking the loops and as shown by the curves, it is very important to be able to compute which block size gives the best performance. We run our code on an IBM RS/6000 that has a cache size of 32kBytes and is 2-way associative. Figure 1 shows the performance in Megaflops versus the block size. The originality of our method is that it allows us, not only to determine which loops should be tiled but also the size of the tiles. As shown in section 4 we are able to deduce automatically that the block size must be less than 62 if we do not want to overflow the cache.

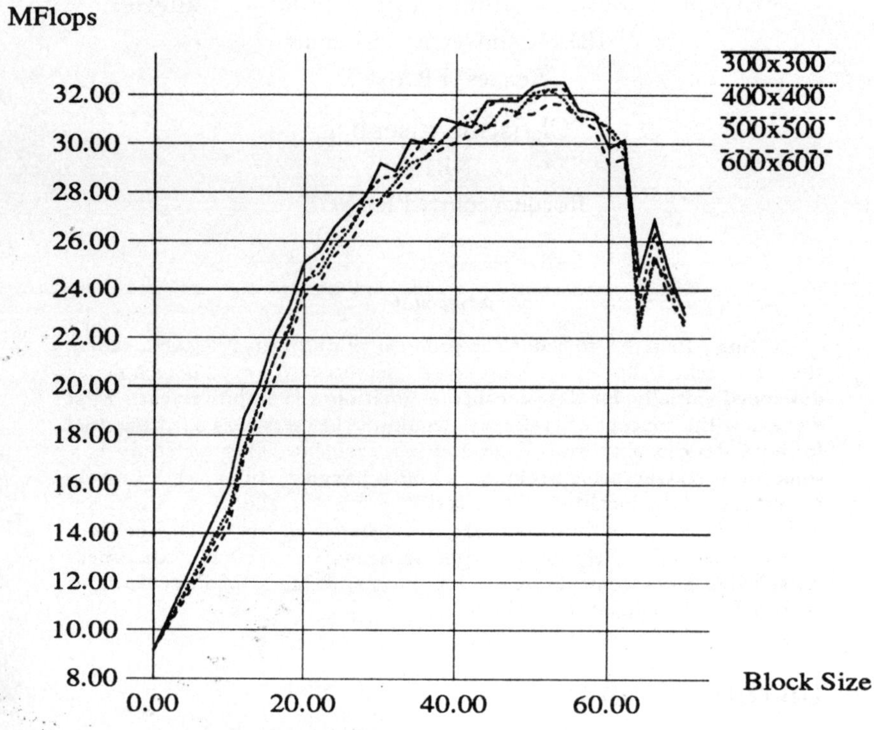

Figure 1: Performance of matrix-matrix multiply on the IBM RS/6000 Model 320

```
DO 1 i1 = 1, N1
  DO 1 i2 = 1, N2
    DO 1 i3 = 1, N3
      A(i1, i2) = A(i1, i2) + B(i1, i3) * C(i3, i2)
1 CONTINUE
```

Figure 2: Matrix-matrix product

1.1 Related Work

In [7], a methodology based on data dependencies is described for detecting and evaluating data locality, and deriving guidelines for driving simple program

```
L1      DO 1 i1 = 1, N1
                 :
Lk      DO 1 ik = 1, Nk
        < S1 >        ··· A[H1(i1,...,ik)]
          :                 :
        < S2 >        ··· A[H2(i1,...,ik)]
1       CONTINUE
```

Figure 3: Structure of perfectly-nested normalized loops

transformations. More precisely, the concept of the window is introduced to characterize "active" portions of arrays which should be kept in the cache memory.

In [17] [18], the emphasis is put more specifically on the problem of developing a strategy to apply loop transformations to optimize data locality and parallelism simultaneously. The scope of these transformations is extensive (including loop reversal and non rectangular tiling) and both temporal and spatial locality are taken into account. This approach is somewhat similar to ours, however in our case the emphasis is put on quantifying the locality, i.e. being able to extract the section of an array that should be kept in a given memory level. We also improved the strategy developed by Wolf et al. [18] by addressing not only the problem of choosing the loops which should be in the tile, but also the problem of determining the order of the loops within the tile. Our study shows that the amount of storage in a given memory level, necessary to achieve the highest reuse of data depends not only on "reuse vector directions", introduced in [18], but also on the order of loop in the block..

However, the previous studies [4, 7, 8, 16, 17] were mainly targeted at cache-based systems, which greatly simplifies the problem in the sense that transfers between memory levels are entirely managed by hardware. With registers or local memory, however, exploiting the locality associated with a memory location referenced several times requires explicit transfer of the content of that memory location either into a register or into local memory [5, 8].

1.2 Overview of the Paper

The objective of the paper is to show how the window concept can be used to optimize the locality of programs. Our main goal is to derive from the window concept a quantification method that allows an accurate computation of the section of an array that must be allocated to a fast memory because of data reuses. Section 2 introduces the general framework, and notation used in the paper. Section 3 presents the main mathematical properties of windows. In particular, an approximation of window is presented. The impact of some loop transformations (loop interchanging, loop tiling) are analyzed in Section 4. Section 5 tackles the problems specific to the register case, i.e explicit movement of data to registers, and Section 6 explains the strategy we use for cache memory.

Section 7 presents some experimental results obtained using our algorithm on an IBM RS/6000.

2 General Framework

2.1 Data Dependencies

In this paper we use the standard definitions for data dependencies. For details on the various definitions and loop transformations see [3, 10, 11, 14, 15]. The reason for using the framework of data dependence analysis, introduced initially for vectorization, is that vectorization and locality optimization have much in common. In the first problem, the issue is to detect whether a specific memory location is referenced at least twice in order to enforce an execution order which preserves the program semantics. For optimizing data locality, the first step is locality detection, which amounts to detecting whether the same memory location is referenced several times. The major difference between the two problems is that, for data locality optimization, a quantitative measure is required (how many times the same memory location is referenced, and which size is necessary to exploit all reuses in a loop). Another difference is that in addition to the three classical dependencies (flow dependence, anti-dependence, and output dependence), we need to consider systematically input dependencies, which arises whenever two successive reads are performed from the same memory location. Although this fourth type of dependency is not of much interest in the case of vectorization or parallelization (because it does not impose any execution order), for data locality optimization, such dependencies have to be taken into account because they reflect the fact that the same memory location is used twice.

2.1.1 Uniformly-Generated Dependencies

It is well known that addressing functions are usually **linear** in scientific programs. Among dependencies resulting from linear addressing functions, it happens that most of data locality is found when both functions are closely related. That is why we restrict our study to **uniformly-generated** dependencies. A uniformly-generated dependency Δ from S_1 to S_2 has the following characteristics:

$$S_1 \cdots A(H_1(\vec{\imath})) \cdots$$
$$S_2 \cdots A(H_2(\vec{\imath})) \cdots$$

where:

$$H_1(\vec{\imath}) = h(\vec{\imath}) + d_1$$
$$H_2(\vec{\imath}) = h(\vec{\imath}) + d_2$$

h() is a linear mapping, called the **common linear part** of H_1 and H_2, d_1 and d_2 are constant vectors.

Considering only uniformly-generated dependencies is not over-restrictive for the sake of data locality optimization, since non uniformly-generated dependencies generally do not carry much locality. For instance, there is not a lot of reuse of data between $A(i_1)$ and $A(i_1+i_2)$ compared to $A(i_1)$ and $A(i_1+2)$ in a 2-nested loop with indexes i_1 and i_2.

In the following, we denote Z the set of integers, $h : Z^k \rightarrow Z^d$, $h(i_1, ..., i_k) = (h^1(), ..., h^d()) = (\lambda_1^1 i_1 + ... + \lambda_k^1 i_k, ..., \lambda_1^d i_1 + ... + \lambda_k^d i_k)$ the linear part of the access function and $H() = h() + d$ the access function. To denote the loop with index i_j we use the notation L_j, as shown on figure 3.

2.2 The Window Concept

Definition 2.1 *The iteration space $C \subset Z^k$, of the loops, is defined by*

$$C = \prod_{j=1}^{k} [1, N_j].$$

We also define the natural basis of Z^k, $(e_1, ..., e_k)$, that corresponds to the induction variables $i_1, \cdots, i_k$.

The basic idea of the window originally introduced in [7] primary for studying data locality, is to quantify the portions of data array which are "alive" at a given time t. Alive array elements are going to be reused later and so they are worth keeping in local memory (that can be either registers or cache). Let $(i_1, i_2, ..., i_k)$ be an iteration. The window for array A with mapping function $H()$ can be defined as the set of elements accessed before iteration $(i_1, i_2, ..., i_k)$ that will also be accessed at or after iteration $(i_1, i_2, ..., i_k)$. In other words, at each time $t = (i_1, i_2, ..., i_k)$, the window contains all the array elements that should be kept in registers or local memory for future accesses because they will be needed again. The window concept is strongly related to data dependence: as a matter of fact, two statements that are not related by any data dependence (input dependencies included) do not share any data.

Definition 2.2 *The* **reference window**, *$W(t)$, for a dependence between two references to array A, $\Delta_A : S_1 \rightarrow S_2$, at time t is defined to be the set of all elements of A that are referenced by S_1 before t that are also referenced after or at t by S_2.*

Usually we distinguish two kinds of data reuse: spatial and temporal. We say that we have a spatial reuse when a reference loads a data (using the cache line mechanism) used by a future reference. We have temporal locality when an instruction accesses an array element which has already been accessed by an instruction in a previous iteration. Spatial reuses do not directly fit in the window concept since the value that is used has not been explicitly accessed by the program. However a straightforward extension of the window concept allows us to take into account such reuses.

If the window is small enough to fit in the lowest level of the memory hierarchy, each array element only needs to be loaded once from main memory (those accesses are often called compulsory accesses); all subsequent accesses can be done from the lower level of memory. In this case, all the locality available in the loop nest is taken advantage of. We say that the data locality is optimal.

Unfortunately, the window may not fit in the lower level of memory. In this case one can try to reduce the size of the windows by restructuring the loop nest. If we succeed to reduce the size of the window so that it fits entirely in the lower level of memory, we have exploited all possible locality. Loop interchanging is used for this purpose. We show later that in order to reduce the size of the window, the loops *carrying locality* should be made innermost. When several loops carry locality, we provide a criterion to choose the order of the internal loops.

In some cases however, loop interchanging can fail to reduce the size of the window sufficiently. In this case our strategy is to optimize data locality only within a subset of the iteration space, which is called a *tile*. Although, each reference in a tile is loaded only once from main memory, an array element may need to be reloaded from main memory when a subsequent tile is executed. As far as tiling is concerned, one of the main issues consists in choosing the size of the tile so that the number of accesses to the main memory is minimum. Since windows can be computed symbolically, as a function of the unknown loop bounds, the problem of choosing the size of the tile can be formulated as an optimization problem.

Definition 2.3 *The* **cost** *of a reference window $Cost(W)$ is defined as the maximum size of the window over the time (the size of the window W is denoted $||W||$).*

Definition 2.4 *The* **benefit** *of a reference window $Ben(W)$ is defined as the number of access to main memory saved.*

For instance if we consider the following loop:

```
      DO 1 i1 = 1, N1
      S1      A(i1) = X(i1)
      S2      D(i1) = X(i1 - 3)
    1 CONTINUE
```

we have the window $W_X = \{X(i_1 - 3), X(i_1 - 2), X(i_1 - 1)\}$ with :

$$Cost(W_X) = 3 \quad \text{and} \quad Ben(W_X) = N_1 - 3$$

2.3 Data Coherence between Windows

In the general case, if an overlap exists between different windows for the same array and if these windows are allocated separately in a memory level, an array element may have two different copies simultaneously alive. This is for instance the case if an array is accessed using functions whose linear parts are different. The problem arises when one of these copies is modified, since the other one needs to be either modified or invalidated accordingly. In order to solve this problem, the idea is to avoid having multiple copies of the array elements. Instead of considering the two windows separately, we can consider the union of the windows (this is usually easy to compute). The resulting window is called the **Dominant Window** . The dominant window is then used by the allocation algorithm. This notion ensures that the approximations made in the window computation are conservative and therefore preserve the semantics of the program.

3 Window Framework

In this section we introduce some basic results concerning the windows. Theorem 3.3 shows that it is not necessary for computing the window to consider all the iteration space. Only the set of innermost loops whose corresponding directions contain the kernel of the index function of an array reference needs to be considered.

Definition 3.1 *We define subsets V_r of Q^k to be*

$$V_r = \{v \in Q^k | v = \sum_{p=k-r+1}^{k} \alpha_p e_p, \alpha_p \in Q\}$$

where Q is the set of rational.

Definition 3.2 *We call a* **partial window**, *denoted $[x]W$ a window obtained by the restriction of the window computation to the x innermost loops ($x < k$) (The window computed over the whole set of loops $[k]W$ will be noted W.)*

Partial windows allow to use an interesting property that simplifies the window computation. Indeed, it may happen that a partial window express all data locality, as explained in the theorem below.

Theorem 3.3 *Let h be a linear function from Z^k into Z^d and r be the smallest integer such that $Ker(h) \subset V_r$ ($Ker()$ is the kernel of a function). The window W associated with $h()$ is such that*

$$W(t = (i_1, \cdots, i_k)) \subset [r]W(t_r = (i_{k-r+1}, \cdots, i_k))$$

Proof: Let C_t^- be the set of iterations that execute before t and C_t^+ be the set of iterations that execute at or after t. Consider two iterations defined by $\vec{\imath} = (i_1, \cdots, i_r, \cdots) \in C_t^-$ and $\vec{\jmath} = (j_1, \cdots, j_r, \cdots) \in C_t^+$ such that $h(\vec{\imath}) = h(\vec{\jmath})$. Thus $\vec{\imath} - \vec{\jmath}$ is in $Ker(h)$ and therefore in V_r by hypothesis. It follows that for every $p \in \{1, \cdots, k-r\}$, $i_p = j_p$, so that $\vec{\imath}$ is in $C_{t_r}^-$ and $\vec{\jmath}$ in $C_{t_r}^+$, hence the result. ∎

For instance if we consider the loop:

```
      DO 1 i=1,10
          DO 1 j =1,20
              DO 1 k = 1,30
                  A(i,j,k) = T(i,j)
1     CONTINUE
```

we get a window $T(i, j)$ for accesses to array T that contains only one element. This window can be computed only considering the loop on k.

Theorem 3.4 *Let h be a linear function from Z^k into Z^d and r be the smallest integer such that $Ker(h) \subset V_r$. The partial windows are such that:*

$$||[k]W|| = ... = ||[r]W|| \geq ||[r-1]W|| \geq ... \geq ||[1]W||$$

As a consequence of theorem 3.3, we can distinguish two aspects in the problem of optimizing data locality:

1. Given a set of nested loops, what is the amount of local memory necessary to exploit all the locality available in the loop, i.e. exploit data reuse so that the number of accesses to the main memory is limited to the intrinsic minimum (i.e. accessing to a main memory cell only one time).

2. Given a set of nested loops how can it be modified to decrease the amount of local memory necessary to exploit all the locality in the loop.

The first problem refers to the window computation and the second to loop transformations that "optimize" the locality. However, even if these problems are perfectly solved, we may not have enough space to keep everything in the local memory. This is the goal of the blocking transformation that allows to consider the reuse of data only on a subset of the iterations. The last problem involved is the explicit management of a memory level, i.e. computing and allocating a window in a memory hierarchy. Those points are discussed in more details in the subsequent sections of the paper.

3.1 Expressing Windows Analytically

In order to characterize windows analytically, we need to introduce the notion of "time", since the definition of reference window involves the concept of **past** and **future** with respect to a given time t. Here for sake of simplicity we consider a two dimensional iteration space. We have chosen to use a **timing function**, that describes at which time step t iteration (i_1, i_2) is run, denoted as $T(i_1, i_2) = t$. Remark that T does not refer to any execution time. It represents only the order in which the iterations are done.

Next, in order to make the window computation easy, we assume that the timing function T is **linear**: $T(i_1, i_2) = P_1.(i_1 - 1) + P_2.(i_2 - 1) + 1$, where P_1 and P_2 are real or integer constants. The following form of T refers to the case when the loop is run sequentially: then $T(i_1, i_2) = N_2(i_1 - 1) + i_2$, so that $P_1 = N_2$ and $P_2 = 1$. Taking P_1 and P_2 as parameters allows us to handle the computation in a symbolic form, so that window computation does not apply only to a given order of iterations, but to any one, provided that the order preserves the semantics of the original loop. It is easy to show that the condition for a timing function to be legal is that, for any dependence vector (d_1, d_2), $T(d_1, d_2) > 0$.

Now we consider the iteration space $C = [1, N_1] \times [1, N_2]$ and for a given time step t, we split the iteration space into two parts: C_t^- is the set of iterations that execute before t and C_t^+ is the set of iterations that execute at or after t. Geometrically, the limit between the two parts is the hyperplane $\mathcal{H}_t$ defined by the equation $T(i_1, i_2) = t$ (see Figure 4). Let us consider the (potential) dependence δ_{S_1,S_2} from S_1 to S_2 of loop of Figure 3. Then, by definition, the window associated with that dependence is (the set of data accessed by any iteration before t and another one, after or equal to t):

$$\boxed{W(t) = H_1(C_t^-) \cap H_2(C_t^+)}$$

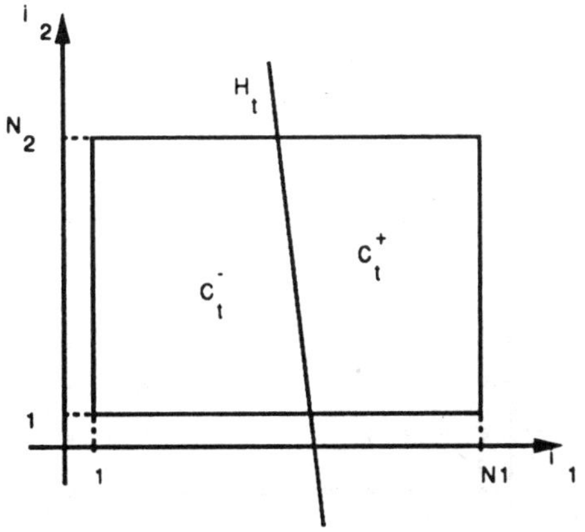

Figure 4: Splitting the iteration space: C_t^- is the set of iterations that occur before t and C_t^+ is the set of iterations that occur at or after t.

To visualize this fact, let us give values to function H_1 and H_2: $H_1(i_1, i_2) = i_1$ and $H_2(i_1, i_2) = i_1 - 3$, then Figure 5 shows the window as intersection of $H_1(C_t^-)$ and $H_2(C_t^+)$.

3.2 Approximating the Windows

In this section, we highlight some problems that make the computation of the **exact** window either complex, intractable or even unprofitable so that approximations of the window are needed (the reader is referred to [6] for a detailed description of the window computation):

1. The first problem is that the window is composed of points lying on the integer lattice instead of the whole real space. The problem of counting or characterizing the integer points inside a convex polytope is known to be a rather complex problem. Therefore we approximate the exact window by a **larger** one, whose integer points are easier to handle.

2. Another problem that appears in window computation is that the shape of the window varies during the execution. The window grows at the beginning of the loop execution then decreases at the end.

3. The third problem that is closely related to both previous ones concerns the variation of the window over t: it can be shown that the windows corresponding to t and $t+1$ are related by a translation by a vector depending on t. However it may happen that the movement of the window is not regular over time (recall that only integer points are considered). Hence we will use instead a larger window (called an **extended window**) consisting of several consecutive windows, that has the attractive property that it moves with integer offsets. A by-product of this approximation is that the window does not need to be updated at each time step, but only at regular time intervals.

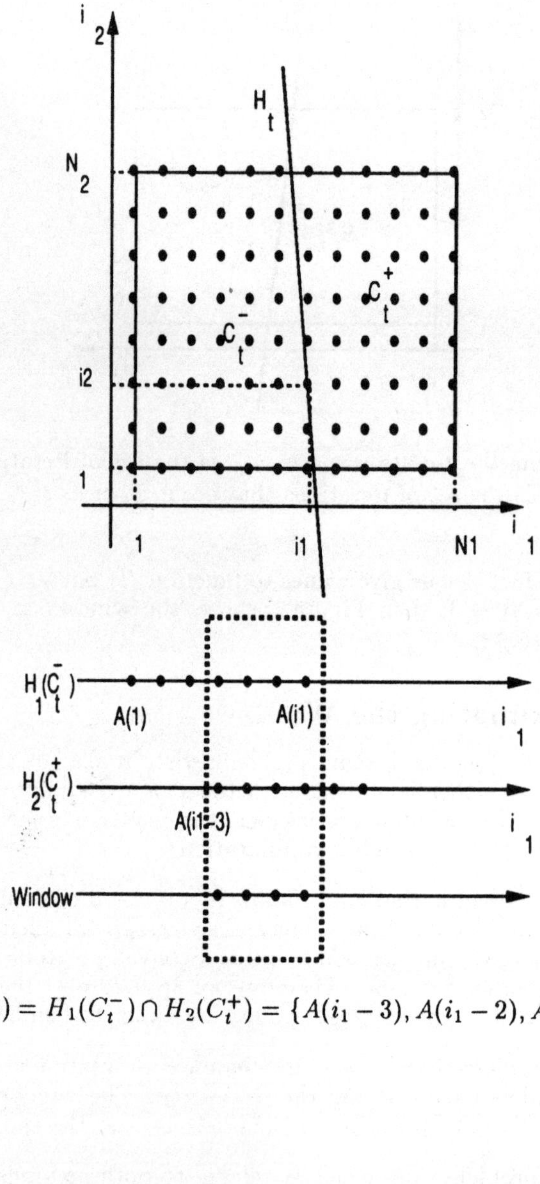

Figure 5: $W_A(t) = H_1(C_t^-) \cap H_2(C_t^+) = \{A(i_1-3), A(i_1-2), A(i_1-1), A(i_1)\}$

Definition 3.5 *The* **extended window** *for a function $H() : Z^k \rightarrow Z$, $H(i_1, ..., i_k) = \lambda_1 i_1 + ... + \lambda_k i_k + d$, is defined by*

$$[r]\overline{W}(i_{k-r+1}) = (\lambda_{k-r+1}(i_{k-r+1} - 1) + W) \cap \delta Z$$

where δ is the greatest common divisor of the λ_i and W is an interval depending on the loop bounds, and independent on the value of i_{k-r+1}. The value of r is the one obtained in theorem 3.3. The interval W, in the case of a two dimensional loop is delimited by

$$\begin{cases} [\lambda_2 + 1, \lfloor \frac{\lambda_1}{N_2} + \lambda_2 N_2 \rfloor + \lambda_1] & \text{if } \lambda_1 \geq 0 \\ [\lambda_2 + 1 + \lambda_1, \lfloor \frac{\lambda_1}{N_2} + \lambda_2 N_2 \rfloor] & \text{if } \lambda_1 < 0 \end{cases}$$

The definition 3.5 gives the shape of an extended window. The extended windows have a simple shape that allows explicit allocation of the windows in a memory hierarchy level (for instance registers).

```
      DO 1 i1 = 1, N1
            DO 1 i2 = 1, N2
S                 B(i1, i2) = A(i1 + i2)
1     CONTINUE
```

For instance the loop above contains a self input-dependence on S due to array A. At the beginning of iteration (i_1, i_2), the corresponding window $W(t = (i_1, i_2))$is given by :

$$\begin{cases} \text{if } 1 < i_1 < N_1 & \{A(j_1 + j_2) /\ i_1 + 1 \leq j_1 + j_2 < i_1 + N_2\} \\ \text{if } i_1 = 1 & \{A(j_1 + j_2) /\ 2 \leq j_1 + j_2 < 1 + i_2\} \\ \text{if } i_1 = N_1 & \{A(j_1 + j_2) /\ N_1 + i_2 \leq j_1 + j_2 < N_1 + N_2\} \end{cases}$$

An extended window is obtained by taking:

$$\overline{W}(i_1) = i_1 + [1, N_2]$$

An extension of this formula for multidimensional array is easily obtained by considering the window on each dimension:

Corollary 3.6 *Let h be a linear function from Z^k into Z^d defined as:*

$$(i_1, \cdots, i_k) \rightarrow (h^1(i_1, \cdots, i_k), \cdots, h^d(i_1, \cdots, i_k))$$

Let r be the smallest integer such that $Ker(h) \subset V_r$. The window W associated with $h()$ is such that

$$W(t = (i_1, \cdots, i_k)) \subset ([r]W_1(t_r) \times [r]W_2(t_r) \times \cdots \times [r]W_d(t_r))$$

Where $[r]W_p$ is the partial window associated with h^p restricted to the r innermost loops and t_r is the iteration $(i_{k-r+1}, \cdots, i_k)$.

4 Loop Transformations

In this section we present the two basic transformations used to optimize the data locality within a loop nest. The first transformation we discuss, is tiling or blocking. We then discuss the strategy for ordering the loops, using interchanging, within the tile considered. This transformation can be expressed using the framework of unimodular transformations [2].

4.1 Tiling for Locality

Block algorithms have been the subject of a lot of research in numerical analysis. They are generally used to reduce the data memory traffic by inducing a high degree of data reuse. Block algorithms break the iteration space defined by a loop structure into blocks or tiles of a regular shape. The blocks are chosen in order to improve the memory hierarchy utilization. Iteration space tiling is used to get a block algorithm via a program transformation. A tiled iteration space is obtained by dividing the iterations space into tiles (or blocks). The shapes of the tiles are typically squares or cubes. The transformation is logically equivalent to a combination of strip mining and loop interchanging. Strip mining transforms a loop into two new loops. For instance

```
        DO 1 i = 1, N
          ...
1       CONTINUE
```

becomes

```
      DO 1 i = 1, N by I
              DO 1 ii = i, min(N, i+I-1)
                  ...
1     CONTINUE
```

the inner loop is called the *tile*. Figure 6 illustrates the tiling of the loop of Figure 3. For the condition of validity of iteration tiling, the reader is referred to [10] and [19]. In the following, for the sake of simplicity, we assume that $N_i \bmod B_i$ is zero.

Loop tiling consists in dividing the iteration space into smaller blocks and modifying the way the iteration space is swept. The innermost loops consist in sweeping over the iterations within a block while the outermost loop (called controlling loops) defines the order in which the blocks themselves are executed. Because a given level of memory may not be large enough to keep all the data that are going to be reused, blocking allows us to reduce the number of data to be kept by considering the locality only inside a block. Four problems need to be solved for applying this transformation:

1. Choosing the loops that should be in the block.
2. Choosing the loop ordering within the block (this is subject of section 4.3).
3. Transforming the nested loops to get the block.

```
DO 1 ii_1 = 1, N_1 by B_1
  DO 1 ii_2 = 1, N_2 by B_2
    ...
    DO 1 ii_k = 1, N_k by B_k
      DO 1 i_1 = ii_1, min(ii_1 + B_1 - 1, N_1)
        DO 1 i_2 = ii_2 , min(ii_2 + B_2 - 1, N_2)
          ...
          DO 1 i_k = ii_k , min(ii_k + B_k - 1, N_k)
            LOOP BODY
1 CONTINUE
```

Figure 6: Loop after tiling

4. Computing the analytical expressions of the windows and computing the tiles bound. The tile bounds are computed such that all the selected windows fit in the memory hierarchy level considered.

Let us overview the overall process as it is presented in the remaining subsections:

1. For each array A, we determine the loops which carry locality (i.e. the loop levels which have an impact on the locality for array A); this will be achieved by computing LDS_A (Locality Direction Set associated with array A) as described in subsection 4.2.

2. For each array A, the vectors in the locality direction set (LDS_A) is classified according to their impact on window size (cf subsection 4.3.3).

3. Then globally, for the whole loop nest, loops are reordered: this includes selecting the loops which are going to be tiled and determining the loop order inside the tile (cf subsection 4.3).

4. Computing the tile bounds: this is achieved by using the analytical expressions obtained for the windows and expressing the tile bounds computation as a standard integer optimization problem (cf subsection 4.4).

4.2 Computation of Locality Direction Set

In this subsection, the effect on locality of a given loop is analyzed. This leads to the computation of Locality Direction Sets (LDS_A) consisting of the vectors relevant to the locality properties of array A. This is very close to the localized vector space defined by Lam [18].

With respect to an array A, all the loop levels do not have the same effect on its locality properties. In fact, we want to determine the loops which are good candidates to be put as innermost loops. This intuitive notion is made more precise by the following definitions:

Definition 4.1 *The direction e_j is said to* **carry locality** *in the iteration space C if there exists a set of references to an array A with access functions $H_l = h() + d_l$ such that:*

$$\exists\ (i_1, ..., i_j, ..., i_k) \text{ and } (i'_1, ..., i'_j, ..., i'_k) \in C,$$

$$\text{and } (l, l') \quad \text{such that} \left\{ \begin{array}{l} i_j \neq i'_j \\ h(i_1, ..., i_j, ..., i_k) + d_l = h(i'_1, ..., i'_j, ..., i'_k) + d_{l'} \end{array} \right.$$

In other words, if we consider the associated distance dependence vector between the two references, the jth coordinate is non null.

For instance if we consider $H(i_1, i_2, i_3) = (i_1 + i_2, i_3)$, e_3 does not carry locality but e_1 and e_2 do.

Definition 4.2 *We call the* **locality direction set (denoted LDS_A)** *associated to the references to array A the set of directions that carry locality according to the access functions of array A.*

For instance, for the array reference $A(H(i_1, i_2) = i_1 + i_2)$ in a two deep nested do loop (without any other access to array A), $LDS_A = \{e_1, e_2\}$.

In the following, the computation of LDS_A is shown as well as the relationship between data reuse and locality direction sets. Since we have restricted our analysis to uniformly generated dependencies, we will consider two access functions $A[H_1() = h() + d_1]$ and $A[H_2() = h() + d_2]$ (the more general cases of more than 2 access functions can be easily derived from that simple case).

1. **if** $Ker(h) = \emptyset$: In this case, $A[H_2()]$ is dependent on $A[H_1()]$ and we have a single constant distance dependence vector z ($h(z) = d_1 - d_2$), possibly with all coordinates equal to zero.
   (a) **if** $d_1 = d_2$ **then** $LDS_A = \emptyset$. This corresponds to the case where the array element accessed by $A[H_1()]$ is reused by $A[H_2()]$ in the same iteration. Therefore this array element does not belong to the window.
   (b) **if** $d_1 \neq d_2$ **then** $LDS_A = \{e_j / z_j \neq 0\}$. In this case the array element accessed by $A[H_1()]$ is reused by $A[H_2()]$ in subsequent iteration. If the jth coordinate of the distance dependence vector z, denoted z_j, is different from zero, the direction e_j belongs to LDS_A.
2. **if** $Ker(h) \neq \emptyset$: in this case, there are potentially many distance dependence vectors.
   (a) **if** $d_1 = d_2$ then LDS_A is the smallest set of vectors in the basis $(e_1, ..., e_k)$ such that $Ker(h)$ is included in the span defined by those vectors.
   (b) **if** $d_1 \neq d_2$ then LDS_A not only contains the directions due to the linear part, but also the directions corresponding to non zero coordinates in a particular dependence distance vector.

Whence for each array, Locality Direction Sets have been computed, Global Direction Set as defined below can be easily obtained.

Definition 4.3 *Let us assume that we have a set of arrays A_i referenced in the loop. We call the* **global locality direction set (denoted $GLDS$)** *the set:*

$$GLDS = \bigcup_i LDS_{A_i}$$

If $GLDS = \emptyset$ then the loop nest does not have any locality.

The global locality iteration space $GLDS$ defines the set of loops to be considered for the tiling procedure. The other loops are irrelevant for the optimizations, more precisely as shown in Section 4.3 considering loops that do not carry locality just contribute to increase the size of the window without improving data reuses.

4.3 Loop Reordering

In this section, we detail our loop ordering strategy. In the first 3 subsections, the various impacts of loop ordering on locality optimization are analyzed providing the basis for our global algorithm which is described in the last subsection.

4.3.1 Importance of Loop Reordering

Loop reordering has many consequences on the locality of a loop. Let us consider the following example to illustrate this fact:

```
      DO 1 i1 = 1, N1
              DO 1 i2 = 1, N2
      < S1 >          ··· A[i1, i2]
        ⋮                 ⋮
      < S2 >          ··· A[i1, i2 + 1]
1     CONTINUE
```

Using the order (L_2, L_1) the size of the window necessary to exploit the locality between the two array references is $2 \times N_1$. This size of the window is due to the fact that we have to keep all the values reached during the inner loop L_1. On the other hand, if the order (L_1, L_2) is considered, the resulting window size is 2. This is illustrated on the figure 7. The impact of reordering on window size is taken into account in subsection 4.3.3 where locality direction vectors are classified according to their impact on the window size.

In addition to that effect, another more complex constraint has to be taken into account: when selecting an order for the loops, all the windows related to different arrays have to be considered. This leads to the problem that the best order for array A might be the worse for array B or vice versa. This phenomenon (called interference effect) is analyzed in subsection 4.3.2. The interference effect is due to the presence of windows for which the optimization objectives differ.

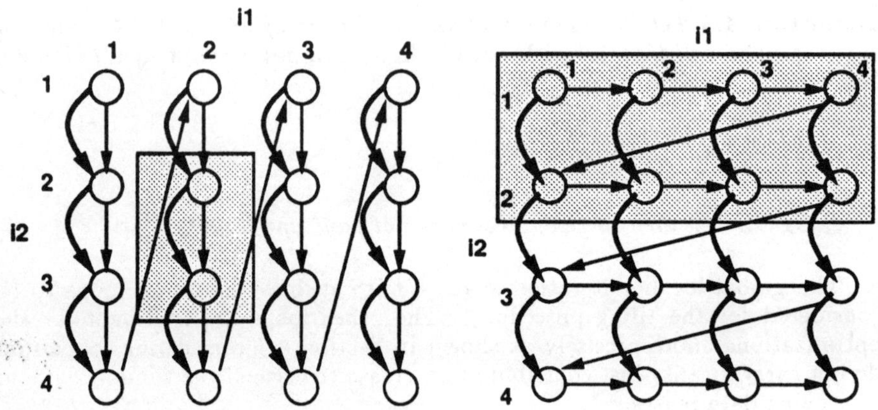

Figure 7: Illustration of the effect of loop reordering on the window size (Bold arrows indicate data dependencies)

4.3.2 Interference Effects

For analyzing more precisely the interference effect, let us consider the following example with two references to two different arrays $A(H_A())$ and $B(H_B())$, such that:

$$GLDS \not\subset LDS_A$$

In such a case, trying to optimize locality on array B may introduce, as an innermost loop, a loop that does not carry any locality for array A. The net result will be a much larger window for A and potentially, another loss in the locality properties.

For making that intuitive notion more precise, the proposition 4.4 below shows the impact of the choice of the innermost loops in the block on the size of the window associated to an array reference.

Proposition 4.4 *Let $A(H())$ be a reference to array A and let us assume that the associated locality direction set is $LDS_A = \{e_2, ..., e_k\}$. The windows relative to the original ordering $(L_1, ..., L_k)$ are denoted by W whereas the windows relative to the interchanged loop $(L_2, \ldots, L_k, L_1)$ are denoted by W^I.*

$$\bigcup_{n\in[1,N_1]} W(n, i_2, \ldots, i_k) \subset W^I(i2, \ldots, i_k, 1)$$

proof: Let n be any value in $[1, N_1]$ and $A[\alpha]$ be an element in $W(n, i_2, \ldots, i_k)$. Then, by definition of the window, there exist $j = (j_1, ..., j_k)$ and $j' = (j'_1, ..., j'_k)$ in C such that

$$\begin{cases} A[H(j)] \equiv A[H(j')] \equiv A[\alpha] \\ T(j) < T(n, i_2, \ldots, i_k) \leq T(j') \end{cases}$$

Moreover, since the direction e_1 does not carry any locality, necessarily $j_1 = j'_1 = n$.

In the interchanged loop, the following relations are valid:

$$\begin{cases} T^I(j_2,\ldots,j_k,n) < T^I(i_2,\ldots,i_k,1) \leq T^I(j'_2,\ldots,j'_k,n) \\ A[H^I(j_2,\ldots,j_k,n)] \equiv A[H^I(j'_2,\ldots,j'_k,n)] \equiv A[\alpha] \end{cases}$$

which shows that $A[\alpha]$ belongs to $W^I(i2,\ldots,i_k,1)$.

■

It should be noted that, since direction e_1 does not carry locality:

$\forall (l,l') \in [1,N_1] s.t. l \neq l'$,

$W(l,i_2,\ldots,i_k) \cap W(l',i_2,\ldots,i_k) = \emptyset$

The previous proposition states that if loop L_1 does not carry locality and if it is made the innermost loop, the window is roughly N_1 times bigger than if loop L_1 were outermost.

When many windows are considered, proposition 4.4, shows that to get a good use of the locality, we need to get the loops carrying the more reuses as the innermost one.

For selecting the loops and windows of interest, we will use the following procedure. After having computed all the LDS_{A_l} for all the relevant arrays, we will build a function θ by the following formula.

$$\theta(e_j) = \sum_{LDS_{A_l}} \begin{cases} 1 & \text{if } e_j \in LDS_{A_l} \\ 0 & \text{if } e_j \notin LDS_{A_l} \end{cases}$$

Where $\sum_{LDS_{A_l}}$ denotes the summation over all the locality direction sets.

The θ function will be used in conjunction with proper weights reflecting the number of references and the window size effect for computing the most appropriate loop order.

4.3.3 Window Size Effect

In this section, the impact of loop reordering on the window size is taken into account. The goal here is to identify among the locality direction vectors, what are the most valuable ones in terms of space usage (i.e. the ones which are most economical). This is achieved by classifying the direction vectors into groups which are themselves ordered. For that purpose, each vector e_l belonging to a Locality Direction Set is considered in turn: first we compute the window size assuming that loop level I_l is made innermost. Two cases need to be distinguished:

- The resulting window size is constant. In such a case, e_l is allocated to Group 1. And inside that group, the e_l are sorted in a list of increasing window size.
- The resulting window size is not constant. In such case, e_l is allocated to Group 2. Inside that group, using the analytical expressions of the windows generated in the previous sections, the directions vectors are again ranked. For sake of clarity, the relatively complex ordering strategy is not detailed, we will just mention that a variant of lexicographic ordering on the polynomial expressions of the window size [6] is used.

More precisely, given a set of functions $H_i() = h() + d_i$ that represent the set of access functions for an array A, let us assume that the locality direction set has been computed (LDS_A). The 2 groups are built in the following manner (the numbering is important and will be used later):

Group 1: the Group 1 contains all the locality direction vectors e_l such that $h()$ does not depend on i_l (all the coefficients for the variable i_l are zero) or e_l belongs to $Ker(h)$ or to the direction vectors that carried directly locality due to constant vectors d_1 and d_2. In fact, the first condition insures a stronger subcase: window size equal to 1, while in general, the second one only enforces constant window size, in the case where L_l is the innermost one. For example, if we have loops (L_1, L_2, L_3) and an array reference $A(i_1, i_2)$[1], the direction e_3 belongs to Group 1. Another example, if we have loops (L_1, L_2, L_3) and two array references $A(i_1 + i_3, i_2 + 1)$ and $A(i_1 + i_3, i_2)$, the direction e_2 belongs to Group 1.

Group 2: The Group 2 contains all the remaining locality direction vectors which could not be allocated to Group 1.

For instance if we consider the following loops:

```
      DO 1 i1 = 1, N1
            DO 1 i2 = 1, N2
      < S1 >        ... A[i1, i2]
        :               :
      < S2 >        ... A[i1 + 1, i2 + 2]
1     CONTINUE
```

the locality direction set is $LDS = \{e_1, e_2\}$. If we choose the order (L_1, L_2) we have a window size of $N_2 + 2$ and if we consider the order (L_2, L_1) we have a window size of $2 \times N_1$. As shown by this example the two directions carry locality. Because the value of N_1 and N_2 may be unknown at compile time we decide to favor the expression of the window that has the smallest expression in term of loop bounds. This decision taken statically at compile time is somewhat arbitrary and could be refined by using tests at run time.

4.3.4 A Strategy to Order the Loops

The strategy to order the loop works in two steps, the interference effect is taken into account first, then the order is refined using the Window size effect. A priority list is first built using the locality direction set:

1. Computation of the LDS_{A_l} (cf subsection 4.2), generation of the groups and the relative order inside each group (cf subsection 4.3.3).
2. Computation of the global θ function (cf subsection 4.3.2).
3. The loops are ordered using the values of $\theta()$, weighted by the number of references associated with the windows. If two loops have the same $\theta()$ values, then the group number and the order inside each group is used to order the two loops (Group 1 having priority over Group 2).

---

[1]Spatial locality is also considered in that case.

Let us give a full example to follow how the procedure given above works:

```
      DO 1 i1 = 1, N1
         DO 1 i2 = 1, N2
            DO 1 i3 = 1, N3
      < S1 >   A(i1, i2, i3) = B(i1, i2) + C(i1 + i2, i3)
               +D(i1, i2, i3) + D(i1, i2, i3 + 1)
               +E(i1, i3)
   1  CONTINUE
```

First step, computation of the Locality Direction Sets:

- $LDS_A = \emptyset$
- $LDS_B = \{e_3\}$, group 1
- $LDS_C = \{e_1, e_2\}$, group 2
- $LDS_D = \{e_3\}$, group 1
- $LDS_E = \{e_2\}$, group 1

So we have $GLDS = \{e_1, e_2, e_3\}$. All the dimensions in the loop nest have to be a priori considered to get all the locality. To choose the order inside the block, the $\theta()$ functions are computed.

Second step:

- $\theta(e_1) = 1$
- $\theta(e_2) = 2$
- $\theta(e_3) = 2$

Following our strategy we choose disadvantage the window on array C instead of the window on B, D, E. Now, either loop L_2 or L_3 have to be selected as the innermost loop:

1. Choice of L_2 : e_2 belongs to Group 1 (cf section 4.3.3) for array E and to Group 2 for array C.
2. Choice of L_3 : e_3 belongs to Group 1 (cf section 4.3.3) for array B and to Group 1 for D.

To see the effect of the two options, the effect of different loop orderings on the locality of the innermost loop has to be compared:

inner-most	$\|W_B\|$	$\|W_C\|$	$\|W_D\|$	$\|W_E\|$	Benefit
L_3	1	0	2	0	$N_1N_2N_3$ - N_1N_2 + $N_1N_2N_3/2$
L_2	0	0	0	1	$N_1N_2N_3$ - N_1N_3
L_1	0	0	0	0	None

4.4 Computing the Tile Bounds

In this section, we detail how the analytical expressions for the windows can be exploited for performing a deep quantitative analysis allowing a very good optimization of the tile bounds.

Given a set of nested loops, as illustrated in Figure 6, the basic problem is to compute the value of the tile bounds $B_1, ..., B_k$ such that all the associated extended windows $\overline{W}_i$, $i = 1, ..., n$ fit in the memory level considered (R is the assumed size). The constraint over the window size can be written formally as

$$\sum_{i=1}^{n} ||\overline{W}_i|| \leq R$$

The general form of the constraints to be satisfied are:

$$\begin{cases} \sum_{i=1}^{n} ||\overline{W}_i|| & \leq & R \\ B_1 & \leq & N_1 \\ & \vdots & \\ B_k & \leq & N_k \\ B_1, B_2, \cdots, B_k & > & 0 \end{cases}$$

Figure 2 shows the initial code of the matrix-matrix product. We have these expressions corresponding to the window sizes for loop order (L_1, L_2, L_3):

$$\begin{aligned} ||\overline{W}_A|| &= 1 \\ ||\overline{W}_B|| &= B_3 \\ ||\overline{W}_C|| &= B_2 B_3 \end{aligned}$$

which give the following system of inequalities:

$$\begin{cases} B_3 + B_2 B_3 + 1 & \leq & R \\ B_1 & \leq & N_1 \\ B_2 & \leq & N_2 \\ B_3 & \leq & N_3 \\ B_1, B_2, B_3 & > & 0 \end{cases}$$

With these constraints we want to minimize the number of reads from the main memory. Using the windows we can automatically compute as a function of $N_1, N_2, N_3, B_1, B_2, B_3$ the number of reads resulting from a block size. In the case of the example we have:

- matrix A: $N_1 B_2 \frac{N_2}{B_2} \frac{N_3}{B_3}$
- matrix B: $N_1 B_3 \frac{N_2}{B_2} \frac{N_3}{B_3}$
- matrix C: $B_3 B_2 \frac{N_2}{B_2} \frac{N_3}{B_3}$

So finally we get the following problem: minimize the number of reads (denoted L) which is equivalent to maximize the benefit at a maximum cost of R:

$$L = \frac{N_1 N_2 N_3}{B_3} + \frac{N_1 N_2 N_3}{B_2} + N_2 N_3$$

```
        DO 1 i = 1,N                      R1 = A[1]
           S1 : Z[i] = A[i + 2]           R2 = A[2]
           +A[i] + B[K]                   R3 = A[3]
     1  CONTINUE                          DO 1 i = 1,N
                                                Z[i] = R3 + R1 + B[K]
                                                C update the window
                                                R1 = R2
                                                R2 = R3
                                                R3 = A[i+3]
                                     1    CONTINUE
```

Figure 8: Register allocation with the window $((i-1)+[1,3])$

under the constraint

$$B_2 + B_2B_3 + 1 \leq R$$

However in many cases N_1, N_2, N_3 are unknown, making the computation of such a solution difficult. Another formulation of the problem is to consider the relative number of reads carried out in the block relatively to the number of reads without the windows. In other words we do not consider the controlling loops. The number of iterations executed by a block is $N_1B_2B_3$, so we want to minimize:

$$\frac{N_1B_2}{N_1B_2B_3} + \frac{B_3}{N_1B_2B_3} + \frac{B_3B_2}{N_1B_2B_3}$$

Which is equivalent to minimize

$$\frac{1}{B_2} + \frac{1}{B_3}$$

under the previous constraints. Solving this problem is a classical optimization problem [13]. For our studies, we used Maple to generate and manipulate the various windows expressions as well as solving the resulting optimization problem. The overall scheme was extremely efficient because the number of variables involved is small (the depth of the original loop nest). It should be noted that the results are similar to those published by Gallivan et al. [9], but automatically deduced.

5 Register Allocation on Uniprocessor Machines

This section shows how reference windows can be used to improve register allocation by keeping frequently used data in registers, thus eliminating expensive memory accesses. We study the case of a uni-processor with a bounded number of registers, R.

The algorithm transforms the source program by introducing temporary scalar variables to be allocated to registers by the compiler. The improvement in performance results both from the decrease in the number of memory accesses and in the number of address computations. The basic idea is to allocate an **extended window** in the register file and then to unroll the innermost loop to replace the accesses to array elements in memory by register reads or writes. Figure 8 illustrates the use of windows to improve register allocation on a simple example. For the reference to array A, the window is:

$$A((i-1)+[1,3])$$

and contains all the references to A that are done in the current iteration but also the one that will be used later in the execution of the loop. To improve the register allocation we allocate the window in registers, then all array references to A are replaced by a register access. Some code is then added to update the memory content and the window. Values discarded from the window are copied back to memory if the window was modified. The register contents are then shifted and new elements of the array are loaded. This simple scheme of code generation is possible because the extended window always has a motion defined by the function $\lambda_j i_j$ and the window interval is also invariant according to the inner loops. The result obtained after dead code elimination [1] is equivalent to the solution method of Callahan et al. [5]. If an access such as $B[K]$ for instance, is invariant in the loop we have a window with $\lambda_j = 0$ so the window is invariant in the loop. The method can be extended to nested loops.

Let the window under consideration be

$$\overline{W} = (\lambda_j(i_j - 1) + W) \cap \delta Z$$

Figure 9 shows the general form of the code after code generation. The loops with indexes i_2,...,i_k are unrolled[2]. The initialization of the windows loads the windows in registers. The updating of the windows loads the $\frac{\lambda_j}{\delta}$ new elements and copies back to memory the elements removed from the window. This part also shifts all the registers. After unrolling the inner loops, it is easy to replace the array reference by a register access. The coherence of memory references is easy to verify since the window moves by λ_j as the index expression of the array.

The overhead of shifting registers can be removed by unrolling the innermost loop after register allocation. We have the following proposition:

Proposition 5.1 *Let us consider the window* $\overline{W} = (\lambda_j(i_j - 1) + W) \cap \delta Z$. *If the loop with index* i_j *is unrolled* α *times* ($\lambda_j \neq 0$), *where*

$$\alpha = \frac{lcm(\lambda_j, ||\overline{W}||)}{\lambda_j}$$

then there exists a correct register allocation on the unrolled loop without any shift operations.

---

[2]The unrolling also allows us to use fine grain parallelism.

```
              Init Windows
              DO 1 i1 = 1, N1
      < S(i1,1,···,1) >              ···Ry
              ⋮                                    ⋮
      < S(i1,N2,···,Nk) >            ···Rx
                          Update Windows
      1 CONTINUE
```

Figure 9: General shape of the code after register allocation

Proof: We want a cyclic allocation CA such that

$$CA^n(R_1,\cdots,R_{\|W\|}) = (R_1,\cdots,R_{\|W\|})$$

where

$$CA(R_1,\cdots,R_{\|W\|}) = (R_{1+\lambda_j mod\|W\|},\cdots,$$

$$R_{i+\lambda_j mod\|W\|},\cdots,R_{\|W\|+\lambda_j mod\|W\|})$$

This is equivalent to proving that

$$(i+\lambda_j\alpha)\ mod\ \|W\| = i,\ \forall\ 1 \le i \le \|W\|$$

which is true since $(\lambda_j\alpha) mod\|W\| = 0$

■

Applying Proposition 5.1 to the example given in Figure 8 we obtain the result shown in Figure 10. Unfortunately the amount of unrolling necessary to remove register shifting may be very large, since the values of λ_j are generally small.

6 Cache Usage Optimization

The strategy described in section 4.3.4 can also be applied to cache optimization. However many differences are due to the cache dynamic management:

1. Windows cannot be directly allocated to the cache.
2. Even if a data is not reused it is loaded in the cache, if the architecture does not provide bypassing.

The cache interference problem is handled using copies of data [12]. The windows are allocated in an array so that interference are limited. To deal with registers and caches we have chosen the following strategy: The window corresponding to the locality carried by the innermost loop are allocated in registers, the others are allocated in the caches. We made that choice because usually the number of registers (for instance 32 floating point registers for the IBM/RS6000) does not allow a lot of tiling when the window size depends on the tile bounds.

```
         R1 = A[1]
         R2 = A[2]
         R3 = A[3]
         DO 1 i = 1, N, 3
                  Z[i] = R3 + R1 + B[K]
                  R1 = A[i+3]
                  Z[i+1] = R1 + R2 + B[K]
                  R2 = A[i+4]
                  Z[i+2] = R2 + R3 + B[K]
                  R3 = A[i+5]
1        CONTINUE
```

Figure 10: Register allocation with the window $((i-1)+[1,3])$, without shifting

To take into account spatial locality, for purpose of optimizing cache line uses, we need to add in the locality direction set $Ker(h')$ where $h'()$ is $h()$ with the access function on the line (address with stride one) of the matrix set to null. For instance if we consider $A(i_1 + i_2, i_1)$, and we assume column-wise storage, we have $h'(i_1, i_2) = (0, i_1)$ meaning that $Ker(h') = i_2$. The coefficient on i_2 in $h()$ must be less than the cache line size.

7 Experimental Results

Our window-based locality algorithm, for cache memory and registers, has been tested on a set of well-known loops. We used the standard C compiler since it allows the user to specify whether a scalar variable should be assigned to a register, by mean of the *register* flag. The codes were generated by hand. The loops used for testing the algorithm are a subset of the Livermore loops, the matrix-vector product (Smxpy) and the matrix-matrix product. Not all the Livermore loops were tested because some do not exhibit data locality, or they have similar behavior in regard to the optimization algorithm. The machine used for the experiments was the IBM RS/6000 model 320 with a 32-kB cache (peak performance is 40 Megaflops).

7.1 Results of Experiments

Table 1 shows the results in Megaflops for the IBM RS/6000. Column **Original** gives the performance of the original loops before locality optimization. Column **Using Window** gives the performance after register allocation. Column **Speedup** is the ratio $\frac{UsingWindow}{Original}$. All computations were done using double precision floating-point arithmetic. The array size was chosen to be 600 so that the working set does not fit in the cache, except in the case of smxpy where it is equal to 900. We used the IBM AIX XL C compiler version 1.01.

The Livermore loops we selected exhibit good opportunities for data locality optimization. In some cases, the data locality would be naturally exploited

Loop	Original	Using Window	Speedup
LLL 1	16.42	23.15	1.40
LLL 5	5.77	5.80	1.01
LLL 7	22.48	37.18	1.65
LLL 8	7.89	8.44	1.06
LLL 11	6.45	7.79	1.21
LLL 18	11.29	15.39	1.36
Matrix	9.12	31.03	3.40
Matrix B^tC	9.01	31.53	3.49
Matrix BC^t	0.89	31.83	35.7
Matrix B^tC^t	0.90	31.44	34.9
Smxpy (str 1)	11.98	13.59	1.13
Smxpy (str 8)	2.53	13.19	5.21

Table 1: Execution results on IBM RS/6000 Model 320 in Megaflops (data N=600 except for Smxpy where N=900)

thanks to the cache. For instance, the first livermore loop contains two references $z[k+10]$ and $z[k+11]$, so the second reference makes effective use of the cache line.

In the case of the matrix-matrix multiply we have considered the cases of the product with the transpose of matrix B and C (denoted respectively B^t and C^t). The performances of the loop with simple blocking (no data copy) are respectively for the case B^tC, BC^t and B^tC^t 17.48 Mflops, 29.61 Mflops and 28.69 Mflops.

For the *Smxpy* loops we have tested two strides for the vector: first a stride of one (*Smxpy (str 1)*) which usually allows good use of the memory cache line, and a stride of eight (*Smxpy (str 8)*) which does not. A substantial speedup appears for stride 8, since in this case the cache line was not used effectively in the original loop.

8 Conclusion

In this paper we present a general framework for optimizing the data locality embedded in the array references occurring within a loop nest. This framework relies on the notion of reference window which identifies the part of an array which is going to be reused later and should be kept in local memory. In a previous paper it was shown that reference windows can be computed at compile-time. The ability to evaluate the amount of storage required for exploiting data locality at compile-time allows us to apply loop interchanging and loop blocking in an adequate way. As a matter of fact loop interchanging is applied in order to reduce the overall size of the reference windows by making loops carrying locality innermost and loop blocking is applied so that the reference windows corresponding to a tile entirely fit in the local memory. Efficient loop blocking requires a quantitative criterion.

Moreover, since we have an explicit characterization of the part of each array which needs to be kept in local memory, we can generate optimized code not only for caches but also for software-managed local memory and registers for which explicit transfers of data are needed.

This work is currently being extended along several directions:

- Extend the scope of loop transformations to unimodular transformations.
- Combination of parallelization and data locality optimizations in the same framework in order to address the multiprocessor case.
- Interaction between register allocation and instruction scheduling: saving a load from cache which turns out to be overlapped with a floating point operation (superscalar architecture) will not necessarily improve performance.

References

[1] Aho AV., Sethi R, Ullman JD. Compiler Principles, Techniques and Tools, Addison-Wesley, 1986.

[2] Banerjee U. Unimodular Transformations of Double Loops, Advances in Languages and Compilers for Parallel Processing. Research Monograph in Parallel and Distributed Computing, The MIT Press, 1991.

[3] Burke M, Cytron R. Interprocedural analysis and parallelization, Proceedings of the Symposium on Compiler Construction, July 1986, pp. 162-175.

[4] Chi CH, Dietz H. Unified Management of Registers and Cache Using Liveness and Cache Bypass, Proceedings of the Conference on Programming Language Design and Implementation, 1989.

[5] Callahan D, Carr S, Kennedy K. Improving Register Allocation for Subscripted Variables, Proceedings of the Conference on Programming Language Design and Implementation, 1990.

[6] Eisenbeis C, Jalby W, Windheiser D, Bodin F. A Strategy for Array Management in Local Memory, Advances in Languages and Compilers for Parallel Processing, MIT Press, 1991.

[7] Gannon D, Jalby W, Gallivan K. Strategies for Cache and Local Memory Management by Global Program Transformation, Proceedings of the International Conference on Supercomputing, Springer Verlag, New York, 1987 and Journal of Parallel and Distributed Computing, October 1988.

[8] Gallivan K, Gannon D, Jalby W. On the Problem of Optimizing Data Transfers for Complex Memory Systems, Proceedings of International Conference on Supercomputing, 1988, pp. 238-253.

[9] Gallivan K, Jalby W, Meier U. The use of BLAS3 in linear Algebra on a Parallel Processor with Hierarchical Memory, SIAM Journal on Scientific and Statistical Computing, Vol. 8, N. 6, November 1986.

[10] Kennedy K. Automatic translation of Fortran programs to vector form, Technical Report, Rice University, Houston, Texas, 1980.

[11] Kuck D, Kuhn R, Leasure B, Wolfe, MJ. Dependence graphs and compiler optimizations, Proceedings of the Eighth Symposium on the Principles of Programming Languages, January 1981.

[12] Lam M, Rothberg E, Wolf M. The Cache Performance and Optimizations of Blocked Algorithms, Proceedings of the Fourth ACM ASPLOS conference, April 91, pp 63-75.

[13] Minoux M. Programmation mathématique : théorie et algorithmes , Dunod, Paris, Collection technique et scientifique des télécommunications 1983.

[14] Padua D, Kuck D. High-speed multiprocessors and compilation techniques, IEEE Transaction on Computer, C-29, 9, pp. 763-776.

[15] Padua D, Wolfe MJ. Advanced compiler optimizations for supercomputers, CACM, 29, 12, pp. 1184-1201.

[16] Porterfield A. Compiler management of program locality, Technical Report, Rice University, Houston, Texas, January 1988.

[17] Wolf M, Lam M. An algorithm to generate sequential and parallel code with improved data locality, Technical Report, Stanford University 1990.

[18] Wolf M, Lam M. A Data Locality Optimizing Algorithm ACM Conference on Programming Language Design and Implementation, June 26-28, 1991.

[19] Wolfe MJ. Optimizing Supercompilers for Supercomputers, PhD thesis, University of Illinois, October 1982.

Phase Ordering of Register Allocation and Instruction Scheduling

Stefan M. Freudenberger
Hewlett-Packard Laboratories
Palo Alto, Calif., USA

John C. Ruttenberg
Silicon Graphics
Milford, Conn., USA

1 Introduction

Register allocation and instruction scheduling are often separated due to the complexity of each. But if register allocation is performed before scheduling, it may introduce artificial data precedence, keeping the instruction scheduler from doing its best job. On the other hand, waiting until after scheduling to perform register allocation may produce impossible schedules. In this paper we present a unified approach to instruction scheduling and global (beyond basic blocks) register allocation.

We assume that we compile for a machine with deep, exposed pipelines and a large amount of instruction set parallelism that must be statically specified; instruction scheduling is required in order to exploit the performance potential of this machine. We also assume that registers are often the most critical instruction scheduling resource; therefore we must delay register binding decisions until scheduling time in order to give the instruction scheduler the greatest possible freedom in picking registers.

We have implemented this technique in a commercial product, Multiflow's Trace Scheduling compilers. At Multiflow, we focused on scientific code written in Fortran, and our results show that this approach is both viable and effective.

1.1 Instruction Scheduling, Scientific Code and Register Allocation

Instruction scheduling at compile time is a powerful technique, one that can have profound influence on hardware design [1,2]. It is especially potent in addressing the class of floating point intensive problems that have been traditional supercomputer applications. Recently, machines with exposed pipelines and multiple instruction issues have begun to supplant machines with vector units in this area. Starting in 1985, we at Multiflow designed, built and brought to market such a system [3,4][1]

In this context we quickly discovered that the "standard" register allocation techniques were inadequate. For floating point loops that can actually approach the machine's full performance, it is often necessary to use all or most of the floating point registers. It is often registers that are the most critical instruction scheduling resource. It is hard to see how one could generate the best code without taking registers into account while scheduling. Register allocation before scheduling would introduce artificial data precedence, something to be avoided when trying to fill up a machine with as much instruction level parallelism as the *Trace* has. Scheduling before register allocation also seems to miss point; when registers are the critical resource, a scheduler that operates in ignorance of them is not doing its job.

Given the desire to integrate instruction scheduling closely with register allocation, we had to depart from the mainstream global register allocation tradition. Since its introduction, *register coloring* [5,6,7,8,9] has become the register allocation method of choice in optimizing compilers. But register coloring assumes that operations do not move relative to one another. In the presence of instruction scheduling, this assumption is plainly wrong.

1.2 Most of the Compute Time is Spent in Long Trip Count Loops

Scientific floating point code tends to have some special properties that an instruction scheduler can exploit: they have a high degree of fine grained parallelism, and they have loops with large trip counts.

We found that inner loop code is by far the most important factor in good performance. We'll pay for tight inner loops with some extra cycles in less frequently executed code. Our approach is therefore geared toward giving our instruction scheduler the freedom it needs to generate the best code for inner loops instead of being geared toward avoiding spilling. We'll gladly spill outside a loop if doing so will allow better code to be generated for the loop body.

The remainder of this paper is organized as follows. Section 2 gives an overview over the organization of our compiler backend and describes our global register allocator. Section 3 presents an example to show how the algorithm works. Section 4 presents some quantitative data on how well our method works. Related work is presented in section 5, followed by our conclusions and acknowledgements.

---

1. Hardware and software development was tightly integrated at Multiflow. In fact, the Multiflow hardware had absolutely no hardware interlocks leaving it to the compiler to observe all hardware resource and memory constraints.

2 Trace Scheduling as a Global Register Allocation Framework

It is well known that trace scheduling [10,11,12,13] is a simple way to allow an instruction scheduler to find parallelism in code sections longer than basic blocks. A less publicized aspect of the Multiflow trace scheduling design is a unique method for global register allocation. This technique relies on trace scheduling to make register allocation trade–offs and communicate binding decisions between discrete invocations of the instruction scheduler.

2.1 Code Generation and Binding Decisions

The basic idea of our design is:

- Trace scheduling is used to give priority to values referenced in the highest frequency traces.
- Complete freedom over register usage is given to the instruction scheduler in the highest frequency traces.
- Values are bound to locations (register or memory) only when the instruction scheduler sees an actual reference to them.
- Binding decisions are communicated between invocations of the instruction scheduler.
- The live ranges of values are extended outward from the highest frequency traces. Compiler introduced data motions (spills, restores, and register transfers) are pushed outward to low frequency traces.

Freedom to choose register bindings should itself be viewed as a scarce resource; its universal application across an entire program would not produce correct code, yet it can yield significantly better code where applied (given an instruction scheduler that can make use of it.[2]) We'd like to apply as much of this freedom as possible to the places where it matters most for the dynamic performance of the program and decrease it only as required for correct compilation and in proportion to the contribution a particular code sequence is likely to have on overall performance. The intended result is that data motions such as spilling, restoring, and register transfers, are executed infrequently. Within reason, it does not matter how much of this sort of data motion is generated, what matters is only its effect on actual dynamic performance.

2.1.1 Code Generator Structure

Figure 1 is a block diagram of the Multiflow code generator. It shows two major modules: the *trace scheduler* and the *instruction scheduler*. These two modules work together to transform the program flow graph of intermediate code operations into a semantically equivalent flow graph of machine code schedules. Initially, the

2. An assumption that runs through the rest of this paper is the existence of such a scheduler.

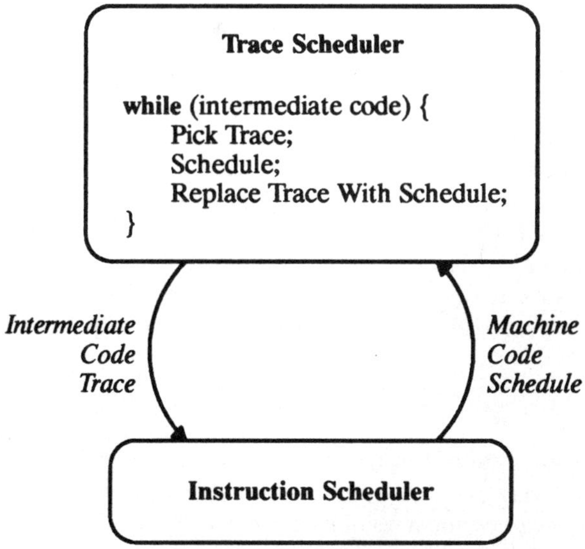

Figure 1. Code Generator Block Diagram

graph consists of operations whose operands are values, not yet assigned registers. They may represent constants, globally renamed scalar variables, or temporaries.

The process of code generation is the process of transforming *traces* of intermediate code operations into *schedules* of machine code instructions. At its highest level, here is the trace scheduler's algorithm:

1. Check whether there are any intermediate operations left in the flow graph. If not, we are done.
2. Find an intermediate operation of highest expected frequency. Choose a sequence of successors and predecessors starting from the chosen operation. (There are a number of termination conditions for these sequences, but the important thing to keep in mind is that the sequences stop at the boundaries of machine code schedules and at loop back edges.)
3. Pass this sequence to the instruction scheduler as a trace, and receive back a machine language schedule with completely bound register references.[3]
4. Remove the operations that compose the trace from the flow graph and replace them with the machine code schedule.

For the purposes of this paper it is only important to understand that the traces are visited in order of their expected execution frequency. This will almost always result in innermost loop bodies being picked first, followed by their direct flow successors and predecessors.[4]

---

3. Although our implementation binds physical registers to values during instruction scheduling, our framework only requires that compiled code can be colored without the introduction of additional operations. See also section 5.

4. Connecting the incoming and outgoing flow edges to the schedule and maintaining legality in the face of various code motions is one of the entertaining aspects of trace scheduling. The method for doing so is extensively described in [13] and is not directly relevant to this paper.

2.2 Recording Register Binding Decisions

Each time the instruction scheduler is invoked and given a trace, it has to decide how to treat the upward and downward exposed values in that trace. Initially, no decisions have been made and the instruction scheduler is free to reference these values in the locations which result in the best schedule. Subsequently, it will have to deal with traces that enter or exit machine code schedules where binding decisions have already been made. When a trace is an exit from a machine code schedule, it has to read its upward exposed values from the locations into which the machine code last wrote them. Traces entering machine code schedules have to write downward exposed values into the locations assumed by the upward exposed references.

2.2.1 The VLM Data Structure

The information about value–location bindings within scheduled code is recorded and communicated via a data structure called a *Value–Location Mapping* (VLM). A VLM maps a set of values into a set of locations (so that one value may have more than one location, but each location will have at most one value.) VLMs are created by the instruction scheduler after it has generated the machine code for each trace. A distinct VLM is required for each split from and for each join to the schedule. The VLM at a split from a schedule tells where the schedule has placed its downward exposed values. The VLM at a join to a schedule tells where the schedule reads its upward exposed values.

Figure 2 shows a simple one operation trace and resulting schedule with a VLM data structure at its top and bottom. The scheduler chose to use register *ir1* to hold the address of the vector *A*, *ir2* to hold the variable *i*, and it chose to leave the variable *z* in floating register *fr1*. The VLMs contain this information.

2.2.2 Communicating Binding Decisions

After the VLMs are created, they are added to the flow graph to guard the borders of the schedule from the surrounding intermediate code. The trace scheduler then

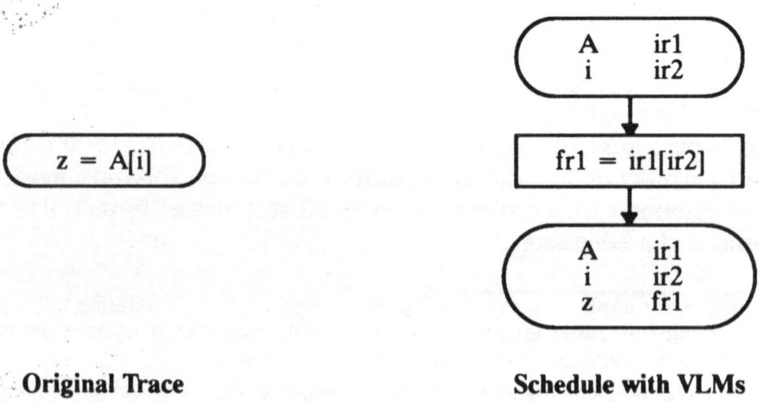

Figure 2. A Trace Transformed to a Schedule with VLMs

treats them almost exactly like other intermediate code operations; they can be chosen as trace elements and passed to the instruction scheduler. Since each VLM forms a border between a schedule and intermediate code, it will always either be the first element of a trace which is an exit from a schedule or the final element of a trace that joins into a schedule.

When a trace contains a VLM, it tells the instruction scheduler how to treat the trace's upward and downward exposed references. When a VLM is the first operation on a trace, the instruction scheduler must generate code that reads any upward exposed values from one of the locations given by the VLM. When a VLM is the final operation on a trace, the instruction scheduler must make sure to *satisfy* the VLM, i.e., it has to generate code that leaves a copy of each value in the VLM in each of the locations associated with it.

We will refer to four distinct types of traces:[5]

1. *Seed.* This is a trace without a VLM at either the top or bottom. The scheduler has complete freedom to choose registers for seed traces.
2. *Entry.* A trace with a VLM only at the bottom. The scheduler must satisfy the VLM at the bottom of the trace.
3. *Exit.* A trace with a VLM only at the top. The scheduler must assume the VLM holds at the top of the trace.
4. *Transition.* A trace with a VLM at both the top and bottom. The scheduler must make sure to move the values from the locations assumed at the top to the locations required at the bottom.

2.3 Delayed Bindings

Some values are live at the top and bottom of a trace, but are not actually referenced on the trace itself. We want to avoid making binding decisions for these values at the time the trace is scheduled, yet we do have to ensure that the values can pass safely though the resulting schedule. In order to do so, the value must reside *somewhere* while the schedule executes. Eventually, we'll have to decide on at least one location for each value during all the schedules that make up its live range. Notice that it is not necessary, though it is desirable, that each value reside in the same location in all the schedules that make up its live range.

Delaying our binding decision for each value until we actually schedule an operation that references it has two advantages:

1. We implicitly prioritize the values by the expected frequency of the access to them. This allows us to weigh the benefits of keeping various different values in registers; given a conflict, we'd most like to keep those values in registers that are accessed in the highest frequency code, relegating spills and restores to the low frequency "suburbs".
2. We can wait to choose locations until the scheduler actually sees *how* each particular value is accessed. This is especially important in the presence of

---

5. We have given names to these different types of traces for expository convenience only. Our instruction scheduler distinguishes them only by assuming the initial VLMs when they are present and by satisfying the final VLMs when they are present.

function calls, which will generally require that their arguments and return values be in certain prespecified locations.[6]

In order to delay the binding decisions for unreferenced live values, we devised a mechanism which we call *delayed bindings*. A delayed binding is a sort of pseudo–location that may be assigned to an unreferenced value by the instruction scheduler. The idea is that a delayed binding represents a connected subset of the value's live range – a set of schedules that have already been generated and through which the value must pass without data motion. For each given value, the same delayed binding is used in the VLMs at all the boundaries of the connected set of schedules. As the connected subgraph of schedules grows or when a binding decision is finally made, the delayed binding is side effected to reflect the new information.

A delayed binding accumulates information that will later be needed to choose a physical location for a value so that it can pass through a completely scheduled subset of its live range. For each schedule, we maintain a set of registers not yet allocated in the schedule. In order to resolve a delayed binding to a register, we must pick a register in the intersection of the unallocated register sets of the delayed binding's set of schedules.

Figure 3 shows an example of a delayed binding and the effect of resolving it. In the example, the binding decision for *Z* has been delayed as each of the schedules

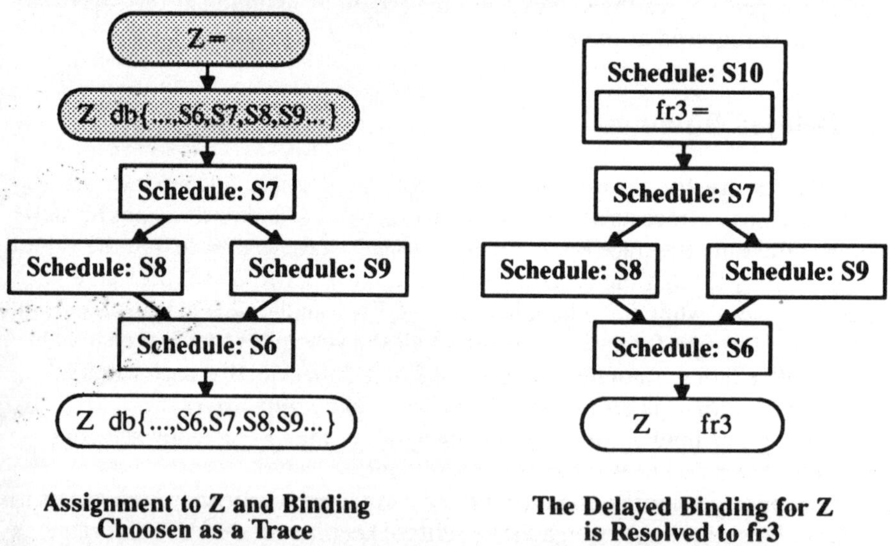

Figure 3. The Effect of Resolving a Delayed Binding

6. For the *Trace* architectures, this has another use. There were many separate register banks, and each functional unit was connected to a distinct register bank. In order to be an operand of a functional unit, a value had to be in the proper register bank. In this context it is very helpful to see a reference to a value when deciding where to bind it.

S6, *S7*, *S8*, and *S9* were created. At this point VLMs exist at the entry and exit to the subgraph which map *Z* into a delayed binding that contains the schedules in the subgraph. When the trace containing the assignment to *Z* and the entry VLM is scheduled, register *fr3* is chosen and the binding is resolved. Note the effect on the exit VLM.

2.3.1 Operations on Delayed Bindings

We implemented delayed bindings as objects that could perform the following operations:

1. *Creation*. A delayed binding is created as a place holder for an actual location whenever the instruction scheduler sees a live but unreferenced value in a seed trace. Exactly one delayed binding is created for each such value and that *very same* delayed binding is given as the value's location in every VLM created for the schedule.
2. *Addition of a schedule*. The live subrange of an unbound value is extended as it passes unreferenced through an entry or exit trace. The resulting schedule is destructively added to the delayed binding, which is then reused in the VLMs generated at the borders of the new schedule.
3. *Merger of delayed bindings*. The VLMs at the top and bottom of transition traces will typically give a different delayed binding to the same value. This represents the fact that two subgraphs of schedules which had previously been connected only by intermediate code will now be joined by a schedule of machine code. The delayed bindings are destructively merged to reflect the merger of the two subranges.
4. *Available registers*. When at last an actual reference to the value is seen, we want to be able to find out which registers are available as choices to hold it through the subrange. This operation returns the set of such choices.
5. *Resolution*. When an actual location has finally been chosen, we resolve the delayed binding. All the VLMs at the borders to the subrange that it represents now reflect the location we choose, which may be either a register or a memory location.

3 An Example

To show how our technique works, we'll present a simple example. Consider the program fragment in Figure 4. There are two loops. The first loop has a conditional assignment to *Y*, and the second is a typical DAXPY-like vector loop. The lifetime of *Z* encompasses the two loops, though *Z* is not referenced in either. Let's follow the major steps our code generator takes as it produces schedules for this program.

```
FUNCTION CRUNCH(A,B,Z,N)

DO I=1,N
    IF ... THEN
        Y=
    ELSE
        Y=
    ENDIF
ENDDO

DO I=1,N
    A(I)=A(I)+Y*B(I)
ENDDO

RETURN Z

END
```

Figure 4. Code Fragment with Two Loops

3.1 Inner Loop and Back Edge

The first trace picked in our example will be the body of the second loop.[7] For the sake of our example, we'll assume that the loop body is unrolled or software pipelined [14,15,16,17,18,19] and that we need to use every floating point register to produce a peak performance schedule. The important thing for our purposes is that this code is picked as a seed trace, giving the instruction scheduler freedom to use the registers in any way that will make the most effective code. It may assume any initial locations for upwards exposed values at the joins to the trace and may leave the downwards exposed values in any locations at its splits.

3.1.1 Avoiding Data Motion on the Back Edge

The back edge of a scheduled loop body is a trace with exactly two operations: it consists of the VLM from the split at the bottom of the loop body followed by the VLM from the join to the top of the loop body. Since the back edge connects the bottom of the loop to the top of the loop, any mismatch between the locations used for the loop's upward exposed references and its downward exposed definitions has to be corrected by the addition of data motion code on the backedge. Probably the single most important aspect of global register allocation for scientific and engineering code is avoiding such backedge data motion. After all, the back edge will be executed as many times as the loop body.

---

7. The exact order in which the traces are considered is less important for this example than the fact that we consider the inner loops first and grow our subranges outward. When exactly the back edges are considered is not important since they contain no code. Our choice was made for expository reasons, as the first loop is more complex than the second loop.

Fortunately, it is fairly easy to make schedules for loop bodies that obviate the need for back edge data motion. In the simple case it is sufficient to avoid gratuitously perturbing the locations used for upward and downward exposed values. All other things being equal, the instruction scheduler should follow two rules:

1. Values should be redefined into the same register from which they are read.
2. Loop invariants should be read from as few registers as are needed to generate the tightest code, and these registers should not be reallocated within the loop body.

The situation is somewhat complicated by loop bodies that either contain function calls or have sections in which they make extreme demands on the registers.[8] In these cases, it is not just a matter of refraining from unnecessarily choosing different locations at the tops and bottoms of the loops; the best code for the loops may require data motion in the loop bodies themselves instead of on the backedges. For a wide machine, there may be opportunities to perform this data motion "for free" using unused resources in cycles that will be required anyway. Since no such "holes" initially exist on the backedge, any data motions that are left for the backedge schedule are certain to have a cost. For this reason, our instruction scheduler always matches the initial and final locations of values for loop bodies, examining both the top and bottom of the schedule for "holes" to fill with data motion.[9] The only information required by the instruction scheduler is that the current trace is a loop body.

3.2 Growing the Subrange from a Seed Trace

Returning to our example, let us consider how scheduling takes place in the loop with the conditional. We chose this piece of code to demonstrate how our technique propagates binding information outward from a seed trace to its neighborhood. Once again, the trace scheduler chooses the loop body as a trace. This time it has to pick one of the two directions of the branch and ignore the other for the time being. One of the controversial aspects of trace scheduling is that it requires that this decision be made. For our purposes, it seems not to matter very much which path is chosen. The important thing is that having chosen a trace, we are able to propagate the binding decisions from the resulting schedule so that when the side branch is scheduled, we'll be able to do a good job of targeting downward exposed results choosing initial locations for upward exposed operands. In short, we'd like to glue the side branch onto the main trace as seamlessly as possible, i.e., with no data motion. Figure 5 shows the intermediate code for the loop and highlights the section chosen as the main trace.

8. The situation is also complicated by the many separate register banks of the *Trace* architectures. Good parallelism may require the same value to be broadcasted to a number of different locations after it is defined.

9. To be honest, our policy of unrolling loops to find parallelism probably makes this simple strategy more effective than is would be in the context of software pipelining. After all, the main criticism of unrolling compared to software pipelining is that it leaves some "holes" at the tops and bottoms of loops.

In our example, the purpose of the side branch is the conditional assignment to *Y*. Figure 6 shows a section of the flow graph after the main trace and the back edge have been scheduled, at the time the side branch is chosen as a trace. Because this trace is an entry into the schedule for the main trace, it is extended to include the appropriate VLM for the join which includes the association of *Y* with *fr10* because that binding must hold true at the bottom of the main trace and *fr10* is not set below the join. Given this final binding, the instruction scheduler knows how to target the assignment to *Y*.

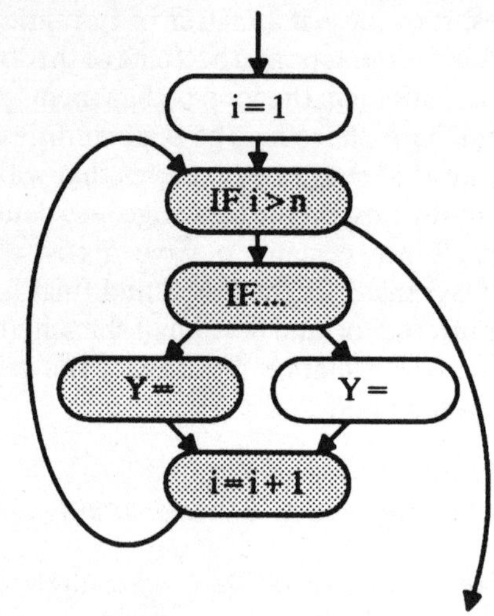

Figure 5. Intermediate Code for 1st Loop

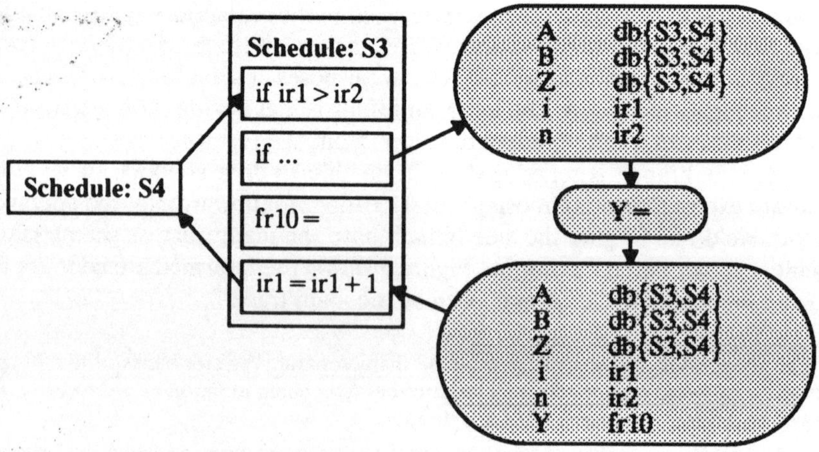

Figure 6. The Side Branch with VLMs

3.3 The Transition Between the Loops

At last we have completed making the schedules for the two inner loops and must now generate a schedule to connect them. The *transition trace* between the two loops consists of just two VLMs: one to represent the state at exit from the first loop and one for the entry to the top of the second loop.[10] Where a value–register pair appears in the second set of bindings, it means that there is an upward exposed reference to the value in the given location somewhere in the lower loop. We'll have to make sure that the upper loop actually leaves the value in that location in order to ensure program legality.

Figure 7 shows the flow graph before and after scheduling of the transition. We have assumed that the code for each of the two loop bodies was compiled without any knowledge of the other.[11] This led us to bind *Y* and *n* to different registers in each of the two sections of the flow graph. So we'll have to generate code to move them in the transition.

3.3.1 *Resolving Delayed Bindings*

More interesting is the treatment of the delayed bindings. The addresses of the two arrays, *A* and *B* were referenced in the DAXPY loop but not in the conditional assignment loop. Consequently, the VLM at the bottom of the transition maps them into actual registers whereas at the top, they are mapped to delayed bindings. Our instruction scheduler uses the final bindings as preferences in resolving the delayed bindings: it would prefer to resolve the binding for *A* to *ir2* and the binding for *B* to *ir3*. The delayed bindings carry the information necessary to determine whether these preferences can be satisfied. In our example, *ir2* is unavailable, and we assume that *ir3* is available. This allows *B*'s delayed binding to be resolved without data motion. *A*, on the other hand, will have to be moved since *ir2* is unavailable as a resolution for its delayed binding in the upper subrange. We've chosen a memory location as its resolution, for the sake of illustration. In reality, our compiler would use a register if there was one available. Notice how this decision is reflected in the VLM at the entry for the first loop. The spill to satisfy this binding will be performed when this VLM and the subroutine entry are picked as a trace and scheduled.

3.3.2 *Merging Delayed Binding Subranges*

Since *Z* is not referenced in either of the two loops, we can further delay binding decisions for it by merging its initial and final delayed bindings. Refer to Figure 7 to see how scheduling the transition trace affects the delayed binding given for *Z* by

10. We do not show the initialization code for the loop index: it only complicates the picture without offering any additional insight.

11. The Multiflow compiler actually used a *clue cache* to help it avoid this kind of arbitrary bad decision. Every time a value is assigned to a register, we make an entry in a global table. Every time a binding choice is made, we consult the clue cache and (all other things being equal) use the last register assignment for the value. This heuristic works out fairly well in practice.

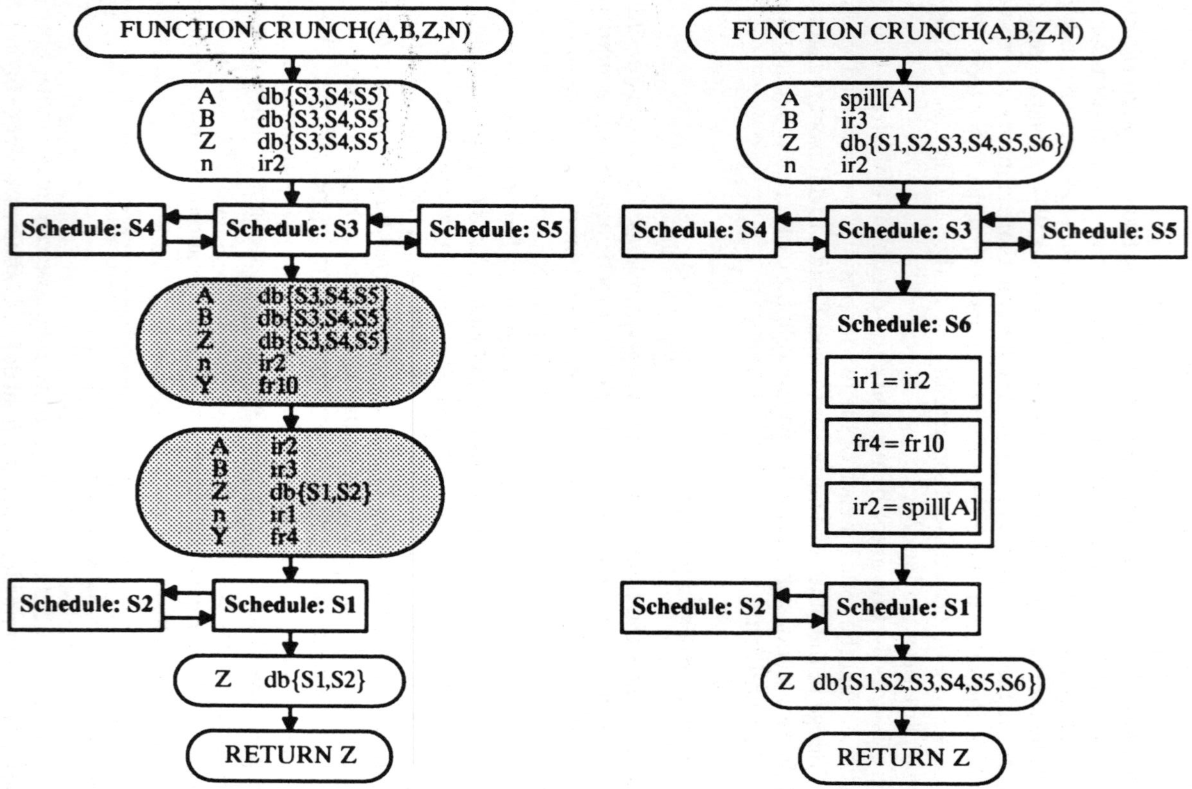

Before *After*

Figure 7. The Effect of Scheduling the Transition between the Loops

the VLMs at the entry to the first loop and the exit from the final loop. *Z*'s delayed binding will be resolved later when either the subroutine entry or its return is scheduled (whichever happens first). At that time, the register availability for its complete live range will be available, as well as its location on entry (or return) to the subroutine. Resolution at either the entry or the return will be reflected in the VLM at the other side of the flow graph, enabling the scheduler to perform any necessary data motion when *that* trace is finally scheduled.

4 Some Measurements

How well does our technique work in practice? To answer this question we undertook two experiments: one to see how well our method performs, and one to support our assumption that registers are often a critical instruction scheduling resource.

The experiments were done on a Multiflow *Trace 14/300* with compilers based on Multiflow's Trace Scheduling Compilers version 2.2. Multiflow's compilers had been tuned for scientific applications written in Fortran and the *Trace* series */300* computers.

The cycle time of a *Trace* is 130ns, subdivided into two minor cycles of 65ns. A *Trace 14/300* can issue four integer operations per minor cycles (two of which may be memory references), and four floating point operations plus two conditional branches per cycle, for a total of 14 operations per cycle. The load pipeline is seven minor cycles, the floating point pipeline four minor cycles, and the branch delay is two minor cycles after the branch condition has been set. A branch must be issued at a cycle boundary, and hence it may take two full cycles to set the branch condition and to complete the branch. The *Trace* has 16 64–bit registers in each floating register bank and 32 32–bit registers in each integer register bank. A *Trace 14* has four register banks of each kind, each of which supplies the operands of exactly one ALU. One register in each register bank is reserved to hold the value zero; three additional registers are reserved in each integer register bank for use by the operating system.[12]

All operations on a *Trace* either complete in a single cycle or are explicitly pipelined. All operations are RISC–like three address operations with explicit load and store operations to access memory. All pipelines are self–draining. The *Trace* does neither perform dynamic scheduling nor does it have any hardware interlocks, and resources can be oversubscribed. It is the compiler's responsibility to manage the machine resources and to schedule the operations.

The memory system is interleaved and does not have a data cache. The *Trace* we used for our experiments has 128Mbytes of main memory and an instruction cache for 8k instructions.

12. In addition, there are two register banks that hold values on their way to memory, and four branch register banks that hold the condition code bits. Their connectivity largely determines when they are allocated, and hence they are omitted in the following discussion.

4.1 First Experiment

Our first experiment tries to answer the question of how well our register allocator performs. The short answer to this question is that our register allocation method leaves very little room for improvement. We used the SPEC floating point benchmarks [20] for our experiment.[13] We analyzed dynamic instruction and operation counts to examine the relative frequency of spills, restores and local moves. These cover all the operations that the register allocator introduces. We are interested in these numbers because they allow us to compare our method with register coloring and to obtain an upper bound on how much other register allocators could improve over our approach.

We used an analysis tool that takes the output of the compiler and inserts frequency counters. Thus we obtained accurate counts about how often each instruction is executed. Since the tool is intrusive, it does not count dynamic stalls (icache miss or DRAM bank stall); and since it modifies the output of the compiler rather than the linked image, it does not include the time spent in library routines, and instructions executed in library routines are not included in our dynamic operation counts.

Chart 1 shows the number of spills, restores and local moves as a percentage of all operations. These counts overstate the number of operations introduced by the register allocator.[14] We see from this chart that the total number of spills, restores and local moves is small when compared to the total number of operations executed: in particular, local moves are always less than 5% of the operation count, and less than 3% for the floating point benchmarks.

How relevant are operation counts for a machine like the *Trace*? Chart 2 compares the dynamic instruction and operations counts for the SPEC floating point benchmarks with the operation counts for the *MIPS* and *SPARC* RISC processors, as reported in [21]. We adjusted the operation counts for the *MIPS* and *SPARC* to exclude the time spent in libraries. The chart shows that the operation counts are comparable in magnitude. This indicates that the *Trace* did not execute many more operations than comparable RISC processors. The execution time for

13. We excluded the SPEC integer benchmarks from this chart because, to be honest, the results are not as good. We feel that this is more a reflection on Multiflow's marketing focus than on the strength of our register allocation method. There are architectural reasons why it is difficult for the *Trace* to compete on C system codes. To give but one example, the unrestricted pointer semantics of C made it difficult both to use the multi-ported, interleaved memory system effectively (it is a resource error when two memory references go through the same memory card) and to schedule memory references out of order. This situation was aggravated by the lack of a data cache and the resulting memory latency. Given this handicap, the compiler implementation effort concentrated on achieving good performance for scientific Fortran codes.

14. The counts for spills and restores include all direct references to the stack frame whose address is the sum of the stack pointer plus a constant. This type of reference includes local variables (and structures but not array references unless indexed by a constant) that require a memory home, e.g., because their address is taken or because they are passed by reference to a subroutine. Likewise, local moves may be required to move values into architected registers, e.g., to pass a value in a register to a subroutine.

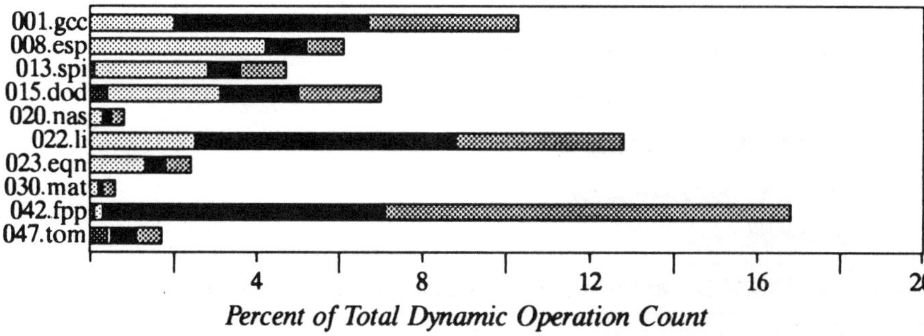

Each bar from the origin:

1. local fmoves 2. local imoves 3. spills 4. restores

The operation counts do not include time spent in system libraries. Spills and restores include all scalar references to the stack frame.

Chart 1. Operation Count Details

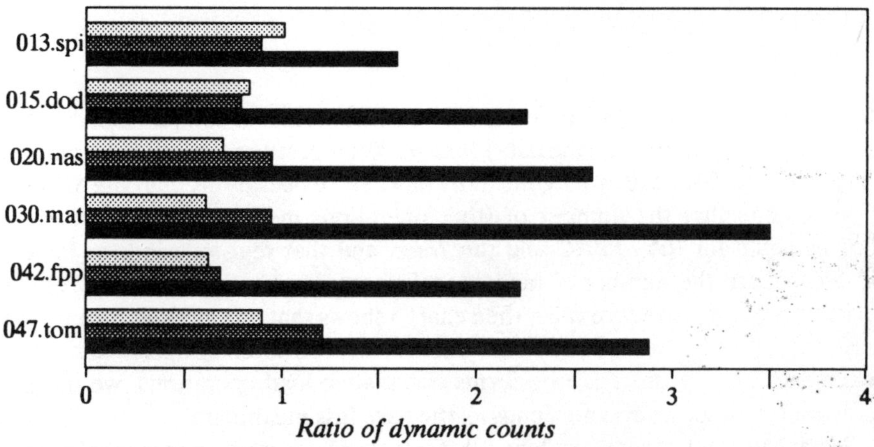

Each benchmark from the top:

SPARC/MIPS SPARC/Trace operations SPARC/Trace instructions

The operation counts do not include time spent in system libraries. A ratio > 1 implies that the SPARC executes more operations or instructions. Trace counts exclude dynamic stalls.

Chart 2. Ratio of Dynamic Operation Counts for *MIPS, SPARC* and *Trace*

a *Trace*, of course, depends on the dynamic instruction counts, not the operation counts. The ratios of the dynamic instruction counts for the *SPARC* over the *Trace* are also shown in chart 2.

Chart 3 compares the dynamic store operation counts for the same set of processors and benchmarks. In four of the six cases, the *Trace* executes fewer

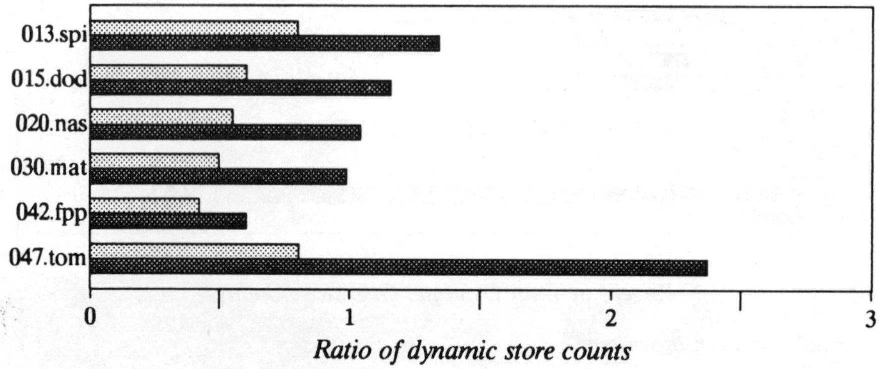

Each benchmark from the top:
SPARC/MIPS *SPARC/Trace operation count*
The operation counts do not include time spent in system libraries. A ratio > 1 implies that the SPARC executes more operations.

Chart 3. Ratio of Dynamic Store Operation Counts for *MIPS*, *SPARC* and *Trace*

stores than the *SPARC* (we included the *MIPS* numbers for comparison, but the lack of 64–bit stores distorts the data); *matrix300* it is pretty much a tie; and only for *fpppp* does the *Trace* execute significantly more store operations than the *SPARC*. If we assume that the number of store operations in the source program are roughly equal for the *SPARC* and the *Trace*, and that register windows for the *SPARC* reduce the number of memory references required to save and restore registers around procedure calls, then chart 3 shows that our method presumably performs a similar number of spills when compared to coloring on this set of benchmarks. Since the *Trace* performs speculative load operations, we did not compare operation counts for loads as they are less meaningful.

Having presented some evidence that our approach will do a reasonable job in placing spills and restores, do we achieve this at the cost of much redundant data motion in transition traces? To answer this question, we looked at the number of local moves and determined an upper bound on the improvement that a more traditional coloring register allocator could achieve over our approach.

We obtain the upper bound for the possible improvement as follows. At worst, each local move is executed in isolation, i.e., each local move will require the latency–weighted number of instructions. Therefore we subtract the maximum number of cycles required for local moves from the dynamic instruction count. This gives us the desired upper bound on the possible improvement. Chart 4 shows the ratio between the actual instruction count and the adjusted instruction count. For four of the Fortran benchmarks, another register allocation strategy might gain at most a 1% improvement by this measure; in all cases, the improvement is less than 5.5%.

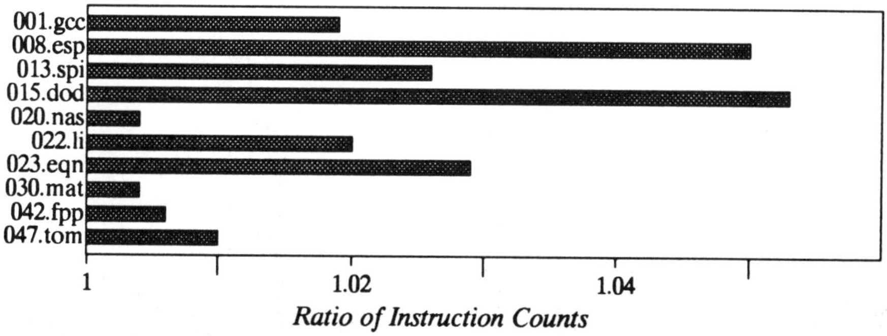

Ratio of actual instruction count over dynamic instruction count minus latency weighted local moves. A ratio of 1.02 means that 2% instructions could be saved if all local moves are counted at maximum latency and could be eliminated by a competing method.

Chart 4. Actual vs. Worst Instruction Counts

4.2 Second Experiment

Our second experiment aims to support our conjecture that registers are a critical resource. For this experiment we reduced the number of registers available for allocation and looked at the SPEC benchmark suite [20] and the Livermore Fortran Kernels [22,23].

For our experiment we changed the number of registers in the compiler's machine description but did not re-tune various optimization parameters and heuristics to account for the different number or registers. We felt that we did not have the time or resources to address this problem.

We increased the number of registers in each floating register bank from 8 to 16 in steps of 2, and the number of registers in each integer register bank from 16 to 32 in steps of 4. We made corresponding changes to the number of function arguments and return values that are passed in registers, and adjusted the maximum length for vector intrinsic functions (e.g., vector-*exp*, which computes *exp* for *n* argument values); the latter adjustment was needed for *spice2g6*, *nasa7* and *LFK kernel 22*. We used unmodified system run-time libraries throughout our experiment, i.e., library routines were always compiled for the full register set.

We are fully aware that our experiment measures the combined effect of global and local register allocation, but we did not see a simple way to measure the effect of global register allocation in isolation.

Chart 5 shows SPEC ratios for the four hypothetical machines and a Multiflow *Trace 14/300*. The results confirm that registers can be a critical scheduling resource.

There are six floating-point intensive benchmarks in the SPEC suite: *spice2g6*, *doduc*, *nasa7*, *matrix300*, *fpppp* and *tomcatv*.

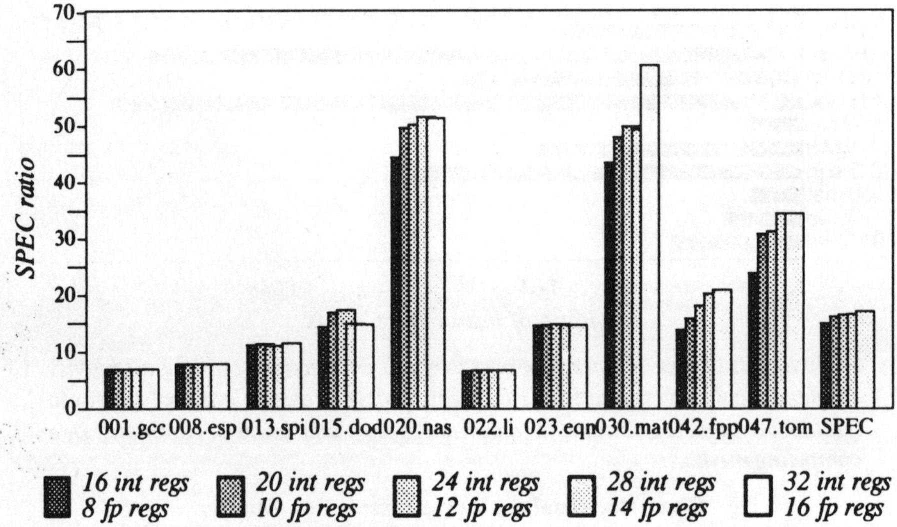

Chart 5. SPEC Ratios for Different Number of Registers

matrix300 and *tomcatv* are vectorizable benchmarks. *matrix300* spends more than 93% of its execution time in the inner loop trace for subroutine *saxpy*. In fact, each instruction of this loop counts for at least 3% of the total execution time, making the benchmark very sensitive to even a small perturbation in the instruction sequence generated for this loop. In the 14 fp register case, a small load balancing error unrelated to register allocation adds an exposed memory pipeline delay to this loop resulting in the observed increase in execution time: here re-tuning for the number of available registers would have improved the result.

tomcatv also spends most of its execution time in a small number of traces: here, the top trace accounts for more than 70% of the execution time, and the top six traces account for more than 98% of the execution time. Therefore we are not that worried that the five run did not produce a proportional improvement but rather believe that the monotonic improvement shows that our register allocator was able to effectively use the additional registers.

fpppp is a scalar benchmark, but its key routine represents a completely unrolled loop with a large amount of instruction level parallelism. This routine represents a very good test on how well a compiler is capable of processing a very large basic block and of handling of large register pressure within a basic block.

nasa7 is a Fortran vector benchmark, but approximately 25% of its execution time is spent in a loop that has three memory accesses through the same memory card of the interleaved memory system, and a fourth access with an unknown stride, severely limiting performance.

spice2g6 and *doduc* show different icache behavior across the five runs. When the execution times are adjusted for the time spent to fill the icache, the execution times for *spice2g6* are the same for all five cases, and the execution times for *doduc* monotonically decrease (i.e., the SPEC ratios monotonically increase) for the five runs. We believe that it is permissible to adjust the execution times for icache miss because the scheduler does not know about (or control) the icache behavior of the program, and changes in the icache behavior should not be taken as a sign that our register allocation approach is flawed. *spice2g6* and *doduc* are scalar programs, and we did not expect any performance improvement when we increased the number of registers. This expectation was confirmed for *spice2g6*, but *doduc* actually had more fine-grain parallelism than we realized, and its icache-adjusted execution time improved. Chart 6 shows SPEC ratios with execution times adjusted for icache miss

There are four integer benchmarks in the SPEC suite: *gcc1.35*, *espresso*, *li* and *eqntott*. They are all written in C, whose unrestricted pointer semantics exposes much less instruction level parallelism than found in typical Fortran programs. We did not expect to see any improvements for these benchmarks, and found our expectations confirmed by our experiment.

Chart 7 shows Livermore Fortran Kernels. This benchmark represent more specialized examples of kernels found in scientific code. The results basically confirm our belief that the register allocator can make effective use of available registers. Note in particular kernels 7 and 9, both of which present very good examples of codes that have a large amount of instruction level parallelism.

5 Related Work

In the five years since we implemented this compiler, some papers have been published describing approaches that take the higher control structure of a program into account.

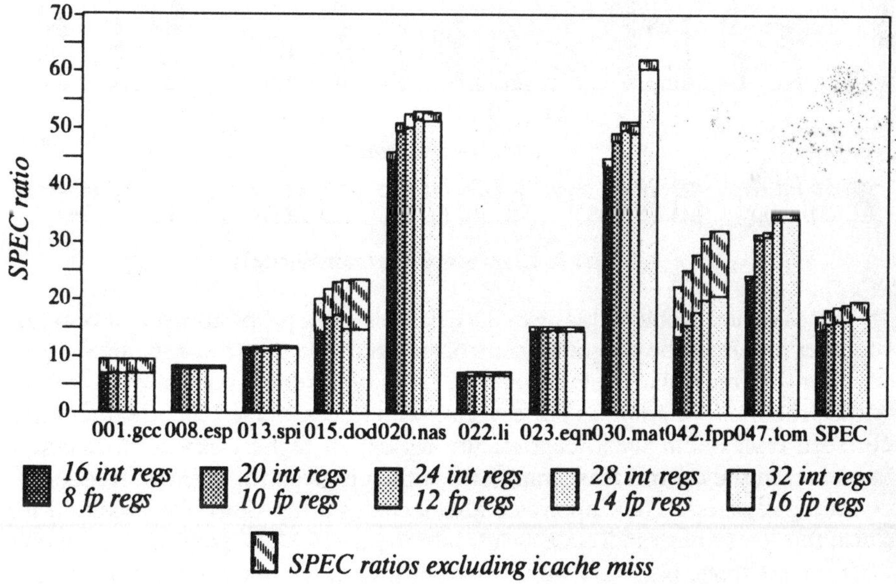

Chart 6. SPEC Ratios for Different Number of Registers

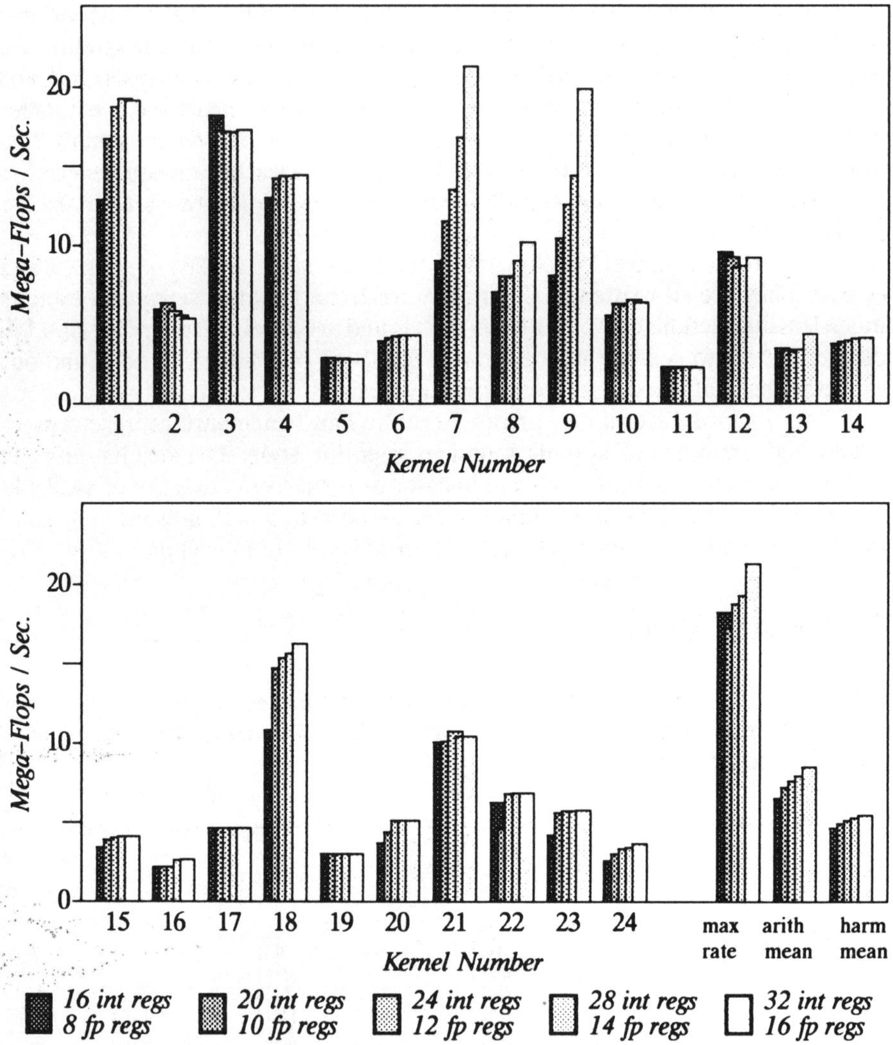

Chart 7. Livermore Fortran Kernels

Callahan and Koblenz [24] extend Chaitin's work [6] by covering a program with tiles to reflect the program's control structure and then color the tiles during a bottom–up tree walk. Their hierarchy of tiles represents a comparable covering of the program flow graph as our covering with traces; in fact, their leaf tiles and our seed traces both try to capture the regions of highest expected execution frequency in the control flow graph, which then is given the greatest freedom in allocating registers. Their approach also includes a top–down tree walk during which they try to push spill code as low into the control flow graph as reasonable, whereas our single pass very well may push spill code higher in the control flow graph than is desirable. Their approach assigns symbolic registers during the bottom–up walk and defers the assignment of physical registers to the top–down pass, whereas our implementation assigns physical registers immediately. Our approach simplifies the amount of bookkeeping, but in retrospect it may have been better to defer physical register assignments, either until delayed bindings are resolved or, assuming that the resolution of delayed bindings introduces additional constraints on the final register assignments, until the entire program has been scheduled.

Briggs, Cooper and Torczon [25] build on their earlier work [8] by using the loop structure of a program to split live ranges at loop boundaries. This approach extends the basic block recognition to loop structures but does not include conditionals as a higher control structure.

Bradlee, Eggers and Henry [26] have looked at the effect of integrating register allocation and instruction scheduling; however, their scheduling is limited to basic blocks and they do not perform global, parallelism-enhancing optimizations. In addition, they target RISCs with very little parallelism and moderate pipeline depths, namely the *MIPS R2000*, the *Motorola 88000* and the *Intel i860*. These limitations greatly diminish the validity of their experiments as regards deeply pipelined machines targeted at floating point computing, machines such as the *Trace*.

6 Conclusions

We have presented the global register allocation method used in the Multiflow compiler. This method places first priority on giving the instruction scheduler the freedom to use whatever registers it needs to generate the best schedules for the most frequently executed parts of a program. This is different from schemes such as coloring that place a greater emphasis on keeping a value in the same register throughout its lifetime. We feel that given the choice, our system will give better results for floating point intensive scientific and engineering codes when targeting architectures requiring extensive instruction scheduling.

The compiler is a finished commercial quality product that has been in use for a number of years. It has been used extensively in benchmarking and production. Due to the nature of our machine, we believe that our compiler has been used on almost all the important CPU intensive floating point applications in use today, with mostly good results. Given the novel nature of both our compiler and our architecture, that is an accomplishment in itself.

7 Acknowledgements

The authors appreciate the contributions of Tom Karzes to the design and implementation of the delayed binding idea. We also appreciate the comments and suggestions of Geoff Lowney, Josh Fisher and Bob Nix on earlier versions of the paper. Last not least we wish to thank the members of Multiflow's compiler group, which provided the environment in which we could develop our ideas, and our current managers, who let us spend the time required to prepare this manuscript.

References

[1] Cocke J and Markstein V. The evolution of RISC technology at IBM. *IBM J. Research and Development 34*:1 (January 1990), pp. 4–11.

[2] Hennessy JL and Patterson DA. *Computer Architecture A Quantitative Approach.* Morgan Kaufmann Publishers, Inc., San Mateo, Calif., 1990.

[3] Colwell RP, Nix RP, O'Donnell JJ, Papworth DB, and Rodman PK. A VLIW architecture for a trace scheduling compiler. In *Proc. 2nd Intl. Conf. Architectural Support for Programming Languages and Operation Systems* (ASPLOS II) (Palo Alto, October 1987). ACM, New York, 1987, pp. 180–192.

[4] Colwell RP, Hall WE, Joshi CS, Papworth DB, Rodman PK, and Tornes JE. Architecture and implementation of a VLIW supercomputer. In *Proc. IEEE Supercomputing '90 Conference*, IEEE, New York, 1990, pp. 910–919.

[5] Chaitin GJ, Auslander MA, Chandra AK, Cocke J, Hopkins ME, and Markstein PW. Register allocation via coloring. *Comput. Lang. 6*,1 (January 1981), pp. 47–57.

[6] Chaitin GJ. Register allocation and spilling via graph coloring. In *Proc. ACM SIGPLAN '82 Symp. Compiler Construction* (Boston, June 1982). ACM, New York, 1982, pp. 98–105.

[7] Bernstein D, Goldin DQ, Golumbic MC, Krawczyk H, Mansour Y, Nahshon I, and Pinter RY. Spill code minimization techniques for optimizing compilers. In *Proc. ACM SIGPLAN '89 Conf. Programming Language Design and Implementation* (Portland, June 1989). ACM, New York, 1989, pp. 258–263.

[8] Briggs P, Cooper KD, Kennedy K, and Torczon L. Coloring heuristics for register allocation. In *Proc. ACM SIGPLAN '89 Conf. Programming Language Design and Implementation* (Portland, June 1989). ACM, New York, 1989, pp. 275–284.

[9] Chow FC and Hennessy JL. The priority–based coloring approach to register allocation. *ACM Trans. Program. Lang. Syst. 12*,4 (October 1990), pp. 501–536.

[10] Fisher JA. The optimization of horizontal microcode within and beyond basic blocks: An application of processor scheduling with resources. Ph.D. Thesis, New York Univ., New York, N.Y., 1979.

[11] Fisher JA, Ellis JR, Ruttenberg JC, and Nicolau A. Parallel processing: A smart compiler and a dumb machine. In *Proc. ACM SIGPLAN '84 Symp.*

Compiler Construction (Montreal, June 1984). ACM, New York, 1984, pp. 37–47.

[12] Nicolau A. Parallelism, memory anti–aliasing and correctness for trace scheduling compilers. Ph.D. Thesis, Yale Univ., New Haven, Conn., 1984.

[13] Ellis JR. *Bulldog: A Compiler for VLIW Architectures*. MIT Press, Cambridge, MA, 1986. Also Ph.D. Thesis, Yale Univ., New Haven, Conn., February 1985.

[14] Charlesworth AE. An approach to scientific array processing: the architectural design of the AP–120B/FPS164 family. *IEEE Computer 14*:9 (September 1981), pp. 18–27.

[15] Rau BR and Glaeser CD. Some scheduling techniques and an easily schedulable horizontal architecture for high performance scientific computing. In *Proc. 14th Annual Microprogramming Workshop* (October 1981). IEEE, 1981, pp. 183–198.

[16] Aiken A and Nicolau A. Optimal loop parallelization. In *Proc. ACM SIGPLAN '88 Conf. Programming Language Design and Implementation* (Atlanta, June 88). ACM, New York, 1988, pp. 308–317.

[17] Aiken A. Compaction–based parallelization. Ph.D. Thesis, Cornell Univ, Ithaca, N.Y., 1988.

[18] Lam M. Software Pipelining: An effective scheduling technique for VLIW machines. In *Proc. ACM SIGPLAN '88 Conf. Programming Language Design and Implementation* (Atlanta, June 1988). ACM, New York, 1988, pp. 318–328.

[19] Dehnert JC, Hsu PY, and Bratt JP. Overlapped loop support in the Cydra 5. In *Proc. 3rd Intl. Conf. Architectural Support for Programming Languages and Operation Systems* (ASPLOS III) (Boston, April 1989). ACM, New York, 1989, pp. 26–39.

[20] Uniejewski J. SPEC Benchmark Suite: Designed for today's advanced systems. *SPEC Newsletter 1*,1 (Fall 1989).

[21] Cmelik RF, Kong SI, Ditzel DR, and Kelly EJ. An analysis of MIPS and SPARC instruction set utilization on the SPEC benchmarks. In *Proc. 4th Intl. Conf. Architectural Support for Programming Languages and Operating Systems* (ASPLOS IV) (Santa Clara, April 1991). ACM, New York, 1991, pp. 290–302.

[22] McMahon FH. The Livermore Fortran Kernels: A computer test of the numerical performance range. Tech. Report UCRL–53745, University of California, Lawrence Livermore National Laboratory, December 1986.

[23] Feo JT. An analysis of the computational and parallel complexity of the Livermore Loops. *Parallel Computing 7* (1988), pp. 163–185.

[24] Callahan D and Koblenz B. Register allocation via hierarchical graph coloring. In *Proc. ACM SIGPLAN '91 Conf. Programming Language Design and Implementation* (Toronto, June 91). ACM, New York, 1991, pp. 192–203.

[25] Briggs P, Cooper K, and Torczon L. Aggressive live range splitting. Tech. report, Rice Univ., Houston, Tex., 1991.

[26] Bradlee DG, Eggers SJ, and Henry RR. Integrating register allocation and instruction scheduling for RISCs. In Proc. *4th Intl. Conf. Architectural Support for Programming Languages and Operating Systems* (ASPLOS IV) (Santa Clara, April 1991). ACM, New York, 1991. pp. 122–131.

Formal Methods

From Programs to Object Code using Logic and Logic Programming

Jonathan Bowen
Oxford University Computing Laboratory
Programming Research Group
11 Keble Road, Oxford OX1 3QD, England
E-mail: Jonathan.Bowen@comlab.ox.ac.uk

Abstract

A compiler may be specified by a description of how each construct of the source language is translated into a sequence of object code instructions. If the machine that interprets the object code is specified in the source language itself, then the compiler may be verified using algebraic laws about the programming language constructs. By adopting a subset of the programming language occam, we can benefit from the large number of existing laws which have already been proved for this language.

The compiling specification theorems are all Horn clauses in general. Thus it is possible to produce an executable compiler prototype almost directly from this specification in the form of a logic program. The target object code for the transputer has variable-length instruction sequences. Thus in some cases it is necessary to transform the theorems into a form which can be more efficiently executed by avoiding unnecessary backtracking, particularly when there are jumps in the code. However the relational nature of logic programming allows a number of solutions to be returned if desired.

1 Introduction

A compiler may be specified by a set of theorems, each relating a construct in the high-level programming language with the allowed machine instruction sequence that implements that construct. In general the two descriptions act on a different data space (i.e., program variables and memory locations). Thus a symbol table describing this relationship will also be needed.

Hoare has suggested a novel way of verifying such a description [1]. This involves specifying the semantics of the low-level machine using an interpreter written in the high-level programming language (or an extension of it if necessary). This allows algebraic laws about the language to be applied to gradually transform one description into the other. These laws may either be held to be self-evident, or can themselves be proved correct with respect to another semantics [2].

This technique has been applied to a subset of the programming language occam [3] and the transputer [4], both of which are in industrial use. Using occam means that the well-understood semantics and algebraic laws already formulated for this language [5] can be readily adapted and applied to the verification proof. This work has been adequately described elsewhere [6, 7,

8]. In addition the language has been extended to include more complicated constructs such as recursion, to demonstrate that the technique is applicable to non-trivial programming constructs [9]. This work forms the basis for an even more ambitious task that is currently being undertaken, to prove the correctness of a *compiler* written in the high-level language [10].

The compiling specification theorems are in general formulated as Horn clauses. Thus they are already very close in form to a logic program. In some cases the programs may be transliterated almost directly from the specification. In other cases, the specifications may be transformed using logic into a form that is more efficiently executable. The rest of this paper describes this process, and some of the particular problems encountered in generating code for the transputer. The minimum development to achieve a reasonably efficient executable program is carried out and a *rigorous argument* [11] is presented to help ensure the correctness of the compiler.

1.1 Logic programming and Prolog

As the name suggests, logic programming has a well established mathematical basis [12, 13, 14]. Prolog [15] is the most widely available logic programming language. However, Prolog includes many non-logical features in an attempt to make it into a usable, practical and efficiently executable language. Even so, if the features used in Prolog are restricted, it is possible to use it in a logical manner. For example, the Prolog Horn clause

$$P \texttt{ :- } Q_1, \ldots, Q_n .$$

is equivalent to the following formula in first order predicate logic:

$$\forall x, y, \ldots \cdot ((Q_1 \wedge \ldots \wedge Q_n) \Rightarrow P)$$

where $x, y, \ldots$ are all the free variables in the predicates P and Q_i $(1 \leq i \leq n)$. Note that the "`:-`" of Prolog can be considered as a reverse implication ($\Leftarrow$ or "**if**") in predicate logic. This theorem is in turn equivalent to:

$$\forall x_1, \ldots, x_l \cdot ((\exists y_1, \ldots, y_m \cdot Q_1 \wedge \ldots \wedge Q_n) \Rightarrow P)$$

where $x_1, \ldots, x_l$ are the free variables in P (normally mentioned in the Q_i predicates as well) and $y_1, \ldots, y_m$ are the variables mentioned in Q_i but not in P. The quantifiers may be omitted when there are no relevant free variables. Additionally, if there are no Q_i clauses, this part of the formula reduces to *true* and the implication may be omitted since $true \Rightarrow P = P$. Such formulae, in which all the variables are set to some specific value are known as *facts* [15].

A set of such clauses form a program. Queries (or *goals*) may be posed to this program as the conjunction of a set of goal clauses:

$$\texttt{?- } G_1, \ldots, G_n .$$

This is equivalent to the following in predicate logic:

$$\neg \exists y_1, \ldots, y_m \cdot (G_1 \wedge \ldots \wedge G_n)$$

The Prolog system searches for a contradiction to this clause. If it finds one (or more), these are output successively as they are discovered. A very simple left-to-right and depth-first search of the database of clauses is used because it is efficient to implement. This can result in non-termination in practice if a search is made down an infinite branch of the proof tree. Thus some judicious ordering of the clauses is often necessary to ensure that an answer is found in finite time.

Using the form of clauses described above results in a restricted form of predicate logic. Note in particular that none of the Q_i and G_i predicates may be negated (e.g., $\neg Q_i$). In practice this can be too much of a limitation sometimes, and the restricted form of negation, *negation by failure*, is allowed in Prolog [13, 16]. This type of negation normally limits the modes in which the logic program can be used (i.e., which variables must be instantiated, and which can be left uninstantiated). In practice this may not be too restrictive since the logic program can be designed knowing which variables are to be inputs and outputs. Where negation is necessary in the logic program presented in this paper, its use is justified informally.

The use of logic programming has at least two advantages compared with functional languages:

1. It is essentially relational and undirectional; *backtracking* allows the possibility of a number of solutions being returned.

2. It is possible to compute with unknown values ("*logic variables*") due to the *unification* algorithm, with the proviso that non-termination and negation (apart from negation by failure) must be avoided, as discussed above

2 Programming and Machine Languages

2.1 The programming language

The programming language presented here is a sequential subset of occam [3]. It consists of the occam constructs, SKIP, STOP, assignment, SEQ, IF and WHILE. The syntax of the subset language is as follows:

$$
\begin{array}{rcl}
blk & ::= & \texttt{INT}\ var : blk \mid p \\
p & ::= & \texttt{SKIP} \mid \texttt{STOP} \mid var := e \mid \texttt{SEQ}[p_1, \ldots, p_n] \mid \\
 & & \texttt{IF}[b_1 \rightarrow p_1, \ldots, b_n \rightarrow p_n] \mid \texttt{WHILE}(b, p) \\
e & ::= & var \mid int \mid \texttt{TRUE} \mid \texttt{FALSE} \mid mop\ e \mid e_1\ dop\ e_2 \\
mop & ::= & - \mid \texttt{NOT} \\
dop & ::= & + \mid - \mid * \mid / \mid \texttt{REM} \mid = \mid <> \mid < \mid > \mid <= \mid >= \mid \texttt{AND} \mid \texttt{OR}
\end{array}
$$

where b is a Boolean expression e, *var* is a variable name and *int* is a machine word integer value.

Note that the concrete syntax is selected such that the program may easily be read directly by Prolog by defining each keyword and symbol as a Prolog operator with some suitable priority, associativity, etc. This obviates the need to write a parser in Prolog.

This subset of occam has been formally specified using an operational semantics and also a specification-oriented semantics [9]. These semantics have been related and the algebraic laws necessary for the proof of correctness of the compiling specification have been proved with respect to the latter [2].

2.2 The machine language

Each machine language instruction can be considered to be constituted out of a sequence of basic byte-sized transputer instructions. Thus a machine instruction occupies some contiguous bytes of memory. Note that in a machine language program the argument of a jump instruction is the byte offset from the *end* of the jump instruction to the *start* of the target instruction. Below, we briefly summarise the repertoire of instructions available in the target machine language.

The machine language instructions include an operand:

Instr	::=	`ldc`(w)	load a constant
	|	`ldl`(w)	load from a local memory location
	|	`stl`(w)	store to a local memory location
	|	`eqc`(w)	compare with a constant
	|	`j`(w)	jump by a specified offset
	|	`cj`(w)	conditionally jump by a specified offset
	|	...	

where w ranges over machine word integer values.

Other "operations" have no explicit operand (at this level of abstraction):

Operation	::=	`stopp`	stop process
	|	`stoperr`	stop on error
	|	`add`	add operands on stack
	|	...	

Together these make up the target instructions for the compiler:

$$Instr_{ML} \ ::= \ Instr \mid Operation$$

These instructions and operations actually consist of a sequence of basic byte-sized instructions, the number of which depends on the size of the operand or the type of the operation. These byte instructions have a 4-bit opcode (allowing 16 basic instructions) and a 4-bit operand. Operations are invoked using the "`opr`" instruction with an operand that determines the operation to be executed. If the operand is greater than a 4-bit value, one or more "`pfix`" instructions are first executed to prefix the higher bit values into an internal register. Negative values are first prefixed with an "`nfix`" instruction. Thus each instruction sequence normally consists of first an optional "`nfix`" instruction if the operand is negative, zero or more "`pfix`" instructions, followed by one of the basic instructions or an "`opr`" instruction.

The byte-sized transputer instructions (used by the code generated by the compiling specification presented here) are:

$$Instr_{TR} \ ::= \ Instr \mid \texttt{opr}(w) \mid \texttt{pfix}(w) \mid \texttt{nfix}(w)$$

where $0 \leq w < 16$.

The formal semantics of the machine language and the transputer instructions have been specified as an interpreter [9] and in the Z notation [17].

2.3 Translating instruction sequences into basic instructions

The function *Operand(minstr)* gives the operand part of a machine language instruction *minstr* as follows:

$$minstr \in Instr \Rightarrow Operand(minstr) = w$$
$$minstr \in Operation \Rightarrow Operand(minstr) = OperationOpCode(minstr)$$

where $minstr = op(w)$ in the first case and the function *OperationOpCode* defines the numeric opcode for each of the defined transputer operations.

The size of a machine language instruction *minstr* in bytes is given by a function *Size(minstr)*:

$$\begin{array}{rcl}
0 \leq Operand(minstr) < 16 & \Rightarrow & Size(minstr) = 1 \\
-16 \leq Operand(minstr) < 0 & \Rightarrow & Size(minstr) = 2 \\
16^i \leq Operand(minstr) < 16^{i+1} \ \wedge\ 1 \leq i & \Rightarrow & Size(minstr) = i + 1 \\
-16^{i+1} \leq Operand(minstr) < -16^i \ \wedge\ 1 \leq i & \Rightarrow & Size(minstr) = i + 1
\end{array}$$

The function *Mtrans(minstr)* may be specified as follows [4]. Instructions from *Instr* are implemented using the corresponding instructions in transputer. The instructions from *Operation* are implemented using the `opr` instruction of the transputer. The loading of a large operand requires a sequence of `pfix` instructions before the actual instruction. A negative operand is normally generated using a prefixed `nfix` instruction. Thus the minimum size of instruction for a positive operand is one byte, whereas for a negative operand it is two bytes (see the definition of *Size* above) [18].

$$Mtrans(minstr) \stackrel{\text{def}}{=} \begin{array}{l} \textbf{if}\ \ minstr = op(w)\ \ \textbf{then}\ \ Prefix(op, w) \\ \textbf{else}\ \ Prefix(\texttt{opr}, Operand(minstr)) \end{array}$$

$$\begin{array}{l}
Prefix(op, w) \stackrel{\text{def}}{=} \\
\quad \textbf{if}\ \ 0 \leq w < 16\ \ \textbf{then}\ \ op(w) \\
\quad \textbf{else}\ \ \textbf{if}\ \ w \geq 16 \\
\quad\quad\quad \textbf{then}\ \ Prefix(\texttt{pfix}, (w \gg 4))^\frown op(w \wedge 15) \\
\quad\quad\quad \textbf{else}\ \ Prefix(\texttt{nfix}, ((BITNOT\ \ w) \gg 4))^\frown op(w \wedge 15)
\end{array}$$

Each machine language instruction is represented as a finite sequence of basic transputer instructions.

3 Compiling Specification

The compiling specification is defined as a predicate relating a high-level programming language process with the corresponding machine language code. Section 3.1 presents this relation and section 3.2 presents some theorems concerning this compilation predicate $\mathcal{C}$. Enough theorems must be included to enable the implementor to select correct machine code for each construct of the programming language. Each theorem has been proved using algebraic laws of process refinement [9].

3.1 Compiling specification predicate

The compiler of the programming language is specified by the predicate $\mathcal{C}\ p\ s\ f\ m\ \Psi\ \Omega$ where

- p is a process, described as a high-level program.
- s and f are the start and finish addresses of a section of object code in memory to be executed. Note that f is the address immediately *after* the object code.
- $m[s], \ldots, m[f-1]$ is the object code for p. This is denoted $m[s:f)$ for brevity.
- The symbol table Ψ maps each identifier (denoting global variables) of p to its address in the memory M. m (used to store the code) and M (used to store data) must be disjoint.
- Ω is a set of locations of the memory M, which can be used to store the values of local variables or the temporary results during the evaluation of expressions. Here we assume that $ran\Psi$ and Ω are disjoint (i.e., $ran\Psi \cap \Omega = \emptyset$). Thus Ω only contains those addresses which have not been allocated yet; it is the responsibility of the compiler designer to ensure that this is so.

3.2 Theorems of compiling specification

We present some of the theorems of compiling specification for the programming language to machine language translation from [6]. Note that machine language instructions are of variable length; each such instruction is implemented as a sequence of simpler single-byte transputer instructions. In a machine language program the argument of a jump instruction is the byte offset from the *end* of the jump instruction to the *start* of the target instruction. All free variables are assumed to be universally quantified.

Theorems of process compilation:

(1) $\mathcal{C}(\texttt{INT}\ var:\ blk)\ s\ f\ m\ \Psi\ (\{loc\} \uplus \Omega)$ **if**
$\quad \mathcal{C}(blk)\ s\ f\ m\ (\{var \mapsto loc\} \uplus \Psi)\ \Omega$

(2) $\mathcal{C}(\texttt{SKIP})\ s\ f\ m\ \Psi\ \Omega$ **if** $f = s$

(3) $\mathcal{C}(\texttt{STOP})\ s\ f\ m\ \Psi\ \Omega$ **if** $m[s:f) = Mtrans(\texttt{stopp})$

(4) $\mathcal{C}(var := e)\ s\ f\ m\ \Psi\ \Omega$ **if**
$\quad \exists l_1 \cdot\ l_1 \leq f\ \wedge$
$\quad\quad \mathcal{E}(e)\ s\ l_1\ m\ \Psi\ \Omega\ \wedge\ m[l_1:f) = Mtrans(\texttt{stl}(\Psi var))$

(5) $\mathcal{C}(\texttt{SEQ[]})\ s\ f\ m\ \Psi\ \Omega$ **if** $\mathcal{C}(\texttt{SKIP})\ s\ f\ m\ \Psi\ \Omega$

(6) $\mathcal{C}(\texttt{SEQ}[p_1, \ldots, p_n])\ s\ f\ m\ \Psi\ \Omega$ **if**
$\quad \exists l_1 \cdot\ l_1 \leq f\ \wedge$
$\quad\quad \mathcal{C}(p_1)\ s\ l_1\ m\ \Psi\ \Omega\ \wedge\ \mathcal{C}(\texttt{SEQ}[p_2, \ldots, p_n])\ l_1\ f\ m\ \Psi\ \Omega$

(7) $\mathcal{C}(\texttt{IF[]})\, s\, f\, m\, \Psi\, \Omega$ **if** $\mathcal{C}(\texttt{STOP})\, s\, f\, m\, \Psi\, \Omega$

(8) $\mathcal{C}(\texttt{IF}[b_1 \rightarrow p_1, \ldots, b_n \rightarrow p_n])\, s\, f\, m\, \Psi\, \Omega$ **if**

$$\begin{array}{l} \exists l_1, l_2, l_3, l_4 \cdot \quad l_1 \leq l_2 \leq l_3 \leq l_4 \leq f \quad \wedge \\ \quad \mathcal{E}(b_1)\, s\, l_1\, m\, \Psi\, \Omega \quad \wedge \\ \quad m[l_1 : l_2) \;=\; Mtrans(\texttt{cj}(l_4 - l_2)) \quad \wedge \\ \quad \mathcal{C}(p_1)\, l_2\, l_3\, m\, \Psi\, \Omega \quad \wedge \\ \quad m[l_3 : l_4) \;=\; Mtrans(\texttt{j}(f - l_4)) \quad \wedge \\ \quad \mathcal{C}(\texttt{IF}[b_2 \rightarrow p_2, \ldots, b_n \rightarrow p_n])\, l_4\, f\, m\, \Psi\, \Omega \end{array}$$

(9) $\mathcal{C}(\texttt{WHILE}(b, p))\, s\, f\, m\, \Psi\, \Omega$ **if**

$$\begin{array}{l} \exists l_1, l_2, l_3 \cdot \quad l_1 \leq l_2 \leq l_3 \leq f \quad \wedge \\ \quad m[s : l_1) \;=\; Mtrans(\texttt{j}(l_2 - l_1)) \quad \wedge \\ \quad \mathcal{C}(p)\, l_1\, l_2\, m\, \Psi\, \Omega \quad \wedge \\ \quad \mathcal{E}(\texttt{NOT}\ b)\, l_2\, l_3\, m\, \Psi\, \Omega \quad \wedge \\ \quad m[l_3 : f) \;=\; Mtrans(\texttt{cj}(l_1 - f)) \end{array}$$

Theorems of expression compilation follow a similar form. We include a small number of them here as an example. The predicate $\mathcal{E}$ has the same parameters as $\mathcal{C}$, except the first parameter is an expression rather than a process.

Theorems of expression compilation:

(10) $\mathcal{E}(var)\, s\, f\, m\, \Psi\, \Omega$ **if** $m[s : f) \;=\; Mtrans(\texttt{ldl}(\Psi\, var))$

(11) $\mathcal{E}(int)\, s\, f\, m\, \Psi\, \Omega$ **if** $m[s : f) \;=\; Mtrans(\texttt{ldc}(int))$

(12) $\mathcal{E}(\texttt{NOT}\ e)\, s\, f\, m\, \Psi\, \Omega$ **if**

$$\begin{array}{l} \exists l_1, l_2, l_3 \cdot \quad l_1 \leq l_2 \leq l_3 \leq f \quad \wedge \\ \quad \mathcal{E}(e)\, s\, l_1\, m\, \Psi\, \Omega \;\wedge\; m[l_1 : f - 1) \;=\; Mtrans(\texttt{eqc}(0)) \end{array}$$

(13) $\mathcal{E}(e_1 + e_2)\, s\, f\, m\, \Psi\, (\{loc\} \uplus \Omega)$ **if**

$$\begin{array}{l} \exists l_1, l_2, l_3, l_4, l_5 \cdot \quad l_1 \leq l_2 \leq l_3 \leq l_4 \leq l_5 \leq f \quad \wedge \\ \quad \mathcal{E}(e_1)\, s\, l_1\, m\, \Psi\, (\{loc\} \uplus \Omega) \quad \wedge \\ \quad m[l_1 : l_2) \;=\; Mtrans(\texttt{stl}(loc)) \quad \wedge \\ \quad \mathcal{E}(e_2)\, l_2\, l_3\, m\, \Psi\, \Omega \quad \wedge \\ \quad m[l_3 : l_4) \;=\; Mtrans(\texttt{ldl}(loc)) \quad \wedge \\ \quad m[l_4 : l_5) \;=\; Mtrans(\texttt{add}) \quad \wedge \\ \quad m[l_5 : f) \;=\; Mtrans(\texttt{stoperr}) \end{array}$$

4 Compilation Strategy

Section 3.2 presented a number of theorems about the compiling specification predicates $\mathcal{C}$ and $\mathcal{E}$. In this section we discuss how these theorems may be used in actually generating code for the high-level programs. These theorems can function as clauses of a logic program implementing the compiler. To make such an approach practicable, it is necessary to transform the compiling specification (using logic) to derive theorems which may be efficiently "executed". This involves first selecting which parameters will be provided as inputs and which will be expected as outputs. We shall choose to supply the program to be compiled, the desired start address of the object code and the locations available for program variables. The object code and the finish address are to be returned. It may be assumed that the symbol table is initially empty.

The standard search strategy for Prolog is left-to-right and depth-first. To avoid unnecessary backtracking, which is desirable for an efficient implementation, we must ensure that inputs to clauses are provided by outputs (instantiated values) from previous clauses. In most cases, this is easy to do, by simply ordering the clauses appropriately.

However, the transputer has variable-length instruction sequences, depending on the size of the operand. If the operand is known or can be calculated at the time that the instruction sequence is to be generated as object code, then code generation can proceed normally. This is not the case for forward jumps since the length of the jump is unknown until the intervening code has been generated. A solution to this problem is to generate this code into a separate memory, then generate the jump code and relocate the intervening code into the actual object code memory. This is allowable since all the transputer instructions generated by the compiler are relocatable.

4.1 Relocatability of machine code

The following theorems, stating that code generated by the compiler is relocatable, are useful in implementing this strategy. The theorems may be used to find the size of code even when its position in memory is unknown.

$$(14)\quad \mathcal{C}(p)\, s\, f\, m\, \Psi\, \Omega \quad \textbf{if} \\ \qquad \exists s', f', m' \cdot\ \mathcal{C}(p)\, s'\, f'\, m'\, \Psi\, \Omega \ \wedge\ m[s:f) \ =\ m'[s':f')$$

$$(15)\quad \mathcal{E}(e)\, s\, f\, m\, \Psi\, \Omega \quad \textbf{if} \\ \qquad \exists s', f', m' \cdot\ \mathcal{E}(e)\, s'\, f'\, m'\, \Psi\, \Omega \ \wedge\ m[s:f) \ =\ m'[s':f')$$

If a block of memory is relocated, the length of the block is unchanged:

$$(16)\quad (f-s) = (f'-s') \quad \textbf{if} \quad m[s:f) \ =\ m'[s':f')$$

The theorem below can be derived from the above and Theorem 8.

$$\begin{array}{l}(17)\quad \mathcal{C}(\texttt{IF}[b_1 \rightarrow p_1, \ldots, b_n \rightarrow p_n])\, s\, f\, m\, \Psi\, \Omega \quad \textbf{if} \\ \qquad \exists l_1, l_2, l_3, l_4, l_{23}, l_{34}, l_{4f}, m', m'' \cdot \quad l_1 \le l_2 \le l_3 \le l_4 \le f \quad \wedge \\ \qquad\quad \mathcal{E}(b_1)\, s\, l_1\, m\, \Psi\, \Omega \quad \wedge \\ \qquad\quad \mathcal{C}(p_1)\, 0\, l_{23}\, m'\, \Psi\, \Omega \quad \wedge \\ \qquad\quad \mathcal{C}(\texttt{IF}[b_2 \rightarrow p_2, \ldots, b_n \rightarrow p_n]\, 0\, l_{4f}\, m''\, \Psi\, \Omega \quad \wedge \\ \qquad\quad m'[l_{23} : l_{24}) \ =\ Mtrans(\texttt{j}(l_{4f})) \quad \wedge \\ \qquad\quad m[l_1 : l_2) \ =\ Mtrans(\texttt{cj}(l_{24})) \quad \wedge \\ \qquad\quad m[l_2 : l_4) \ =\ m'[0 : l_{24}) \quad \wedge \\ \qquad\quad m[l_4 : f) \ =\ m''[0 : l_{4f})\end{array}$$

4.2 Optimisation of backward jumps

As well is the problem mentioned above concerning forward jumps, there is also a problem concerning backward jumps. This is because the offset of the jump is between the location to be jumped to and *end* of the jump instruction sequence.

Thus the total offset is dependent on the size of the instruction sequence used to implement the jump itself.

The implementation of the **WHILE** construct requires a backward conditional jump "cj". We first formulate a scheme for optimising backward jumps. Let s be the target address of the jump, and let l be the start address for the cj instruction. We design a function *BackJump* which has the following properties:

$$\begin{aligned} & s \leq l \leq f \\ & Size(\mathtt{cj}(s-f)) = (f-l) \\ & BackJump(s,l) = (s-f) \end{aligned}$$

These can be solved to give the following specification of *BackJump*:

$$\begin{aligned} & l - s = 0 \Rightarrow BackJump(s,l) = -2 \\ & 0 \leq i \wedge (16^i - i) \leq (l-s) < 16^{i+1} - (i+1) \Rightarrow \\ & \quad BackJump(s,l) = -(i+2+(l-s)) \end{aligned}$$

We may now formulate a compiling specification for the **WHILE** construct as follows:

$$\begin{aligned} (18)\ & \mathcal{C}(\mathtt{WHILE}(b,p))\, s\, f\, m\, \Psi\, \Omega \ \ \textbf{if} \\ & \quad \exists l_1, l_2, l_3, l_{12}, m' \cdot \ l_1 \leq l_2 \leq l_3 \leq f \quad \wedge \\ & \quad \mathcal{C}(p)\, 0\, l_{12}\, m'\, \Psi\, \Omega \quad \wedge \\ & \quad m[s:l_1) = Mtrans(\mathtt{j}(l_{12})) \quad \wedge \\ & \quad m[l_1:l_2) = m'[0:l_{12}) \quad \wedge \\ & \quad \mathcal{E}(\mathtt{NOT}\ b)\, l_2\, l_3\, m\, \Psi\, \Omega \quad \wedge \\ & \quad m[l_3:f) = Mtrans(\mathtt{cj}(BackJump(l_1, l_3))) \end{aligned}$$

The compiling specification theorems for the IF and **WHILE** constructs outlined in this section, together with the other original theorems in section 3.2, have been used to implement a compiler in the logic programming language Prolog. Extracts of this compiler are included in section 5.

4.3 Jumps in general

Astute readers will have noticed that the **WHILE** loop was compiled in a slightly non-standard manner. Instead of immediately checking the loop expression and then conditionally jumping out of the loop, the expression check is negated and placed at the end of the code. This avoids the problems of having two interlocking jumps, the size of each of which is dependent on the other. Since the compiler only generates a standard set of jump sequences, we can benefit from this fact, avoid interlocking jumps, and generate code in a single pass. If arbitrary jumps are allowed, as in an assembler for instance, the situation is much worse, and a multipass strategy is necessary if optimal jumps are to be generated. The standard methods are to start with zero-sized jumps and gradually increase their size at each pass, or start with maximal-sized jumps and gradually reduce their size until a fixed-point is reached. The former is better for reaching an optimal solution [4]. Details of the verification of assembling a subset of **transputer** instructions may be found in [19].

The problems of forward and backward jumps mentioned in this paper are peculiar to the **transputer** because of their variable length depending on the size of the jump if one wishes to produce optimised code. If the maximal size were allocated for the jump instructions, or the machine did not include variable length jump instructions (as is the case for many processors) then these problems would not arise. Indeed, it would then be possible to make use of logical variables as discussed in [12] for the forward jumps, which could be instantiated with the correct value later in the program's execution when the value became known. However, no *real* compiler for the **transputer** would leave jumps unoptimised, so it was felt desirable to present a compiling specification with a realistic level of optimisation.

5 Prolog Implementation

The idea of using Prolog [15] for the construction of compilers has been accepted for some time [20]. Advantages include the fact that the code for the compiler can be very close to the compiling specification and thus the confidence in its correctness is increased. It can be used both for a prototype compiler and even for a "real" compiler since the Prolog code itself may be transformed and compiled for increased efficiency [16].

The following sections include parts of a Prolog compiler from the programming language to the machine instruction set which follows the compiling specification outlined in section 3.2 as closely as possible. The strategy presented in section 4 is followed to produce a working compiler. Efficiency has sometimes been sacrificed for clarity in the example that follows to aid the reader.

5.1 Process compilation

Each program construct is compiled using a separate Prolog clause. Individual instructions are assembled using the `mtrans` function. Prolog clauses are relations rather than functions in general. However, in the interest of readability, functions in the specification have been implemented using an infix operator "`:=`" which may be invoked as follows:

$$output := function(inputs)$$

Prolog may be used to simulate interpreted functions by substituting Prolog *functors* in place of the *function*, and even within the *inputs* above, and then encoding the lower-level clauses to handle all the different cases of functors used in this manner. This allows the higher-level clauses to be encoded in a form that is very close to the original theorems. Additionally, because of the relational and undirectional nature of Prolog, it is sometimes possible to provide the output and infer the inputs instead, with the usual provisos concerning the use of negation by failure and irreversible clauses.

Declarations cause a free location in Ω to be allocated in Ψ. These are implemented as *lists*; in general any free location may be extracted from Ω, but we choose to extract the first element for efficiency, the reasoning being that a more deterministic program is "better" than a less deterministic one.

```
c(int Var: Blk,S,F,M,Psi,[Loc|Omega]) :-
    c(Blk,S,F,M,[Var->Loc|Psi],Omega).
```

Variables that are only mentioned once are normally indicated by a "_" in Prolog.

```
c(skip,S,F,_,_,_) :- F=S.
```

Constraints on the ordering of intermediate locations l_i may be omitted in practice since the ordering is automatically ensured by **mtrans**.

```
c(stop,S,F,M,_,_) :- M@(S:F) := mtrans(stopp).

c(Var:=E,S,F,M,Psi,Omega) :-
  e(E,S,L1,M,Psi,Omega), M@(L1:F) := mtrans(stl(Psi@Var)).

c(seq[],S,F,M,Psi,Omega) :- c(skip,S,F,M,Psi,Omega).

c(seq[P|Ps],S,F,M,Psi,Omega) :-
  c(P,S,L1,M,Psi,Omega), c(seq Ps,L1,F,M,Psi,Omega).
```

The **if** and **while** constructs involve variable-length jump instructions that must be handled slightly differently from the specification in order to produce an efficiently executable program. More details concerning the implementation of the relocation of memory are included later. **backjump** implements the *BackJump* function.

```
c(if[],S,F,M,Psi,Omega) :- c(stop,S,F,M,Psi;Omega).

c(if[B->P|BPs],S,F,M,Psi,Omega) :-
  e(B,S,L1,M,Psi,Omega),
  c(P,0,L23,M1,Psi,Omega),
  c(if BPs,0,L4f,M2,Psi,Omega),
  Mp@(L23:L24) := mtrans(j(L4f)),
  M@(L1:L2) := mtrans(cj(L24)),
  M@(L2:L4) := M1@(0:L24),
  M@(L4:F)  := M2@(0:L4f).

c(while(B,P),S,F,M,Psi,Omega) :-
  c(P,0,L12,M1,Psi,Omega),
  M@(S:L1)  := mtrans(j(L12)),
  M@(L1:L2) := M1@(0:L12),
  e(not B,L2,L3,M,Psi,Omega),
  M@(L3:F)  := mtrans(cj(backjump(L1,L3))).
```

Expressions are handled separately and straightforwardly [6]. E.g.:

```
e(Var,S,F,M,Psi,_) :- M@(S:F) := mtrans(ldl(Psi@Var)).

e(Int,S,F,M,_,_) :- M@(S:F) := mtrans(ldc(Int)).

e(not E,S,F,M,Psi,Omega) :-
  e(E,S,L1,M,Psi,Omega), M@(L1:F) := mtrans(eqc(0)).
```

```
e(E1+E2,S,F,M,Psi,[Loc|Omega]) :-
  e(E1,S,L1,M,Psi,[Loc|Omega]),
  M@(L1:L2) := mtrans(stl(Loc)),
  e(E2,L2,L3,M,Psi,Omega),
  M@(L3:L4) := mtrans(ldl(Loc)),
  M@(L4:L5) := mtrans(add),
  M@(L5:F)  := mtrans(stoperr).
```

The first entry in the free memory list is selected for the temporary storage location for efficiency. In general, any free location in the list could be extracted of course; this would result in a non-deterministic program.

5.2 Transputer instructions

Each instruction `Ins` is located at a particular byte address `S` in a memory `M`. The sequence of basic byte instructions, including all necessary prefixed `nfix` and `pfix` instructions must be calculated; the position of any following instructions `F` is then known. Each instruction is assembled into a list of byte values `Code` which is subsequently set in memory.

```
M@(S:F) := mtrans(Ins) :-
  Ins := ins(Op,Operand),
  W := Operand,
  Minstr := ins(Op,W),
  instr(Minstr),
  Code := prefix(Op,W),
  M@(S:F) := code(Code).

M@(S:F) := mtrans(Opr) :-
  operation(Opr),
  Operand := operand(Opr),
  Code := prefix(opr,Operand),
  M@(S:F) := code(Code).
```

Happily, bitwise arithmetic for conjunction (x/\\y), complement (\\(x)), shifting (x>>y), etc., are provided by Quintus Prolog:

```
[I] := prefix(Op,W) :- 0=<W, W<16, I := ins(Op,W).

Prefix := prefix(Op,W) :-
  W>=16, X is W>>4, Y is (W/\15), I := ins(Op,Y),
  P := prefix(pfix,X), append(P,[I],Prefix).

Prefix := prefix(Op,W) :-
  W<0, X is \(W)>>4, Y is (W/\15), I := ins(Op,Y),
  P := prefix(nfix,X), append(P,[I],Prefix).

Operand := operand(Minstr) :-
  instr(Minstr), Minstr := ins(_,Operand).

Operand := operand(Minstr) :-
  operation(Minstr), operationOpCode(Minstr,Operand).
```

An instruction may be split into its name and its operand using the built-in Prolog operator "=.." for splitting and combining Prolog functors:

```
Ins := ins(Op,W) :- Ins =.. [Op,W].
```

5.3 Correspondence between variables and memory locations

The memory location **Loc** for a particular variable **Var** may be retrieved from the symbol table Ψ using the following Prolog code:

```
Loc := ([Var->Loc|_]@Var).

Loc := ([Var0->_|Psi]@Var) :-
  Var\==Var0, Loc := (Psi@Var).
```

It is assumed that the symbol table is fully instantiated at the time of the call, and thus the negation `Var\==Var0` may be used safely.

Operands may simply consist of an integer value, in which case the identify function suffices:

```
Int := Int :- integer(Int).
```

integer is a built-in Prolog clause that is only true if its argument is instantiated to an integer value.

5.4 Machine instructions

The class of instructions is defined as:

```
instr(ldc(W))  :- integer(W).
instr(ldl(W))  :- integer(W).
instr(stl(W))  :- integer(W).
instr(eqc(W))  :- integer(W).
instr(j(W))    :- integer(W).
instr(cj(W))   :- integer(W).
...
```

The class of operations is defined as:

```
operation(stopp).
operation(stoperr).
operation(add).
...
```

The combination of these give the available machine language instructions:

```
instrML(Minstr) :- instr(Minstr).
instrML(Minstr) :- operation(Minstr).
```

The basic byte-sized transputer instructions are:

```
instrTR(Tinstr)   :-
  instr(Tinstr), Tinstr := ins(_,W), nibble(W).

instrTR(opr(W))   :- nibble(W).
instrTR(pfix(W))  :- nibble(W).
instrTR(nfix(W))  :- nibble(W).

nibble(W) :- 0=<W, W<16.
```

5.5 Relocation of machine code

Compilation may proceed in a straightforward sequential manner following the original specification directly except where forward jump instructions (`j` and `cj`) are involved. This occurs in the case of `IF` and `WHILE` constructs. In these cases the size of the relative jump and hence the size of the jump instruction itself are not known in advance.

The solution adopted in the Prolog program is to first compile the code which is to be jumped over into a separate piece of memory, starting at location zero for convenience. This temporary memory may subsequently be relocated into the actual position in memory once the jump instruction involved has been calculated and the real location (following the jump instruction) is known. This is possible because all the instructions in the machine language are relocatable; that is to say, they have the same effect wherever they are in memory.

The following Prolog code relocates a list of instructions from `S0` up to (but not including) `F0` in memory `M0` into `M`, starting at position `S` and ending at `F`:

```
_@(S:S) := _@(S0:S0).

M@(S:F) := M0@(S0:F0) :-
  S0<F0,
  M0@(S0) := code(I), S01 is S0+1,
  M@(S)   := code(I), S1  is S+1,
  M@(S1:F) := M0@(S01:F0).
```

A code sequence may be loaded into a memory:

```
_@(S:S) := code([]).

M@(S:F) := code([I|R]) :-
  M@S := code(I), S1 is S+1, M@(S1:F) := code(R).
```

An individual byte-sized instruction may be loaded into a single location in memory:

```
[I|_]@0 := code(I).

[_|M]@N := code(I) :-
  integer(N), N>0, N_1 is N-1, M@N_1 := code(I).
```

5.6 Backward jumps

Backward jumps occur only in `WHILE` loops in the programming language. Here the distance of the jump from the *start* position of the jump instruction is known. However the jump is actually effective from the *end* position of the jump instruction which depends on the size of the backward offset to be jumped.

```
-2 := backjump(S,L) :- 0 is L-S.

BackJump := backjump(S,L) :-
  I := upto(7), I16 := 16^I,
  I16-I =< L-S, L-S < 16*I16-(I+1),
  BackJump is -(I+2+(L-S)).
```

Note that the minimum size of instruction for a backward jump is two bytes, even for a zero offset (from the beginning of the instruction) [18].

To enable the code to terminate in finite time, a maximum value for `I` of seven is assumed in this example. (This allows 32-bit address.)

```
0 := upto(N) :- N>=0.

I := upto(N) :-
  N>0, N_1 is N-1, I_1 := upto(N_1), I is I_1+1.
```

Standard Prolog does not normally implement a power operator in arithmetic, and thus this must be coded explicitly:

```
1 := _^0.
Z := X^N :- N>0, N_1 is N-1, Y := X^N_1, Z is X*Y.
```

The code for `backjump` could be further optimised if desired to avoid the backtracking involved in checking all the possible values of `I`.

5.7 Performance

A half-page program compiles to object code in memory locations in about a second using compiled Quintus Prolog [16] on a Sun SPARCstation. However the performance of the prototype compiler is not linear with the size of input. It has been formulated to be as close to the original compiling specification as possible to help ensure its correctness. This is acceptable for a prototype, but further semantics-preserving transformations would be necessary to produce something approaching a "real" compiler. Prolog has been found to be especially suitable for code generation and can be in the same order of magnitude of efficiency as conventional imperative programming languages when used for this purpose [21].

6 Discussion

In this paper, we have outlined a compiling specification for a simple subset of the occam programming language and its rapid implementation using logic programming. The compiling specification is given as a set of theorems that have been proved using algebraic laws of process refinement. The complete specification as well as the full correctness proof may be found in [6]. Further work investigating more complicated language constructs such as recursion may be found in [9].

There are several advantages in following this approach:

- Each theorem and its proof is independent of the other theorems. This modularity is important if the verification method is to be practicable. The specification, its proof and the program can be developed one theorem and clause at a time. New theorems can be added to capture different ways of compiling the same construct. For example, the specification may be extended with the following theorem.

  (19) $\mathcal{C}(\texttt{SKIP})\, s\, f\, m\, \Psi\, \Omega$ **if**
  $\exists l_1 \cdot l_1 \leq f \;\wedge\; m[s : l_1) \;=\; Mtrans(\mathtt{j}(f - l_1))$

  The compiler algorithm can then generate code using any of the alternative theorems; or possibly using several of them, choosing the "best" (e.g., the smallest) code. For example, the following theorem applies to **IF** clauses where one of the guards is **TRUE** since subsequent guards can be ignored:

  (20) $\mathcal{C}(\texttt{IF}[\texttt{TRUE} \rightarrow p_1, \ldots, b_n \rightarrow p_n])\, s\, f\, m\, \Psi\, \Omega$ **if** $\mathcal{C}(p_1)\, s\, f\, m\, \Psi\, \Omega$

  A logic program defines a relation between the parameters of its clauses and thus may be non-deterministic in general. The prototype compiler could be used as a *compiler checker* to compare the output generated by a particular compiler implementation, thus increasing the confidence in the correctness of a particular compilation by that compiler. Alternatively, a code selection mechanism could decide which compilation should be chosen [22].

- The compiling specification for this programming language subset and its correctness proof are envisaged to be valid even for a larger language such as occam. The proofs given in [6, 9] will remain valid provided that the algebraic laws continue to hold for the full language.

The form of compiling specification is very similar to a logic program, with each theorem corresponding to a clause. However, such literal translation of the specification into a logic program may be inefficient. Hence, a strategy for executing the specification has been devised where necessary and a prototype Prolog compiler has been developed following this strategy. We have not given here a formal proof, but rather a rigorous argument that the compiler satisfies the compiling specification [11]. A more formal proof could be attempted since the Prolog compiler is very close to the compiling specification. Of course, the resulting compiler will generate "verified code" only if the compiler itself is executed on a trusted implementation of Prolog (which itself must be running on trusted hardware). In the practical use of formal methods, an engineering decision must be made as to where formal proofs are beneficial to increase the confidence of the correctness of a product within the prevailing financial constraints of a particular project.

6.1 The future

Some aspects of practical logic programming using Prolog involve using clauses in which one or more parameters must be instantiated at the time of invocation of the clause. For instance, the infix "`is`" clause for evaluating arithmetic expressions is actually nothing more than the standard assignment statement in imperative programming; the left-hand side must be instantiated before use. Such features restrict the modes in which the Prolog clauses can be used. More recent research has concentrated on mechanisms to make logic programs more declarative. For instance, *constraint logic programming* [23] allows extra constraints over a particular domain to be added to each of the clauses. Such systems are now becoming commercially available [24]. This enables, for example, more declarative arithmetic to be included if constraints on numerical expressions are allowed. This in turn means that clauses may be used in a more versatile manner.

As an example of this more declarative approach, instead of supplying a high-level program and returning the corresponding object code, it is possible to do just the opposite, and thus obtain a *decompiler* [25]. This is even possible using standard Prolog, although, care must be taken to ensure termination, for example, when negation by failure is used; in addition, irreversible clauses like the arithmetic "`is`" clause must be recoded. A decompiler could be useful in the area of *reverse engineering* during the software maintenance process if the original source program has been lost or if existing low-level code is to be verified. Of course, some semantics-preserving transformations of the logic program will normally still be necessary to produce a useful decompiler in practice.

The compiler presented here has been rigorously developed, but ongoing research into the synthesis of logic programs from inductive proofs [26] and also the study of termination of logic programs [27] could ensure even more confidence in the correctness of the compiler. The scalability of such approaches will be important if they are to be used in practice.

Despite the fact that generated instructions are optimised in length, much further optimisation could be considered. In particular, the issues of expression optimisation could be addressed by providing a number of theorems which could be selectively applied.

As well as targeting the code to a processor such as the transputer, it is also possible to compile a language like occam directly into hardware, in the form of a *netlist* of simple components such as Boolean gates and latches [28]. These netlists may be encoded into a form that can be loaded directly into a *Field Programmable Gate Array* (FPGA). These devices contain a memory that may be loaded under computer control with an object "program" like any other more standard memory. However, the code defines interconnections of components within the chip so that a hardware circuit may be configured (and also reconfigured) very rapidly (in the order of milliseconds). This approach enables parallel constructs to be compiled truly concurrently, thus allowing the possibility of greatly speeding up some algorithms. Because the size of FPGAs is limited (currently to around 10,000 gate-equivalents), and because interconnectability between FPGAs is limited by the number of I/O pins available on each chip, it will also be desirable to produce compilers that produce hybrid code for both a standard processor and programmable hardware. This technology is likely to become much more widely used in the next decade and will provide compiler writers with new problems to investigate and solve in the area of code generation.

Acknowledgements

Thank you to Prof. Tony Hoare, He Jifeng and Paritosh Pandya (now at the Tata Institute of Fundamental Research, Bombay, India) for their contribution to the work presented here. Mark Josephs suggested the reordering of the `WHILE` loop code. The anonymous reviewer provided helpful and constructive comments.

The work was undertaken as part of the European ESPRIT BRA **ProCoS** ("Provably Correct Systems") project [29] and the UK IED **safemos** project. The financial support of the IED **safemos** project (no. IED3/1/1036) is gratefully acknowledged.

Copies of **ProCoS** project deliverables are available from the project coordinator: Department of Computer Science, Technical University of Denmark, Building 344Ø, DK-2800 Lyngby, Denmark.

References

[1] Hoare CAR. Refinement algebra proves correctness of compiling specifications. In: Morgan CC, Woodcock JCP (eds) 3rd Refinement Workshop. Springer-Verlag, 1991, pp 33–48 (Workshops in computing)

[2] He Jifeng. Specification oriented semantics for the ProCoS level 0 language. ESPRIT BRA ProCoS project document [OU HJF 5], Oxford University Computing Laboratory, UK, 1990

[3] INMOS Limited. Occam 2 Reference Manual. Prentice Hall International Series in Computer Science, 1988

[4] INMOS Limited. Transputer instruction set: A compiler writer's guide. Prentice-Hall International, 1988

[5] Roscoe AW, Hoare CAR. Laws of occam programming. Theoretical Comput Sci 1988; 60:177–229

[6] He Jifeng, Pandya PK, Bowen JP. Compiling specification for ProCoS level 0 language. ESPRIT BRA ProCoS project document [OU HJF 4], Oxford University Computing Laboratory, UK, 1990

[7] Bowen JP, He Jifeng, Pandya PK. An approach to verifiable compiling specification and prototyping. In: Deransart P, Małuszyński J (eds) Programming Language Implementation and Logic Programming. International Workshop PLILP 90. Springer-Verlag, 1990, pp 45–59 (Lecture notes in computer science no. 456)

[8] Hoare CAR, He Jifeng, Bowen JP, Pandya PK. An algebraic approach to verifiable compiling specification and prototyping of the ProCoS level 0 programming language. In: Directorate-General of the Commission of

the European Communities (eds) ESPRIT '90 Conference Proceedings, Brussels. Kluwer Academic Publishers B.V., 1990, pp 804–818

[9] He Jifeng, Olderog ER (eds). ESPRIT BRA 3104 Provably Correct Systems ProCoS Draft Final Deliverable, vol 2, Interfaces between Languages for Concurrent Systems. 1991 (To be published)

[10] von Karger B (ed). ESPRIT BRA 3104 Provably Correct Systems ProCoS Draft Final Deliverable, vol 3, Compiler Development. 1991 (To be published)

[11] The Procurement of Safety Critical Software in Defence Equipment, Interim Defence Standard 00-55. Ministry of Defence, Directorate of Standardization. Kentigern House, 65 Brown Street, Glasgow G2 8EX, UK, 1991

[12] van Emden MH, Kowalski RA. The semantics of predicate logic as a programming language. J ACM 1976; 23(4):733–742

[13] Lloyd JW. Foundations of Logic Programming, 2nd edition. Springer-Verlag, 1987

[14] Hogger CJ. Essentials of Logic Programming. Oxford University Press, 1990

[15] Clocksin WF, Mellish CS. Programming in Prolog, 3rd edition. Springer-Verlag, 1987

[16] Quintus Prolog – Sun 4 User Manual, Release 2.5. Quintus Computer Systems, Inc., Mountain View, California, USA, 1990

[17] Bowen JP. Formal specification of the ProCoS/safemos instruction set. Microprocessors and Microsystems 1990; 14(10):631–643

[18] Nicoud J-D, Tyrrell AM. The transputer T414 instruction set. IEEE Micro 1989; 9(3):60–75

[19] Pandya PK, He Jifeng. A simulation approach to verification of assembling specification of ProCoS level 0 language. ESPRIT BRA ProCoS project document [OU PKP 3], Oxford University Computing Laboratory, UK, 1990

[20] Warren DHD. Logic programming and compiler writing. Software—Practice and Experience 1980; 10:97–125

[21] Paakki J. Prolog in practical compiler writing. The Computer Journal 1991; 34(1):64–72

[22] Giegerich R. Considerate code selection. In: Giegerich R, Graham SL (eds) CODE'91 Proc. International Workshop on Code Generation. Springer-Verlag, 1992 (Workshops in computing, this volume)

[23] Cohen J. Constraint Logic Programming languages. Commun ACM 1990; 33(7):52–68

[24] Colmerauer A. An introduction to Prolog III. Commun ACM 1990; 33(7):69–90

[25] Bowen JP, Breuer PT. Decompilation. In: van Zuylen H (ed) The REDO Handbook: A Compendium of Reverse Engineering for Software Maintenance, chapter 9, Wiley, 1992 (To appear)

[26] Bundy A, Smaill A, Wiggins G. The Synthesis of Logic Programs from Inductive Proofs. In: Lloyd, JW (ed) Computational Logic. Springer-Verlag, 1990, pp 135–149 (Basic research series)

[27] Apt KR, Pedreschi D. Studies in pure Prolog: Termination. In: Lloyd JW (ed) Computational Logic. Springer-Verlag, 1990, pp 150–176 (Basic research series)

[28] Page I, Luk W. Compiling Occam into field-programmable gate arrays. in Moore W, Luk W (eds), FPGAs, Oxford Workshop on Field Programmable Logic and Applications. Abingdon EE&CS Books, 15 Harcourt Way, Abingdon OX14 1NV, UK, 1991

[29] Bjørner D. A ProCoS project description: ESPRIT BRA 3104. Bulletin of the EATCS 1989; 39:60–73

An Approach to Automatic Proof Support for Code Generator Verification

Bettina Buth Karl-Heinz Buth

Institut für Informatik und Praktische Mathematik
Christian-Albrechts-Universität zu Kiel
Preußerstr.1-9, W-2300 Kiel 1, Germany
email: bb@causun.uucp, khb@causun.uucp

Abstract

In principle, program verification is the only adequate means to ensure the correctness of software with respect to precise specifications. But since realistic programs such as code generators and other parts of compilers tend to be large and complex, some mechanical support is necessary for the verification of these programs. In this paper we present the ideas of the verification support system PAMELA that is intended for the verification of programs written in a subset of Meta IV that are specified by pre- and postconditions. PAMELA organizes the proof for such programs and is based on a special kind of term rewriting.

1 Introduction

The increasing use of computer systems, especially in safety related applications, leads to increasing demands on their reliability. To ensure this property high level specification techniques and programming languages are employed. This also leads to stronger requirements for the correctness of compilers and code generators.

The safest way to ensure the correctness of all kinds of software is rigorous development including program verification. This means an accurate correctness proof of a program with respect to a formal specification. Specifying a code generator is usually straightforward: the generated code must be syntactically correct and semantically equivalent to the original program. The equivalence predicate usually takes into account that for the overall correctness certain properties of the target program (such as final states of auxiliary variables) can be disregarded.

But code generators, as most realistic programs, are large and involved, and therefore verification becomes very complex. This means that it is impracticable to do the verification for code generators and other parts of a compiler completely by hand. At least some mechanical support is necessary. But such a support system requires that the program to be proved and all necessary information be supplied in a suitable formal way.

We are developing a proof support system that is applicable for programs written in a subset of the specification language Meta IV [2]. Meta IV is the predecessor of the standardized specification language VDM-SL [9] used in VDM (the *Vienna Development Method*). The philosophy of VDM is to develop software by stepwise refinement starting with a set of pre- and postconditions which are intended as the specification of a set of function definitions. The programs resulting from this development must be correct with respect to their specification, i.e. each function definition with respect to its pre- and post-conditions. The starting point for our work were partial correctness proofs for code generators in the CAT system [18, 19, 20].

Our aim is to construct a proof system that can easily be understood even by persons not acquainted with the theory of program verification, that needs a minimum of additional information and that can deal with program texts without having to transform them. The system PAMELA (*Proof Assistant for Meta IV-like Languages*) is mainly based on term rewriting, i.e. information necessary for the proofs is stated in form of conditional rewrite rules. In addition to the program, PAMELA requires a pair of pre- and postconditions for each function contained that form the invariants for the proof. Furthermore, rules have to be stated that in an appropriate way describe the application area of the program.

This paper is organized as follows: In the next section we describe the subset of Meta IV that PAMELA can handle, followed by a brief description of the CAT system and a short survey of the theoretical background. After a small example, the main ideas of the proof system are introduced including an example from the code generator verification. The last section contains a conclusion comprising a short comparison with other systems.

2 Meta IV'

The language Meta IV [2] is a very high level specification language originating from VDM [14]. At the University of Kiel it was essentially used for the formal specification of partially automated compiler generation within the CAT system [see section 3]. Compilers of this kind have been developed and are employed by Norsk Data. The subset of Meta IV (called *Meta IV'*) that PAMELA can handle comprises all constructs that are used in the specification of code generators in the CAT system. Meta IV' is an expression language, i.e. there is no distinction between expressions and statements; a program is a set of recursive function definitions together with a set of global variables.

Meta IV' contains the following constructs:

- constants,
- global variables,
- conditionals (`IF-THEN-ELSE` , McCarthy conditionals)
- `LET`-expressions (non-recursive),
- recursive function definitions,
- function calls,
- assignments,

- sequential composition.

The semantics of these constructs is the usual one (applying a call-by-value strategy).

The main restriction of this subset of Meta IV is that no loop constructs (**REPEAT**, **WHILE** etc.) are allowed. Furthermore we demand that predicates must not have side-effects on global variables.

3 The CAT System

The CAT system is a multi-language multi-target compiler generating system. It has been developed by U. Schmidt and R. Völler at the University of Kiel between 1980 and 1983. Here, we will only give a very brief survey of it; for details see [18, 19, 20].

The basic idea of the system is to compile a program of a high level imperative language in two separate steps. In the first step, the programs of the source language (e.g. PASCAL, C, Basic) are compiled by a target machine independent *front-end* into a common intermediate language called *CAT* (*Common Abstract Tree language*). In the second step, CAT programs are translated by machine dependent *back-ends* or code generators into the target language (assembler format, linker format, machine code, etc.).

In the following, we only consider the code generators. Hence, we start from a CAT program and deal with its translation into the target language for a certain machine M. This phase is again separated into several subphases. First, declarations and higher level statements are evaluated (machine independent except for the variable allocation that has to respect the memory structure of M). The result of this step is a program of another intermediate language called $\mathrm{CAL}_{\mathrm{CAT}}$. CAL (*CAT Assembly Language*) is a language scheme parameterized with a signature. CAL programs consist of sequences of assignments (of arbitrary complexity), jumps, and procedure and label statements. The signature of $\mathrm{CAL}_{\mathrm{CAT}}$ is derived from the source language CAT, and is therefore machine independent.

In the next phase, $\mathrm{CAL}_{\mathrm{CAT}}$ is translated into $\mathrm{CAL}_{\mathrm{M}}$, the signature of which is determined by the target machine M. At first, the machine independent $\mathrm{CAL}_{\mathrm{CAT}}$ operators are substituted by suitable machine dependent $\mathrm{CAL}_{\mathrm{M}}$ operators (*substitution phase*), and then the resulting (still complex) $\mathrm{CAL}_{\mathrm{M}}$ expressions are split into sequences of simple $\mathrm{CAL}_{\mathrm{M}}$ expressions (*decomposition phase*). These simple $\mathrm{CAL}_{\mathrm{M}}$ expressions are translated 1:1 into the target language in the third phase of code generation. Summing up the structure of a compiler in the CAT system, we come to the diagram in Figure 1.

The code generator specifications are written in Meta IV'. Hence they are systems of recursive function declarations with a set of global variables (e.g. for the registers). In addition to the functions for the two phases *substitution* and *decomposition* there are some predicates for controlling the translation (mainly the *is-wellformed-predicates*, describing the static semantics of $\mathrm{CAL}_{\mathrm{CAT}}$ and $\mathrm{CAL}_{\mathrm{M}}$ expressions). The specifications become executable by translating them into PASCAL and including this code into a general compiler frame. The main data type of the specification is that of CAL "typed expressions" (*Te*). These are trees consisting of an operator, a result type (*mode*), and a finite number of subexpressions. The primitive operations available contain constructor (*mk-*), selector (*sel-*), and recognizer (*is-*) functions.

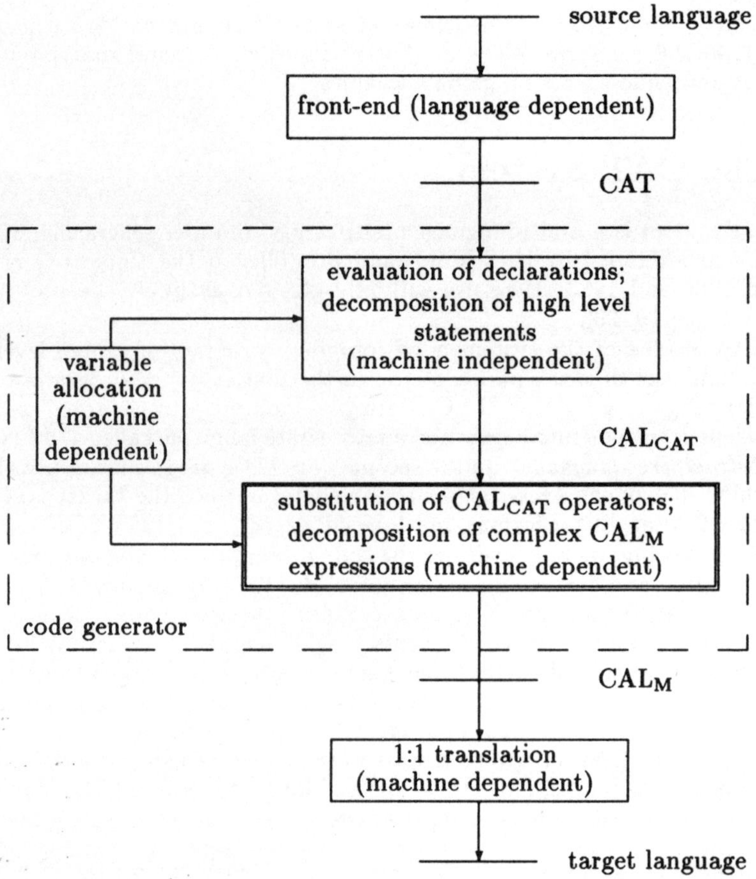

Figure 1: Structure of the CAT-system

As a working example we have used a simplified code generator for the translation of PASCAL into MC68000 assembler. So, we have to deal with CAL_{CAT} and CAL_M, where M is the MC68000 processor. The parts we are concerned with are

- the ***substitution functions***: for each possible CAL_{CAT} operator there is a special function that selects the corresponding CAL_M operator;
- the ***decomposition functions***: for each possible operator of an expression resulting from the substitution phase there is a special decomposition function,
- predicates used for controlling the phases (e.g. *is-well-formed* functions),

- the *mop-map*, containing the information which substitution or decomposition function is to be used for which operator (*mop* is the set of all CAL operators),
- type declarations and (PASCAL) code for some primitive operators.

An example for a substitution function is given in Figure 2.

```
.1 subst-addi (e) =
.2  LET e1  = sel-e1 (e),
.3      e2  = sel-e2 (e),
.4      m   = sel-mode (e),
.5      len = max (sel-len (e1), sel-len (e2))
.6  IN
.7    ( is-quick-pos (e1)
.8        -> mk-exp2 (ADDQ, sel-mode (e2),
.9                          e1,
.10                         subst-cat-ops (e2))
      , ...
.11   , is-quick-neg (e2)
.12       -> mk-exp2 (SUBQ, sel-mode (e1),
.13                         c-neg (e2),
.14                         subst-cat-ops (e1))

.15   , (is-subrmode (sel-mode (e1)) AND
.16      is-subrmode (sel-mode (e2)) )
.17       -> mk-exp2 (ADD, set-modelen (m, len),
.18                        subst-cat-ops (e1),
.19                        subst-cat-ops (e2))
      , ...
.20   , TRUE
.21       -> wrong (''illegal operand'')
      )

.22 TYPE: Te -> Te
```

Figure 2: Example for a substitution function

This function is the substitution function for $\mathrm{CAL}_{\mathrm{CAT}}$ expressions with operator **ADDI** or **ADDO**, denoting simple integer addition or integer addition with overflow check. The parameter of the function, **e**, is a $\mathrm{CAL}_{\mathrm{CAT}}$ expression (**Te**, see .22). Both of the two subexpressions and the mode are selected in the **LET**, which is a declaration of local constants. The body of the function (.7-.21) is a conditional, describing the selection of a machine dependent operator that is to be replaced for the original one. This selection is determined by the subcomponents. In the first case (.7-.10), the selection is defined for the case where the first subexpression **e1** is a small integer constant in the range of 1 to 8. In this case, we can choose the fastest addition operator available (**ADDQ**, "add quick").

A new expression is built with this operator, a suitable mode and two subexpressions. The first subexpression **e1** is the unmodified first subexpression of **e**; the second is the result of substituting the second subexpression **e2**. The function **subst-cat-ops** (.10) is the main function of the substitution phase; here we have a recursive call of another specification function. The two other cases are similar. In the second case (.11-.14) the second subexpression of **e** is a small negative integer constant between -8 and -1. Here we selected fast subtraction (**SUBQ**) and hence the constant has to be negated (.13). The third case (.15-.19) is the most general case. No special properties of the operands can be exploited, and hence the general addition operator (**ADD**) is selected. Both subcomponents have to be treated in the recursion. The predicates **is-quick-pos** (.7), **is-quick-neg** (.11) and **is-subrmode** (.15,.16) are examples for predicates that are used for controlling the substitution process. The last clause (.20,.21) is the error clause of the function. The case selectors of the other clauses, together with the precondition of the function, have to guarantee that this clause can never be reached.

The result of the substitution process is a CAL expression that is neither $\mathrm{CAL}_{\mathrm{CAT}}$ nor $\mathrm{CAL}_{\mathrm{M}}$: the operators are machine operators, but the complexity is not that of $\mathrm{CAL}_{\mathrm{M}}$, so they are $\mathrm{CAL}_{\mathrm{M}}$ expressions, but are not well-formed. The decomposition of these expressions is done in the decomposition phase.

4 Theoretical Background

It is part of the philosophy of VDM to develop functions (and whole programs as well) by first specifying them through pre- and postconditions. Afterwards a function (or set of functions) is developed that satisfies these pre- and postconditions, i.e. a function whose result satisfies the postcondition whenever the input that leads to this result satisfies the precondition.

For the proof of code generator specifications of the CAT system it was necessary to supply the pre- and postconditions for each function afterwards (since they are not developed by refinement from a specification). In this case one must be very careful to choose them since otherwise the proof might fail because the conditions are not strong enough.

These pre- and postconditions form the invariants, the unchangeable information that is necessary for the proof. Both are predicates, possibly of higher order predicate calculus. The precondition describes which restrictions are to be fulfilled by the input to guarantee a correct result (in the sense of the specification); the postcondition describes the result of the function and its side-effects, for example the status of global variables after the execution of the function (usually in terms of the values before the execution).

Since the programs to be proved are sets of recursive functions, their meaning can be defined as a fixed point. Therefore, it is possible to employ Scott's Fixpoint Induction method [1, 15] for the partial correctness proof. Partial correctness means that if the program terminates then it fulfils the requirements (in contrast to total correctness: the program terminates and fulfils the requirements).

The result of these theoretical considerations is that for the proof of partial correctness it remains to show that each function **f** of a program satisfies its pre- and postcondition. For these smaller proofs we can use as an induction hypothesis the fact that our assumption is fulfilled for each function call inside the body of `f`.

This is the point where the support with PAMELA is possible. Similar to testing or symbolic execution we have to prove that each path through the program, resp. the result of such a path, satisfies the postcondition under the assumption that the precondition is fulfilled for the input leading to this result. But in contrast to testing we do not only check our assumption for a small subset of the possible inputs but for all of them.

To cope with the assertion, it is necessary to state all additional information not available in the program itself. Since PAMELA employs rewriting techniques, this information must be stated in form of (conditional) rules. These are used to transform the assertion (like in mathematical proofs) until no more rules can be applied or the assertion has been transformed to the special terms `TRUE` or `FALSE`. In order to realise these transformations the rules are regarded as an transformation system that is essentially a term rewriting system [13, 10] but allows for higher order variables.

5 A Small Example

To demonstrate the way our proof method works, let us consider a very small example of a system of recursive function definitions. Suppose we want to define a function *mult* that is to implement the multiplication of non-negative integers and that only makes use of additions. The desired properties can be expressed by the following pre- and postconditions:

$pre\text{-}mult(x, y) = x \geq 0 \land y \geq 0$
TYPE: INTG INTG → BOOL

$post\text{-}mult(x, y) = mult(x, y) \equiv x \cdot y$
TYPE: INTG INTG → BOOL,

where '$\cdot$' is the normal multiplication on integers and $mult(x, y)$ is the result of function *mult* applied to arguments x and y.

We are looking for a function *mult* that satisfies

(*) $\forall x, y \in \texttt{INTG} : pre\text{-}mult(x, y) \Rightarrow post\text{-}mult(x, y)$.

One possible solution for this problem is the following:

```
(.1) mult(x, y) =
(.2)      IF x = 0 THEN 0
(.3)               ELSE y + mult(x - 1, y)
(.4) TYPE: INTG INTG → INTG
```

For the second case (.3), we need some information about the recursive call of *mult* for our proof, because without this knowledge we cannot succeed. This information is given by the induction hypothesis which states that (*) is fulfilled for the arguments $x - 1$ and y.

We can demonstrate our method on this very small "system of recursive function definitions". We must prove:

1. For the recursive call of *mult* (.3), the precondition is fulfilled. This is necessary to employ the induction hypothesis.

2. If the precondition of *mult* is valid, then the postcondition is valid as well for all possible results of *mult*. That is, (*) is valid for all x and y.

[By fixpoint induction, 1. and 2. suffice to prove partial correctness.]

First we determine the paths of this function. It contains two paths according to the two branches of the `IF-THEN-ELSE`.

The first one (.2) is represented by condition

$$\begin{aligned}&\textit{pre-mult}(x, y) \wedge x = 0, \text{ i.e.}\\ &x \geq 0 \wedge y \geq 0 \wedge x = 0\end{aligned}$$

and result 0.

Since the second path (.3) contains the recursive call of function *mult*, the condition of this path is not only determined by the precondition and the negation of the condition of the `IF-THEN-ELSE` but it must be enlarged by the postcondition of the recursive call.

For this, first the precondition has to be checked:
The condition valid for the proof of the precondition of $mult(x - 1, y)$ is

$$\begin{aligned}&\textit{pre-mult}(x, y) \wedge \neg(x = 0)\\ &= x \geq 0 \wedge y \geq 0 \wedge \neg(x = 0)\\ &= x > 0 \wedge y \geq 0\end{aligned}$$

The precondition of $mult(x - 1, y)$ is

$$\begin{aligned}&\textit{pre-mult}(x - 1, y)\\ &= (x - 1) \geq 0 \wedge y \geq 0\end{aligned}$$

The second part of this precondition follows directly from the second part of the valid condition, the first follows from the first part with the following law of integer arithmetic:

$$x > 0 \Rightarrow (x - 1) \geq 0.$$

So the second path (.3) is represented by the condition

$$\begin{aligned}&\textit{pre-mult}(x, y) \wedge \neg(x = 0) \wedge \textit{post-mult}(x - 1, y)\\ &= x \geq 0 \wedge y \geq 0 \wedge \neg(x = 0) \wedge mult(x - 1, y) = (x - 1) \cdot y\end{aligned}$$

and its result $y + mult(x - 1, y)$.
Now let us consider the proof for the second case. We have the following hypotheses:

1. $x \geq 0$

2. $y \geq 0$

3. $\neg(x = 0)$

4. $mult(x - 1, y) = (x - 1) \cdot y$,

all from the path condition of the second path.
The claim in this case is:

$$y + mult(x - 1, y) = x \cdot y.$$

We can transform the left-hand side of our claim in the following way which proves the claim:

$$\begin{array}{ll}
\quad y + mult(x-1, y) & \\
= y + (x-1) \cdot y & (.4) \\
= y + x \cdot y - 1 \cdot y & \text{Distributivity} \\
= y - 1 \cdot y + x \cdot y & \text{Commutativity} \\
= y - y + x \cdot y & 1 \cdot z = z \\
= 0 + x \cdot y & z - z = 0 \\
= x \cdot y & 0 + z = z \\
 & \text{q.e.d.}
\end{array}$$

6 Proofs with PAMELA

6.1 Organization of the Proof

For the proof of partial correctness of a specification function it is necessary to inspect all possible results and check whether the postcondition is valid for each result assuming validity of the precondition. Since it is not possible to inspect each concrete possible result in our formal approach, we need to classify them and prove the correctness for each class. This is done in a very natural way: each result belongs to one particular path through the function body. Therefore, we determine all possible paths (which is possible since we do not have loops inside function bodies) and show the validity of the postcondition for the result of each path.

PAMELA determines the result of a path during the splitting of the body into its constituent paths. The splitting is essentially determined by the structure of the function body. It corresponds to application of proof rules for Meta IV expressions similar to those of [16].

The idea is to represent a path by a pair of condition and result. The condition is a Boolean expression comprising all conditions of `IF-THEN-ELSE`-expressions and conditionals leading to the result, the instantiated postconditions of function calls along this path and the precondition of the function to prove (i.e. the strongest postcondition of the path). The result may be the empty expression if the function considered has no functional result (i.e. is an operation; in Meta IV there is no syntactical distinction between functions and operations).

The overall organization of the proof of a program is the following: First PAMELA reads all necessary information (rules, pre- and postconditions etc.), then it checks one function after the other. If the body is a conditional, the different cases are treated separately. First the body is split, then the actual assertion is built and afterwards transformed as far as possible by the rewriting system.

6.2 The Induction Hypothesis

Since the proof is essentially based on Fixpoint Induction, we have to check where it is necessary to make use of the induction hypothesis. It says that for each function call inside the body of the function regarded at the moment the validity of the postcondition follows from the validity of the precondition. But since it is necessary to make use of the postconditions for the proof (otherwise we do not have enough information, e.g. about the status of global variables after execution of this function call), we first have to check that for each call of a function inside the body the corresponding precondition is fulfilled. In this way we make use of the invariants for the proof.

The checking of the preconditions of function calls is done during the splitting of the body into its paths whenever a function call is found. If the proof of the precondition is successful, the postcondition is added to the condition of the path. In order to keep track of the results of calls of functions that are used more than once in the body these results are marked with an index during the process of splitting. This is necessary in the presence of functions with side effects, since calling a function with the same arguments twice possibly leads to different results. Therefore, the term representing the function call alone does not suffice to designate the result.

6.3 Proof with Term Rewriting

After the function body has been split into its different paths, each represented by a condition and a result, the actual proof consists of checking the postcondition of the function for each of these paths. That means that the postcondition is instantiated with the result of a path and then the resulting predicate is checked using the term rewriting rules. For this proof, the condition of the path is regarded as valid, i.e. it is the assumption of the proof.

For term rewriting in PAMELA sets of possibly conditional rules are used, which may be conditional ones. This means that a rule is a triple (*cond*, *left*, *right*), also written as

$$cond \Rightarrow left \rightarrow right,$$

where *cond* is a predicate term and *left* and *right* are terms. Applying such a rule to a term t means the following:

> If there exists a substitution (i.e. a replacement of variables by terms) σ and an occurrence of a subterm t' of t such that $\sigma(left) = t'$ and if $\sigma(cond)$ can be rewritten to **TRUE**, the occurrence of t' in t is replaced by $\sigma(right)$; otherwise t is not changed.

The idea for the proof of the validity of the instantiated postcondition is to apply the rules of the transformation system to it until no more rules can be applied.
This process of rule application can either

- stop with the original predicate reduced to **TRUE**:
  in this case the proof has succeeded;

- stop with the original predicate reduced to **FALSE**:
  in this case the proof has failed, indicating that there is an error in the function proved, or that the rules are not correct;

- stop with some other predicate:
  in this case the proof has also failed, but the reason is that not enough or not the appropriate rules have been stated;

- loop forever:
  in this case the set of rules must contain a loop, i.e. the rules describe a possibly non terminating rule system.
  For example:
  $a + b \rightarrow\ b + a.$
  In this case we get a non-terminating sequence of transformations for term $t = x + y$, namely $x + y \rightarrow\ y + x \rightarrow\ x + y \rightarrow\ \ldots)$

For efficiency's sake, the implementation of PAMELA does not use just one large set of rules. The set of rules can be divided by the user into smaller sets. In the example of the code generators of the CAT system there is e.g. one set for arithmetical and logical rules, one set for constructor and selector functions of the data types used in the program, several sets of semantic rules and so on.

PAMELA allows the user to define strategies on these sets of rules. The strategies define in which order the sets of rules shall be applied, whether one set or one substrategy shall be applied only once or repeatedly and whether application shall first be tried on the subterms or on the whole term. In this way the user can influence the order of rule applications, which can be crucial for the length of the proof. It is desirable to choose the strategies in such a way that the terms resulting from the application are as small as possible during the whole proof.

6.4 Proving the Substitution Phase

As described above, the substitution phase of the code generation in the CAT system can be regarded as an independent part of the specification. The definition of this part consists of a set of mutually recursive functions with a certain set of auxiliary functions (e.g. predicates).

We want to prove the correctness of the substitution phase. This means, that we want to prove that for each well-formed CAL_{CAT} expression the substitution yields a well-formed substituted expression with equivalent semantics if the recursive process of substitution terminates. The essential proof consists of the partial correctness proof for each substitution function with respect to its pre- und postcondition, exploiting the correctness of recursive calls.

The input data we need for the proof consist of:

- the set of specification functions to be proved,

- the sets of pre- and postconditions for each function (and of variables that may be changed by the function; this is not relevant for the substitution phase, but it is for the decomposition, where functions have side effects on global variables),

- the auxiliary functions of the specification (like well-formedness predicates for CAL_{CAT} and CAL_{M}),
- conditional rewrite rules describing semantics of CAL_{CAT} and CAL_{M}, resp. of CAL expressions after the substitution (which essentially depends on the semantics of the different operators),
- rules describing constructor, selector and recognizer functions for CAL (*mk-*, *sel-* and *is-* functions),
- general arithmetical and logical laws as conditional rewriting rules,
- a strategy for the proof,
- a set of exceptions, describing the syntactical structure of expressions that are not to be treated according to the strategy.

Since the specifications of the CAT system usually do not contain all the additional information it has to be stated very carefully afterwards. The sets of pre- and postcondition for each substitution function have to be derived from the correctness predicate of the main function. This is not too difficult. For the semantics of CAL expressions we have chosen a continuation semantics. The denotational style of this semantics is very suitable for the representation as rewriting rules. Furthermore, the compositionality of the semantics style is convenient for the structural induction proof, since the semantics of all subcomponents can be determined independently.

For our example specifications (about 3200 lines of Meta IV') we need about 2500 lines of additional information given as Meta IV' functions or rewrite-rules. This seems to be much, but most of it only has to be stated once for all possible code generator specifications (like rules describing general CAL operations, logical and arithmetical rules). So for another specification essentially the pre- and postconditions and the descriptions of the machine instructions (semantics, static semantics etc. of CAL_{M}) have to be stated. We would strongly advise that pre- and postconditions be stated along with the development of the specification functions, as proposed by VDM.

As an example, we state pre- and postcondition for the substitution function **subst-addi** (ref. Figure 2) in Figure 3.

The precondition states that the application of **subst-addi** is only guaranteed to be correct for expressions **e** that are either well-formed CAL_{CAT} expressions or are already substituted. For the proof the precondition can be enlarged by the information concerning the operator of **e** derived from the *mop-map*, i.e.

```
(is-equal (s_op (e), ADDI) OR is-equal (s-op (e), ADDO)).
```

The postcondition contains the semantical correctness (.8) as well as the static semantics condition (.6-.7). The static semantics condition says that the result **e1** of **subst-addi** applied to **e** (.4) is a well-formed substituted expression (.6) and that the modes of **e** and **e1** are compatible. The semantics condition (.8) states that for all denotational environments (essentially variable bindings) **rho** and all continuations **kappa** the semantics of **e** and **e1** are 'equivalent'. Equivalence has to be defined in a suitable way, e.g. such that source and target

```
pre-subst-addi (e) =
  (is-wf-expr-cat (e) OR is-wf-subst-expr (e))
TYPE: Te -> Bool

post-subst-addi (e) =
  LET e1 = subst-addi (e)
  IN
   (is-wf-subst-expr (e1) AND
   (is-appropriate-mode (sel_mode (e), sel_mode (e1)) AND
    is-equiv (sem (e, rho, kappa), sem (e1, rho, kappa)) ))
TYPE: Te -> Bool
```

Figure 3: Pre- and postconditions for **subst-addi**

states are regarded as equivalent if they are equal except for the contents of auxiliary variables.

The proof with PAMELA proceeds as described above. First all necessary information is retrieved from the relevant files. The user may choose between an interactive or automatic run where interactive means that there is a choice of different actions (interrupt, repetition, continuation) at certain points of the proof (after proof of a function, a clause, an error). One after the other, the specification functions are read, split into their paths and proved. Splitting into paths with **subst-addi** essentially means that for each clause of the conditional a separate proof is done. This proof again is divided into several smaller proofs depending on the disjunctions in the preconditions. This is what would have been done by a proof by hand.

Even this simple example shows that the proof is divided into a lot of different cases; for **subst-addi** there are 56 paths. Some of these can be sorted out immediately, since the path condition can be reduced to **FALSE**, which means that the result cannot be reached. But nevertheless, a proof by hand would be very tedious, since similar proof steps have to be done for the different cases. PAMELA supports this process by structuring the proof and doing all transformations. This is only possible, since the main work for the proof is the fixpoint induction and the proof for each single specification function is not mathematically complex, but rather consists of simple rewritings.

The errors we found applying this method are typical for the development process of the specifications. Since the clauses are very similar, copying is the easiest way to obtain them. Errors are due to disregarding necessary changes for the adaptation of the part copied. These errors can either effect the well-formedness (if e.g. in the second clause **e1** substitutes **e2** in line .13, Figure 1) or the semantical equivalence (e.g. if **e2** is not negated in line .13, Figure 1). Other errors are due to wrong pre- and postconditions (which must be regarded as part of the specification). If a precondition is too strong, it may not be possible to prove it for certain parameters in recursive calls. On the other hand, a weak postcondition may not yield enough information on the recursive call for the proof of the respective path.

7 Conclusion

7.1 Experiences

PAMELA is still under construction and therefore we do not have much experience with the system yet. But there exists a preliminary version of PAMELA, named PACS (*Proof Assistant for Code generator Specifications*) [5, 6, 7] that is suitable for certain parts of the code generators of the CAT system. PACS is not able to cope with global variables; therefore it is only applicable to the ***substitution*** part where no global variables are needed. In PACS the user cannot define strategies of his own on a set of rules; instead one fixed strategy is implemented. Furthermore the idea of splitting is only realized in a less precise kind. These weaknesses of PACS lead to the new concepts of PAMELA.

But we had some encouraging experiences with PACS. One discovery we made is that it is essential for the proof to formulate all information very precisely. If the pre- and postconditions do not contain all features of the function, either the correctness of this function cannot be proved, or for calls of the function either the precondition cannot be proved or the postcondition is not strong enough for the proof of correctness of the calling function.

The way in which a rule is stated is crucial for the applicability of that rule. Furthermore it is necessary to have in mind the order in which the rules are examined for the transformations. Since we treat a set of rules as a list, i.e. we apply the first rule (in order of definition) that is applicable at all, it is necessary to state more general rules after special ones, since otherwise the special rules would never be applied. The order inside one list of rules can be relevant for the efficiency of the transformations, too. But the strategies of PAMELA allow an easier control of these requirements since they allow to define many smaller sets of rules for each of which it is, in general, easier to have an overview.

We made the experience that it is quite easy to determine the sources of errors found by PACS and that we can rely on the system to detect errors in the code generator functions. Errors, inadequacies or incompleteness in the pre- and postconditions or rules are in general also detected and can easily be repaired, but here the user is asked to be very precise when stating these.

7.2 Open Problems

For the moment we can only cope with partial correctness. One of the next steps must be to have a look at the termination property of programs to be able to prove total correctness as well. But first we need to get more experience with the system PAMELA so that we can determine for which types of programs and programming languages this approach is suitable.

Some other problems directly arise from the use of the term rewriting systems. It would be very helpful to exclude errors in the lists of rules (like loops, inconsistencies etc.). In this way we could be sure that the errors arising during the proof of a program are due to errors in the program itself. There are solutions for these problems in the field of term rewriting, but since unfortunately PAMELA possibly makes use of rules with higher order expressions these results are not immediately applicable for our rule systems.

Another problem is the use of several sets of rules. We need to investigate the conditions that guarantee that a set of rules is terminating, consistent etc. if it consists of smaller sets of rules that have these properties. In any case, it is desirable to make use of methods and results already developed in term rewriting. One must be careful, however, not to include techniques that take too much time compared to the whole proof. This would e.g. be the case if we started to use completion procedures [4] on our sets of rules.

Last, but not least, it is an interesting question whether the method of PAMELA can be extended to programs with `WHILE`-loops and which new techniques are necessary to deal with the fixpoints arising when dealing with such programs.

7.3 Comparison with Other Systems

One of the best known proof support systems is the Boyer-Moore prover [3]. The main drawback for using this system for the field of our interest is that the object language is a variant of LISP. To apply the prover to a set of Meta IV' function requires first of all syntactic changes. But since Meta IV' is not a pure functional language (it contains assignments and sequences) further, more complicated transformations are necessary. Additionally suitable data representations have to be found. This is also true if the Boyer-Moore prover were to be applied to programs written in PASCAL or some other imperative languages.

This means that extensive transformations of a Meta IV' program are necessary before the Boyer-Moore prover could be applied to prove its correctness. This is also true for programs written in PASCAL or other imperative languages.

As far as we know the Boyer-Moore prover is the proof system with the highest level of automation, but nevertheless this is not enough for the applications we have in mind. As many others, it requires a high degree of interaction to organize the proof. This, of course, is due to the fact that it is not solely applicable to the verification of programs, but also to general mathematical problems.

LCF [12] and SPADE [17] both have for our application an unacceptably high need for interaction. The only automatic components are just able to achieve the simplification of expressions. We do not think this is adequate for the proof of programs with some hundred functions.

Our experiences with the Larch Prover (LP) [11] show that rewriting based systems can be useful for supporting verification work [8]. But LP needs very much user interaction for controlling the proof, whereas we think that it must be the aim of a program verification system to give the user the possibility to use it like a compiler: detect an error, correct it and let the system start again, but all in an acceptable time. None of the systems mentioned above can be used in that way. We hope that PAMELA is a step in that direction.

References

[1] de Bakker J. Mathematical Theory of Program Correctness. Prentice-Hall, 1980

[2] Bjørner D., Jones CB. The Vienna Development Method: The Meta-Language. Springer, LNCS 61, 1978

[3] Boyer RS, Moore JS. A Computational Logic Handbook. Academic Press, 1988

[4] Buchberger B. "Basic Features and Development of the Critical Pairs/-Completion Procedure". In: Jouannaud JP (ed.) Proceedings of the First International Conference on Rewriting Techniques and Applications. Springer, LNCS 202, pp. 1-45, 1985

[5] Buth B. PACS - Implementierung einer computergestützten Verifikation für die Substitutionsphase von Codegenerator-Spezifikationen im CAT-System. Diplomarbeit, Christian-Albrechts-Universität, Kiel, 1988

[6] Buth K-H. Beweis der partiellen Korrektheit von Codegenerator-Spezifikationen mit Hilfe von Termersetzung. Diplomarbeit, Christian-Albrechts-Universität, Kiel, 1988

[7] Buth B, Buth K-H. "Correctness Proofs for META IV Written Code Generator Specifications Using Term Rewriting". In: Bloomfield R et al. (eds.) VDM '88, VDM – The Way Ahead, Proceedings of the 2nd VDM-Europe Symposium. Springer, LNCS 328, pp. 406-433, 1988

[8] Buth B et al. Experiments with Program Verification Systems. Technical Report [Kiel BB 2], ESPRIT BRA 3104 ProCoS, Christian-Albrechts-Universität Kiel, 1989

[9] Dawes J. The VDM-SL Reference Guide. Pitman, 1991

[10] Dershowitz N. "Termination" In: Jouannaud JP (ed.). Proceedings of the First International Conference on Rewriting Techniques and Applications. Springer, LNCS 202, pp. 180-224, 1985

[11] Garland SJ, Guttag JV. "An Overview of LP, The Larch Prover". In: Dershowitz N (ed.). Proceedings of the Third International Conference on Rewriting Techniques and Applications. Springer, LNCS 355, pp. 137-151, 1989

[12] Gordon MJ, Milner R, Wadsworth CP. Edinburgh LCF. Springer, LNCS 78, 1979

[13] Huet G, Oppen DC. "Equations and Rewrite Rules: A Survey". In: Book RV (ed.). Formal Languages: Perspectives and Open Problems. Academic Press, New York, pp. 349-405, 1980

[14] Jones CB. Systematic Software Development Using VDM. Prentice Hall International, 1990

[15] Loeckx J, Sieber K. The Foundations of Program Verification. Wiley-Teubner, 1984

[16] Milne R. "Proof Rules for VDM Statements". In: Bloomfield R et al. (eds.). VDM '88, VDM - The Way Ahead, Proceedings of the 2nd VDM-Europe Symposium. Springer, LNCS 328, pp. 318-336, 1988

[17] O'Neill IM et al. "The Formal Verification of Safety-critical Assembly Code". In: Ehrenberger WD (ed.). Safety of Computer Control Systems 1988. IFAC Proceedings Series, Vol. 16, Pergamon Press, pp. 115-120, 1988

[18] Schmidt U. Ein neuartiger, auf VDM basierender Codegenerator Generator. Dissertation, Christian-Albrechts-Universität, Kiel, 1983

[19] Schmidt U, Völler R. "A Multi-Language Compiler System with Automatically Generated Codegenerators". In: Proceedings of the SIGPLAN '84 Symposium on Compiler Construction. ACM SIGPLAN Notices, Vol. 19(6), pp. 202-212, 1984

[20] Völler R. Entwicklung einer maschinenunabhängigen Zwischensprache und zugehöriger Übersetzeroberteile für ein Mehrsprachenübersetzersystem mit Hilfe von VDM. Dissertation, Christian-Albrechts-Universität, Kiel, 1983

The Semantics and Syntax of Update Schemes.

Hugh Osborne

Department of Informatics, University of Nijmegen

Nijmegen, The Netherlands

hugh@cs.kun.nl

Abstract

Update schemes are a high level formalism for specifying low level activities, such as the semantics of machine level operations. Update schemes have well defined denotational semantics and simple intuitive operational semantics. They also have a great deal of similarity to low level code. This combination makes it possible to give formal specifications of low level activities.

A compiler for update schemes is under development, and a prototype has been completed. This has been applied to a specification of an abstract machine for a simple functional language.

This paper presents the syntax and semantics, both formal and informal, of update schemes.

1 Introduction

At some point in the specification of computing systems, it becomes necessary to specify low level activities, for example when defining the instruction set of some machine, either concrete or abstract. In the case of abstract machines, or concrete machines under development, such a specification can be useful in reaching design decisions, and optimising the instruction set. In the case of existing concrete machines it can be used for deriving provably correct optimisations on generated code.

Various formalisms have been proposed for such specifications. The functional language community has used transition systems [1], informal description [2], imperative programming style [3, 4] and functional languages [5], to name but a few. The best known contributions from the concrete side are probably ISPS [6] and register transfer languages, for example three address code [7].

These methods all have their drawbacks, lacking either a formal definition, or being impractical in that they are not easily realisable as concrete implementations. Transition systems have a well defined semantics, but quickly become unwieldy as the complexity of the system being specified increases. Even expressing a simple `JUMP` instruction leads, at best, to an inelegant use of the formalism. Functional languages also have a well defined formal semantics, and a functional language specification is *in principle* also implementable. However, current implementations of functional languages are generally too inefficient for realistic prototyping.

At the other end of the scale, a specification in some imperative language will be easy to implement with reasonable efficiency, but will suffer from a lack of formal semantics. The same is true, possibly to a lesser extent, of ISPS and register transfer languages.

The drawbacks of informal specifications are well known.

Update schemes are a formalism combining well defined denotational semantics and intuitive operational semantics with readability and flexibility. Update schemes were originally proposed by Meijer [8] where they are used to specify an implementation of Extended Affix Grammars. This paper extends Meijer's original work by presenting a denotational semantics for update schemes, and by extending the available syntactic sugar to cover simple i/o constructs.

The basis for update schemes is a formal notation for specifying machine configurations. These are then combined in rewriting rules, or *update schemes*, which specify possible machine transitions in which the machine is updated from a configuration specified by the left hand side of the update scheme to a configuration specified by the right hand side. Various notational conventions increase the legibility of update schemes, and facilitate the introduction of command streams and specification involving input and output.

This paper is organised as follows. Section 2 discusses representations of computer memory and introduces the notation used in update schemes for specifying machine configurations. In section 3 this notation is extended to cover the full syntax of update schemes. Update schemes and their semantics are presented. Section 4 is dedicated to the notational conventions used to increase the expressive power of update schemes. These conventions are illustrated in a simple example. A simple application of update schemes is discussed in section 5. Finally, section 6 outlines plans for further research. A glossary of the terms introduced in this paper is included in appendix A.

2 Memory

Computer memory can be viewed in two complementary ways. In the first view the machine on which update schemes operate consists simply of a *memory* containing a countable set of *cells* addressed by a completely ordered set of *locations*. In the second, the memory is a function $\mathcal{M}$ from locations to values. The domain of $\mathcal{M}$, or address space $\mathcal{A}$, is a countable set of locations. Since it is a countable set, there is a complete ordering $<_{\mathcal{A}}$ along with the relevant successor and predecessor functions $succ_{\mathcal{A}}$ and $pred_{\mathcal{A}}$. In update schemes '+' and '−' are used in the usual way: $L + n$ to indicate $succ^n_{\mathcal{A}}\ L$ and $L - n$ for $pred^n_{\mathcal{A}}$. The address space is two way infinite, that is $succ_{\mathcal{A}}$ and $pred_{\mathcal{A}}$ are defined for all elements of $\mathcal{A}$.

2.1 Locators

Rather than addressing the cells as if they were elements in an array, update schemes address the boundaries between cells, so that what in an array notation would be specified as $[2:4] = [\text{'}a\text{'}, \text{'}b\text{'}, \text{'}c\text{'}]$ is specified in an update scheme by

2['a' 'b' 'c']5. A triple of this form, consisting of two locations and a sequence, is called a *locator expression.* 2 is the *left locator* and 5 the *right locator* of the sequence of cells containing 'a', 'b' and 'c'. However, when no confusion can arise a cell may be referred to by its left locator. That is, rather than saying *"the cell with left locator X contains the value Y"* one may say *"X contains Y"*. In exceptional cases the right locator may be used in the same way, but then extra care must be taken to avoid confusion.

A singleton sequence is identified with its element. Everything in memory is considered to be a sequence and is "desequenced" (to a location, number or other basic type) as the context requires.

In the following the term "memory" will be used to refer to the whole memory of the machine. This means that, in the formal view, $\mathcal{M}$ is a total function, possibly returning some special value $\perp$ for undefined values. A subset of the memory function will be referred to as a "configuration". A configuration is *satisfied* by any memory or configuration of which it is a subset. The domain of a configuration c — the subset of $\mathcal{A}$ for which c is defined — is given by Dom c. Update schemes define relations between configurations. An application of an update scheme to a memory, however, defines a relation between memories.

A locator expression defines a configuration. The locator expression L[S]L$'$ expresses the idea *"the cells between L and L$'$ contain the sequence S"*. Since the locator expression contains no information about the cells other than those between L and L$'$, only the values in the cells between L and L$'$ are defined. More formally, there is a function I from locator expressions to configurations given by

$$I[\![l[s_0..s_n]r]\!] = \{(l+i, s_i) \mid 0 \leq i \leq n\}.$$

Locator expressions can be combined to specify larger configurations. A set of locator expressions only specifies a configuration if it is *consistent*, i.e. there are no locator expressions in the set specifying conflicting contents for one and the same cell. For example 3[1 2]5 4[2 3]6 is consistent, but 3[1 2]5 4[1 2]6 is not, due to the conflict between 4[2]5 and 4[1]5. Note the use of layout to separate the elements of a sequence in the above expressions. Elements in sequences are separated by whitespace, rather than commas. There must not be any whitespace between a locator and its brace ('[' or ']'). A tie character '~' may be used to override this, so that "...]~ L ..." is equivalent to "...]L ...".

Consistency can be defined formally as follows. Two configurations c and c' are consistent if $c\ x = c'\ x$ for all x in (Dom c) $\cap$ (Dom c'). A set of locator expressions L is consistent if $I[\![l]\!]$ is consistent with $I[\![l']\!]$ for all l and l' in L.

2.2 Combining Configurations

Configurations can be combined in a manner akin to set union. The 'union' of two configurations must also be a configuration, that is, a partial function. If the two configurations to be combined are not consistent then, by definition, there is an argument for which they give different values. One of the configurations is chosen to consistently provide the result in such cases. By convention this is the left argument of the 'union' operator.

Formally

$$c \uplus c' = c \cup (c' \upharpoonright (\text{Dom } c' \setminus \text{Dom } c)).$$

This is equivalent to

$$\begin{aligned}(c \uplus c')\ l &= c\ l, l \in \text{Dom } c \\ &= c'\ l, l \notin \text{Dom } c\end{aligned}$$

Note that $\uplus$ is equivalent to conventional set union, if the configurations to which it applied are consistent.

The union operator defined above is used to extend the function $I[\![]\!]$ to cover sets of locator expressions. This extension is noted $\mathcal{I}[\![]\!]$, and is defined by

$$\mathcal{I}[\![e_1 \ldots e_n]\!] = (I[\![e_1]\!] \uplus (I[\![e_2]\!] \uplus (\ldots \uplus (I[\![e_{n-1}]\!] \uplus I[\![e_n]\!]) \ldots)))$$

The motivation for this definition can be found in section 3.

3 Update Schemes

Locator expressions are the basic building blocks of update schemes. The locator expressions presented above contain only constants, or instantiated values such as 3 and 'b'. This is not the case in update schemes. These may contain variables, or uninstantiated values. A variable is indicated by a lower case word. Constants are given by a value or, symbolically, by upper case words. The underscore character '_' and the prime character ''' may be part of a word. Thus 5, 's' and PC are all valid constants, x, new_pc and i' are all valid variable names and Call and sTrAnGe are neither. Constant locators play such a special rôle in update schemes that a special, somewhat suggestive terminology is used to refer to them. A constant locator is called a *register*. By application of the convention that a cell may be referred to by its locator, a cell having a register as its left or right locator may also be referred to as a register, if no confusion may arise as to which cell is being referred to.

A locator expression containing variables is instantiated by substituting values for the variables to obtain a closed locator expression. A *substitution* is a mapping from variables to values. A value is a closed term. Given an expression e and a substitution σ, the instantiation of e by σ is noted e^{σ}.

An update scheme is constructed from two sets of locator expressions, forming the *left hand side* and *right hand side* and a boolean expression known as the *guard*. The following is a simple example of an update scheme. Note that this update scheme could be simplified by applying some of the syntactic sugar presented in section 4.

PC[x]pc x[BCC o]y C[0]c =[TRUE]⇒ PC[y+o]pc.

This is a definition for the BCC instruction on the M6800 processor. Intuitively the definition states that if the instruction addressed by the PC is BCC with argument o and the condition code register C bit is 0 then the PC is reset to $y + o$ where y is the address immediately after the $BCC\ o$ instruction.

More formally, this update scheme can be applied to the memory $\mathcal{M}$ if the following conditions hold.

$$\begin{aligned}\mathcal{M}\ x &= BCC, \text{ where } x = \mathcal{M}\ PC \\ c &= 0, \text{ where } c = \mathcal{M}\ C\end{aligned}$$

or, equivalently, $((\mathcal{M} \circ \mathcal{M})\ PC = BCC) \wedge (\mathcal{M}\ C = 0)$. If these conditions hold then the result of applying the update scheme is a new memory $\mathcal{M}'$ defined as follows.

$$
\begin{array}{lcl}
\mathcal{M}'\ PC & = & \text{let } x = \mathcal{M}\ PC \\
 & & \text{in let} \quad \begin{array}{lcl} y & = & x+2 \\ o & = & \mathcal{M}\ (x+1) \end{array} \\
 & & \quad \text{in } y+o \\
\mathcal{M}'\ x & = & \mathcal{M}\ x, x \neq PC
\end{array}
$$

The syntax of update schemes is as follows.

update scheme::= locator*, "$\dashv$[", guard, "$\models\!\Rightarrow$", locator*.

guard::= term.

locator::= term, "[", term*, "]", term.

An update scheme must also satisfy a well formedness condition known as ***traceability*** which requires all variables appearing in the scheme to be expressible as closed terms. The update scheme given for the BCC instruction is well formed. A closed expression for o, for example, is $\mathcal{M}\ ((\mathcal{M}\ PC) + 1)$.

An update scheme is ***applicable*** to a configuration if there is a substitution under which the guard is true and the configuration satisfies the left hand side. The result of applying the update scheme is then this configuration minimally changed so as to contain the instantiation of the right hand side under the same substitution as that applied to the left hand side and the guard.

The following example should clarify these concepts. Consider the update scheme for the BCC instruction given above, and the configuration PC[1234] 1234[BCC 67] C[0]. There is a substitution, $\{(x, 1234), (y, 1236), (o, 67)\}$, under which the left hand side is contained in, and in fact is identical to the given configuration and the update scheme is therefore applicable to the configuration. The result is then the configuration PC[1303] 1234[BCC 67] C[0]. Only the contents of PC have been changed, this being the minimal change necessary to make the configuration satisfy the right hand side of the update scheme under the substitution above.

More formally, an update scheme $(lhs, guard, rhs)$ is applicable to a configuration c if there is a substitution σ such that $lhs^\sigma \subseteq c$ and $guard^\sigma$. The result is the configuration c' defined as follows.

$$c' = \mathcal{I}[\![rhs^\sigma]\!] \uplus c$$

In this configuration one can distinguish three types of cells. There are those cells specified in the configuration c, but not in the right hand side of the update scheme. The values in these cells remains unchanged. Secondly, there are the cells specified both in c and the right hand side of the scheme. The values in these cells are *updated* to the values specified in the right hand side. Finally, there may be some cells specified in the right hand side of the update scheme that do not occur in the c. These cells are then added to the configuration.

The motivation for the definition of $\uplus$ should now be clear. The left argument of $\uplus$ specifies an update of the right argument. Operationally, any cells in memory specified in the left configuration must have their value updated to the value specified in that configuration. The values in cells not specified in the left argument are left unchanged.

The only remaining problem is finding a substitution. The substitution must satisfy the guard and, when applied to the left hand side, it must give a configuration contained in the configuration to which the update scheme is being applied. More formally, a set of possibly open locator expressions L, a guard g and a configuration c together define a set of applicable substitutions as given by the function $\mathcal{S}$.

$$\mathcal{S}\ L\ g\ c = \{\sigma \mid (\mathcal{I}[\![L^\sigma]\!] \subseteq c) \land g^\sigma\}$$

Note that consistency of L under the substitution is not explicitly required. However, if c is consistent the instantiation of L must, implicitly, also be consistent.

The concept of applying update schemes can now be formalised. An update scheme $s = (lhs, guard, rhs)$ defines a relation between configurations, notation $\Rightarrow_s$, given by

$$c \Rightarrow_s c' \equiv \exists \sigma \in (\mathcal{S}\ lhs\ guard\ c) : c' = \mathcal{I}[\![rhs^\sigma]\!] \uplus c.$$

When no ambiguity can arise the subscript s may be omitted.

One update scheme is typically used to specify one possible machine transition, for example, the effect of one specific instruction. A complete machine specification will contain many such update schemes. The transition relation defined above can easily be extended to sets of update schemes, known as ***update plans***. Any update scheme contained in the update plan which is applicable to a given configuration may be applied to that configuration. An update plan P defines the following relation.

$$c \Rightarrow_P c' \equiv \exists s \in P : c \Rightarrow_s c'$$

Again, the subscript may be omitted when no confusion can arise. As usual $\Rightarrow^*$ is the reflexive transitive closure of $\Rightarrow$.

A configuration c' is a *development* of configuration c under an update plan P if $c \Rightarrow_P^* c'$. A combination of a specification of an *initial configuration* c and an update plan P is called a *script*. A *final development* of a script consisting of initial configuration c and update plan P is any configuration c' such that $c \Rightarrow_P^* c'$ and $\neg\exists c'' : c' \Rightarrow_P c''$. To arrive at a final development one keeps on applying update schemes until one arrives at a configuration to which no update schemes in the plan are applicable.

4 Sweetening the Syntax

The basic syntax of update schemes has been introduced in section 3. However, update schemes conforming to this syntax are unwieldy, as the following example shows.

The aim of this example is to construct a parser for the following simple context free grammar.

S ::= "a"| "a", S.

A script consisting of the following initial configuration

PARSE[START]PARSE′ START[S]END IP[I]IP′ I[ω]EOF

where ω is some string, and the three update schemes

PARSE[v]PARSE′ v[S]w
=[TRUE]⇒ PARSE[v′]PARSE′ v′['a']w.

PARSE[v]PARSE′ v[S]w
=[TRUE]⇒ PARSE[v′]PARSE′ v′['a']v v[S]w.

PARSE[v]PARSE′ v['a']w IP[ip]IP′ ip['a']ip′
=[TRUE]⇒ PARSE[w]PARSE′ IP[ip′]IP′.

will have a final development containing PARSE[END]PARSE′ IP[EOF]IP′ if and only if ω is in the language generated by S in the given grammar.

While correct, the update schemes above are unwieldy. Some syntactic sugar will be introduced which provides abstraction capabilities and improves the readability of update schemes. The extensions to the basic syntax fall into two categories. The first category is concerned with omitting redundant information from update schemes, while the second increases readability by making some information implicit.

4.1 Omitting Redundant Information

Update schemes written without syntactic sugar often contain a lot of redundant information. The following conventions make it possible to omit this.

- Contiguous sequences may be concatenated. Two expressions *x[s]y* and *y[t]z* may then be written as *x[s]y[t]z*, allowing the second update scheme to be rewritten as follows.

  PARSE[v]PARSE′ v[S]w
  =[TRUE]⇒ PARSE[v′]PARSE′ v′['a']v[S]w.

- Superfluous locations may be omitted. A location is superfluous if its removal does not lead to any confusion, i.e. it must be possible to rename the occurrence to be removed (to some new name not yet appearing in the update scheme) without changing the semantics of the update scheme. In the following only right locators have been removed, but left locators may of course also be omitted.

  PARSE[v] v[S]w =[TRUE]⇒ PARSE[v′] v′['a']v[S]w.

  Locations may also be omitted when concatenating contiguous sequences so that the update scheme above may be written as

  PARSE[v] v[S]w =[TRUE]⇒ PARSE[v′] v′['a' S]w.

- Tautological guards may be omitted.

PARSE[v] v[S]w ⟹ PARSE[v′] v′['a']w.

- Identical left hand sides may be shared. For example

PARSE[v] v[S]w ⟹ PARSE[v′] v′['a']w
⟹ PARSE[v′] v′['a' S]w.

4.2 Making Information Implicit

There are two more far reaching notational conventions. The first of these is used for specifying input and output activities and the second to increase the readability of a common type of update scheme called a *command*.

i/o The update scheme for parsing the terminal symbol 'a' included a mechanism for reading input, by means of an input pointer.

PARSE[v] v['a']v′ IP[ip] ip['a']ip′ ⟹ PARSE[v′] IP[ip′].

The scheme contains a register IP which points to an input stream. When 'a' is read the pointer is moved over that symbol. The symbol '?IP' is used as shorthand for this mechanism. Any update scheme exhibiting the pattern

... IP[i] i[input]j ... ⟹ ... IP[j] ... .

may then be written

... ?IP[input] ... ⟹ ... .

Though this convention can also be used for standard stack operations it is recommended that its use be restricted to operations that conceptually can be considered to be input operations.

Note that if the input pointer is not moved—the input is looked at, but not read—then this convention cannot be used.

The third update scheme can now be written as

PARSE[v] v['a']w ?IP['a'] ⟹ PARSE[w].

There is a similar convention for output, using the symbol '!'. Any scheme with the pattern

... OP[o] ... ⟹ ... o[output]p OP[p] ... .

may be written as

... ⟹ ... !OP[output] ... .

Programme counter The update schemes obtained by applying all the conventions above satisfy the requirements, namely specifying a parser for the given grammar, but introducing new registers such as PARSE for each routine one wants to implement leads to illegibility and makes coordination between routines difficult. This can be simplified by introducing a command stream and a programme counter to administer it. The constant location PARSE is replaced by the constant 'command' PARSE. When the schemes above are transformed to command stream style

$$\mathsf{PARSE[v]\quad v[s]w} \implies \mathsf{PARSE[v']\quad v'['a'\quad S]w.}$$

becomes

$$\mathsf{PC[pc]\quad pc[PARSE\quad v]qc\quad v[S]w} \\ \implies \mathsf{PC[pc']\quad pc'[PARSE\quad v']qc\quad v'['a'\quad S]w.}$$

The initial configuration becomes

$$\mathsf{PC[GO]\quad GO[PARSE\quad START]\quad START[S]END\quad IP[I]\quad I[}\omega\mathsf{]EOF}$$

The string ω is in the language generated by S if there is a terminal configuration satisfying

$$\mathsf{PC[pc]\quad pc[PARSE\quad END]\quad IP[EOF]}$$

At first sight introducing a programme counter does not seem to have increased the legibility of the update schemes, but the following notational convention puts that right.

If the left hand side of an update scheme exhibits the pattern

$$\mathsf{PC[pc]\quad pc[}OP\quad args\mathsf{]qc}\ \ldots\ .$$

where *OP* is a constant and the locations PC, pc and qc can be omitted without confusion, then it may be rewritten as

$$OP\quad args\ \ldots\ .$$

An update scheme of this type is called a *command*. *OP* is called the *opcode*, and **args** the *arguments* of the command. An update plan containing only commands is called a *command driven* plan.

The same convention may be applied to the right hand side. In most case it will be necessary to apply this convention to the left and right hand sides simultaneously in order to satisfy the conditions under which locations may be omitted. The PARSE update scheme under consideration is a case in point. Rewriting only the left hand side gives

$$\mathsf{PARSE\quad v\quad v[S]w} \implies \mathsf{PC[pc']\quad pc'[PARSE\quad v']qc\quad v'['a'\quad S]w.}$$

which contains the undefined locations pc′ and qc. Similarly, rewriting only the right hand side gives an update scheme with undefined locations pc and qc. Rewriting both sides gives

$$\mathsf{PARSE\quad v\quad v[S]w} \implies \mathsf{PARSE\quad v'\quad v'['a'\quad S]w.}$$

If both sides of an update scheme are rewritten then it is assumed that the command stream grows to the left, as if it were implemented on a stack.

As an aside, note that this update scheme can be simplified again, at the cost of a simple change to the initial configuration. The first step is to eliminate the indirection in PARSE's argument, which gives

$$\mathsf{PARSE\ \ S} \implies \mathsf{PARSE\ \ 'a'\ \ S}.$$

The initial configuration has to be modified to

$$\mathsf{PC[START]\ \ START[PARSE\ \ S]END\ \ ?}[\omega].$$

and the string is accepted if there is a terminal configuration satisfying

$$\mathsf{PC[p]\ \ p[PARSE]END\ \ IP[EOF]}.$$

The complete collection of update schemes for the parser is now

$$\begin{aligned}\mathsf{PARSE\ \ S} &\implies \mathsf{PARSE\ \ 'a'\ \ S}\\ &\implies \mathsf{PARSE\ \ 'a'}.\end{aligned}$$

$$\mathsf{PARSE\ \ 'a'\ \ ?['a']} \implies \mathsf{PARSE}.$$

The PARSE command has now become superfluous since both S and 'a' are constants and can therefore both be used as opcodes. The update schemes can now be rewritten as

$$\begin{aligned}\mathsf{S} &\implies \mathsf{'a'\ \ S}\\ &\implies \mathsf{'a'}.\end{aligned}$$

$$\mathsf{'a'\ \ ?['a']} \implies \ .$$

with initial configuration

$$\mathsf{PC[START]\ \ START[S]END\ \ IP[I]\ \ I}[\omega]\mathsf{EOF}.$$

The configuration that must be satisfied by a terminal configuration is then

$$\mathsf{PC[END]\ \ IP[EOF]}.$$

5 An Application

An abstract machine for a functional language has been implemented in update schemes [9]. The language is called FLIP, which stands for "Functional Language Implementation Prototype". The instruction set is specified in update schemes and there is a translation scheme defined from the language to command sequences.

The command specifications have been compiled, by hand, to C. Hand compilation was necessary because the update scheme compiler is not yet fully implemented. The compilation was as close an imitation of machine compilation as possible. The translation scheme has been implemented, giving a compiler from FLIP to command sequences. This can then be compiled using the prototype update scheme compiler. When combined with the C code for the command specifications this gives a complete C programme. The efficiency of the code produced has been investigated. The nfib function was compiled. The nfib function is given by

$$\begin{aligned} \text{nfib } n &= 1, n < 2 \\ &= 1 + (\text{nfib } n) + (\text{nfib } n - 1), \text{otherwise} \end{aligned}$$

This function has the useful characteristic:

nfib n = the number of applications of nfib necessary to compute nfib n.

and is used to derive the "nfib number" which is defined as

nfib n/time required to compute nfib n.

The higher the nfib number the better. Declarative languages have nfib numbers ranging from the order of 1 [5] to 10^6 [10]. This last value is competitive with imperative languages. The gnu C compiler version 1.36 on a SUN 3/60 running OS 4.1 has an nfib number of 250,000.

The nfib number for the FLIP abstract machine, implemented by the prototype update scheme compiler, was of the same order as that for Miranda[1] (release 2). On a SUN 3/60, running under OS 4.1, Miranda had an nfib number of 1,200 and the FLIP implementation, compiled using the gnu C compiler version 1.36, with optimisation, had one of 1,300. Simple optimisation at an intermediate code level (eliminating unnecessary copying, for example) increased this to 1,400, and optimisation of the update scheme code generated gave an nfib number of 2,200.

6 Further Research

Update plans make it possible to write executable specifications for various abstract machines. They may make it possible to conduct empirical efficiency comparisons of abstract machines.

An interesting challenge is to specify an existing concrete machine using update schemes.

Update plans form an abstract rewrite system. Work on their relation to other ARS's, and to graph rewrite systems in particular should lead to insights into the conditions neccesary to to guarantee one or more of, for example

- finite ambiguity
- the strong Church-Rosser property
- the weak Church-Rosser property
- modularity

The current prototype compiler for update schemes is restricted to deterministic update plans. This will be extended to accept certain classes of non-deterministic update plans as well. This work will be related to the work on update schemes as an abstract rewrite system.

[1]Miranda is a trademark of Research Software Ltd.

A Glossary

applicable An update scheme is applicable to a configuration if there is a substitution under which the guard is true and the left hand side of the update scheme is contained in the configuration.

arguments In a command, the contents of the cells immediately to the right of the opcode.

cell An element of memory.

command An update scheme, in the left hand side of which there is a register PC which contains the left locator of a cell which in turn contains a constant value.

command driven Said of an update plan consisting solely of commands.

configuration A subset of memory.

consistent A set of locator expressions is consistent if there are no two expressions in the set that specify the contents of some cell to have two different values.

development Given an initial configuration and an update plan, a configuration that can be arrived at from the initial configuration by zero or more applications of update schemes occurring in the update plan.

final development A development of an initial configuration under an update plan, to which none of the update schemes in the update plan is applicable.

guard A boolean expression in an update scheme which must evaluate to true if the update scheme is to be applicable.

initial configuration A configuration given in a script, indicating the state of the machine at the start of computation.

left/right locator For a given sequence, the location immediately to the left (right) of that sequence.

location The boundary between two cells in memory.

locator expression An expression specifying a partial configuration of the machine by specifying the contents of a sequence of cells.

memory A two way infinite countable set of cells.

opcode The constant value in a command which is contained in the cell, the left locator of which is in the register PC.

register A constant locator occurring in an update scheme and, by extension, the cell of which that locator is the left locator or, in exceptional circumstances, the right locator.

satisfy A configuration is satisfied by any memory or configuration of which it is a subset.

script An initial configuration, and an update plan to be applied to that configuration.

substitution A mapping from variables to values.

traceable A variable (in an update scheme) is traceable if a closed term can be derived for it.

update The configuration to which an update scheme is applied, minimally transformed so as to be consistent with the instantiation of the right hand side, said substitution being one under which the update scheme is appicable to the given configuration.

update plan A set of update schemes.

update scheme A rewrite rule consisting of a left hand side, a guard and a right hand side. Both the left hand side and the right hand side consist of sets of locator expressions. The guard is a boolean expression. An update scheme may contain variables.

References

[1] Fairbairn J, Wray S. Tim: A simple, lazy abstract machine to execute supercombinators. In Kahn G (ed), Functional Programming Languages and Computer Architecture: Lecture Notes in Computer Science, 274. Springer Verlag, 1987.

[2] Warren DHD. An abstract Prolog instruction set. Technical Report 309, Artificial Intelligence Center, SRI International, Menlo Park, California, USA, 1983.

[3] Lock HC. An abstract machine for the implementation of functional logic programming languages. Technical report, ESPRIT Basic Research Action No. 3147 (the **Phœnix** Project), 1990. Draft version.

[4] Peyton Jones SL, Salkild J. The spineless tagless G-machine. University College, London, 1989.

[5] Koopman P. Functional Programs as Executable Specifications. PhD thesis, University of Nijmegen, Toernooiveld 1, Nijmegen, The Netherlands, 1990.

[6] Siewiorek DP, Bell CG, Newell A. Computer Structures: Principles and Examples. Computer Science Series. McGraw-Hill, 1982.

[7] Aho AV, Sethi R, Ullman JD. Compilers: Principles, Techniques and Tools. Addison-Wesley, 1986.

[8] Meijer H. Programmar: A Translator Generator. PhD thesis, University of Nijmegen, Toernooiveld 1, Nijmegen, The Netherlands, 1986.

[9] Osborne HR. Update plans. In Proceedings of the Hawaii International Conference on System Sciences. IEEE Computer Society Press, 1992.

[10] Implementation of CLEAN on MAC II-fx, see [11].

[11] van Eekelen M. Parallel Graph Rewriting. PhD thesis, University of Nijmegen, Toernooiveld 1, Nijmegen, The Netherlands, 1988.

Additional Topics

Attributed Transformational Code Generation for Dynamic Compilers*

John Boyland
Computer Science Division, University of California, Berkeley
Berkeley, CA 94720 USA

Charles Farnum
Department of Computer Science and Engineering, Wright State University
Dayton, OH 45435 USA

Susan L. Graham
Computer Science Division, University of California, Berkeley
Berkeley, CA 94720 USA

Abstract

The design of dynamic compilers, that is, compilers that preserve execution state when newly compiled code is patched into an executing image, presents the compiler writer with a number of difficulties. First, all the complexity of a standard compiler is present. Second, enough intermediate information must be maintained to allow the compilation to proceed incrementally. Third, the incremental incorporation of newly compiled segments of code must disturb the existing execution state as little as possible. The last two factors are compounded when the desired level of granularity is small, such as at the level of statements or expressions. We describe our proposed method for automatically generating dynamic compilers and explain how the method will handle these issues.

1 Introduction

The role of an interactive source-language debugger is to allow the user to inspect the state of an executing program, usually by setting breakpoints. In some debuggers it is possible to change the values of variables, the subsequent control flow, or even the program itself. Typically, changes to the program are supported by interpreted execution of the modified code or by recompilation and dynamic linking of a modified subroutine or module [1,2]. If the debugger does not support changes to the program, it is necessary to abandon the execution state and possibly even the debugging session to recompile the whole program. In the case of programs with long execution times or difficulties in reproducing input data, these methods may have drawbacks. The goal of our research is to provide the user the ability, at least conceptually, to "patch" compiled code through source-level modification and to continue execution without

*Research sponsored by the Defense Advanced Research Projects Agency (DoD), monitored by Space and Naval Warfare Systems Command under Contract N00039-88-C-0292, by a National Science Foundation Graduate Fellowship to John Boyland, and by the California MICRO program.

losing execution state. We call the underlying technology needed to support that capability ***dynamic compilation***.

Dynamic compilers share a number of characteristics with incremental compilers and may incorporate incremental compilation in their design. In both types of compilers, a local change in the program text leads to a corresponding change in the target code. ("Local" is of course a relative term; a minor textual change may lead to a major change in the target code.) However, the two kinds of compilers have different purposes. An incremental compiler compiles local changes incrementally only in order to save compilation time. The choice of degree of granularity balances decreased code performance and the extra information that must be maintained against a shorter compilation time. The design of a dynamic compiler, on the other hand, is driven not so much by efficiency, as by the need to maintain an execution state with the greatest consistency possible.

Because of the painstaking nature of incrementality and consistency management, we are developing a method to generate dynamic compilers automatically from declarative descriptions. The compiler writer will specify the code generator as a sequence of attribute-directed tree transformations, separating the task of translation from the problem of dynamically linking segments of small granularity. Applying techniques akin to those for attribute coupled grammars [3,4,5], the sequence of transformations can be composed to form a single-level attribute grammar that generates target code from an abstract syntax representation of the source program. With this code generator, a change to the source code will cause a corresponding change to the target code. A form of fine-grained dynamic linking can then be used to update the executable image.

2 Research Context

This research is an outgrowth of our work at Berkeley on the *Pan* system, which provides language-based support for interactive software development environments [6]. Much of the previous work on Pan has dealt with the interactive "front-end" that provides language-based editing and browsing of (static) language documents [7,8,9], using description-based components. It is natural to extend the Pan system to support execution services.

In order that the debugger work with a variety of languages and a diversity of target architectures, we will build the debugger (and also the execution environment) using dynamic compilers. Each dynamic compiler will translate a particular programming language to a particular target machine.

For example, suppose that execution is paused at the point marked "*":

```
    procedure max(a : array <> of integer) returns integer is
        maxval : integer;
        begin
            for i in a'range loop
*               if maxval < a[i] then
                    maxval := a[i];
                endif;
            endloop;
            return maxval;
        end max;
```

Suppose, further, that the user wishes to view the value of expression $a[i]$. Using some language-specific rule, the Pan system will modify the program temporarily at the current execution point, perhaps to insert *put*($a[i]$). The dynamic compiler will be invoked and will generate the code to accomplish the printing. Execution will then be continued past the print expression, causing the value to be printed. If the user has indicated a one-time inspection of the value, the "put" statement will be removed and the execution state will be the same as it was before the operation.

At present we are not tackling the more complex issues associated with maintaining a correspondence between the source text and highly optimized target code. Dynamic compilation will only be available for computation units in which such optimization has not been applied. Even with that limitation, the execution of compiled code is sufficiently faster than interpretive execution that there will be considerable benefit from our techniques.

3 The Problems That Must Be Solved

3.1 Consistency

When a program is executing, there is an execution state consisting of values of the program counter, variables, parameters, return addresses, frame pointers, etc. If a portion of an executing program is modified by changing the value of a variable, or the executable code, it is possible that the modification will be at odds with the previously existing execution state. For example, the value of a global variable might be altered to some value never achieved during a normal execution, or a function might be redefined to contain a new local variable. In our model of debugging, all such actions are performed by adding or deleting sections of the program; a global variable is changed by adding code to perform the assignment, running it, and then deleting it. Thus to consider changes to the computation we need only consider how to handle additions or deletions to the program.

We would like to describe the semantics of making a program change dynamically. First we assume we have a denotational semantics of the programming language[1] that allows us to determine which sections of the program have a changed denotation. We view the semantics of program changes by considering every changed piece of executable code to be embedded in a conceptual conditional clause. The condition is true exactly for those execution states occurring before the change, and so the old version of the code is chosen when the state is original and the new version is chosen hereafter: an addition will have the first part empty; a deletion will have the second part empty. For this model, we use the model of state provided by the denotational semantics. The semantics of the change is thus that the program is restarted and executed to the point of change (determined by comparing the state to that state existing just before the change) and then program execution is continued as indicated by the client.

It may seem unclear how to conditionalize a change in a declarative part of a program. For example, how does adding a declaration to the local scope of a procedure affect executable code? This question answers itself for the most

[1] We gloss over whether the compiler actually satisfies the denotational semantics when run non-incrementally.

part; there are changes in a section of executable code exactly when the new declaration changes its denotation. So any uses of a (now) shadowed declaration in the executable part of the procedure are changed and can be conditionalized.

We now have a semantics of program change. If a dynamic compiler maintains this semantics, we say it provides *consistent* execution. Sometimes the dynamic compiler is unable to compile a certain change with full execution consistency, and execution becomes inconsistent. Certain inconsistent executions are "worse" than others; to distinguish between cases, we define the terms *partially consistent* and *erroneous*. An execution is partially consistent if the conditions used to choose between old and new code sometimes choose old code when the consistent semantics executes new code. This definition ensures that the partially consistent execution is consistent at least to the point of code change. We say that an execution state is *erroneous* if there is not any program at all that could induce the state from the start state.[2]

For example, suppose a local variable is added to a procedure that is currently active but not on the top of the call stack (i.e., it has an active call site within its body), and suppose further that a use of this variable is added to the procedure right after the active call site. Then execution is continued. In consistent execution, the use of the variable would execute as soon as the active call returns. A dynamic compiler supporting only partial consistency might replace the entire procedure for future calls but leave the old code in place to be executed when the active call returns. Execution would be inconsistent but not erroneous if the call stack were rolled back to the affected procedure and execution restarted from there. Execution would be erroneous if, for example, it continued back to the new use which then modified internal information by writing into a non-existent slot in the current (old) procedure frame.

A dynamic compiler can be the main vehicle for interactive debugging only if it supports at least partial consistency for all program changes. Partial consistency is needed so that the execution state current at the change is the one that is used for further execution. If the current execution state is lost, then any queries or changes on the state may have unintended results. Moreover, no dynamic compiler can be considered correct if it yields an erroneous state. One must note, however, that partial consistency is still inconsistent and with partial consistency, old code may be executed after a change is made. We imagine it may prove useful if the user is notified when old code is executed with an option to forbid such execution.

3.2 Why Conventional Incremental Compilers Don't Solve the Problem

For incremental compilation, there are few constraints, other than correctness, on the form in which a change is reflected in the modified target code. The design of a dynamic compiler, on the other hand, must take into account that execution may be active in or near to the region of code being changed. In order that execution *near* the change remain consistent, it is necessary for the dynamic compiler to generate code at the smallest granularity possible and

[2] Note that the definitions of *consistent*, *partially consistent*, and *erroneous* are not decidable in general.

then make a surgical patch. If execution is active within the change, even more care is necessary.

Another feature of many compilers which makes them unsuitable for dynamic compilation is that they structure the program in terms of lines rather than in terms of the underlying syntactic structure. Not only do statements and lines only partially correspond, but the hierarchical structure of program statements and expressions is not reflected in line numberings. For example, a *while* loop may cover several lines and include several statements and yet remain a single statement itself.

4 The General Structure of a Dynamic Compiler

There are two major components of a dynamic compiler. One component is the run-time support system. All dynamic compilers for a particular target machine will share a run-time support system that handles the following tasks: 1) loading foreign code,[3] 2) using the target code generator in the form of the code templates (to be explained subsequently), 3) communicating input/output for the program being debugged, and 4) honoring requests from the debugger (both interrogative and imperative) concerning the current execution state. The language implementor will describe the execution environment of the language being compiled in order that the run-time support system can locate such information as function return addresses. The dynamic compiler can implicitly provide much of the information needed in traditional debuggers, such as the values of variables, as illustrated by the example of printing `a[i]`. Similarly, to change the value of a variable, the debugger makes a source program change to store a value, incrementally compiles the change, and undoes the change.

The other significant component of a generated dynamic compiler is the incremental compiler. In our research effort, the front-end functionality is provided by Pan, which generates and maintains an annotated abstract syntax representation of the program. The incremental code generator is itself generated from a sequence of tree transformations and attributes. As currently envisaged, the generated incremental code generator will consist of two parts: a set of target machine code templates keyed by syntactic node labels, and a set of attribute equations specified for the source language abstract syntax. The code templates will be loaded by the run-time support system when required. The attribute equations will be accessed by an incremental attribute evaluator.

The structure of the generated code corresponds to that of the abstract syntax representation of the program, so that the code corresponding to a subtree of the abstract syntax tree can always be found. To allow the code to be patched arbitrarily, the template for a node contains 'holes' into which the code for each subtree is patched. Each hole consists of an unconditional jump; patching provides the target of the jump instruction. Additionally, each template has a number of parameters whose values depend on the context of the abstract syntax node. For example, the template for a *while* statement with parameter *size* might look like the following, where the *predicate* is assumed to provide a value for **temp**.

---

[3] That is, code compiled by other compilers, including standard system functions

```
While[body,predicate](size : integer)
        allocate-temp(size)
        jump-to label2
label1: jump-to body
label2: jump-to predicate
        read-temp
        jump-if-true-to label1
        deallocate-temp(size)
```

That structure permits code to be generated top down, provided that no information needs to be synthesized from below. Certain kinds of changes, such as insertion of declarations, necessarily cause information to propagate up the tree, and therefore require top down code generation to start at the highest node in the tree to which changes have propagated. Consequently, in specifying the code generator, the compiler writer should avoid complex patterns (such as those used for optimization) and synthesized attributes that transmit information a long distance up the tree.

A similar approach to compilation is "threaded-code compilation" in which the program is compiled to a sequence of abstract machine operations each of which is implemented by a subroutine [10,11]. The generated code consists of a sequence of parameterized subroutine "calls," and is usually compact. In practice, the code is not directly executed; each subroutine is responsible for jumping to the next subroutine in the sequence. Threaded code typically has a specialized machine model (for example, one register is typically reserved for the threaded code program counter), and thus is not as easily integrated with conventional code as code produced using our approach.

In the following two sections, we describe the description and creation of the incremental compiler component. We then discuss the run-time system in greater detail.

5 Patterns, Attributes, and Transformations

In this section, we explain the basis for compiler descriptions used in our system. Compilation can be viewed as a sequence of horizontal and vertical transformations of a program, where a vertical transformation maps from one representation to another, and a horizontal transformation maps to an equivalent but 'better' computation in the same representation. Vertical transformations are often called *lowerings*, and horizontal transformations are usually known as *optimizations.* If the representations are tree-structured, the transformations can often be implemented by a sequence of smaller more local pattern-based rewrites of attributed trees, combined with an attribute-style analysis system for capturing global information [12,13,14]. Instruction selection can be described in this way [15,16], as can intraprocedural optimization [17].

In our system, a compiler will be written as a sequence of code attributes and transformations. Our attribution and transformation languages were originally developed in the context of Dora, an optimizing compiler workbench [17]. Dora is implemented in Lisp; consequently the pattern language syntax is also based on Lisp. In this section, we summarize the languages used to write the code attributes and transformations.

5.1 The Pattern Language

Our pattern language is based on the traditional notion of a tree pattern as a tree with some of the subtrees replaced by pattern variables. Efficient automaton-based pattern matchers can be constructed for such simple patterns [18]. We have made some useful extensions to the pattern language, while maintaining the ability to build an efficient matcher.

5.1.1 Trees

Our trees are labeled and ordered. We write tree nodes by enclosing the label and (possibly empty) list of children in brackets: `[ ]`. For example, a tree with root label `A` and leaves labeled `B` and `C` is written `[A [B] [C]]`.

In order to construct an efficient pattern matcher, it is important that the set of labels be finite. But applications often require the use of potentially infinite sets of "labels" at leaves of the tree, such as integers. We therefore define trees over a tuple of two disjoint finite sets of labels: the *internal* labels and the *leaf* labels. A node with an internal label has an ordered, possibly empty, list of subtrees as children. A node with a leaf label has a single value of arbitrary type. We write leaf nodes by enclosing the label and the value in brackets. For example, the tree for the infix expression **x+2** could be written as `[Plus [var x] [int 2]]`. (For the purposes of this paper, we use capitalized symbols for internal node labels, and lower case symbols for leaf node labels.)

5.1.2 Simple patterns

A tree pattern is a tree with some of the subtrees replaced by pattern variables. Additionally, an operator or the value of a leaf node may be replaced by a pattern variable. Syntactically, pattern variables are alphanumeric symbols preceded by a question mark, for example, `?x`. A pattern matches a tree if there is a substitution of subtrees for pattern variables that transforms the pattern into the tree. We do not permit a pattern variable to appear twice in the same pattern.

A pattern match is found by considering all subtrees of the subject tree and trying to find appropriate substitutions for the variables named in the pattern. Note that there may be multiple possible matches for a pattern within a single tree. Matching the following pattern against the subject yields the single set of bindings shown:

```
pattern:     [A [B ?x] ?y]
subject:     [X [A [B [n 1]] [B [n 2] [C]]]]
        x =  [n 1]
        y =  [B [n 2] [C]]
```

No additional matches are possible.

Pattern variables may be constrained to match only a subset of trees by employing a syntactic typing facility. A type for a pattern variable is written by appending a dot and the name of the type to the variable, for example, `?x.expr`. In our examples, we will only attach types to variables in the operator position. Operator types are defined by listing the (finite) set of operators acceptable for a given type. There are two built-in types, `internal` and `leaf`, that contain, respectively, all internal and all leaf operators.

5.1.3 Iterators

There are two major extensions to simple patterns in Dora: *horizontal iterators* and *vertical iterators*. Horizontal iterators enhance the pattern matcher's ability to deal with variable-arity labels. Vertical iterators allow a pattern to specify a repetitive "backbone" between the root of the pattern and a leaf. These extended constructs can be handled without slowing down the pattern matcher; an automated reduction to the simple pattern matching language allows automaton-based solutions to be used for the enhanced language [17].

A *horizontal iterator* matches an indefinite number of subtrees at a particular position in the tree. Horizontal iterators are written by enclosing one or more subpatterns in an internal node within braces: `{ }`. A horizontal iterator denotes zero or more insertions of its subpatterns into the pattern. For example, the pattern `[X { [A] }]` matches the trees `[X]`, `[X [A]]`, `[X [A] [A]]`, and so on.

Horizontal iterators provide the power to match zero or more children of a node. On occasion, it is desirable to describe trees with zero or more identical "wrappers" built up on some base node. For example, suppose we have a binary `Plus`-labeled node, and `Plus`-trees are made left-heavy by convention. We might want to identify all trees with zero or more additions to a constant, such as `[int 3]`, `[Plus [int 3] [int 4]]`,
`[Plus [Plus [int 3] [int 4]] [var x]]`, and so on.

We can match such trees with a *vertical iterator* pattern. A vertical iterator has two parts: a base pattern (`[int ?x]` in our example) to match the base node, and a wrapper (`[Plus ... ?y]` in our example) that matches the (possibly repeated) surrounding context. The vertical iterator is written by prefixing the wrapper with a `$` and enclosing the base pattern in dots, in its appropriate place within the wrapper. The left-heavy `Plus`-trees are matched by the pattern `$[Plus ... [int ?x] ... ?y]`.

When a variable is contained within a horizontal and/or vertical iterator, it conceptually "matches" several (or perhaps zero) subtrees. A pattern variable in an iterator is bound to a list of the matched subtrees. The list is ordered left-to-right for horizontal iterators, and top-down for vertical iterators. For example:

```
pattern: [A { ?x ?y } ]
subject: [X [A [B] [C] [D] [E] ]]
        x = ([B] [D])
        y = ([C] [E])

pattern: $[Plus ... [int ?x] ... ?y]
subject: [Plus [Plus [int 3] [int 4]] [var x]]
        x = [int 3]
        y = ([var x] [int 4])
```

Note that variables in the base of a vertical iterator correspond to exactly one subtree, and so are bound to that tree and not to a list.

Iterators may be nested. Matching of nested iterators is conceptually straightforward, but appropriate bindings for variables becomes complicated. Variables get bound to lists of lists, in a way that maintains the structure of the tree. Details are omitted here, as nested iterators have not been used heavily in practice and do not occur in the examples of this paper.

5.2 Attributes

We use the notion of *attribute* familiar from attribute grammars: an attribute is a function on tree nodes, computable given the node and the tree in which it exists. As with attribute grammars, attributes in Dora are specified by giving semantic rules that describe how to compute an attribute in terms of attribute values at nearby nodes. But whereas attribute grammars associate semantic rules with grammar productions, Dora associates semantic rules with tree patterns, and additionally allows semantic constraints to be placed on the applicability of a given rule.

A compiler implementor defines an attribute using **def-attribute**:

```
(def-attribute name
  (pattern1
    defining-clause1,1
    defining-clause1,2 ...)
  (pattern2
    defining-clause2,1
    defining-clause2,2 ...)
  ...)
```

(Here '...' denotes ellipsis and is not a syntactic component of the macro). Each defining clause contains at least one semantic rule of the form

```
(:= (name node-expr) Lisp-form)
```

that states that the named attribute, at the node specified by *node-expr*, can be computed by evaluating the *Lisp-form*. The *Lisp-form* must be purely functional and may contain attribute evaluations of other nodes. The **def-attribute** form must be read declaratively, not imperatively; it states that, for all matches of each $pattern_i$ in a tree, each $defining\text{-}clause_{i,j}$ applies. The **def-attribute** compiler takes this declarative specification and determines a suitable evaluation method, defining a function of the given name that evaluates the attribute at any given node. This function may be used anywhere, and in particular may be used in defining attribute values, or in conditions used in attribute and transformation definitions.

In addition to the pattern variable bindings, the variable **self** is bound to the node corresponding to the root of the pattern. We can now show an example that computes the value of a simple constant expression tree:

```
(def-attribute val
  ([int ?v]
    (:= (val self) v))
  ([Plus ?x ?y]
    (:= (val self) (+ (val x) (val y))))
  ([Minus ?x ?y]
    (:= (val self) (- (val x) (val y)))))
```

In this example, the attribute **val** is defined to be either the value at an **int** leaf, the sum of the values of the subtrees of a **Plus** node, or the difference of the values of a **Minus** node.

Defining clauses may also place restrictions on the bindings taken on by the variables in semantic rules. The restrictions are specified by enclosing the rules in constructs such as **let**, **when**, and **dolist**[4]. The sequence of defining

[4] **dolist** is a Common Lisp iteration construct in which the first parameter is the loop variable and the second parameter is the list of elements that are successively bound to it.

clauses can be used to construct a case analysis, providing a different attribute equation for each context in which a successful match occurs.

For a trivial example of conditions, we define an attribute **frame-depth** on an intermediate language with **Block** expressions. The **frame-depth** attribute computes the lexical stack-frame depth of a node. **Blocks** contribute to this depth unless it is determined that they can be merged inline, as computed by a separately defined attribute **inline-block**:

```
(def-attribute frame-depth
  ([Block { ?kids }]
    (when (inline-block self)
      (dolist (kid kids)
        (:= (frame-depth kid) (frame-depth self)))))
  ([Block { ?kids }]
    (dolist (kid kids)
      (:= (frame-depth kid) (+ 1 (frame-depth self)))))
  ([?op.internal { ?k1 } ?kid { ?k2 }]
    (:= (frame-depth kid) (frame-depth self)))
  (?      ;must be root of tree - all others defined by previous rules
    (:= (frame-depth self) 0)))
```

This example is meant to demonstrate various features of **def-attribute**, not to demonstrate good form. As shown here, it is possible for two different rules to apply for an attribute value at a given node. In our system, the equation that occurs syntactically first in the **def-attribute** definition takes precedence. Note also that the **kid** variable used in the first two rules is bound by a **dolist** form, not by pattern matching.

In Dora, any pure Lisp construct can enclose semantic rules in a defining clause. Attributes are evaluated by traversing the whole tree, collecting the rules to be evaluated at each node, and dynamically determining an appropriate order for rule evaluation. This dynamic ordering supports any noncircular attribute definition, albeit executing less efficiently than a static ordering would. We are currently investigating the restrictions that must be placed on **def-attribute** to permit efficient implementation via attribute couplings.

Dora also has *recursive attributes* which permit multiple and circular definitions. The programmer specifies a lattice for the computation and the evaluator attempts to find a least fixed point solution. Since recursive attributes are not used in our examples, they are not further discussed in this paper.

5.3 Transformations

Transformations are described using the **def-transformation** macro:

```
(def-transformation name composition-rule
  (pattern_1
     rewrite-clause_1,1
     rewrite-clause_1,2 ...)
  (pattern_2
     rewrite-clause_2,1
     rewrite-clause_2,2 ...)
  ...
)
```

Each rewrite clause has at least one rewrite rule of the form

```
(-> node-expr partial-tree)
```

A partial tree looks like a pattern except that it has ***instantiations*** instead of pattern variables. It indicates how the tree node defined by ***node-expr*** is to be rewritten. An instantiation is a pure Lisp expression (usually a variable) preceded with an exclamation point, for example, **!x**. As in **def-attribute**, the **def-transformation** macro is to be read declaratively: for all matches of each *pattern*$_i$ in a tree, each *rewrite-clause*$_{i,j}$ describes a possible node rewrite given the pattern variable bindings for the match. As in the attribute definitions, restrictions on the matches of variables in the node expression and partial tree can be placed around the rewrite rules.

The composition rule determines whether the node rewrites described by the rewrite rules should be repeatedly applied, how to handle multiple rewrite rules applicable at a given node, and in what order the tree is traversed. Dora has a wide variety of composition rules needed for optimization applications. In this paper, we only consider the simplest composition rule, ***partial-tiling***, in which at most one rewrite rule is applicable at each node. In a partial tiling, the set of rewrites is computed in one pass over the tree and then all are applied "simultaneously."

Partial tilings are appropriate for the simple lowering transformations required for dynamic compiling. These transformations typically expand a tree while renaming some of the nodes. The following example rewrites simple binary expressions into a sequence of three-address machine instructions, making use of an attribute **temporary-for-result** that specifies a temporary location for the result of a node:

```
(def-transformation tree-to-three-address-code partial-tiling
  ([?op.binop ?x ?y]
   (-> self [Sequence !x !y
              [!(binop-to-three-address-op op)
                !(temporary-for-result self)
                !(temporary-for-result x)
                !(temporary-for-result y)]])))
```

As with attributes, Dora allows virtually any Lisp form to enclose rewrite rules in rewrite clauses. Combined with the many different forms of rewrite rules, this feature makes it easy to write very powerful transformations, at the expense of a slow implementation that must make many decisions at runtime. We have been investigating limitations to the acceptable wrappers and composition rules that make possible efficient implementation via attribute couplings.

5.4 Attribute Couplings

Attribute couplings were first formulated in the work of Ganzinger and Giegerich [3]. Work on attribute couplings has continued [4,5]. For our purposes, an attribute coupling is a closed collection of attribute definitions, similar to an attribute grammar, that defines a tree transformation. (Here "closed" means that every attribute definition is complete and every named attribute has a definition.) One particular attribute is distinguished as the "transformation." The value of this attribute at the root of a tree is another tree that is the transformation of the original tree. Attribute couplings differ from the attributes and transformations defined above in that they use pattern matching only superficially and have no disambiguation rules.[5] Attribute couplings are declared in the following manner in our system:

```
(def-attribute-coupling name
  (attribute-declaration1
   attribute-declaration2 ...)
  (node-pattern1
    defining-clause1,1
    defining-clause1,2 ...)
  (node-pattern2
    defining-clause2,1 ...)
  ...
  )
```

Each attribute declaration names an attribute and additionally may declare various properties of the attribute, such as its direction as in an attribute grammar (`:inherited` or `:synthesized`) or type. The first attribute declaration refers to the "transformation."

A *node-pattern* is a pattern matching a single node type and simply naming its direct children, for example, `[Minus ?expr1 ?expr2]`. The attribute coupling must have exactly one node-pattern for every node in the intermediate language. A defining clause has the same syntax in **def-attribute-coupling** as in **def-attribute**.

Attributes computing portions of the output of the transformation are called *syntactic* valued attributes. For example, the following defining clause for the syntactic valued attribute `operation` creates a MIPS assembly instruction in tree form:

```
(:= (operation self)
    (make-Add-node
     (make-temp-node 0)
     (make-temp-node 1)
     (make-temp-node 0)))
```

For complex transformations, named constructors (such as **make-temp-node**) may obscure the meaning. For clarity, therefore, we provide the operator '->*', allowing the previous equation to be written in the style of a transformation:

```
(->* (operation self) [Add [temp 0] [temp 1] [temp 0]])
```

This operator may be used in defining clauses of either **def-attribute** forms or **def-attribute-coupling** forms.

The following example of an attribute coupling compiles a simple intermediate language to MIPS assembly code:[6]

---

[5] Our attribute couplings are less restrictive than those of Ganzinger and Giegerich; we permit conditional attribution, default attribute values and attributes of mixed semantic and syntactic type.

[6] This example was generated from a transformation (see appendix) by the system described in the next section.

```
(def-attribute-coupling ir-to-mips-ac
  ((ir-to-mips :type :output :direction :synthesized))
  ([Minus ?expr1 ?expr2]
   (->* (ir-to-mips self)
    [Seq [Seq !(ir-to-mips expr1) [Push [temp 0]]]
         [Seq !(ir-to-mips expr2)
              [Seq [Pop [temp 1]]
                   [Sub [temp 0] [temp 1] [temp 0]]]]]))
  ([Plus ?expr1 ?expr2]
   (->* (ir-to-mips self)
    [Seq [Seq !(ir-to-mips expr1) [Push [temp 0]]]
         [Seq !(ir-to-mips expr2)
              [Seq [Pop [temp 1]]
                   [Add [temp 0] [temp 1] [temp 0]]]]]))
  ([int ?val]
   (->* (ir-to-mips self)
        [Lwi [temp 0] [imm16 !val]])))
```

This example has only one attribute; it computes the assembly code tree for all nodes in the intermediate language. The attribute has type **:output** (meaning it computes trees in the output language) and direction **:synthesized**.

Our system provides two other ways for declaring attribute couplings:

(**def-attribute-coupling-from-transformation** *name*
transformation-name)

(**def-attribute-coupling-composition** *name*
name-of-part1 name-of-part2)

These declarations create an attribute coupling from respectively a transformation or two attribute couplings. The methods used are described in the following section.

5.5 Summary

In this section, we described the various tools available to a compiler writer in our system. The compiler writer may define operations on trees: attributes, transformations and attribute couplings. While these tools are useful in their own right, in the next section we show how they can be used to describe a dynamic compiler.

6 The Incremental Component of a Dynamic Compiler

In this section, we discuss some of the ideas we are pursuing to achieve the automatic generation of the incremental component of the dynamic compiler. This transformation occurs in two parts. First, a compiler specification written as Dora attributes and transformations is composed into a single attribute coupling. Second, this attribute coupling is broken up into the two pieces of the incremental compiler: the attribute grammar to be evaluated incrementally and the code templates.

6.1 The Compiler Specification

The specification for the incremental part of the dynamic compiler consists of descriptions of intermediate languages and transformation stages. The transformation stages are ordered and represent the compilation process. The intermediate languages serve as interfaces between stages. Although the compiler description is multi-stage, the generated incremental component does not create any intermediate tree forms. A complete, albeit grossly simplified, example is given in the appendix.

Although we are using these methods for producing dynamic compilers for use with debugging, the specifications could also be used for production compilers. The resulting attribute coupling need not be evaluated incrementally and need not be implemented in Lisp.

6.1.1 The Intermediate Languages

The compiler writer first must describe the syntactic form of the intermediate languages being used. The term "intermediate language" is used rather loosely, in that the syntactic form of the input and of the machine code are also considered "intermediate" languages. The compiler writer may use inheritance to allow intermediate languages to share node types; transformations between languages with a common core (including transformations which operate within a single tree language) can therefore omit rewrites which simply copy node types from this shared core.

From the appendix, we have the following example of a very simple intermediate language with two internal node types **Plus** and **Minus**, each of which has two children and one leaf type **integer**, which contains an integer. The macro **def-tree-language** generates a number of functions for creating and analyzing trees of this type.

```
(def-tree-language ir
  (:node Plus
         (:child-slot expr1)
         (:child-slot expr2))
  (:node Minus
         (:child-slot expr1)
         (:child-slot expr2))
  (:leaf int
         (:data-slot val (:type integer))))
```

Considerable benefit can be obtained from widespread sharing of intermediate languages. It is expected, for example, that all implementations of dynamic compilers for the same machine will share the same "assembly" intermediate language for the particular machine[7]. More interestingly, it is possible that a

[7] The recent work by David Wall on Mahler [19] demonstrates additional advantages of such sharing.

few intermediate forms may be used in a wide variety of compilers for various languages and machines.

One of the most immediate benefits of sharing is that if two compilers share two intermediate languages, it is likely they can share the transformation stages converting one intermediate form to the other. As a result, later compilers can be described mainly using pieces from existing compilers. The benefit of sharing intermediate languages in compilers is, of course, well known [20].

6.1.2 The Transformation Stages

Each transformation stage consists of a transformation and the required attributes for this transformation. The compiler writer uses **def-attribute** and **def-transformation** for this purpose. Other macros are necessary for "glue" purposes. The syntax given is not crucial to our approach; it merely reflects the Lisp implementation framework.

From the appendix, we have the following example of a transformation stage:

```
(input-tree-language calc)
(output-tree-language ir)

(def-transformation calc-to-ir partial-tiling
  ([Binexpr ?e1 [operator "+"] ?e2]
      (-> self [Plus !e1 !e2]))
  ([Binexpr ?e1 [operator "-"] ?e2]
      (-> self [Minus !e1 !e2]))
  ([integer ?val]
      (-> self [int !val])))

(def-attribute-coupling-from-transformation
    calc-to-ir-ac calc-to-ir)
```

The transformation stage begins with declarations of the two intermediate languages in which the translation is expressed, one before and one after the transformation. In this example we are transforming a simple programming language (called "**calc**") into an intermediate language (called "**ir**") which has integer addition and subtraction. Following these declarations, we have a single transformation declaration. The final line declares the composable transformation stage. Originally we considered composing transformations directly, but the partial pattern matching necessary was overly complex and insufficiently powerful.

Converting transformations to composable attribute couplings requires several steps summarized here. First the given transformation must be converted to a syntactic valued attribute. The conversion involves making explicit the implicit recursion in rewrite clauses and generating default copying rewrites for the shared core between the input and output intermediate languages. Next, all the necessary attributes and transformations need to be gathered together and the priority between attribute equations must be eliminated. The major part of the conversion process is the expression of pattern matching through attribute computation. We are investigating various methods; for the examples in this paper, we generate a match attribute for each subpattern. We are also considering generating two tree automata to handle all necessary pattern matching.

The resulting attribute coupling is then cleaned up (using a specialized Lisp simplifier) and the direction and type are inferred for each attribute, including those attributes introduced in the conversion. As a result of this process, the following attribute coupling for the above transformation stage is produced:

```
(def-attribute-coupling calc-to-ir-ac
  ((calc-to-ir :type :output :direction :synthesized)
   (match2363 :type boolean :direction :synthesized)
   (match2045 :type boolean :direction :synthesized))
  ([Binexpr ?expr1 ?operator ?expr2]
    (when (match2045 operator)
      (->* (calc-to-ir self)
           [Plus !(calc-to-ir expr1) !(calc-to-ir expr2)]))
    (when (match2363 operator)
      (when (null (match2045 operator))
        (->* (calc-to-ir self)
             [Minus !(calc-to-ir expr1)
                    !(calc-to-ir expr2)]))))
  ([operator ?name]
    (:= (match2045 self) (string-equal name "+"))
    (:= (match2363 self) (string-equal name "-")))
  ([integer ?val]
    (->* (calc-to-ir self) [int !val])))
```

The conversion process has introduced two synthesized attributes, `match2363` and `match2045`, to take the place of the two-level pattern matching that existed in the transformation. The transformation has been converted to a synthesized attribute (which is the attribute coupling "transformation") of type `:output`. In this case, there is little expansion; in more complex examples, the resulting attribute coupling can be very large.

6.2 Composing Transformation Stages

Composition is carried out on the attribute couplings using the method given by Ganzinger and Giegerich extended to handle conditional attribution. Composing the example in the appendix yields the following attribute coupling which computes the binary MIPS program for the extremely simple language defined there. (The long numbers inside `code32` leaf nodes are the decimal equivalents of 32 bit machine instructions.)

```
(def-attribute-coupling calc-to-mips-binary-ac
  ((calc-to-ir-+-e-raw-mips
              :type :output :direction :synthesized)
   (match2363 :type boolean :direction :synthesized)
   (match2045 :type boolean :direction :synthesized))
  ([Binexpr ?expr1 ?operator ?expr2]
     (when (match2363 operator)
       (when (null (match2045 operator))
         (->* (calc-to-ir-+-e-raw-mips self)
              [Seq [Seq !(calc-to-ir-+-e-raw-mips expr1)
                        [Seq [code32 2946826236]
                             [code32 599654396]]]
                   [Seq !(calc-to-ir-+-e-raw-mips expr2)
                        [Seq [Seq [code32 2409955328]
                                  [code32 599588868]]
                             [code32 10756130]]]]))))
     (when (match2045 operator)
       (->* (calc-to-ir-+-e-raw-mips self)
            [Seq [Seq !(calc-to-ir-+-e-raw-mips expr1)
                      [Seq [code32 2946826236]
                           [code32 599654396]]]
                 [Seq !(calc-to-ir-+-e-raw-mips expr2)
                      [Seq [Seq [code32 2409955328]
                                [code32 599588868]]
                           [code32 10756128]]]]])))
  ([operator ?name]
    (:= (match2363 self) (string-equal name "-"))
    (:= (match2045 self) (string-equal name "+")))
  ([integer ?val]
    (->* (calc-to-ir-+-e-raw-mips self)
         [code32 !(+ 536870912 0 262144 (mod val 65536))])))
```

6.3 Generating the Incremental Compiler

The resulting attribute coupling is transformed so that it can be used as an incremental code generator for a dynamic compiler. We convert the code attribute into one that simply fills a slot in an instantiated template. The slot is the value of an inherited attribute. The template descriptions are owned by the dynamic linker.[8] Templates may have slots (the templates **add-tp** and **sub-tp** each have two, **int-tp** has none) and arguments (the templates **add-tp** and **sub-tp** have none, **int-tp** has one: **val**). This change allows the code generation process to proceed in a top-down fashion; each new piece of code is inserted into a slot in the code for its parent.

Finally we add a new synthesized attribute that depends on the code for the subtree rooted at that node. This attribute will serve as a "handle," as the system can bring the compilation up to date by requesting the current value of this attribute at the root.

[8] In our example, we give them names; in the actual system they will be numbered.

Applying this process to the composed attribute coupling in the preceding section may yield the following two parts.[9] The functions **make-slot** and **make-handle** can be evaluated in the context of the attribute grammar. The functions **fill-slot** and **instantiate-template** on the other hand represent remote procedure calls to the dynamic linker, as explained in the following section.

```
(def-attribute-grammar calc-to-mips-ag
  ((handle          :type handle :direction :synthesized)
   (slot            :type slot :direction :inherited)
   (calc-to-raw-mips :type :output :direction :synthesized)
   (match2363       :type boolean :direction :synthesized)
   (match2045       :type boolean :direction :synthesized))
  ([Binexpr ?expr1 ?operator ?expr2]
   (:= (slot expr1) (make-slot (calc-to-raw-mips self) 0))
   (:= (slot expr2) (make-slot (calc-to-raw-mips self) 1))
   (:= (handle self)
       (make-handle (calc-to-raw-mips self)
                    (handle expr1) (handle expr2)))
   (when (match2363 operator)
     (when (not (match2045 operator))
       (:= (calc-to-raw-mips self)
           (fill-slot (slot self)
                      (instantiate-template 'add-tp)))))
   (when (match2045 operator)
     (:= (calc-to-raw-mips self)
         (fill-slot (slot self)
                    (instantiate-template 'sub-tp))))
  ([operator ?name]
   (:= (match2363 self) (string-equal name "-"))
   (:= (match2045 self) (string-equal name "+")))
  ([integer ?val]
   (:= (calc-to-raw-mips self)
       (fill-slot (slot self)
                  (instantiate-template 'int-tp val)))
   (:= (handle self) (make-handle (calc-to-raw-mips self)))))
```

[9] This final example, unlike the previous compositions, was created by hand.

```
(def-code-templates calc-to-mips-temp
  ((add-tp 2)
     [Seq [Seq [slot 0]
               [Seq [code32 2946826236] [code32 599654396]]]
          [Seq [slot 1]
                [Seq [Seq [code32 2409955328]
                          [code32 599588868]]
                     [code32 10756130]]]])
  ((sub-tp 2)
     [Seq [Seq [slot 0]
               [Seq [code32 2946826236] [code32 599654396]]]
          [Seq [slot 1]
               [Seq [Seq [code32 2409955328]
                         [code32 599588868]]
                    [code32 10756128]]]])
  ((int-tp 0 val)
     [code32 !(+ 536870912 0 262144 (mod val 65536))]))
```

7 The Dynamic Linker

The largest part of the run-time system is a "dynamic linker" which handles code generation, code linking and execution state maintenance. In addition, the run-time system contains operating system virtualization and debugger support. In this section, we discuss the issues concerning the dynamic linker.

7.1 Dynamic Code Generation

The dynamic linker executes in a different process from the incremental attribute evaluator and links the compiled program in the linker's own address space. The compiled program consists of instantiated templates and foreign code. The dynamic linker communicates with the incremental evaluator in terms of tree paths—each node is designated by a sequence of node positions and names starting from the root.[10] When a source tree node changes, the incremental compiler passes to the dynamic linker the node designation, a template name, and a list of parameters which are the non-code values used in the template for this node.

The dynamic linker creates an instance of the given template and links it with the code for its parent. The parameters passed to the dynamic linker provide information about the context in which the code will be executed, and are used to tailor the template to the context. For instance, in the previous section, we had a template for integer constants in which the value of the integer constant is such an parameter.

Code segments are linked in the same way that assembly language code is typically patched "by hand." There is a jump from the previous instruction to the beginning of the inserted sequence, and a jump from the end of the sequence to the instruction that logically follows the insertion.

[10] Names are used instead of positions when the subtrees are logically unordered. For instance, the ordering of global function objects is unimportant for code generation purposes.

This model of code generation allows great latitude for handling inconsistency without causing erroneous execution. Since the new code is not written over the old code, the execution state is not affected. The debugger could thus allow execution to continue even when it is only partially consistent with the current program text.

7.2 Execution State Maintenance

The top-down nature of code generation ensures that whole subtrees are replaced at a time. If the compiler were to "optimize" by not replacing certain subtrees of the changed subtree, then active execution within those subtrees could be rendered erroneous. For example, the new surrounding code might push another word on the stack. Under certain conditions, the dynamic compiler may have enough information to do this properly and thus provide complete execution consistency, but the danger of erroneous execution is great.

Removing other types of inconsistency might likewise prove difficult; the surrounding context might require a different stack frame. The return addresses could be found and made to point to new addresses, but removing or adding words to the stack means we need to traverse all data structures which might point into the stack.

Instead of modifying a current execution state in order to remove inconsistency, the run-time system could unroll computation back to the last consistent point and then restart computation. This capability was provided in the LOIPE system [2], though side-effects were not unrolled—the execution environment popped procedure frames off the stack until no changed procedures were active. Such a system abandons partial consistency and thus is not suitable for debugging.

7.3 Foreign Code

Foreign code — modules compiled by the standard system compiler, including standard library functions — are linked with the dynamically compiled code using traditional dynamic linking methods (such as *dld*[22]). Direct operating system entry points are linked with virtual functions in the run-time system so that, for example, input and output is appropriately redirected.

In order to use dynamic compilation for compute-intensive applications, it is possible to integrate sections of optimized code with the code generated by the dynamic compiler. The optimized code segments would be treated like foreign code, in the sense that they would not be accessible internally by the debugger. If the code segments were annotated with attributes that indicated what external changes would invalidate them, then the dynamic compiler could invoke a batch optimizer on the appropriate subtrees.

8 Previous Work

Since dynamic compilers provide a powerful interactive environment for the programmer, it is not surprising that many programming environments have been proposed and developed which allow some degree of dynamic compilation.

The paucity of truly dynamic compilers is thus surprising. We summarize briefly the previous work in this area.

In order to provide incremental or dynamic compilation, a programming environment must allow the compiler to save its state somehow, and in the case of the dynamic compiler, the compiler must be able to communicate with the process executing the compiled code. These requirements are more easily met within the scope of an integrated programming environment that controls all access to the program: its text, machine code and execution state. A number of integrated programming environments provide some sort of incremental or dynamic compilation to the programmer [2,23,24,25,26]. Some environments provide facilities similar to dynamic compilation using an interpreter [27,28,29, 30]. Typically, such systems provide incremental compilation at the procedure level and many allow a procedure definition or redefinition to be added to a program already in execution.

Though several authors mention that dynamic compilation in their systems could *theoretically* be used for debugging purposes [2,24], in the same manner as interpreted Lisp, they do not pursue this capability seriously. For example, in Feiler's proposed system LOIPE [2], the compiler would be able to partially replace a procedure with a new definition including a new statement (in our case, a debugging statement) right at the current execution point and then execution would be permitted to continue. Unfortunately for this scenario, the system actually implemented by Feiler did not allow execution to continue in a procedure that had been recompiled. The goal of fine granularity dynamic compilation was apparently too difficult to achieve using his method of *partial replacement*, which patched in whole new procedure objects at a time rather then patching the code locally at the statement or expression. We believe that one of the factors leading to LOIPE not meeting its goals was that Feiler relied on transforming execution state to make it consistent with the new code.

In Tektronix's integrated programming environments [24,25,31], the programmer could leave part of a procedure definition unspecified, leaving an explicit hole, or, in the systems' terminology, *workspace*. When execution reached a workspace, execution would be suspended. The programmer could then put some (temporary) code in the workspace and continue execution. This allows for certain controlled debugging actions which are executed just like the rest of the program. But since workspaces have to be specified before a procedure is compiled and because compilation is incremental only to the procedural level, this feature does not give the dynamic compiler enough granularity to be the only venue of execution for a debugger.

Lisp environments often provide a powerful stepping facility that allows the programmer to break execution at any point (for interpreted code) or at any place so marked at compile time (for compiled code). The programmer may then examine or modify the execution state by evaluating any Lisp expression or by invoking special built-in commands. The debugger only has to handle these special commands; the interpreter already supports the rest. In fact most Lisp implementations allow the programmer to redefine active or inactive procedures during execution. Redefining active procedures leads to inconsistency, which is allowed to persist—an inconsistent state does not lead to erroneous execution because the system maintains the old version of the procedure until it is no longer needed.

9 Current Status

Much work remains in the implementation of the generator of dynamic compilers. We can convert transformation stages into attribute couplings, and can compose attribute couplings that do not make use of variable length children lists and that create a bounded number of output nodes for each input node. We are currently working to support such extensions to the composition method given by Ganzinger and Giegerich. The other aspects of the system, the generator of the incremental compiler, the incremental attribute evaluator and the dynamic linker, are still under design.

10 Acknowledgement

We thank John Hauser for his careful reading of the manuscript and his helpful comments.

11 References

1. Chase B B, Hood R T. Selective interpretation as a technique for debugging computationally intensive programs. Proc ACM SIGPLAN 1987 Symp on Interpreters and Interpretive Techniques, ACM SIGPLAN Notices 1987; 22(7):113–124
2. Feiler P H. A language-oriented interactive programming environment based on compilation technology. PhD thesis, CMU-CS-82-117, Carnegie-Mellon University, 1982
3. Ganzinger H, Giegerich R. Attribute coupled grammars. 1984 Symp on Compiler Construction, ACM SIGPLAN Notices 1984; 19(6):157–170
4. Ganzinger H, Giegerich R, Vach M. MARVIN: a tool for applicative and modular compiler specifications. Report 220, University Dortmund, 1986
5. Giegerich R. Composition and evaluation of attribute coupled grammars. Acta Inform 1988; 25:355–423
6. Ballance R A, Graham S L, Van De Vanter M L. The Pan language-based editing system. ACM Trans on Soft Eng and Meth 1992; 1(1):95–127
7. Ballance R A. Syntactic and semantic checking in language-based editing systems. PhD thesis, UCB/CSD 89/548, University of California, Berkeley, 1989
8. Black C. PPP: a pretty-printer for Pan. Master's report, UCB/CSD 90/589, University of California, Berkeley, 1990
9. Butcher J. LADLE. Master's report, UCB/CSD 89/519, University of California, Berkeley, 1989
10. Bell J R. Threaded code. Comm ACM 1973; 16(2):370–372
11. Kogge P M. An architectural trail to threaded code systems. IEEE Computer 1982; 15:22–33

12. Alt M, Fecht C, Ferdinand C, Wilhelm R. The Trafola-H system. In The PROSPECTRA system (to appear)

13. Ganzinger H, Giegerich R, Möncke U, Wilhelm R. A truly generative semantics directed compiler generator. 1982 Symp on Compiler Construction, ACM SIGPLAN Notices 1982; 17(6):172–184

14. Lipps P, Möncke U, Wilhelm R. OPTRAN—A language/system for the specification of program transformations: system overview and experiences. In Compiler Compilers and High Speed Compilation, 2nd CCHSC Workshop 1988; 52–65

15. Pelegrí-Llopart E, Graham S L. Optimal code generation for expression trees: an application of BURS theory. In 15th ACM Symp on Princ of Prog Lang 1988; 294–308

16. Henry R R, Damron P C. Algorithms for table-driven code generators using tree-pattern matching. 89-02-03, University of Washington, Seattle, 1989

17. Farnum C. Pattern-based languages for prototyping compiler optimizers. PhD thesis, UCB/CSD 90/608, University of California, Berkeley, 1990

18. Hoffman C M, O'Donnell M J. Pattern matching in trees. J ACM 1982; 29(1):68–95

19. Wall D W. Experience with a software-defined machine architecture. In ACM Trans on Prog Lang and Sys (to appear, 1992)

20. Strong J, Wegstein J, Tritter A, Olsztyn J, Mock O, Steel T. The problem of programming communications with changing machines: a proposed solution. Comm ACM 1958; 1(8):12–18

21. Dybvig R K. The Scheme programming language. Prentice-Hall, Inc., Englewood Cliffs, New Jersey, 1987

22. Ho W W, Olsson R A. An approach to genuine dynamic linking. University of California, Davis, CSE-90-25, 1990

23. Deutsch P, Schiffman A M. Efficient implementation of the Smalltalk-80 system. In 11th ACM Symp on Princ of Prog Lang 1984; 297–302

24. Schwartz M D, Delisle N M, Begwani V S. Incremental compilation in Magpie. 1984 Symp on Compiler Construction, ACM SIGPLAN Notices 1984; 19(6):122–131

25. Ross G. Integral C—A practical environment for C programming. In Proc ACM SIGSOFT/SIGPLAN Soft Eng Symp on Pract Soft Dev Env 1986; 42–48

26. Fritzson P. Preliminary experience from the DICE system: a distributed incremental compiling environment. Proc ACM SIGSOFT/SIGPLAN Soft Eng Symp on Pract Soft Dev Env 1984; 19(5):113–123

27. Teitelman W. Interlisp reference manual. Xerox PARC, 1978

28. Teitelbaum T, Reps T. The Cornell program synthesizer: a syntax-directed programming environment. Comm ACM 1981; 24:563–573

29. Standish T A, Taylor R N. Arcturus: a prototype advanced Ada programming environment. Proc ACM SIGSOFT/SIGPLAN Soft Eng Symp on Pract Soft Dev Env 1984; 19(5):57–64

30. Saber Inc. Saber C. 1989

31. Delisle N M, Menicosy D E, Schwartz M D. Viewing a programming environment as a single tool. Proc ACM SIGSOFT/SIGPLAN Soft Eng Symp on Pract Soft Dev Env 1984; 19(5):49–56

A Compiler Specification Example

The following compiler specification describes the compilation of a "language" which has addition, subtraction and small integer constants.

```
(def-tree-language calc
  (:node Binexpr
         (:child-slot expr1)
         (:child-slot operator)
         (:child-slot expr2))
  (:leaf integer
         (:data-slot val (:type integer)))
  (:leaf operator
         (:data-slot name (:type string))
         (:equal string-equal)))
```

```
(def-tree-language ir
  (:node Plus
         (:child-slot expr1)
         (:child-slot expr2))
  (:node Minus
         (:child-slot expr1)
         (:child-slot expr2))
  (:leaf int
         (:data-slot val (:type integer))))
```

```
(def-tree-language binary
  (:node Seq
         (:child-slot in1)
         (:child-slot in2))
  (:node Skip)
  (:leaf code32
         (:data-slot data (:type integer))))
```

```
(def-tree-language raw-mips-asm
  (:includes-lang binary)
  (:node Add
        (:child-slot rd)
        (:child-slot r1)
        (:child-slot r2))
  (:node Addi
        (:child-slot rd)
        (:child-slot r1)
        (:child-slot imm))
  (:node Sub
        (:child-slot rd)
        (:child-slot r1)
        (:child-slot r2))
  (:node Lw
        (:child-slot rd)
        (:child-slot r1)
        (:child-slot imm))
  (:node Sw
        (:child-slot rs)
        (:child-slot r1)
        (:child-slot imm))
  (:leaf reg
        (:data-slot num (:type integer)))
  (:leaf imm16
        (:data-slot num (:type integer))))
```

```
(def-tree-language mips-asm
  (:includes-lang raw-mips-asm)
  ;; some syntactic sugar
  (:node push
        (:child-slot r))
  (:node pop
        (:child-slot r))
  (:node Lwi
        (:child-slot rd)
        (:child-slot imm))
  (:node nop)
  (:leaf temp
        (:data-slot num (:type integer))))
```

```
;;;; Converting to Intermediate format

(input-tree-language calc)
(output-tree-language ir)

(def-transformation calc-to-ir partial-tiling
  ([Binexpr ?e1 [operator "+"] ?e2]
     (-> self [Plus !e1 !e2]))
  ([Binexpr ?e1 [operator "-"] ?e2]
     (-> self [Minus !e1 !e2]))
  ([integer ?val]
     (-> self [int !val])))

(def-attribute-coupling-from-transformation
    calc-to-ir-ac calc-to-ir)
```

```
;;;; Converting intermediate form to MIPS assembly language

(input-tree-language ir)
(output-tree-language mips-asm)

(def-attribute operation
  ([Plus ?e1 ?e2]
    (->* (operation self) [Add [temp 0] [temp 1] [temp 0]]))
  ([Minus ?e1 ?e2]
    (->* (operation self) [Sub [temp 0] [temp 1] [temp 0]])))

(def-opvar-type binop
    Plus Minus)

(def-transformation ir-to-mips partial-tiling
  ([?op.binop ?e1 ?e2]
    (-> self [Seq [Seq !e1 [push [temp 0]]]
                  [Seq !e2 [Seq [pop [temp 1]]
                                !(operation self)]]]))
  ([int ?val]
    (-> self [Lwi [temp 0] [imm16 !val]])))

(def-attribute-coupling-from-transformation
    ir-to-mips-ac ir-to-mips)
```

```
;;;; Removing syntactic sugar from MIPS assembly language

(input-tree-language mips-asm)
(output-tree-language raw-mips-asm)

(def-transformation lower-mips partial-tiling
  ([temp ?r]
    (-> self [reg !(+ 4 r)]))

  ([push ?r]                              ; NB: reg29 = stack pointer
    (-> self [Seq [Sw !r [reg 29] [imm16 -4]]
                  [Addi [reg 29] [reg 29] [imm16 -4]]]))
  ([pop ?r]
    (-> self [Seq [Lw !r [reg 29] [imm16 0]]
                  [Addi [reg 29] [reg 29] [imm16 4]]]))
  ([Lwi ?rd ?imm]
    (-> self [Addi !rd [reg 0] !imm]))
  )

(def-attribute-coupling-from-transformation
    lower-mips-ac lower-mips)
```

```
;;;; Assembling MIPS assembly language

(defconstant *SPECIAL* #o00)
(defconstant *ADD* #o40)
(defconstant *SUB* #o42)
(defconstant *ADDI* #o10)
(defconstant *LW* #o43)
(defconstant *SW* #o53)

(input-tree-language raw-mips-asm)
(output-tree-language binary)

(def-opvar-type arith3r Add Sub)
(def-opvar-type arithi Addi Lw Sw)

(def-transformation assemble-raw-mips partial-tiling

  ([?op.arith3r [reg ?rd] [reg ?r1] [reg ?r2]]
    (-> self [code32 !(+ (ash *SPECIAL* 26)
                         (ash r1 21)
                         (ash r2 16)
                         (ash rd 11)
                         (op-case op
                           (Add *ADD*)
                           (Sub *SUB*)))]))

  ([?op.arithi [reg ?rd] [reg ?r1] [imm16 ?val]]
    (-> self [code32 !(+ (ash (op-case op
                                (Addi *ADDI*)
                                (Lw *LW*)
                                (Sw *SW*)) 26)
                         (ash r1 21)
                         (ash rd 16)
                         (mod val (ash 1 16)))])))

(def-attribute-coupling-from-transformation
   assemble-raw-mips-ac assemble-raw-mips)

;;;; Define compositions

(def-attribute-coupling-composition calc-to-mips-ac
   calc-to-ir-ac ir-to-mips-ac)

(def-attribute-coupling-composition assemble-mips-ac
   lower-mips-ac assemble-raw-mips-ac)

(def-attribute-coupling-composition calc-to-mips-binary-ac
   calc-to-mips-ac assemble-mips-ac)
```

The RTL System: A Framework for Code Optimization

Ralph E. Johnson
Carl McConnell
J. Michael Lake

Department of Computer Science

University of Illinois at Urbana-Champaign

Urbana, Illinois USA

{ johnson, mcconnel, jmlake }@cs.uiuc.edu

Abstract

The construction of compiler front and back-ends is understood well enough for a great deal of the work to be automated, but such is not the case for the rest of a modern compiler, the optimizer. This paper describes the RTL System, a flexible set of classes with a large number of predefined algorithms that the compiler writer can customize. The RTL System differs from systems to construct compiler front and back-ends because it does not specify the optimizations with a specialized language, but is instead an object-oriented framework. This paper describes the framework and how it can be used to build a code optimizer.

1 Introduction

Compiler front and back-ends are understood well enough for them to be generated automatically. A parser generator can create the parser from a grammar describing the language, and a code generator can be built automatically from a description of the machine. However, the construction of an optimizer is much less straightforward. This paper describes the RTL (Register Transfer Language) System, a framework for code optimization.

RTL is a register transfer language that compilers can use to represent programs during optimization. The RTL System is a set of classes for representing and manipulating programs, along with a large number of predefined algorithms that the compiler writer can customize. These algorithms include the common optimizations found in a typical compiler textbook [1][8], and it is easy to implement new optimizations. Thus, the RTL System is a toolkit for constructing code optimizers.

Such a toolkit is necessary because no code optimizer can be completely language- and machine-independent: when an optimizer is retargeted to a new language or machine, optimizations must nearly always be added, deleted, or modified to achieve the best results. For example, elimination of array bounds checks may be a worthwhile optimization for Pascal, but it is not for C; likewise, the criteria for when to perform constant propagation are different for a CISC architecture than for a RISC one. Such differences are best handled by providing a set of algorithms and components that can be "mixed and matched" to construct an optimizer for a given target. This is the philosophy behind the design of the RTL System.

The RTL System is not just a set of reusable software components, it is also a theory of how to represent and optimize programs. This theory is represented as a *framework* that is designed to be customized and extended [21]. An object-oriented framework is a reusable design for an application or a part of an application. It consists of a set of classes and a model of how instances of these classes interact.

The theory behind the RTL System is a combination of two different lines of work. The idea of using a register transfer language as an intermediate language in a compiler was borrowed from the work of Davidson and Fraser [5] [7] [6]. The RTL System also uses their algorithm for peephole optimization and code generation. The data dependence representation and the machine independent optimizations are based on SSA form [2][4][17]. Combining these two ideas was not trivial [15], but is not discussed here. This paper focuses on the object-oriented framework, not the details of the underlying theory.

The RTL System is part of TS, an optimizing compiler for Smalltalk. TS is one part of the Typed Smalltalk project [12]. The project has several components, such as developing a type system for Smalltalk [9] and redesigning some of the tools in the Smalltalk-80 programming environment to ensure that the compiler is compatible with the rapid-prototyping style of Smalltalk [22]. However, the largest component of the project is the TS compiler. The front-end of TS performs some optimizations, such as early-binding of message sends and in-line substitution, that are important because of peculiarities of Smalltalk. These optimizations convert Smalltalk programs into C-like programs, at which point conventional code optimization and generation is needed.

TS uses RTL not only as an intermediate form for programs, but also to define primitive Smalltalk methods (*i.e.*, procedures). After the TS front-end performs Smalltalk-specific optimizations on a method, it converts the entire method into RTL. Most optimizations are done by the RTL System, which also generates machine language. Thus, the RTL System also acts as a back-end.

The following begins by describing the register transfer language and the representation of RTL programs within the implementation of the RTL system. In section 4, some of the algorithms in the RTL System are described, followed by a discussion of the code generation subsystem in section 5. Section 6 shows how to customize the RTL System. Together, these sections describe the framework for code optimization. Section 7 describes some lessons on framework design that we learned by developing the RTL System.

2 The Register Transfer Language RTL

The key lesson learned from the work of Davidson and Fraser was that a universal intermediate language for a compiler should be the *intersection* of machine languages, not the *union*. This implies that its operations should be so elementary that every machine has them, thus ensuring that every RTL program

```
Compute the sum of 10 integers
starting at memory location 1000,
and put the result in memory location 500.

r1 ← 1000.          Initialize pointer to address 1000.
r2 ← 0.             Initialize sum to 0.
r3 ← 0.             Initialize counter to 0.

L1:
r3 >= 10 ↑ L2       If counter ≥ 10, jump to L2.
r4 ← *r1.           Fetch integer pointed to ...
r2 ← r2 + r4.       ... and add it to sum.
r1 ← r1 + 4.        Increment pointer.
r3 ← r3 + 1.        Increment counter.
↑ L1.               Jump to L1.

L2:
r5 ← 500.           Set pointer to 500 ...
*r5 ← r2.           ... and store sum there.
@.                  Return.
```

Figure 1: An RTL program.

corresponds to some machine program. Unfortunately, this ideal is impossible to reach, since there are no operations that all machines use. An optimizer for a machine that lacks common operations like multiplication will have to transform missing operations into simpler ones, giving one more reason to customize the optimizer. In spite of this, we have found that a simple register transfer language makes an effective intermediate language for a compiler.

The sample program in Figure 1 illustrates the constructs available in RTL. RTL provides a typical set of numeric operations, as well as operations to read and write memory and to change the flow of control. RTL programs can use an infinite number of logical registers. Logical registers can be preassigned to particular physical registers, enabling RTL to describe subroutine calling conventions.

The simplicity of RTL means that a relatively large quantity of RTL code is sometimes needed to represent high-level operations. However, this is exactly the idea: provide verbose but simple code to the RTL System, thus enabling it to uncover all possible optimizations.

The RTL System forms machine instructions by combining as many RTL statements together as it can; it never breaks them down into simpler ones. It works best when the RTL code it receives is as simple as possible. Computations that could be expressed using one RTL statement are instead broken up into several, with temporary registers holding intermediate results. A complex RTL statement may keep the RTL System from discovering an optimization. That is why the statements

```
r4 ← *r1.
r2 ← r2 + r4.
```

are used instead of

```
r2 ← r2 + *r1.
```

in Figure 1, even though the latter is equivalent and shorter.

One construct not shown in Figure 1 is the concurrency operator ";". For example,

```
r2 ← *(r1 - 4) ; r1 ← r1 - 4
```

expresses a pre-decrement memory access that might be written as

```
r2 = *--r1
```

in C. The concurrency operator is used to represent complex instructions and addressing modes that are discovered by the RTL System during optimization and instruction selection, and does not usually appear in the RTL System's input.

3 Program Representation

The RTL System represents RTL programs using objects of four kinds of classes. A **RTLProgram** contains the flow graph of a program. **RTLFlowNode** represents the nodes of the flow graph. **RTLTransfer** represents the register transfers in each flow node. **RTLExpression** represents the expressions in each register transfer.

Like most frameworks, the most important classes in the RTL System are abstract. **RTLFlowNode**, **RTLTransfer**, and **RTLExpression** are abstract, *i.e.* it is really their subclasses that are used to represent programs. **RTLProgram** is concrete, but it is just used to contain information global to the optimization process, and is never subclassed.

Figure 2 illustrates how a program is represented in terms of objects in these classes by showing the flow graph for the RTL program in Figure 1. It contains one instance of **RTLProgram** (representing the entire graph), four instances of subclasses of **RTLFlowNode**, nine instances of subclasses of **RTLTransfer**, and over a dozen instances of subclasses of **RTLExpression**. Memory references are represented as functions taking an explicitly named memory object as an argument. This streamlines the treatment of memory operations, and is discussed in more detail later.

3.1 Static Single Assignment Form

Global optimizations require information about the global data flow properties of a program: Which transfers create the values used by a given transfer? This question is easy to answer if each register is assigned a value exactly once, and this is guaranteed by static single assignment (SSA) form, a program representation developed by researchers at IBM [4]. The RTL System uses SSA form to simplify algorithms for common subexpression elimination [2], code motion out of loops [17], and other optimizations.

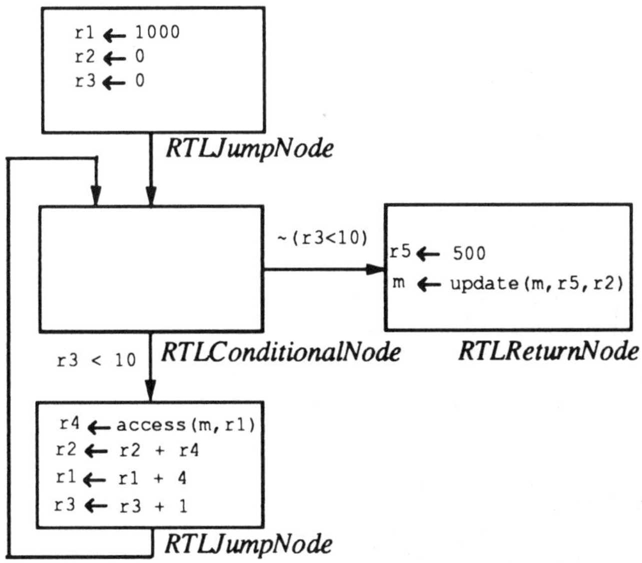

Figure 2: Flow graph for an RTL Program

It is simple to rename registers in a basic block so that there is only one assignment to (*i.e.*, definition of) each register. However, this isn't possible in the presence of conditionals or loops, since a given point in the program may be reached by conflicting definitions. SSA form avoids this problem by using an operator that merges (chooses) distinct registers defined on different paths. The first node reached by a set of conflicting definitions starts with a *ϕ-assignment* that merges them. As a consequence, each register is defined by no more than one register transfer.

A ϕ-assignment is an assignment whose right hand side is a ϕ function. Each operand of ϕ is a register, and there is one register for each predecessor of the flow node in which the ϕ-assignment appears. If control reaches the ϕ-assignment through the j-th predecessor, then the result of ϕ is the value of the j-th operand. Each execution of a ϕ-assignment uses only one of the operands, but which one depends on how control reached the flow node containing the ϕ-assignment.

SSA form makes computing data flow information easy. It also makes thinking about optimizations easy, since the case where different definitions reach the same point no longer occurs. Figure 3 shows how the flow graph in Figure 2 looks after SSA conversion. Note how conflicting definitions of loop variables are resolved by ϕ-assignments, which are shown as assignments with `phi(...)` on their right-hand sides in the figure. Also note the addition of *implicit assignments*, shown as assignments with --- on their right-hand sides; these indicate that the destination was initialized outside the RTL program. Thus, every register is the destination of exactly one register transfer.

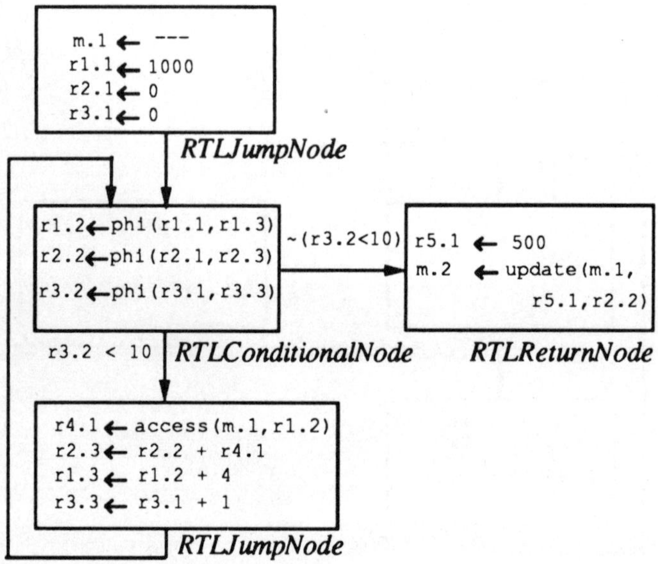

Figure 3: Flow graph for an RTL program after SSA conversion.

3.2 The Flow Graph Level

RTLProgram represents the control flow graph of a program. It acts as a container for the flow nodes, and for anything that is global with respect to the optimization process. For example, it contains an instance of **MachineDescription** that describes the target machine: all machine-dependent operations consult this object. **RTLProgram** also has methods for optimizing the RTL program, and for generating machine code, as well as for traversing the flow nodes in various ways.

RTLFlowNode and its subclasses represent vertices of flow graphs, and act as containers for register transfers. **RTLFlowNodes** also capture the structure of the flow graph by maintaining pointers to the nodes that precede and succeed them, as well as to their dominators and intervals. All flow-of-control optimizations, such as branch elimination, take place at the flow node level.

The **RTLFlowNode** protocol includes many of the same kind of optimization and code generation methods as **RTLProgram**; in fact, many **RTLProgram** methods do little more than delegate the message to the flow nodes. Since flow nodes are responsible for maintaining the structure of the flow graph, there are methods for changing a flow node's predecessors and successors.

Loops require special attention since a program spends most of its time executing them. In the RTL System, a loop is referred to as an *interval* [19]; a single-entry, strongly connected region of the flow graph. Sometimes it is convenient to treat an interval itself as a flow node. For this reason, an interval is represented by an instance of **RTLIntervalNode**, which is a kind of flow node that may act on behalf of the nodes inside it. Intervals can be nested, so **RTLIntervalNode** has a pointer to the surrounding interval.

Except for **RTLIntervalNode**, the subclasses of **RTLFlowNode** represent basic blocks. Thus, they are all subclasses of **RTLBasicBlock**, which is a subclass of **RTLFlowNode** that contains register transfers and is able to add, remove, and iterate over them.

The flow node hierarchy is

RTLFlowNode
  RTLBasicBlock
    RTLJumpNode
      RTLCallNode
      RTLConditionalNode
    RTLReturnNode
  RTLIntervalNode

The reason for having a class hierarchy for basic blocks instead of a single class is that *the class of a flow node implicitly represents how control changes after the basic block in that flow node finishes executing.* In other words, rather than ending basic blocks with a register transfer indicating how control changes, the flow node itself indicates this. This principle has three corollaries:

- Basic blocks always end (by the flow node that contains them) with a change of control. They never just "fall through" to a successor.
- Basic blocks consist only of assignments. They never contain a register transfer representing a change of control.
- The targets of jumps are always flow nodes. Flow nodes play the role that labels do in conventional representations.

This scheme simplifies the implementation of the RTL System, since methods that depend on how control changes are implemented differently by each flow node class.

The subclasses play the following roles:

RTLJumpNode: basic blocks that end with a jump.

RTLCallNode: basic blocks that end with a call followed by a jump.

RTLConditionalNode: basic blocks that end with a conditional jump followed by a jump.

RTLReturnNode: basic blocks that end with a return.

3.3 The Register Transfer Level

RTLTransfer and its subclasses represent the register transfers that make up the program. They are components of basic blocks, and maintain the data flow information of the program. Each register transfer is able to find the register transfers that creates the values it uses and that use the values it creates.

A register transfer describes either a transfer of data—in other words, an assignment—or a transfer of control, such as a jump. However, as discussed in the previous section, control flow is represented at the flow node level. Control register transfers are not used during the optimization phases of the RTL System, but are only used during machine code generation.

The register transfer class hierarchy is

RTLTransfer
- **AbstractAssignment**
  - **ImplicitAssignment**
  - **Assignment**
  - **PhiAssignment**
- **RegisterTransferSet**
- **Call**
- **Jump**
  - **CondJump**
- **Return**

Some of these classes represent the transfer of data, and so are the main register transfer classes.

AbstractAssignment: the abstract superclass of all classes representing assignments to some storage.

ImplicitAssignment: assignments having an unknown source. These are used, for example, to define registers containing arguments.

Assignment: assignments having a destination and a source. These are the most common kind of **RTLTransfer**.

PhiAssignment: ϕ-assignments.

RegisterTransferSet: sets of concurrent **RTLTransfers**.

The other register transfers represent the transfer of control. They are used primarily during machine code generation, where each register transfer produces machine code for itself.

Call: procedure calls.

Jump: unconditional jumps.

CondJump: conditional jumps.

Return: returns.

3.4 The Expression Level

Except for **RegisterTransferSet**, the components of a register transfer are expressions. Both the source and destination of a register transfer are instances of subclasses of **RTLExpression**. The expression hierarchy is

- **RTLExpression**
  - **Storage**
    - **Register**
      - **SpecialRegister**
    - **Memory**
  - **MemoryAccess**
  - **MemoryUpdate**
  - **BinaryExpression**
  - **Constant**
  - **UnaryExpression**

Storage is the abstract superclass of all classes representing expressions that can be the target of an assignment. **Register** is one subclass, with a subclass **SpecialRegister** that represents special registers such as the stack pointer. **Memory** is less naturally (at least at first glance) another subclass. However, as mentioned earlier, memory references are represented explicitly as functions in order to allow a unified treatment of operations on memory and operations on registers where dependency analysis and optimization are concerned. Instances of **Memory** serve as one argument to these functions. The functions themselves are

```
access(m, x)
```

which returns the item at address `x` in memory `m`, and is represented by **MemoryAccess**; and

```
update(m, x, v)
```

which returns a fresh **Memory** after storing value `v` at address `x` in memory `m`, and is represented by **MemoryUpdate**.

3.5 Creating an Expression

Since **RTLExpressions** are complicated objects, it is useful to have an object to build them. **RTLExpressionBuilder** plays this role. **RTLExpressionBuilder** makes testing the equality of **RTLExpressions** cheap by ensuring that only one version of each **RTLExpression** exists. Thus, two **RTLExpressions** are equal if and only if they are the same object. One consequence of this scheme is that an **RTLExpression** can never be altered, since changing one occurrence of an expression would change all of them. Therefore, the only way to update an expression is by creating a copy having the desired changes.

4 Optimizations

Some optimizations are performed by the objects that make up a RTL program, *i.e.* by the flow nodes and register transfers. Other optimizations are implemented by separate classes. Optimizations with their own classes are easier to customize and can encapsulate data local to the optimizations, but simple optimizations are better done by the objects that make up the RTL program. Also, some optimizations are naturally distributed, and it is easier to implement them as methods on flow nodes and register transfers.

Distributed optimizations help solve one of the main problems in in designing an optimizing compiler: deciding on the order in which to apply the optimizations. One optimization creates opportunities for another. The wrong order will miss optimizations, but there is often no ordering that is always best.

One way to keep from missing optimizations is to repeatedly retry optimizations until no further improvements can be made. However, this can be expensive and can even cause infinite loops if optimizations do not always shrink the program. Sometimes a single algorithm can carry out several optimizations, but no algorithm has been discovered that can perform all the optimizations that are needed.

The RTL System can sometimes solve the ordering problem by making each object responsible for optimizing itself. All the control flow optimizations are implemented this way, as well as dead assignment elimination. On the other hand, optimizations like register allocation and scheduling are better implemented as separate objects. It can be difficult to decide which implementation strategy is best for each optimization, and the strategy used for a particular optimizations often changes with experience.

4.1 Control Flow Optimizations

Optimizations that depend only on the control flow graph can be implemented entirely by the subclasses of **RTLFlowNode**. All of the control flow optimizations rely on the self-optimizing nature of the RTL program representation, and are performed whenever flow nodes lose predecessors or register transfers.

Each of these optimizations has two parts. The first part makes an invariant true, such as that there is no unreachable code. The second part maintains the invariant. It would be possible to require the front-end to take care of the first part by ensuring that these invariants are true from the start, but it is easier to check the invariants in the RTL System. Requiring as little as possible from the front-end also makes the RTL System more robust.

4.1.1 Eliminating Unreachable Code

Unreachable code is code to which there is no control path. An RTL program is effectively an acyclic graph, since the back edges of an interval are to a node inside an **IntervalNode**, not to the **IntervalNode** itself. Therefore, an unreachable flow node is one that is not the root node of the flow graph and that has no predecessors. Whenever a flow node is removed, it recursively removes any of its successors that consequently become unreachable.

4.1.2 Eliminating Jump Chains

A jump chain is a sequence of "jumps to jumps", and corresponds to an empty **RTLJumpNode**. Whenever a flow node removes its last register transfer, it eliminates itself.

4.1.3 Maximizing Basic Block Sizes

A pair of nodes is part of a larger basic block (and so should be merged) if the first has the second as its sole successor, and the second has the first as its sole predecessor. A node checks whenever its number of predecessors becomes 1 to see if it can merge with its predecessor.

4.2 Data Flow Optimizations

A data dependence exists between two register transfers if one writes to storage—either a register or memory—that the other uses. Traditional program representations have three kinds of data dependence [13]: flow dependence, anti dependence, and output dependence. By ensuring that a register is written by only one register transfer, SSA form has only one kind of data dependence, ***flow dependence***. If transfer A defines storage that transfer B uses, then A is a ***flow supporter*** of B, and B is a ***flow dependent*** of A. This information is an integral part of SSA form; each register is responsible for knowing the register transfer that defines it and each register transfer is responsible for knowing the register transfers that use its result.

An RTL program is initially converted to SSA form using the algorithms in [4]. After SSA conversion, flow dependencies are easily computed in two steps. The first step associates each storage unit with the register transfer that defines it. The second step uses this information to link each transfer to its flow supporters by examining the storage used by the transfer. Once an RTL program is in SSA form and dependencies have been computed, the RTL System must maintain the dependencies. We do not have general incremental algorithms for updating a program in SSA form, but all the SSA-based optimizations maintain SSA form.

Not all storage can be modeled by registers in SSA form. Memory (*i.e.* arrays and records accessed by pointers) and registers that are preassigned to physical registers also have ***anti dependencies***. Anti dependencies are not stored explicitly, but instead are computed whenever they are needed from the flow dependencies.

4.2.1 Propagating Copies

Copy propagation replaces the destination of a register-to-register assignment with the source everywhere it appears in the program. A transfer r2 ← r1 finds all register transfers that use r2 and tells them to replace r2 with r1.

4.2.2 Eliminating Dead Assignments

Dead assignments are assignments whose destination is never used; in other words, assignments with no flow dependents. Thus, dependence information makes it easy to remove dead assignments. Register transfers with no dependents automatically remove themselves from the program.

4.2.3 Eliminating Common Subexpressions

Common subexpression elimination replaces expressions by equivalent but simpler expressions. The RTL System uses the algorithm described in [2], which detects when computations produce equivalent values. The algorithm is conservative in that any expressions found to be equivalent are in fact equivalent, but not all equivalences are found. The SSA representation makes the algorithm fast, simple, and powerful. The algorithm is complex enough that it is implemented in its own class.

4.2.4 Code Motion

Code motion moves invariant code out of intervals, where it will be executed less often; it also moves redundant code from different branches of a conditional to a common ancestor, thus reducing program size. The RTL System uses the algorithm described in [17], which globally recognizes invariant and redundant expressions, even those that are lexically different.

4.2.5 Eliminating Constant Conditionals

A constant conditional is a conditional jump in which the condition can be evaluated at compile time, thus making the jump unnecessary. The RTL System can eliminate conditional jumps even when the value of the condition is not constant in the flow node containing it. Sometimes the condition is constant in the preceding flow node, so duplicating the conditional node for each preceding flow node converts the conditional node into a set of jump nodes. These jump nodes usually consist only of dead assignments and so are eliminated. The value of this particular optimization is dependent on the source language and its implementation. It is useful for our implementation of Smalltalk due to aggressive early binding and procedure inlining. For conventional implementations of procedural languages it may bring less benefit.

5 Code Generation

The task of code generation is to impose a linear order on the register transfers in the program. High-quality code generators attempt to find an ordering executing in as few time units as possible without violating control and data dependences. In general, different machine architectures will require somewhat different code generation strategies, however, much of the implementation remains the same. While constructing code generators for the Motorola 68020, the National Semiconductor Series 32000, and the SPARC, we have developed a framework for code generators based largely on the Davidson-Fraser approach. The framework continues to evolve as it is extended to handle other architectures.

The structure of the code generator is conventional, consisting of four phases. In the first phase, register transfers are combined to form more complex transfers corresponding to machine instructions. Next, the transfers are ordered to minimize register lifetimes. The optional third phase orders the transfers to minimize pipeline interlocks. Finally, register allocation is performed by graph coloring.

5.1 Machine Descriptions

An instance of a subclass of **MachineDescription** serves as the central repository for machine specific information needed during code generation. The machine description functions somewhat as a catch-all for information not provided elsewhere, but this aspect is secondary. Of greater importance is the protocol it provides for mapping register transfers to machine instructions.

Since a single register transfer may correspond to many machine instructions, it is necessary to provide a means for selecting the most desirable instruction. One approach to this problem is to explicitly provide *cost* information with each instruction or instruction component. In many cases, such cost information is redundant, or can be made so by appropriately ordering the search. In recognition of this, the register transfer mapping process is broken into two primary components: *canonicalization* and *instruction binding*. Canonicalization is invoked during instruction binding, which is invoked by the scheduler.

Canonicalization puts register transfers into the format "preferred" by the instruction binder. Consider the SPARC's load instruction, which forms its address from the sum of two registers. The register transfer `r4` ← `*r1` (Figure 1) then presents a slight problem. Two solutions are readily apparent: rewrite the transfer as `r4` ← `*(r1+g0)`, or code the instruction binder to recognise several formats for the same instruction. The latter solution lacks generality, since such problems are not limited to the recognition of special format instructions. On the Motorola 68020, integer multiplication by two is much more efficiently implemented as an addition instead. Having an explicit canonicalization process as part of the machine description increases the portability and maintainability of the register transfer classes, as well as reducing the cost and complexity of the instruction binder.

Instruction binding maps canonicalized register transfers into machine instructions. In order to promote retargetability, the machine description is responsible for performing the mapping. The machine description in turn delegates to the *instruction builder*, which performs its task by table lookup. This is where the problem of a single register transfer having several possible implementations is handled. The order in which instructions are added to the table serves as a simple prioritizing scheme, terminating instruction binding when the first matching instruction is found.

As a side effect of instruction binding, *constraints* on register assignment may be added to the graph. These constraints reflect the differences between three address SSA form and a two address machine.

5.2 Retargeting

Instructions are represented by instances of subclasses of the class **MachineInstruction**. The primary function of such objects is to generate machine code, but protocol checking for legality of operands during instruction binding is also found here. Retargeting the RTL System to a new architecture requires a new machine description, part of which is an instruction table. Designing the class hierarchy for a new instruction set is simplified by the following rule: each field in the machine instruction should be represented by a separate instance variable. By implication, each instruction format should correspond to a subclass of **MachineInstruction**. This sort of correspondence allows fairly clean handling of instruction set idiosyncrasies.

When instruction operands may have complex structure, as is the case with most CISC architectures, a separate operand class hierarchy has been found desirable. The first machine targeted was the MC68020, and the initial implementation did not separate operands into a separate structure. When the NS32000 series code generator was written, the need for structured treatment of operands was apparent. On the 68020, the number of operand combinations is relatively small, and the internal structure of the combinations is simple. The 32000 presents a richer set of combinations, each of which has approximately the complexity of an instruction. Subsequently, the 68020 instruction classes were factored to represent the addressing modes as separate objects. The new structure is easier to understand and smaller. The SPARC's operand structure is much simpler than either of the CISCs, and thus no SPARC operand classes have been defined.

5.3 Scheduling

The scheduling phase uses a variation of an algorithm for peephole optimization and code generation invented by Davidson and Fraser [5] [6] [7]. This algorithm was first used in a code generator called PO. PO has many phases; the *combiner* is the one whose design was borrowed for the RTL System. It was chosen because it seemed simple and easy to implement, easy to retarget to new machines, and the original papers showed it gave good results.

As in PO, the scheduling phase scans the program once, combining each transfer with members of its *window*—flow supporters, and possibly their flow dependents—and replacing the original transfers with the result if it corresponds to a machine instruction. For example, combining the third register transfer with the second (its flow supporter) in the RTL fragment

```
r2 ← r1 + 8.
r4 ← r3 + r2.
r5 ← *r4.
```

would yield `r5 ← *(r3 + r2)`, which does not correspond to a 68020 instruction. However, combining this new transfer with the first transfer in the fragment (one of the flow supporters of the new transfer) yields `r5 ← *(r1 + r2 + 8)`, which does correspond to an instruction. The RTL System would then replace the third transfer above with this new transfer, and delete the other two.

PO also forms instructions using a window. The difference is that SSA form automatically determines the window for the RTL System, while PO has to explicitly manage the window, which we found to be complex and error-prone. Thus, SSA form made RTL scheduling simpler and more reliable.

5.4 RISC Scheduling

The optional "third" phase of code generation attempts to minimize the number of pipeline interlocks per basic block and fill branch delay slots. Since a register spill is much more costly than a pipeline interlock, the RISC scheduler gives priority to minimization of register lifetimes.

Potential interlocks can be treated in almost the same way as true dependencies. For hardware with pipeline interlocks, ignoring such dependencies does not alter the correctness of the generated code. For this reason, our scheduler maintains three sets of transfers during scheduling: those ready to be scheduled, those schedulable but likely to cause an interlock, and those not yet ready to schedule. The class **PotentialInterlock** represents a potential interlock between two transfers. Instances of this class are responsible for maintaining a set of transfers which could be scheduled between the transfers and avoid the interlock. Once this set becomes unitary, the potential interlock attempts to claim the transfer to guarantee the interlock will not occur. Multiple claims may be placed on a single transfer, but a single potential interlock will be arbitrarily chosen.

The transfer scheduled is the one with the highest priority. Priorities are computed based upon the distance between a transfer and its flow supporters, if the supporter dies in the current block, and the number of flow dependents a transfer has. This priority computation reflects the desire to minimize register lifetimes so as to reduce the potential for spilling, but allows some rearrangement of the schedule when an interlock can be avoided.

One of the consequences of this implementation is that our scheduler works best when interlocks cause a single cycle delay. Longer delays do not affect the correctness of the scheduler, but may result in suboptimal schedules.

5.5 Register Assignment

Register assignment is based on the classical graph coloring algorithm [3]. Constructing the graph to be colored is complicated by SSA form.

SSA form breaks the lifetime of each physical register into many pieces, each represented by a logical register. Each assignment of a register becomes a new logical register and each place where logical registers have their values merged also becomes a logical register. The first task of register assignment is to merge these register lifetimes together again. However, optimizations performed since putting a program in SSA form might prevent register lifetimes from being merged.

Another way of looking at the problem is to note that the least expensive way to implement a ϕ-assignment `r3` $\leftarrow$ ϕ`(r1,r2)` is to assign `r1`, `r2`, and `r3` to the same physical register. However, this works only if the lifetimes of `r1` and `r2` don't extend beyond the ϕ-assignment. Otherwise, copy instructions must be introduced.

Moreover, the scheduling phase places constraints on register assignment. Many machine instructions require that their destination be the same register as one of their sources. Some machines have several kinds of registers, and each instruction must use the right kind. Thus, each instruction includes a *constraint* object that describes the constraint that it places on the registers it uses. The assigning phase checks each constraint to see whether it can be satisfied by merging register lifetimes. Otherwise, it must satisfy the constraints by introducing instructions to copy values from one register to another.

Register assignment can be customized in several ways. It is simple to replace the register assigner, and we have experimented with several versions[18]. The register assigner is an object, and there is a class hierarchy of the various register assignment algorithms that we have implemented. It is also easy to invent new kinds of constraints and to associate them with machine instructions so that scheduling will place constraints on register assignment correctly. Adding new kinds of constraints might require changing the register assigner.

Several parts of register assignment are machine-dependent. The number and type of registers is machine-dependent, and the way that registers are spilled is not only machine-dependent but run-time system dependent. Thus, parts of register assignment are delegated to the machine description, which can provide the list of available registers, and which is able to spill registers.

6 Customizing the RTL System

There are two ways to customize the RTL System. One way is to extend the RTL language that is used to represent programs. This is done by creating subclasses of the classes that represent RTL programs, namely **RTLFlowNode**, **RTLTransfer**, and **RTLExpression**. The other way is to modify or create algorithms that manipulate RTL programs. Algorithms implemented as single objects are usually easier to understand and modify than algorithms implemented as a collection of methods in various classes, but they are somewhat harder to create.

A good example of extending RTL by creating a new kind of register transfer or expression is the way that support for debugging was added to TS. The debugger required the compiler to produce functions that recovered the unoptimized values of variables at particular points in the program. Each point in the program at which the debugger might be invoked is an "inspection point" and is labeled with a new kind of register transfer, a **DebuggingUseMarker**. Each **DebuggingUseMarker** keeps track of the variables for which it computes a recovery function. As the various optimizations transform and manipulate the register transfers, the **DebuggingUseMarker** updates its recovery functions.

As might be expected, debugging support required more changes to the RTL System than simply adding a new class. Although debugging support required little change to most of the RTL System, some of the algorithms that manipulated register transfers were too specialized for **Assignment** and so had to be generalized to work with **DebuggingUseMarker**. However, these changes usually improved the clarity of the RTL System and made it easier to change in the future. Thus, the changes were essentially fixing "reusability bugs" in the RTL System.

The second way to customize the RTL System is to add new algorithms to it or to change the algorithms that it uses. Many of the optimizations are represented by objects, so a new algorithm is often a new class definition. The compiler can control the optimizations that will be performed by specifying the class of each optimization. The instance of **MachineDescription** keeps track of the classes used for each optimization. Thus, each machine can use a slightly different set of optimizations. This will probably be changed in the future, since the set of optimizations that should be used also depends on the source language, not just the target machine.

A good example of customizing the RTL System by modifying an algorithm expressed as an object is the scheduler. RISC machines may not need the peephole optimizations provided by the combining algorithm, but will instead need to fill branch delay slots or minimize pipeline delays. Representing the scheduler as an object means that it is easy to make slight variations using inheritance. Data structures that are not needed by other algorithms can be encapsulated in the new class, and the machine description can determine which scheduling algorithm is used by creating a scheduler of the appropriate class.

The machine description is involved in almost all customizations of the RTL System. It is responsible for mapping register transfers to their equivalent machine instructions, so it determines which table to use. It creates objects that perform register allocation, scheduling, and other optimizations. Thus, a new use of the RTL System often requires a new subclass of **Machine Description**. Fortunately, machine descriptions are not large and are always simple. For example, the largest subclass of **MachineDescription** that we have written, which is for the Motorola 68020, is 242 lines long.

7 Lessons Learned

The RTL System is not just a set of reusable software components, it is also a theory of how to represent and optimize programs. Probably any system for code reuse is also a theory of its application domain, so this should not have been surprising. Every time we discovered a weakness in our theory, we have had to revise the software. A brief history of the RTL System illustrates this.

The first version of the RTL System was written in 1986-1987 [20]. It was designed to be an object-oriented version of PO, so its design was as much like that of PO as possible. The only initial difference was that it recognized legal instructions by looking register transfers up in a hash table instead of by matching them with a parser, as in PO.

The first version of the RTL System differed greatly from the current one. RTL programs were represented by several classes in addition to the ones that the RTL System now uses. **RTLFlowNode** had no subclasses, in large part because the control flow graph was unimportant and only used by a few optimizations. An **RTLProgram** was a stream of register transfers, not a directed graph. Data dependencies were represented by def-use chains, and sets of register transfers were not considered a register transfer, so the **RTLTransfer** class hierarchy was different. None of the optimizations were implemented as separate objects, but as collections of methods in the classes representing RTL programs. Of the RTL classes that are now important, only **RTLExpression** has been relatively unchanged.

The first changes were primarily to correct errors and to make the RTL System easier to understand. The first major change was to make the flow graph the basis of the RTL program. This led to a class hierarchy for **RTLFlowNodes** that is similar to the current one. The RTL System worked well enough to compile some benchmarks for TS[12], but the optimizations were unreliable and hard to understand. It was clear that a less ad-hoc basis for code optimization was needed.

We read the papers on SSA form in mid-1988 and were convinced that they would provide a sound theoretical basis for code optimization. The RTL System was converted to use SSA form in 1989 [11][14]. A major change that occurred just prior to this (and partly in preparation for it) was to merge several classes used to represent RTL programs into the **RTLTransfer** hierarchy. A class that contained data-flow information was merged into **RTLTransfer**, and the list of register transfers that it contained was replaced by adding **RegisterTransferSet** to represent a group of simultaneous transfers. Also, the first instance of representing an optimization by an object occurred when the first version of the graph coloring based register allocator was built.

An important way of improving a framework is to use it in a way that was not originally foreseen. There were two such uses of the RTL System during this time. The first was by Javalina [10], a system for converting abstract specifications of digital filters to microcode for digital signal processors. This use showed a weakness in the way machine-dependent information was represented, and resulted in the design of **MachineDescription**. The second was in research on debugging optimized code [22]. This use verified the flexibility of the RTL System, and did not result in any major changes to it.

To test the representation of machine-dependent information, we wrote code generators for the National 32032 and the SPARC [16]. This led to making the scheduler a component, and to a class hierarchy for schedulers. This work showed a problem with memory references, which was subsequently fixed, but otherwise the basic representation of programs held up well.

The RTL System has constantly been revised to make it easier to understand and to change. However, the biggest changes have been caused by changes to the underlying theory. This includes the shift from viewing a program as a stream of instructions to viewing it as a directed graph, generalizing the notion of a register transfer to include a set of transfers, and SSA form. Changes such as converting optimization algorithms into separate classes are much easier to implement, and have little effect on the rest of the RTL System.

Uses of the RTL System usually point out ways to improve it, and we expect it to continue to improve as we use it in new applications. In addition to porting it to new architectures and adding new optimizations, we are also planning to use it with new source languages. In particular, we plan to use the RTL System as the back-end of a C compiler. These uses will help us refine and improve the RTL System.

8 Conclusion

The RTL System shows that object-oriented frameworks are valuable for application domains other than user interfaces. Code optimization is an example of an application domain that depends on complex algorithms. The RTL System provides ways to customize both the data structures that represent programs and the algorithms that manipulate these data structures. There are several families of classes, each family having a standard interface. Each family provides a different way to customize the optimizations, and the standard interfaces make it easy to combine new features.

The RTL System is relatively easy to understand and modify, and hence can significantly reduce the effort required to create new optimizations. This is not just the effect of implementing it in an object-oriented language; reusable software requires a theory upon which to base the system design. SSA form and the use of register transfers to describe both the program and the target architecture have been the foundations of the RTL System. The role of object-oriented programming is to express this theory in a natural and simple way, and the RTL System shows that this can be done much more concisely in a language like Smalltalk than in a language like C.

Acknowledgements

We thank Gary Leavens for his comments on earlier versions of this paper.

This research was supported by the National Science Foundation under grant CCR-8715752 and by a gift from Tektronix.

References

[1] Aho AC, Sethi R, Ullman JD. Compilers, Principles, Techniques, and Tools. Addison-Wesley, 1986.

[2] Alpern B, Wegman MN, Zadeck FK. Detecting equality of variables in programs. In: Conference Record of the Fifteenth Annual ACM Symposium on Principles of Programming Languages, pp 1–11, 1988.

[3] Chaitin GJ, Auslander MA, Chandra AK, Cocke J, Hopkins ME, Markstein PW. Register allocation via coloring. *Computer Languages*, 6(1):47–57, 1981.

[4] Cytron R, Ferrante J, Rosen B, Wegman M, Zadeck FK. An efficient method of computing static single assignment form. In: Conference Record of the Sixteenth Annual ACM Symposium on Principles of Programming Languages, pp 25–35, 1989.

[5] Davidson JW. Simplifying Code Generation Through Peephole Optimizations. PhD thesis, University of Arizona, 1981.

[6] Davidson JW, Fraser CW. Code selection through object code optimization. ACM Transactions on Programming Languages and Systems, 6(4):505–526, 1984.

[7] Davidson JW, Fraser CW. The design and application of a retargetable peephole optimizer. ACM Transactions on Programming Languages and Systems, 2(2):191–202, April 1980.

[8] Fischer CN, LeBlanc, RJ. Crafting a Compiler. Benjamin-Cummings, 1988.

[9] Graver J, Johnson RE. A type system for Smalltalk. In: Conference Record of the Seventeenth Annual ACM Symposium on Principles of Programming Languages, pp 136–150, 1990.

[10] Hebel KJ. An Environment for the Development of Digital Processing Software. PhD thesis, University of Illinois at Urbana-Champaign, 1989.

[11] Heintz R. Low Level Optimizations for an Object-Oriented Language. Master's thesis, University of Illinois at Urbana-Champaign, 1990.

[12] Johnson RE, Graver JO, and Zurawski LW. TS: An optimizing compiler for Smalltalk. In: Proceedings of OOPSLA '88, pp 18–26, November 1988. printed as SIGPLAN Notices, 23(11).

[13] Kuck DJ. The Structure of Computers and Computations. John Wiley and Sons, 1978.

[14] McConnell C. An Object-Oriented Code Optimizer Using Static Single Assignment Form. Master's thesis, University of Illinois at Urbana-Champaign, 1989.

[15] McConnell C, Johnson RE. SSA form, dependencies, and peephole optimization. 1991. University of Illinois at Urbana-Champaign.

[16] Roberts JD. A Highly Portable Code Generator. Master's thesis, University of Illinois at Urbana/Champaign, 1990.

[17] Rosen BK, Wegman MN, Zadeck FK. Global value numbers and redundant computations. In: Conference Record of the Fifteenth Annual ACM Symposium on Principles of Programming Languages, pp 12–27, 1988.

[18] Schoening CB. A Family of Register Allocation Algorithms. Master's thesis, University of Illinois at Urbana-Champaign, 1991. forthcoming.

[19] Tarjan RE. Testing flow graph reducibility. J. Comp. Sys. Sci., 9:355–365, 1974.

[20] Wiegand JD. An Object-oriented Code Optimizer and Generator. Master's thesis, University of Illinois, Urbana-Champaign, 1987.

[21] Wirfs-Brock RJ, Johnson RE. Surveying current research in object-oriented design. Communications of the ACM, 33(9):104–124, 1990.

[22] Zurawski LW. Source-Level Debugging of Globally Optimized Code with Expected Behavior. PhD thesis, University of Illinois at Urbana-Champaign, 1990.

Systems for Late Code Modification

David W. Wall
Digital Equipment Corporation
Western Research Laboratory
Palo Alto, California, U.S.A.

Abstract

Modifying code after the compiler has generated it can be useful for both optimization and instrumentation. Several years ago we designed the Mahler system, which uses link-time code modification for a variety of tools on our experimental Titan workstations. Killian's Pixie tool works even later, translating a fully-linked MIPS executable file into a new version with instrumentation added. Recently we wanted to develop a hybrid of the two, that would let us experiment with both optimization and instrumentation on a standard workstation, preferably without requiring us to modify the normal compilers and linker. This paper describes prototypes of two hybrid systems, closely related to Mahler and Pixie. We implemented basic-block counting in both, and compare the resulting time and space expansion to those of Mahler and Pixie.

1 Introduction

Late code modification is the process of modifying the output of a compiler after the compiler has generated it. The reasons one might want to do this fall into two categories, optimization and instrumentation.

Some forms of optimization have to be performed on assembly-level or machine-level code. The oldest is peephole optimization [16], which acts to tidy up code that a compiler has generated; it has since been generalized to include transformations on more machine-independent code [4, 5]. Reordering of code to avoid pipeline stalls [6, 9, 25] is most often done after the code is generated because the pipeline stalls are easier to see then.

Other forms of optimization depend on having the entire program at hand all at once. In an environment with separately-compiled modules, this may mean we must apply the optimization to machine-level code. Global reorganization of code to reduce instruction cache misses [15] is one example. Intermodule allocation of registers to variables is another; the Mahler system [21] chose the register variables during linking and modified the object modules being linked to reflect this choice. Register allocation is a fairly high-level optimization, however, and other approaches have been taken, such as monolithic compilation of source modules or intermediate-language modules [3, 10, 20] or compilation with reference to program summary databases [19].

Optimization removes unnecessary operations; instrumentation adds them. A common form of machine-level instrumentation is basic block counting. We transform a program into an equivalent program that also counts each basic block as it is executed. Running the instrumented program gives us an execution count for each basic block in the program. We can combine these counts with static information from the uninstrumented program to get profile information either at the source level, such as procedure invocation counts, or at the instruction level, such as load and store counts [14, 17].

Some events that we might want to count require inter-block state. Counting pipeline or coprocessor stalls, for example, can be done with basic-block counting only if any stall is guaranteed to finish before we leave the basic block. Counting branches taken or fallen through, or the distribution of destinations of indirect jumps, are other examples. Counting these events is no harder than counting basic blocks, but requires different instrumentation [23, 25].

Still other kinds of instrumentation are easy to do by code modification. Address tracing for purposes of cache modeling [1, 17] can be done by instrumenting the places where loads and stores occur and also the places where basic blocks begin. A 1988 study [22] compared software register allocation with hardware register windows, by instrumenting the code to keep track of procedure call depth, and counting the times when a machine with register windows would overflow its buffer of windows.

Naturally, certain kinds of transformation are best done before we reach machine-level code. Global movement of operations out of loops could in principle be done at the machine level, but it makes more sense to do it earlier, when more of the semantics of the program are easily available. Inline procedure expansion is often most useful if it can be followed by normal global optimizations, because the latter act to specialize the body of such an expansion; inline expansion might therefore be done higher than at the machine-level.

Nevertheless, it is clear that a wide variety of transformations for purposes of optimization and instrumentation can be done on machine-level code. This paper compares two existing systems for late code modification, discusses advantages and disadvantages in each, and then describes two new systems we have built that represent compromises between these two, combining the advantages (and a few of the disadvantages) of both.

2 Overview of late code modification

There are two different questions to address. How do we decide what modifications to make? How do we make those modifications and still get a working program?

The former depends on the transformation. In basic block counting, we simply insert a load, add, and store at the beginning of each block, to increment the counter associated with that block. In interprocedure register allocation, we decide which variables to keep in registers – the hard part – and then we delete loads and stores of those variables and modify instructions that use the values loaded and stored. In any case this paper will not discuss how to decide what changes to make, except in passing.

There are two main problems associated with making the modifications correctly. The first is that adding and deleting instructions causes the addresses of things to change. We must be able to correct for these changes somehow, or references to these addresses will not work right. The second is that the modifications may themselves need resources that must somehow be acquired. Most commonly these resources are registers: for example, in block counting we need at least one register in which to do the increment, and another to hold the address of the count vector.

A code-modification system that knows enough about the program can address both these problems without introducing much or any overhead in the transformed program. This makes the system a suitable medium for optimization as well as for instrumentation. If we are forced to introduce overhead, to deal with the problems dynamically rather than statically, optimization is unlikely to be feasible, and a large overhead will reduce the usefulness of the system even for instrumentation.

Next we will look at two systems for late code modification, and compare their approaches.

3 Mahler

The Mahler system [21, 23, 24, 25] is the back-end code generator and linker for the Titan [12, 18], an experimental workstation built at DECWRL. The Mahler system does code modification in the linker. A wide variety of transformations are possible: intermodule register allocation, instruction pipeline scheduling, source-level instrumentation compatible with gprof [8], and instruction-level instrumentation like basic block counting and address tracing [1]. The linker decides in the usual manner which modules to link, including modules extracted from libraries. Each is passed to the module rewriter, which modifies it according to the transformations requested. The transformed modules are then passed back to the linker proper, which links them just as if they had originally come from object files.

Correcting for changed addresses is easy in this context. An object module contains a loader symbol table and relocation dictionary, which mark the places where unresolved addresses are used. An unresolved address may be one that depends on an imported symbol whose value is not yet known, or may be one that is known relative to the current module but will change when the module is linked with other modules. In either case the linker is responsible for resolving it, and the relocation dictionary tells the linker what kind of address it is. This same information lets us correct the value, if only by leaving the relocation entry in place so that the linker will give it the right value.

Other addresses are not marked for relocation, because they are position-relative addresses and will not change when the module is linked with others. These are all manifest in the instruction format itself, as in a pc-relative branch instruction. If instructions are inserted between a branch and its destination, we increase the magnitude of the displacement in the instruction word.[1]

If the module rewriter is applying a transformation that requires some new registers, such as block counting, they are easy to obtain, because global register allocation is also done in the linker. Thus we can choose to allocate fewer registers than the maximum, reserving a few for the use of the instrumentation code. This leads to some overhead, because the variables that would have used

[1] Although this might seem to handle all the cases, in theory there is another that would be troublesome. If we did an unrelocated computation of some kind, added the result to the pc, and jumped to that address, it would be very difficult to correct this address statically. Such a computation is one possible implementation of a case-statement, but the more common one is to use the computation to select the destination from a table of complete addresses, each marked for relocation.

those registers must now live in memory and must be loaded and stored as needed. However, the Titan has 64 registers, and losing the last few never made much difference to performance.

Mahler code modification is made still easier by the combination of two circumstances. First, the presence of the loader symbol table means that the compiler can pass hints through it. Second, the Mahler compiler is the back-end of all the high-level language compilers, and is also the only assembler available for the Titan, which means that *any* code the module rewriter sees is guaranteed to have been produced by the Mahler compiler. For example, the Titan has no variable-shift instruction; this operation is implemented as an indexed jump into a series of 32 constant-shift instructions. The code modifier must be careful not to damage this idiom, and would wreak havoc if for example it blithely changed the order of these shifts. The Mahler compiler flags this idiom with a symbol table entry, which tells the module rewriter what it is.

Mahler's approach of code modification in the linker arose from the desire to do intermodule register allocation without giving up separate compilation. With that machinery in place, it was natural to do instrumentation there as well. This unfortunately means that to request instrumentation a user must relink, and so must have access to the object modules and libraries that the program is built from. On the other hand, this approach means the user need not recompile, and means we need not maintain instrumented versions of the libraries, as has been the usual practice, for example, in systems that support gprof [8]. The need to relink is inconvenient, however, and it is interesting that another approach is possible.

4 Pixie

Pixie [14, 17], developed by Earl Killian of MIPS, does block counting and address tracing by modifying a fully-linked executable.[2] The executable file may even have had its symbol table removed, though the block counts are normally analyzed by tools that need to see the symbol table. This approach is much more convenient for the user, who does not have to be able to rebuild the executable. It is less convenient for Pixie, however, which must work harder to preserve program correctness, and introduces run-time overhead in doing so.

As with Mahler, some address correction is easy. Pc-relative branches and direct jumps are easy to recognize, and Pixie can change their destinations just as Mahler can. Indirect jumps pose more of a problem, because their destinations are computed at other points in the program, and we no longer have the relocation dictionary to let us recognize those points. Pixie solves this problem by including a big translation table in the modified program. The table is as big as the original code segment, and gives the correct new address for each code address in the original program. Each indirect jump is then preceded by new code that translates its destination at run time by looking it up in this table. Even when Pixie knows it is computing a code address, it computes the old version of that address, so that the run-time translation lookup will always work correctly regardless of where the address came from. This leads to a rather odd transformation of a jump-and-link instruction, which expands

[2] A predecessor, moxie [2], translated a MIPS executable into an equivalent VAX executable, allowing the MIPS compilers to be tested extensively before MIPS hardware existed.

to an ordinary jump together with a pair of instructions that load what would have been the return address in the unmodified program.

Fortunately for Pixie, data addresses do not change even though the code segment gets larger. By convention, data segments on MIPS systems occupy a place in the address space that is far removed from the code segment; there is ample room for a code segment to grow manyfold before it affects data addresses. Without this convention, data addresses might change (as in fact they do under Mahler on the Titan); Pixie would have to do loads and stores with an extra level of indirection, just as it does indirect jumps.

The instrumentation added by Pixie needs three registers for its own use, which it must steal from the registers already used by the program. Pixie accomplishes this by maintaining three *shadow registers* in memory. The shadow registers contain the "user" values of these three registers, and Pixie replaces uses of these registers in the original program by uses of the three memory locations. Since the MIPS processor has a load-store architecture, this adds some overhead, but it is typically small compared to the overhead of the instrumentation itself. These three registers can then be used for Pixie's purposes, and also as temporaries to access the shadow registers. To pick the registers to steal, Pixie looks for the registers that have the fewest number of static references.

Pixie uses no hints from the compiler, and in fact does not even use knowledge about the patterns of code the compiler generates. This means it can usually tolerate assembly code and sometimes even code from "foreign" compilers, neither of which is sure to adhere to the MIPS compiler conventions.

5 What more do we need?

Pixie is convenient to use, but incurs a fair bit of runtime overhead. By far the majority of indirect jumps are subroutine returns, and most of these are from ordinary direct calls. In these cases the overhead of going through the address table is logically unnecessary. If all we want to do is instrumentation, the overhead is probably acceptable, though there are certainly times when we might want to do lightweight or time-critical instrumentation. In any case, the overhead makes it an unsuitable vehicle for optimization.

Mahler's use of the loader information lets it transform a program with much smaller runtime overhead. It is built into the linker, however, and probably depends on the integration of the back-end compiler and the linker. This degree of integration is not common in most language systems. In our case we wanted a Mahler-like facility for low-overhead code modification on MIPS-based workstations, but we did not want to make wholesale changes to the standard MIPS compilers and linker.

It therefore seemed to us that a compromise between Mahler and Pixie might be in order. Much of Pixie's overhead is not logically necessary: for instance, if a procedure is certain to be called only directly, those calls and returns can safely be translated as calls and returns, without going through the address table. Moreover, all of the MIPS compilers have the same back-end code generator, so we can be almost as sure of understanding coding conventions as we are with Mahler on the Titan. A variant of Pixie that paid attention to compiler conventions and other information might be able to reduce the overhead significantly, perhaps enough to let us use it for optimization as well as instrumentation. The rest of this paper describes prototypes of two such compromises that we have built at DECWRL.

6 Nixie

The first compromise we built was a system called Nixie. Nixie works very much like Pixie, but makes certain assumptions about the code it modifies. The framework of this approach is threefold. First, the MIPS architecture [13] has a strong bias in favor of using r31 as the return address register. Second, the procedure linkage activity of a jump-and-link (JAL) or jump-and-link-register (JALR) instruction will work fine in the modified code, provided that we return from the procedure in the normal way, with an unmodified jump-register (JR) instruction. Third, all of the MIPS compilers use the same back-end code generator, whose coding conventions are therefore uniform over all compiled code.

Nixie therefore assumes that any JR via r31 is in fact a return, and (sensibly) that any JAL or JALR is a call, and simply leaves them both in place. The destination of the call, however, must still be translated into the new address space. For a JAL this is easy because the destination is encoded literally in the instruction. The destination of a JALR is an address in the instruction's operand register, so we precede this instruction by address translation code to look up the procedure address and convert it from the old space to the new.

We would not be far wrong if we further assumed that any other JR is the indexed jump from a case-statement. These we can handle by noting that the MIPS code generator produces only a few distinct code templates for these indexed jumps. By examining the instructions before the JR, we can confirm that this JR is indeed the indexed jump from a case-statement, and can also determine the location and size of the associated jump table in the read-only data segment. This allows us to translate the entries in this table statically, so that we need not insert translation code.

The main hole in this argument is that a program can contain code that was originally written in assembly language. Such code was *not* produced by the code generator, and might not follow its conventions. Users tend not to write such code, but it is not uncommon in the standard libraries. Fortunately, most assembly routines in the libraries follow the conventions well enough for our purposes: they return through r31, and they seldom have case-statements at all.

In the standard libraries, Nixie knows of two dozen assembly routines that have unusual jumps. It finds these in an executable by looking for the file name in the loader symbol table, and then pattern-matching the code at that address to confirm that the routine is really the one from the library. If the symbol table is absent, Nixie searches the entire executable for the patterns. When one of these nonstandard routines is found, Nixie marks the violations so that it will know what to make of them later.

Any jump that we have been unable to explain with this whole analysis triggers an error message.[3] In programs without procedure variables, we are

[3]At present this includes jumps corresponding to Fortran's assigned go-to. We are considering ways of coping with these; fortunately, they seem to be comparatively rare in modern programs.

normally able to translate all jumps cleanly, without using the runtime address table, and if so we do not include the address table in the transformed executable. In accomplishing this, we have conveniently also assigned meanings to the jumps in the program, distinguishing between procedure calls, procedure returns, and case-statement indexed jumps. This lets us consider doing global analysis using the control structure of the program. The reduction, often to zero, of the runtime overhead of doing program transformation, together with the ability to do global analysis, means that we should be able to use this technique to do low-level optimization as well as instrumentation.

On the other hand, certain assumptions are necessary. We assumed that a JAL or JALR is used only for procedure call; if this is false our understanding of the global structure may suffer. More seriously, we assumed that any JR via r31 was a return; if this is false we will not translate the destination of the jump correctly, and the transformed program won't even run correctly.

Moreover, we can't always remove the runtime address table. Mahler never needed it, and it would be nice to dispense with it in general. This is the motivation for the second compromise system.

7 Epoxie

Mahler can do all of its address translation statically, because it operates on object files, which still have loader symbol tables and relocation dictionaries. We wanted a Pixie-like tool that would work the same way, but we didn't want to change the standard linker. One option would be to make the tool transform an individual object file, and then apply it to each of the object files in turn, but this would make it inconvenient to include library files. Our solution was to begin by completely linking the program but retaining all of the loader information. In practice this is easy to do: most standard linkers have an option for *incremental linking*, which lets us link together several object files into what is essentially one big object file that can then be linked with others to form a complete executable. In our case we link together everything there is, but we pretend there might be more so that the linker will keep the relocation information we want.

This done, we can modify the result in the same manner as Mahler. Where the code or data contains an address, either the use is marked for relocation or else the use is self-evident, as with a pc-relative branch. Like Mahler, this system translates not only code addresses that appear in the code, but also code addresses that appear in the data, in the relocation dictionaries, and in the symbol table. Unlike Mahler, this system need not translate data addresses, because the addresses of the data segments do not change.

The resulting system is very similar in structure to Nixie, and is called *Epoxie*, because all the glue holding the executable together is still visible. With Epoxie, we never need runtime address translation. For many tools, we also need not do as thorough an analysis of the program's jumps: for basic-block counting, for example, we do not care whether a JR is a case-statement or a subroutine return, and Epoxie does not need to know this for a safe translation.

A somewhat similar approach, which *does* require changing the linker, was recently described by Johnson [11]. A modified linker always retains a compact form of the relocation information, even for completely linked programs. Code

Phase 1:
    Break code into blocks
    Categorize jumps
    Link blocks into flow graph
Phase 2:
    Generate preface code
    Build new version of code, one block at a time
    Nixie: Precede indirect subroutine calls with addr translation code
    Compute mapping from old addresses to new
    Adjust destinations of branches and jumps where needed
    Nixie: Append address table to code if needed
    Nixie: Adjust addresses in indexed-jump tables
    Epoxie: Adjust code addresses marked for relocation in code or data
    Adjust addresses in loader symbol table, if present

Figure 1: Main steps in Nixie and Epoxie

modification can then occur after linking, as it does in Pixie, without sacrificing the type knowledge that Mahler found so useful.

8 Implementation overview

Currently Epoxie and Nixie are in fact the same program, with somewhat different behavior depending on whether the relocation tables are present in the program being modified. Figure 1 lists the sequence of steps required. The first phase analyzes the program to determine its structure, building a description that divides the program into procedures and basic blocks. This structure is then used to guide the second phase, which performs a particular transformation and makes the new version internally consistent. Much of the machinery in this second phase is shared from one transformation to another.

When we read the program into memory, the data structure attaches relocation entries to their instructions, so we can keep them together while inserting, deleting, and moving code. This also makes it convenient to insert new instructions with their own relocation entries.

The first step is to break the code into basic blocks. This requires identifying all the places where transfer of control can happen and all the places to which control can be transferred. The former is easy: we just look for branch, jump, and trap instructions. The latter is more complicated. Branches and direct jumps have explicit destinations in the instructions, so we must mark these destinations as block starts. Indirect jumps to addresses in registers must also be considered, however; such an address may be computed with a load-immediate operation, which requires two MIPS instructions, or it may appear as a data item. Epoxie can easily recognize either of these, because they must be marked for relocation as a code address. Nixie must be more conservative; if a data item or a load-immediate constant looks like a code address, Nixie must assume it is.

Next we categorize the jumps. The bulk of this step involves recognizing patterns of code. Most of these patterns are simply the bodies of the known assembly routines that violate the usual conventions; a few are variations on the code generated by the compiler for indexed jumps in case-statements. In each case the pattern tells us the meaning of the nonstandard jumps it includes. For indexed jumps it tells us the location and extent of the address table indexed: for known assembly routines it tells us explicitly, and for compiled case-statements we deduce it from the code preceding the jump. The known assembly patterns also tell us about subroutine returns via registers other than r31, and about JUMP instructions that correspond to tail-calls. After all the pattern-matching, we confirm that all jumps have been classified.

If our transformation requires it, we next link the blocks into a flow graph and the procedures into a call graph. This process is influenced by the jump categorization. For example, we treat an indexed jump, which has many possible successor blocks, differently from a subroutine return, which has none in that subroutine.

Now we are ready to begin an actual transformation. We start by generating any preface code needed, code that should be executed before starting the original program. For many transformations, particularly those whose purpose is instrumentation, this code allocates some memory on the stack. This may be a big chunk of memory or it may be just enough to accomplish the "register stealing" described in section 4. This is also where we insert any utility routines that we want to call from inserted code.

Next comes the transformation itself, in which we build a new version of the original code. Along with whatever changes are required by the choice of transformation, we may also have to make some enabling changes as well. If the transformation requires register stealing, we must insert code to load or store values from the "shadow registers" in memory whenever the stolen registers are used in the original program.

In Nixie, calls via procedure variables must be preceded by code to translate the destination address. (The translation table used for this will be appended to the program later.) Figure 1 lists this as a separate step, but in fact our implementation does this at the same time as the requested transformation.

As we built the new version of the program, we kept track of which of the instructions in the original program corresponded to each instruction in the new program. When the transformation is complete, we can invert this information to get a mapping from old addresses to new addresses. This is just a look-up table as big as the original program, telling the correct new address for each old address. This mapping may tell us that some branches now have destinations that are too far away to represent in the instruction format. If so, we replace these branches with branches around jumps, and then repeat the process as long as necessary.

When we have a usable address mapping, we step through adjusting the destinations of branches and direct jumps. There may be some we must not adjust: for instance, we might have inserted a new self-contained loop whose branch destination is not even expressible in the old address space because the whole loop corresponds to a single instruction in the original program. As we put instructions in the new code area, we mark those that must be adjusted.

This leaves the problem of indirect jumps via a register. In Nixie, we append the address table to the new code; now that we know the table's address, we fill in the fields that access it wherever we have inserted address translation code.

So that indexed jumps from case-statements will not need dynamic translation, we step through each of the jump tables that our pattern-matching told us about, converting the addresses from the old space to the new. Epoxie need not do any of this. Instead, it goes through all of the code and data, translating addresses wherever an instruction or data item is marked for relocation as a code address.

If the loader symbol table is present, we translate the addresses there as well. This is easy for both Nixie and Epoxie because the values in the symbol table are tagged with types, so we can always recognize a code address and use our translation table to adjust it. This suffices because our transformations to date have been relatively local. When we develop tools that move code across block boundaries, the question will arise of whether a label on a piece of code goes with it or stays behind. This will likely require a new approach to adjusting the symbol table, perhaps by attaching symbols to their code locations in the same way that we attach relocation entries to instructions.

9 Pitfalls

There are several tricky bits worth explaining.

There is occasionally a reason to have code in the data segment. For example, an instruction might be constructed on the fly for emulation purposes. None of the code modification systems discussed here understand this possibility, and therefore will not instrument such code. Fortunately, such code rarely arises. Not counting it as a basic block will probably not skew results much. On the other hand, branching to code in the data segment and then back to the code segment could easily confuse us if we are doing a transformation that requires understanding the control flow.

There is also occasionally reason to have data in the code segment. The MIPS Fortran compiler puts constant arguments of subroutines in the code segment,[4] and Pixie's documentation suggests that the MIPS Fortran compiler at one time used code-segment data as part of the implementation of FORMAT statements. There are two problems with data in the code segment. First, we access this data via an address into the code segment, and code modification will probably change the address. Second, if we mistake the data for code, we may instrument or modify it, causing the computations that depend on it to get the wrong values.

Pixie and Nixie deal with both problems by including a copy of the original code at the beginning of the modified code segment. Since loads and stores do not have their addresses translated the way jumps do, following the untranslated address will lead to the old, unmodified code segment. This means both that we will look in the right place and that we will get an unaltered value.

Because Epoxie corrects all addresses statically according to the relocation dictionary, the address will lead us to the right place in the modified code. It won't help, then, to include a copy of the original code. Instead, we must distinguish between instructions and data in the code segment, and be sure

[4] This way it can pass these arguments by reference, secure in the knowledge that a protection violation will occur if the subroutine tries to modify them. The read-only data segment would be a more logical place for these values, but it did not exist when the compiler was developed.

not to alter the latter. Fortunately, it turns out that the MIPS loader symbol table contains information that makes this possible. This information also lets Nixie determine (if the symbol table is present) whether including the old code is necessary.

Nixie uses the runtime address translation table only if there are indirect procedure calls in the program. Unfortunately, our standard C library has one routine, called *fwalk*, that takes a procedure address as an argument and makes indirect calls to that procedure. *Fwalk* is called in all programs, as part of the normal exit sequence. Rather than surrender and include the translation table all the time, Nixie recognizes the *fwalk* routine, and also recognizes direct calls to it. It inspects the instructions around these calls to find the instructions that compute the procedure address passed. If these instructions compute a literal address, as is usually the case, Nixie simply modifies them to compute the corrected address. Of course, *fwalk* might itself be called indirectly, in which case we can't recognize the call and therefore won't do the translation of its argument; but we can always tell if *fwalk*'s address is taken, and avoid this entire optimization for such programs. Pixie and Epoxie need not give *fwalk* special treatment, because all code addresses are translated at the same time: at run time for Pixie and at modification time for Epoxie.

The MIPS and Titan architectures both have delayed branches: when a branch or jump is taken, the instruction after the branch (sometimes called the "branch slot") is executed before control is transferred. Code modification may replace the branch slot instruction by a series of several instructions. In that case we cannot just leave these instructions in place, because only the first will be executed if we take the branch. Fortunately, a branch slot is often filled with an instruction from before the branch, in which case the expansion of this instruction can be safely moved back before the branch.

If the slot changes a register that the branch uses,[5] however, it is incorrect simply to move the slot back before the branch. In this case there are two possible approaches. One is to duplicate the expansion, so that we replace

```
conditional-branch to L
slot instruction
```

with

```
     reverse-conditional-branch to L1
     nop
     slot expansion
     unconditional-branch to L
     nop
L1:  slot expansion
```

(If we are careful we can do this without the two nops.) This is roughly what Pixie does. Another choice is to expand to

[5]This situation can arise, for example, if the assembler moves an instruction from the destination block or the fall-through block to be executed *speculatively* in the branch slot. The assembler does this only if it is safe; i.e. if the register changed by this instruction is set before it is used in the alternative block.

```
        temp := evaluate condition
        slot expansion
        if temp branch to L
        nop
```

Epoxie and Nixie do this.[6] Pixie's approach is longer but simpler, and works better in the case where the branch slot is itself the destination of some other branch.[7] Pixie can simply consider everything up to L1 as part of the expansion of the branch, and everything at L1 and beyond as the expansion of the slot. In contrast, Epoxie must do an ugly thing: it changes

```
        conditional-branch to L
LL:     slot instruction
```

into

```
        temp := evaluate condition
        branch to L2
        nop
LL:     temp := false
L2:     slot expansion
        if temp branch to L
        nop
```

so that branches to LL will follow the right path. This works, but it is distinctly inelegant.

System calls present a few problems to these systems, especially if we are stealing registers. System call traps are allowed to destroy the first 16 registers, which means our stolen registers should probably not include these. A sigreturn trap restores the values of the other 16 from the *sigcontext* data structure, so Pixie, Nixie, and Epoxie precede this trap with code that copies the sigcontext values of the stolen registers into the shadow registers it maintains in memory, and stores its own values of these registers into the sigcontext data structure. (The values that start out in the sigcontext structure were put there by normal user code somewhere, which would have been translated as usual into code accessing the shadow values.) Even if we are not stealing registers, either a

---

[6]For a bad reason. I didn't understand a tricky property of the relocation dictionaries, which I thought made it impossible to correctly duplicate the code if it was marked for a particular kind of relocation. Specifically, the MIPS loader format has a pair of related operations, R_REFHI and R_REFLO, which it uses to relocate a pair of instructions that compute a 32-bit address by combining two 16-bit parts. These relocation entries must be consecutive in the dictionary, because we must inspect both instructions to know how to relocate the first. The problem arises if the slot instruction is relocated R_REFLO, where the associated R_REFHI relocation appears before the branch. If we duplicate the expansion of the slot, we will have two R_REFLO entries and only one R_REFHI entry, which I thought at first was illegal. In practice, though, a R_REFHI can be followed by any number of R_REFLOs, as long as they all make the same assumptions.

[7]This can happen explicitly in assembly code, of course, but also occurs as the result of pipeline scheduling, if a branch slot is filled from the fall-through block, but the fall-through block is itself the destination of another branch.

sigreturn or a sigvec call involves a code address that will eventually be transferred to by the operating system kernel. The code of the kernel is not modified by our tools, so Pixie and Nixie precede these traps with code to translate the address. Epoxie need not, because the original address computation, wherever it is, has relocation entries that cause Epoxie to translate it. Finally, if we want to do anything just before termination, like write a file of basic block counts, we can insert code to do so before each _exit system trap: Pixie, Nixie, and Epoxie all work this way.

Signals caused by external interrupts or by error conditions detected by the hardware are a problem if the transformation includes register stealing. This is because the three shadow registers are part of the register state that a kernel must preserve before giving control to the user's signal handler, but there is no way for the kernel to know this. This is a problem for Pixie, Nixie and Epoxie, thought not for Mahler, whose instrumentation facility is integrated with its register allocator so that shadow registers are not needed.

Probably the biggest pitfall is the use of pattern-matching to recognize certain library routines. This is relatively fail-soft, because a routine that is listed as present in the symbol table but that does not match the pattern triggers a warning, and a jump that cannot be classified triggers an error. Nonetheless, the patterns are very specific, and a new version of the library routine will probably fail to match. The right solution is to raise the level of the assembly language slightly, so that assembly code adheres to the same conventions as compiled code. One simple way to do this is by requiring the assembly programmer to explain the violations of the conventions, and encoding these explanations in the symbol table. If we do not wish to change the assembler, a less attractive solution is to develop a tool that looks for violations in the libraries themselves, and asks the Nixie/Epoxie maintainer to categorize them. These explanations would in turn generate the patterns used by Nixie and Epoxie. Perhaps the easiest solution is simply to provide clean versions of the problematic library routines, versions that adhere to the conventions of the code generator, so that we need not do anything special at all.

10 A few numbers

We have a prototype version of Nixie and Epoxie. To compare its code modification to that of Mahler and Pixie, we implemented basic block counting. Figure 2 shows the expansion in code size for a variety of programs.

The ratio of code size reflects only the difference in the space needed for the executable instructions between the original and the instrumented versions. In addition, Pixie and occasionally Nixie need the address translation table that converts old addresses to new, which is as long as the original code segment. Moreover, Pixie and Nixie sometimes need the original code to be included before the instrumented code, because data items exist in the code segment.[8] The code expansion from Mahler is noticeably less than for the MIPS-based tools. This is due mainly to the fact that the Titan's instruction set is more

[8]Pixie and Nixie align these pieces on particular boundaries for convenience, resulting in even larger instrumented versions; I believe this is not logically necessary, and so the empty space between pieces is not counted here.

	Mahler	*Epoxie*	*Nixie*	*Pixie*
ccom	1.4	2.1	2.1	3.0+
doduc	1.3	1.6	1.6+*	2.0+*
eco	1.5	2.0	2.0	2.9+
egrep	1.6	2.1	2.1	2.9+
eqntott	1.5	2.1	2.2+	3.0+
espresso	1.5	2.1	2.1+	2.7+
fpppp	1.2	1.6	1.6+*	2.0+*
gcc1	1.6	2.4	2.4+	2.7+
grr	1.5	2.0	2.0	2.7+
li	1.6	2.1	2.1+	3.1+
linpack	1.4	1.9	1.9	2.7+
livermore	1.6	2.0	2.0	2.7+
matrix300	1.6	2.1	2.2+*	3.0+*
met	1.5	2.0	2.0	2.8+
nasa7	1.4	1.9	1.9+*	2.6+*
sed	1.5	2.0	2.0	2.7+
spice	1.3	1.7	1.8+*	2.1+*
stanford	1.4	2.0	2.0	2.8+
tomcatv	1.5	2.1	2.1+	2.9+
whetstones	1.5	2.0	2.0	2.8+
yacc	1.5	2.1	2.1	2.8+

+ means runtime address table required; add 1.0

* means original code required; add 1.0

Figure 2: Ratio of code size to original

	Mahler	*Epoxie*	*Nixie*	*Pixie*
ccom	1.6	2.1	2.1	3.0
doduc	—	1.2	1.2	1.3
eco	1.7	1.9	1.9	2.5
egrep	1.6	2.0	2.0	2.4
eqntott	1.5	2.1	2.2	2.7
espresso	1.6	1.9	1.9	2.2
fpppp	1.0	1.1	1.1	1.2
gcc1	1.7	2.2	2.2	2.7
grr	1.6	1.4	1.4	1.7
li	1.7	2.0	2.0	2.7
linpack	1.1	1.1	1.1	1.1
livermore	1.1	1.3	1.3	1.4
matrix300	—	1.1	1.1	1.1
met	1.5	1.7	1.7	2.3
nasa7	1.0	1.1	1.1	1.1
sed	1.6	=	=	=
spice	1.2	1.3	1.3	1.4
stanford	1.5	1.7	1.7	2.1
tomcatv	1.1	1.1	1.1	1.1
whetstones	1.2	1.3	1.3	1.6
yacc	1.6	1.9	1.9	2.4

— means runtime error in unmodified program
= means run too short for resolution of system clock

Figure 3: Ratio of runtime to original

reduced than the MIPS's. Equivalent basic blocks take more Titan instructions on the average, so the Titan counting code is smaller in proportion.

Figure 3 shows the ratio of execution times. It is interesting that the increase in execution time is typically rather less than the increase in executable code size. Perhaps this is because both the instrumented and uninstrumented versions of the program spend cycles waiting for data-cache misses, which are likely to be comparable in the two versions. Or perhaps long blocks, whose expansion is proportionately smaller, happen to be executed more frequently than short ones.

We can tell Mahler, Epoxie, and Nixie to perform all the transformations for basic-block counting, but to leave out the actual counting code. This tells us how much of the expansion in code space and time is the overhead of stealing registers and possibly doing some runtime address translation, as opposed to the instrumentation itself. Figure 4 shows the result. We can see that the expense of the register-stealing overhead is very small: it is amusing that adding the overhead of Nixie or Epoxie made grr 8% *faster*![9] From this we see that the smaller time and space expansion of Nixie in comparison to Pixie must come

[9]Timer variability, while nonzero, is too small to account for this difference. Perhaps the expansion in the code segment pushed parts of the program to new addresses that accidentally resolved a cache conflict.

	code size			run time		
	Mahler	*Epoxie*	*Nixie*	*Mahler*	*Epoxie*	*Nixie*
ccom	1.00	1.02	1.02	1.01	1.11	1.11
doduc	1.00	1.02	1.03+*	—	1.04	1.03
eco	1.00	1.04	1.04	1.01	1.17	1.17
egrep	1.00	1.06	1.06	1.02	1.00	1.00
eqntott	1.00	1.06	1.07+	0.99	1.01	1.01
espresso	1.00	1.07	1.07+	1.00	1.00	1.00
fpppp	1.00	1.01	1.03+*	1.00	1.01	0.99
gcc1	1.00	1.03	1.03+	1.01	1.08	1.08
grr	1.01	1.05	1.05	1.01	0.92	0.91
li	1.00	1.02	1.02+	0.99	1.00	1.02
linpack	1.00	1.05	1.05	1.00	1.01	1.01
livermore	1.00	1.05	1.05	1.00	1.10	1.10
matrix300	1.00	1.03	1.05+*	—	1.00	1.00
met	1.01	1.05	1.05	1.01	1.00	1.00
nasa7	1.00	1.06	1.07+*	1.00	1.02	1.02
sed	1.00	1.05	1.05	1.00	=	=
spice	1.00	1.05	1.05+*	0.99	1.02	1.02
stanford	1.00	1.04	1.04	1.00	1.00	1.00
tomcatv	1.01	1.02	1.04+	1.00	1.02	1.02
whetstones	1.00	1.04	1.04	1.00	1.00	1.00
yacc	1.01	1.05	1.05	1.01	1.00	1.00

+ means runtime address table required; add 1.0
* means original code required; add 1.0
— means runtime error in unmodified program
= means run too short for resolution of system clock

Figure 4: Ratio of time and space with overhead code but not instrumentation code

from Nixie's ability to do most address translation statically. We can also see that using Nixie or Epoxie to do optimization seems quite feasible, even if it turns out we must steal registers to do so. Mahler's time and space expansion due to overhead alone is nearly negligible: the largest increase in runtime is 2%, and the runtime even decreased slightly in several cases. The overhead is so small partly because the register allocation is integrated more closely with the instrumenter, but mostly because the Titan has 64 registers, so that taking a few away is less important than it is on the 32-register MIPS architecture.

11 Conclusions

A late code modification system that compromises between the integrated approach of Mahler and the conservative stand-alone approach of Pixie is possible. We have prototypes of two such systems, Nixie and Epoxie, that require different amounts of compile-time information to be preserved. The overhead of these systems is usually quite small. Because Nixie and Epoxie correct the symbol table information – something Pixie could do but does not – the resulting modified file can be run under the debugger to the same extent as the original. This may not matter for an instrumenting transformation (except to make it easier to debug the instrumentation process), but it is likely to be important if we use Nixie or Epoxie for optimizing transformations.[10]

Nixie and Epoxie work by understanding enough about the code in a program that in most cases they can assign meanings to all the jumps in a program, allowing the entire control structure to be determined. This should mean that we can do global analysis of that structure. Understanding the global control structure may let us use these tools for low-level global optimizations, such as interprocedure register allocation and pipeline scheduling. In any case we should be able to do instrumentation less intrusively.

12 Acknowledgements

Aaron Goldberg experimented with a less general form of Nixie's approach as part of his summer project [7] at DECWRL, and I am indebted to him for several stimulating discussions.

Most of what I know about Pixie I have learned by disassembling the code it produces, but along the way Earl Killian has given me a hint or three, for which I am most grateful. In particular Earl tipped me off about the run-time address translation, which is, as far as I know, entirely his invention.

My thanks for helpful criticisms of this paper to Anita Borg, Preston Briggs, Chris Fraser, Bill Hamburgen, Earl Killian, and Scott McFarling.

[10] I have recently learned that the MIPS debugger has an option that allows it to run Pixie-instrumented programs. In this mode, it knows about the stolen registers, and to understand the unmodified symbol table it looks at the address translation table included by Pixie. This is a nice idea, and allows it to display either the original code or the instrumented code, but it does require modifying the debugger, in a quite specific way.

References

[1] Borg A, Kessler RE, Lazana G, Wall DW. Long address traces from RISC machines: Generation and analysis. In Seventeenth Annual International Symposium on Computer Architecture, pp 270–279. IEEE Computer Society Press, 1990.

[2] Chow F, Himelstein M, Killian E, Weber L. Engineering a RISC compiler system. In Digest of Papers: Compcon 86, pp 132–137. IEEE Computer Society Press, 1986.

[3] Chow FC. Minimizing register usage penalty at procedure calls. In Proceedings of the SIGPLAN '88 Conference on Programming Language Design and Implementation, pp 85–94, 1988.

[4] Davidson JW, Fraser CW. Code selection through object code optimization. Transactions on Programming Languages and Systems, 6(4):505–526, 1984.

[5] Davidson JW, Fraser CW. Register allocation and exhaustive peephole optimization. Software–Practice and Experience, 14(9):857–865, 1984.

[6] Gibbons PB, Muchnick SS. Efficient instruction scheduling for a pipelined architecture. In Proceedings of the SIGPLAN '86 Symposium on Compiler Construction, pp 11–16, 1986.

[7] Goldberg A, Hennessy J. MTOOL: A method for detecting memory bottlenecks. Technical Report TN-17, Digital Equipment Corp., 250 University Ave., Palo Alto, California, 1990.

[8] Graham SL, Kessler PB, McKusick MK. An execution profiler for modular programs. Software–Practice and Experience, 13(8):120–126, 1983.

[9] Hennessy J, Gross T. Postpass code optimization of pipeline constraints. ACM Transactions on Programming Languages and Systems, 5(3):422–448, 1983.

[10] Himelstein MI, Chow FC, Enderby K. Cross-module optimizations: Its implementation and benefits. In Proceedings of the Summer 1987 USENIX Conference, pp 347–356. The USENIX Association, 1987.

[11] Johnson SC. Postloading for fun and profit. In Proceedings of the Winter 1990 USENIX Conference, pp 325–330. The USENIX Association, 1990.

[12] Jouppi NP, Dion J, Boggs D, Nielsen MJK. Multititan: Four architecture papers. Technical Report 87/8, Digital Equipment Corp., 250 University Ave., Palo Alto, California, 1988.

[13] Kane G. MIPS R2000 Risc Architecture. Prentice Hall, 1987.

[14] Killian EA. Personal communication.

[15] McFarling S. Program optimization for instruction caches. In Third International Symposium on Architectural Support for Programming Languages and Operating Systems, pp 183–191, 1989.

[16] McKeeman WM. Peephole optimization. Communications of the ACM, 8(7):443–444, 1965.

[17] MIPS Computer Systems . RISCompiler and C Programmer's Guide. MIPS Computer Systems, Inc., 930 Arques Ave., Sunnyvale, California 94086, 1986.

[18] Nielsen MJK. Titan system manual. Technical Report 86/1, Digital Equipment Corp., 250 University Ave., Palo Alto, California, 1986.

[19] Santhanam V, Odnert D. Register allocation across procedure and module boundaries. In Proceedings of the SIGPLAN '90 Conference on Programming Language Design and Implementation, pp 28–39, 1990.

[20] Steenkiste PA, Hennessy JL. A simple interprocedural register allocation algorithm and its effectiveness for LISP. ACM Transactions on Programming Languages and Systems, 11(1):1–32, 1989.

[21] Wall DW. Global register allocation at link-time. In Proceedings of the SIGPLAN '86 Symposium on Compiler Construction, pp 264–275, 1986.

[22] Wall DW. Register windows vs. register allocation. In Proceedings of the SIGPLAN '88 Conference on Programming Language Design and Implementation, pp 67–78, 1988.

[23] Wall DW. Link-time code modification. Technical Report 89/17, Digital Equipment Corp., 250 University Ave., Palo Alto, California, 1989.

[24] Wall DW. Experience with a software-defined machine architecture. ACM Transactions on Programming Languages and Systems, to appear. Also available as WRL Research Report 91/10, Digital Equipment Corp., 250 University Ave., Palo Alto, California. August 1991.

[25] Wall DW, Powell ML. The Mahler experience: Using an intermediate language as the machine description. In Second International Symposium on Architectural Support for Programming Languages and Operating Systems, pp 100–104, 1987.

The Design of a Back-end Object Management System

A. Asthana
H. V. Jagadish
P. Krzyzanowski

AT&T Bell Laboratories
Murray Hill, New Jersey 07974

Abstract

We describe the architecture and design of a back-end object manager, designed as an "active memory" system on a plug-in board for a standard workstation (or personal computer). We show how, with minimal modification to existing code, it is possible to achieve significant performance improvement for the execution of data-intensive methods on objects, simply by using our back-end object manager.

1. Introduction

Medium to fine grain multi-processing systems are fast becoming a reality. However, advances in parallel programming have not yet made it possible for the typical user to write efficient programs that can exploit high degrees of parallelism, except in certain limited contexts (cf. [9, 10]). Alongside, object oriented programming is emerging as a popular methodology for constructing and maintaining large complex software systems. We believe that a merger of object oriented programming and parallel processing technologies can provide the basis for building systems that are both modular and efficient. In this paper we attempt to show how an object-oriented view of the world can be used to assist in this task.

Our notion is that there is a front-end host machine that the user interacts with, and a back-end multi-processor that is an "object-server". Each processor in the back-end manages a set of objects that are resident in the memory and/or disks associated with that processor. Upon receiving a message from the host, a back-end processor can execute a specified method on an object that it manages, and then return the results of the computation, if any, to the host. In the process of method invocation other methods may be invoked, on the same or on a different processor. When a processor wishes to invoke a method on a different processor, it does so by means of a message, just as in the case of the host.

Objects remain stationary at a fixed location while messages are passed from the processor managing one object to a processor managing another object, partially mimicking in hardware the way (software) objects are supposed to behave conceptually. While each back-end processor manages a fixed set of objects, in its own individual section of memory, and its own disks, if any, *all processors are part of the address space of the host processor*. Thus, a shared-memory programming model can be constructed on top of a physically shared nothing multi-processor system, by using the encapsulation of objects to provide the necessary programming discipline. One could think of the back-end system as being an "object server", along the lines suggested in [8], following the client-server model. However, we believe that the extremely low communication overhead possible in a parallel processor brings about a qualitative change in the way the system is used.

While our model of computation is similar to the *actor* model, proposed in [7], our intention here is not to design a new parallel-programming language based on the model of computation sketched above. (There are several excellent efforts in this direction [1, 2, 16]). Instead, we wish to use a standard object-oriented language and show how object operations described in it can be accelerated with the help of a back-end object manager. While many of the concepts we present are quite general, we shall describe them in the context of a specific language, C++ [14], and a specific system, SWIM, which is a medium-fine-grained multiprocessor of the type described above. A quick overview of the architecture of the SWIM system is given in Sec. 2.

The main idea and the basic mechanisms for supporting it are presented in Sec. 3. Issues involved in object creation and destruction, and the management of resources, are discussed in Sec. 4. An overview of the compile system is presented in the Sec. 5. Performance figures are provided in Sec. 6 followed by a discussion of some subtleties of the architecture in Sec. 7. Finally, in Sec. 8 we present plans for extending our work, and conclude in Sec. 9.

2. Background

The "von Neumann bottleneck", in the movement of data on the system bus from memory to processor, is a well-recognized performance limiting phenomenon in computer architecture. This problem can partially be ameliorated by the use of cache memory close to the processor. However, such a cache is not likely to be of much help where data-intensive operations are concerned. For data-intensive operations, it appears desirable to perform as much computation as possible close to where the data is stored, and thereby minimize the traffic to the main processor. Early systems following such an idea have been described in [12, 13, 15]. A recent system for this purpose is a back-end medium-fine-grained MIMD message-driven "multiprocessor", called SWIM [5].

SWIM is a high bandwidth, multiported, disk-sized memory system capable of storing, maintaining, and manipulating data structures within it, independent of the main processing units. SWIM increases memory functionality to better balance the time spent in moving data with that involved in actually manipulating it. The memory system is composed of up to thousands of small memory units, called Active Storage Elements (ASEs), embedded in a communication network as shown in Figure 1. Each active storage element has microprogrammable processing logic associated with it that allows it to perform data manipulation operations locally. Simple and small objects can be stored and manipulated entirely within an ASE, while larger and more complex objects are stored within several ASEs, and are cooperatively managed.

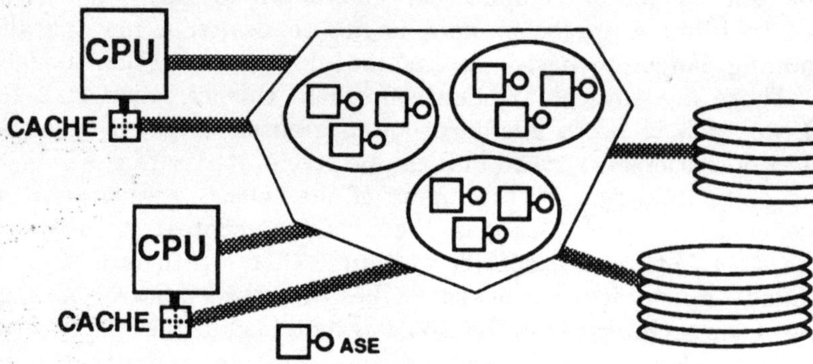

Figure 1. Conceptual View of the Back-End Object Management System

SWIM appears as a very high bandwidth multi-ported shared memory to the processors that connect to it. However, because the SWIM memory is much more functional, it is capable of performing many of the data manipulation tasks that would normally have to be handled by the processor itself in a conventional system. Freeing the processors of the actual data manipulation and transformation allows them to concentrate on the task of coordinating program control instead of wasting cycles on data massaging. SWIM is unique in that it allows both (ordinary) memory read/write in the normal fashion, in addition to higher level transactions.

3. Object manipulation

3.1 The main idea

An object *class* physically comprises a data structure and some member functions. One copy of the data structure is required for each instance of the class. The member functions need be stored only once.

An Active Storage Element (ASE) is *configured* with the member functions for a particular object class. While there is nothing to prevent a single ASE from managing objects of multiple classes, it is easiest to think of each ASE as managing objects of exactly one class. When one ASE manages objects of different classes we think of it as multiple "virtual ASEs". As such, for the rest of this paper, we shall pretend that there is exactly one type of object in each ASE. (Of course, there usually are multiple instances of that one type).

An ASE can be configured to manage objects of a particular class by loading its on-chip microcode memory with the appropriate microcode to execute member functions associated with that class. This microcode can be down-loaded at run time, in the SWIM system. The data memory of the ASE is (conceptually) divided into multiple *object buffers*. Each object buffer is a chunk of memory large enough to hold all the data for an instance of the particular class.

A member function is invoked on a specific object by sending a message to the ASE managing it. This message must identify the particular object of interest, the specific function to be executed, and the values for any parameters that may be required. Any response from the ASE is also in the form of a message.

Execution within an ASE is single-threaded. There is no mechanism for an ASE to switch processes, or to save and restore state (except through explicit program specification). As such, a method, once invoked, runs to completion before any other method can be initiated at that ASE.

Thus we see that, logically, the ASE provides complete encapsulation of the object it is managing from outside agents. External agents accessing the objects need not know about its internal implementation. Only the ASE has knowledge about the structure and semantics of the object. In addition, the ASE can provide any desired measure of security and protection. Physically, the ASE represents close coupling between the memory cells and specialized processing logic in the same local domain, creating the potential for performance benefits.

3.2 Host - SWIM communication

There is a single address space for the entire system, SWIM and the host processor. Every SWIM address has two components: one identifying the ASE, and the other identifying the specific object (or memory location) in the ASE. This division of the address into two components is internal to SWIM and is transparent to any software on the host (and therefore to the user).

Thus, a message invoking a member function has in it the object (and ASE) identifier, a member function identifier (a class dependent "opcode"), and zero or more values that are parameters to the member function invoked. The host writes these values to SWIM on the system bus as if it were writing to regular memory (except that it writes to a part of the address space reserved for SWIM).

It is usually expensive to interrupt the host, on account of a significant amount of interrupt processing that would be required. Instead, messages sent from SWIM to the host are queued up in a buffer, and this buffer is read by the host at its will. There is a "buffer full" flag to coordinate this handshake.

We call a *transaction*, the processing between the receipt of a function invocation by SWIM from the host, and the provision of the corresponding response to the host. In the course of this transaction, multiple additional functions may be invoked. The entire computation has associated with it a system generated transaction identifier. After the host has invoked a member function, it can look for results associated with the corresponding transaction identifier. This is managed in the hardware by providing multiple logical buffers at the output of SWIM, each with a different transaction identifier associated. The host queries only the appropriate buffer and reads it when full.

In terms of the code executed at the host, a member function invocation looks like a series of writes to SWIM memory (to invoke the member function), followed by a series of reads to retrieve any values returned[1]. The mechanism is asynchronous in that there is no need for the host to wait while SWIM executes the member function invoked. (Of course, individual memory reads and writes are synchronous. But these are usually quick enough that the waiting time is not large). Thus, the overhead of member function invocation on SWIM is a few memory operations. This overhead may swamp any benefits from executing code in SWIM rather than the host for the very simplest member functions that operate on data likely to have been cached. However, for any substantial member function, and especially if it is likely that a significant portion of the data is not cached, executing the member function on SWIM will be a win. We verify this intuition in Sec. 6.

1. There may be additional reads and writes to complete an appropriate buffer management protocol for communication in either direction.

3.3 An example

To illustrate the concepts presented in this paper, we use as a running example, a directed graph, maintained as a collection of `Node` objects. The definition of the class `Node` can be found in the Appendix. The example has intentionally been kept simple to emphasize object management rather than present functional software.

A node has a `key` and some non-key information recorded in `attr`. It can have up to `MAX_CHILDREN` (let us assume this is 4) outgoing links (to children nodes). To aid in searching the graph, each node also has a `visit` flag. The data structure for a `Node` object has a size of 28 bytes. Thus an ASE managing this class of objects has its data memory divided into object buffers each of 28 bytes.

There are a few different member functions associated with this class. In addition to a constructor and a destructor (discussed in the following section), there is a function `add_child()` to create links between nodes. There is a function `search()` that returns a node reachable from a specified starting node with a specified key value. Finally there is a function `clean_search()` that cleans up after a search has been performed.

Let us consider the `add_child()` function. When this function is invoked, the appropriate ASE receives a message indicating the function to be invoked, the particular object on which the function is to be invoked (the source of the new edge), and the node object parameter to the method (the destination of the new edge). The last two (object pointers) are placed in registers in the ASE when the message is received. The opcode is decoded and the microcode for the function `add_child()` is executed, utilizing the two values placed in registers. The host performs a couple of writes to SWIM memory to invoke this function. Having done so, it can continue execution, while the function executes on SWIM in parallel. In this case, an asynchronous call was possible because the function did not return any value, or alter its input parameters.

4. Object creation and destruction

4.1 Creation

Objects are created in C++ by calling a constructor for the appropriate class. The constructor is a member function of the class and takes zero or more parameters, whose values are used to determine initial values for the data members of the new object.

Like all other member functions associated with a class, constructors are also compiled into microcode and stored at the appropriate ASEs. The constructor call goes as a message to one of the ASEs managing objects of the specified type (see Sec. 4.4 below on how the specific ASE is determined). The message invokes the constructor function, which allocates an object buffer, initializes values in it and thus creates a new object.

4.2 Destruction

Objects are deleted by calling a destructor member function for the class. Once more, the destructor is invoked like any other member function – by sending a message to the ASE managing the object. Any code in the destructor is executed, and the object buffer released.

4.3 Buffer management

An object buffer is required every time a new object is created, and an object buffer is released every time an object is deleted. Each ASE has a certain fixed number of object buffers for a particular object type. It has to keep track of its own object buffers, and uses a bit vector to do so, one bit for each object buffer indicating whether it is in use. When a constructor is invoked at the ASE, an available buffer is selected and assigned, and the corresponding bit set. When a destructor is invoked, the corresponding bit is cleared.

4.4 Data allocation

When a destructor is invoked in user (source) code, we know which ASE to send a message to since the identifier of the object specified encodes the ASE address. However, we do not have this information when a constructor is invoked. If there is exactly one ASE managing objects of that particular class, then we are fine. If there are multiple ASEs, then there is no way for the programmer, from whom we are trying to hide all the parallelism and even the existence of ASEs, to specify which ASE is meant. We use the concept of a head ASE for this purpose[2]. For each object class there is a single *head ASE*. All constructor requests are sent to this head ASE. This ASE knows about other ASEs currently managing objects of its class, and assigns the constructor calls to one of them. For this to work efficiently, it is useful for the head ASE to keep track of space availability in each of the other ASEs. Since all constructors go through the head ASE any way, this is not too difficult. Each ASE is required to know the head ASE of its type, and sends a message to the head every time it invokes a destructor, to record the freeing up of an object buffer. Due to delays in message transit times, the head ASE will have a slightly conservative picture of the space available (since it records buffers as assigned before the requested ASE assigns the buffer, but records buffers as freed only after the buffer has been freed). We do not see this as a problem.

Free-space collection is an important issue in storage management. Within an ASE, by maintaining bit vectors for buffer usage, we make

2. Alternative schemes are possible. In fact there could even be a different scheme for each class!

sure that object buffers are reused once they are freed. Free memory can thus be reused without having to relocate objects. While this works wonderfully for objects of any one type, it is not sufficient for the purpose of re-allocating memory between objects of different classes. We achieve this end by making it possible to configure additional ASEs to manage objects of a given type, and to free ASEs that are no longer required to manage objects of that type. The mechanism for this ASE configuration is described in the next section. Suffice to say here that as more objects are created of some type, it can consume more ASEs, and as these objects are destroyed, it can give up some of these ASEs. The caveat here is that we currently do not have a mechanism for transparently relocating objects, so an entire ASE will be retained if even one object remains in it.

4.5 ASE configuration

An Active Storage Element is *configured* to manage objects of a particular class by loading it with the microcode associated with that class. This microcode is run-time downloadable in SWIM. What this means is that ASEs can be reconfigured dynamically. As a program runs, it can request and give up ASEs. Due to each ASE being identically equipped, and the almost symmetric nature of communication between ASEs in SWIM, which particular ASE gets assigned to a particular class is not important.

There is an "ASE Assignment Manager", which keeps track of ASEs that are currently free. One head ASE is assigned for each class of objects, with the relative addresses of these head ASEs being fixed at compile time. Being assigned to the class means that the ASE has the appropriate microcode downloaded, and any required data structures initialized (such as marking all object buffers as free).

As new objects are created, the head ASE can request and obtain additional ASEs for its class from the the ASE assignment manager. When all objects of a particular ASE are deleted, the ASE can be de-commissioned. De-commissioning an ASE simply involves recording it to be free at the ASE assignment manager. The head ASE for a class is responsible for requesting and de-commissioning ASEs managing objects of that class. The code for this is automatically generated by our compile system, optionally utilizing user-supplied hints.

4.6 Example - continued

Turning to our directed graph example, let us look at the constructor for the class `Node` defined in the Appendix. Conceptually, a constructor performs two operations: allocating space for an object and executing a user-defined constructor function (which initializes values of data members in the object). The return from a constructor is a handle to the object, and is available immediately after space allocation, *before* the user-defined function is executed. As such, the ASE can send the return value (the handle) back to the host (or other constructor invoking entity) before executing the user-defined code. The execution of the user-defined constructor function occurs in parallel with the next stages of computation on the host processor. (This sort of optimization is possible in other member functions as well, through a dependency analysis).

5. The compile system

The mechanisms described so far are not straightforward, and are certainly not trivial for an ordinary C++ programmer to use directly. Fortunately, most of the complexity described above can be made transparent to the user by means of an appropriate compile system. In this section we describe such a compile system.

5.1 The architecture

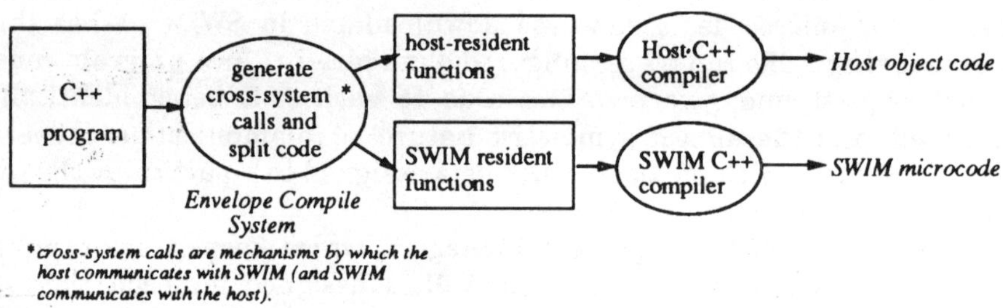

Figure 2. The Compile System

As shown in Figure 2, there are two primary compilers. One is the standard C++ compiler, which generates regular object code for the host machine. The other is an ASE compiler that generates SWIM ASE microcode from class definitions. This compiler is described in [4, 11] and its internals are largely orthogonal to our thrust here. On top of these two is an envelope compile system. This system has to determine which of the two compile paths any individual piece of code has to follow. It also creates stubs for invocations of methods that are to be run on SWIM rather than be regular function calls.

5.2 Object location

Objects can be managed either on SWIM or on the host. Ideally, the compiler should make an intelligent decision based on the structure of the class, the complexity of its member functions, and so on. Until we develop a better understanding of the issues involved, we are leaving it up to the user to specify for each object class where it should be managed. This specification is done by means of *pragmas*. (A *pragma* is treated as a comment by the C++ compiler, but can be used to derive useful information by other front-ends, such as our envelope compile system). Member functions of a class to be managed on SWIM will be compiled into SWIM microcode, and will be executed on the appropriate ASEs. However, the class definer can specify, once more with the use of pragmas, that selected member functions of the class are to be executed directly from the host, exploiting the fact that we have a single shared address space. All member functions of a class managed on the host are executed on the host, with no exceptions.

If a class is managed on SWIM (the host), it is unlikely that a class derived from it will be managed by the host (respectively, SWIM). As such, user specification for where an object is to be managed is inherited, just like data members and member functions, but can be over-ridden. All inheritance is resolved prior to any code generation. In the case of SWIM classes, all inherited functions are replicated (in the output microcode) in each of the classes in which they are inherited.

In general, the structure of an object can be complex. References (pointers) to other objects may be included in an object. These do not cause any new difficulties. A "composite" object may actually have other objects as components of it. When a composite object is located in SWIM, its component objects are also forcibly located on SWIM, even if these component objects belong to classes not in SWIM. The inverse is not true: composite objects managed by the host can have component objects managed by SWIM. Even when a (component) object is located on SWIM, its member functions could be executed on the host. However, it will be more efficient if its member functions are executed in the ASE managing the object. To obtain this efficiency, for composite objects that are compiled for SWIM, code for member functions of component objects is also included. Thus this code is directly available in the ASE managing the composite object.

5.3 Function invocation

A function invoked on the host from the host works as usual. There is no change. A function invoked on SWIM from the host, instead of being a function invocation, is translated into a series of reads and writes to memory addresses in SWIM space. The results returned from the function are obtained as a series of reads from SWIM space. If the compiler is able to determine that some statements are not dependent on the function, these can be moved in between the first and the second series of accesses to SWIM memory, that is between function invocation and result return, thereby obtaining somewhat greater concurrency. Often, functions do not return any results, or the returned value is ignored. In such a case, the second set of reads is completely unnecessary, and the function can execute on SWIM completely in parallel with the rest of the code on the host.

A piece of code (a function) executing in a SWIM ASE can return results to the host by sending a message. This message is explicitly encoded as a sequence of transmits in the ASE microcode. The compiler generates this sequence of transmits based on the return statement encountered.

Execution of a member function on an ASE could require the execution of another member function. If this member function is on the same object, nothing special is required. The second member function is invoked as a subroutine in the course of the execution of the first member function.

A member function may be invoked on a different object in the same or different ASE, by sending a message, just as the host can invoke a member function by sending a message to an ASE. These messages are explicitly encoded as a sequence of transmits in the microcode. The compiler has to translate function calls from code in SWIM to such a sequence of transmits. Within SWIM, inter-ASE message transmission is very efficient, with the time to transfer a message with two 32-bit words of data being only a fraction of the time for a normal main memory access by the host.

When a function is called on a SWIM ASE, whether from within SWIM or from the host, any returned values are sent back to the invoking ASE or host. Both at the host and at an ASE, the physical SWIM function call mechanism is asynchronous: the calling entity can continue operation while the called entity computes the result. Synchronous calls can easily be emulated by forcing the calling entity to look for the returned value (or completion signal, if there is no returned value), immediately after the computation has been initiated, and blocking on this attempt to read. All C++ language function calls are synchronous, so we can exploit the added parallelism of asynchronicity to the extent that the compiler is able to locate code that is independent of the function called. The asynchronous nature becomes really useful when we use Concurrent C++ [6] constructs.

When one ASE invokes a function on another ASE, it is not necessary that the results be returned to the calling ASE. Instead, the called ASE may pass the results along to some third place. This sort of computation becomes feasible due to the asynchronous nature of function invocation. The calling ASE can move on to other business having passed on the "baton" as it were. Such an organization of computation is the core idea of pipelining: a popular means of speeding up computation. Unfortunately there is no language support for this mode of computation in C++. An optimizing compiler is required to recognize when the calling function does not use the results from the called function, but, instead, simply returns. In such cases, an additional parameter to the call can be used to indicate where the results of the computation is supposed to go. Sometimes a few more parameters may be required, to carry the state of the computation along.

5.4 SWIM-Host communication

In general, a host processor could have memory other than SWIM. Some objects may reside in this other memory. Also, addresses of locations in this memory may be specified as parameters in some function invocations. In such cases, an ASE requires access to memory locations outside the SWIM system. ASEs do not have direct access to memory managed by the host system. Any such access is provided by the host through an appropriate (method invocation) interface. This interface is exactly the same for invocations of all functions on the host from SWIM. For instance, if a member function on SWIM requires the computation of `sqrt()`, it may wish to use the `sqrt()` function available in the math library on the host rather than maintain a copy of this function in microcode.

SWIM could cause an interrupt on the host when it requires the host's services. However this is generally undesirable due to the expected high cost of interrupt processing on the host. Instead, as in the case of a returned value, any such requests are left for the host in a communications buffer that the host polls periodically. When the host reads the contents of the buffer, it determines whether this is a function invocation request or a returned value, and behaves accordingly. If a function is invoked on the host, the returned value, if any, is sent back to the requesting SWIM ASE in the form of a message, delivered as always by the host doing a sequence of writes to memory at an address in SWIM space.

When a function is called on the host from a SWIM ASE, results may have to be returned to the ASE. The function on the host cannot be altered for this purpose. The way this works is that there is code on the host that is polling the buffer for messages from the ASE to check if some function is invoked (or results are returned). If a function is invoked, this code calls the appropriate function on the host, and then sends the results back to SWIM by doing a series a writes to the appropriate memory address.

5.5 Resource management functions

Resource management functions are automatically included in the executables for the ASE or host, from a standard library by the loader. Such functions include the microcode required by the head ASE to process constructors, and the microcode to configure an ASE, to manage object buffers, and to free up an ASE.

5.6 Example

Let us assume that the (by now familiar) `Node` class, along with all its member functions, is to be handled on SWIM. We show below a simple C++ program that uses this class, and discuss its compilation.

```
main()
{
    Node a(1,100), b(2,15), c(4,18), d(4,9), e(3,99);
    Node *f;
    int res;

    a.add_child(&b);     // Set up the graph structure.
    a.add_child(&c);     // Nodes b and c are children
    b.add_child(&c);     // of node a, and so on.
    c.add_child(&a); c.add_child(&d); e.add_child(&d);

    // Now let's see if we can find the attr for a
    // key of 4, starting from node e
    if ((res = e.search(4)) >= 0)
        cout << "node e reaches key 4 with attr " <<
                res << "\n";
    else
        cout <<
         "no path from node e to a node with key 4\n";
    e.clean_search() ;

    f = new Node(5,5);   // Add a new node to the graph.
    f->add_child(&a);    // Set up edges from it
    c.add_child(f);      // and to it.
}
```

In this case `main()` is the only function that is compiled on the host. The remaining functions, being methods on the `Node` object, are targeted for the ASE, with the help of the microcode compiler. Let us see how the host-resident code looks.

First, the constructor for the class `Node` is invoked repeatedly for the initializations in the first line. These objects (`a`, `b`, *etc.*) are not themselves physically stored on the stack. Instead, a pointer is stored, along with a reminder that when the stack is popped, these objects must be deleted from (SWIM) memory.[3] Continuing the initialization, space is

3. The benefit of this mechanism is that the stack can be kept smaller. The price paid is that at the end of the routine, the stack cannot be popped by simply changing the stack pointer: items have to be popped individually, and appropriate action taken. However, this price is required any way in C++ in general, since an arbitrary destructor function could have been associated with each object, and has to be executed when the object is deleted.

also created on the stack for two pointers to `Node` objects: `f` and `res`.

Next is a series of member function invocations to SWIM, each accomplished by a couple of writes to a SWIM memory address. Since no values are returned, these functions can be invoked asynchronously, as fast as the SWIM system is able to accept (as opposed to process) these requests.

Next, a search member function is invoked, once more by performing a couple of memory writes. This time, however, there is a returned value for which the host has to wait. The waiting is done by repeatedly reading a memory location for indication that the result is ready, and then reading the result itself when it is there. Rather than a tight busy-wait loop, an implementation dependent delay can be inserted so that the operating system can swap a different process in while the current program is waiting on SWIM. Once the search is complete, a member function is invoked to clean up. Once more, this function returns no result, and need not be waited on.

In the last part of the program, the host requests a new node `f`. Once more, the host has to wait until the allocator returns a handle to this new object. A clever enough compiler may be able to determine that the creation of this new node object does not interfere with the search conducted previously, and generate code in which this constructor call is issued concurrently with the search operation, before an attempt is made to read the search result. Alternatively, user-provided hints can be used for this purpose. We are still studying this issue.

Finally, edges are set up to and from the new node. These function invocations can once more be performed asynchronously from the host, and performed immediately after the constructor call returns a value, even though the ASE executing the constructor may still be initializing the data structure for the new object `f`. Error-free operation is guaranteed due to the single-threading of operations in an ASE.

6. Performance

The goal in having a back-end object manager is to provide improved performance through exploiting a moderate level of parallelism and, in the case of SWIM, by using an architecture whose instruction set is well-suited to data manipulative operations. In this section we examine a few simple fragments of code and show how this design achieves increased performance.

First off, constructors can be virtually free as far as the host's time is concerned. This is because an ASE has only to return a handle for a newly allocated object and can work on the rest of the constructor function (the user-written portion) later. The task of finding a free slot in the object buffer allocation bitmap takes only a few cycles. During that time, the host can do a minimal amount of work, such as preparing an address in which to store the handle and to pass parameters to the user-defined constructor function. Using the `Node` class definition in the appendix, we consider the case of initializing a graph from data in a file with the following loop:

```
for (i=0; i < maxnodes; ++i) {
        fscanf(fp, "%d, %d", &k, &val);
        n[i] = new Node(k, val);
}
```

The compile system translates this to the following source on the host[4]:

```
for (i=0; i < maxnodes; ++i) {
        fscanf(fp, "%d, %d", &k, &val);
        *_swim = _cNode;
        *_swim = k;
        *_swim = val;
        n[i] = (Node *)(*_swim);
}
```

The references to `_swim` are reads and writes of the memory-mapped port for communicating with SWIM. The constructor itself has been replaced with a write of a constant `_cnode` to SWIM, which invokes that member function on the ASE. Note that the optimizer can move the invocation of the constructor before the call to `fscanf()` since there are no dependencies between the two functions.

Once in the loop, the iterative sequence of operations is shown in figure 3. In executing `n[i] = new Node(k, val)`, the first operation which takes place is a memory write on the host which sends a packet to SWIM to execute the `Node` constructor code. While this is running, the host fetches the values of the parameters for the constructor (which will be used by the user-defined function) and performs memory writes to SWIM. Note that in more complex cases, fetching parameters may involve function calls and subsequently take more time. The host then calculates the memory address in which the constructor's result (the object handle) will be stored and then performs a blocking read of the result. In this example, the read will not block since the ASE would already have sent the object handle and be executing the user-defined constructor code, by the time the host is ready to perform the read. In parallel with the ASE running the constructor function, the host continues, testing the loop condition, preparing arguments for calling the `fscanf()` function, and executing `fscanf()`. Then it issues another constructor request. If the constructor function happens to be overly complex and takes longer to run than the tasks on the host, the next read of the object handle blocks until the ASE catches up.

---

4. The code is shown here captures the essence of the actual code, but has been simplified slightly for ease of understanding

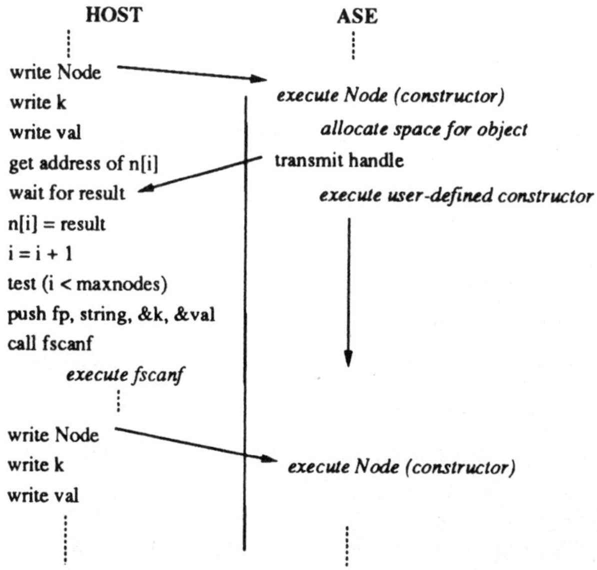

Figure 3. Parallelism in constructor operations

How does this translate to actual time savings? In the loop just examined, the bulk of the performance was used by the `fscanf()` function and associated file input support functions. With a back-end object manager, the performance of a SUN-4/260 increased by only 10%. When the `fscanf()` routine was replaced with explicit settings of `k` and `val` to functions of `i`, the constructor's role became more visible, and the same program run with a back-end object manger ran 383% faster[5]!

Let's examine the overhead and savings of executing methods on objects. Using the same `Node` class, we'll examine a simple loop which calls two support functions to calculate the linkage between two nodes (what these functions do is unimportant here, since we're not interested in what the program does) and then invokes the method that sets up the links. The fragment is:

---

5. The performance difference is obtained by measuring differences in user time. User time measures only the time spent executing user's code. With 10,000 nodes, the program runs in 0.58 seconds real time and 0.23 seconds user time on a Sun-4/260 without a back-end object manager. With a back-end object manager, the same program runs in 0.25 seconds real time and 0.06 seconds user time.

```
for (i=0; i < maxedges; ++i) {
        n[findsource(i)]->add_child(n[finddest(i)]);
```

where `findsource()` and `finddest()` are arbitrary functions computed sequentially on the host (they are not member functions). In tests, with the simple `findsource()` and `finddest()` functions shown below, the program ran 342% faster with SWIM serving as an object manager.

```
int                                 int
findsource(int i)                   finddest(int i)
{                                   {
    return i&3;                         return (5-i)&3;
}                                   }
```

From the simple examples above, we have shown that there is a potential for considerably speeding up existing code by adding a back-end object manager to a regular workstation. In fact, the current version of the SWIM ASE, used for these tests, ran only at 3MHz, whereas we expect to be able to boost the clock rate in the near future to around 20 MHz, which is more in line with rates on most workstations today. Once this happens, the performance improvements achieved should be substantially greater. More important, the code examined here was simple, with only one class. In reality, methods will often be complex and, in a well-structured program, will comprise the bulk of computation. Furthermore, methods will often be invoked on objects of different classes, yielding a greater than two processor utilization of the system. For such programs the benefits of a back-end object manager will be even greater.

On the other hand, we also saw that there can be great variance in the performance improvement of a system due to a back-end object manager. Programs that do not effectively utilize an object oriented design paradigm will typically perform most of their computation on the host (i.e. referencing functions instead of methods). These programs will not enjoy increased performance since the ASEs will be idle most of the time and the host will be computing in much the same manner that it has in the past (without an object manager).

7. Discussion

7.1 Defeating encapsulation

Recall that the entire SWIM system is within the address space of the host. As such, it is possible for the host to address directly any individual memory location within any ASE in SWIM. Direct accesses are transparent to the ASE, and to any method it may have been executing at that time. Any such direct access defeats encapsulation, and is not recommended, except in special circumstances.

One such special circumstance is debugging. A major difficulty with developing parallel systems is that they are hard to debug when problems arise. We have found the provision of transparent direct access of great value in determining (and even controlling) the state of an ASE in the course of some parallel computation. See [3].

Another such special circumstance arises due to the flexibility provided by the language of greatest concern to us, C++. C++ permits any data member and any member function of a class to be declared `private` or `public`[6]. Our discussion so far has assumed that each data member is `private` and each member function is `public`. Providing private member functions creates no special difficulty: these are like sub-routines that can be called only by other member functions associated with the class.

Public data members are an issue. A public data member can be accessed directly from anywhere in the program, just like a member of a `struct`, without the need to invoke any member functions. This implies direct access. Clearly, encapsulation is defeated for such data members, sacrificed to attain greater efficiency. Extensive use of public data members is not good object-oriented programming style, even though C++ provides the facility; in SWIM we can handle direct references to such members from the host, but discourage such access.

However, one ASE cannot access memory locations in the address space of another ASE. If public data members of such "external" objects are to be referenced, this must happen through the message mechanism. We manage this by providing trivial (public) member functions to read and write each public data member of a class. Due to the efficiency of our message system, a message can be sent to invoke this single instruction member function, and a response received, all within approximately the amount of time it would take for the host to perform a single memory read across the system bus.

6. These could also be declared `protected`, which is a point between the two extremes of public and private. We do not consider this here since, once inheritance has been worked out, protected components effectively become private.

With each ASE, we also provide methods to read and to write any specified memory location in the ASE. These methods effectively provide the ability for any ASE to read or alter the memory contents of another ASE. In particular, they are invoked when there are address parameters to a member function call that have to be dereferenced.

7.2 Memory hierarchy

7.2.1 Virtual memory

Most computer systems today provide *virtual memory*. That is, the range of memory addresses available to the processor is larger than the amount of memory physically present. The rest of the memory is stored on some "swap space" on disk, and is paged in, under operating system control, when required. There are sophisticated algorithms, relying on the locality of data access, to determine precisely which part of the virtual memory space should actually be stored in the limited main memory available.

The use of virtual memory is orthogonal to the ideas being discussed here. It is entirely possible for each ASE to address a range greater than the physical memory associated with it, and to swap pages as necessary for the rest. This facility could be built in the standard way with a hardware-supported page table, or in any other way that we choose. As long as the host always sees a specific address range that can be addressed uniformly, irrespective of the actual size of physical memory, the way in which this is implemented in an ASE is immaterial for the purposes of this paper.

7.2.2 Cache

Most computer systems today also exploit the use of high-speed "cache" memory that is placed "close" to the processor, and contains at any time the items that are most likely to be required by the processor in the near future, thereby minimizing the need for the processor to access main memory across the system bus.

In SWIM, the processing logic part of each ASE accesses the memory part as if it were cache. Thus we can effectively utilize a cache even for data intensive applications where many cache misses may be likely in a normal architecture.

However, access to SWIM from the host is as if SWIM were part of main memory. It is not possible to access SWIM at cache speeds. If the host processor wishes to compute intensively on some section of SWIM memory, it may transfer the relevant portion of memory to its own cache, just as it can from normal main memory. Obviously, this cacheing mechanism can be used only with respect to code that has been compiled for the host processor.

7.3 Parallelism

From the description seen so far, it should be evident that there is scope for two types of parallelism. The first is parallelism between the host and SWIM. The second, and more interesting one, is between multiple ASEs in SWIM. We have already seen how the first type of parallelism is obtained. Member functions are invoked asynchronously from the host. Computations that do not depend on the results of this member function being available can go on before the results of the member function are retrieved by the host from SWIM. These computations may be determined through dependency analysis by the compiler, may be indicated explicitly by the programmer using concurrency constructs such as in [6], or may be obtained at run-time due to the operating system swapping processes. In all cases, this concurrency remains non-scalable, and has little special in it on account of object orientation. As such, we do not discuss it further.

We have seen how one ASE can invoke a member function in another ASE. Since such invocations are asynchronous, they provide a natural mechanism for parallelism. There is absolutely NO change to the program or data on account of this parallelism. We simply get it for free by using SWIM.

In addition to the natural parallelism discussed above, we can orchestrate data parallelism for set operations. Conceptually, we do this by making each ASE that is configured to manage objects of class *foo*, also to manage a single object of (implicit) class *set-of-foo*. Member functions can be defined for this set class. These member functions can iterate over all elements of the set, which are the objects of type foo managed by the particular ASE. (The identifiers for these member functions will have to be distinct from those for the member functions associated with the class *foo* itself). Now a single member function invocation from the host can cause the ASE to iterate over all the objects of the appropriate type, invoking appropriate member functions on each individual object directly, with no need for the host to invoke these member functions directly on the objects by Itself. Data parallelism is achieved when there are multiple ASEs responsible for objects of a particular class. Each of them can start iterating over the objects they manage concurrently. The host need not know about this (conceptually meaningless) allocation of objects to ASEs. In particular, it need not be responsible for concurrently starting of the iteration methods in several ASEs. Instead, the head ASE asynchronously invokes corresponding iteration methods at the other ASEs of the class, before it actually begins iterating over its own objects.

8. Extensions

8.1 Persistence

Recall that each ASE has (or at least, could have) its own disk. It is possible for ASEs to save objects on disk in some persistent manner.

SWIM can thus be used for persistent object management, and is likely to prove even more of a performance benefit since data will not have to be moved in and out of SWIM, even for initializing objects. We are working on this at present.

8.2 Concurrency control

Execution within each individual ASE is single-threaded. All member-functions run to completion without interruption. (An interruption can be permitted, if desired, but this requires explicit specification). In consequence, there is a good measure of concurrency control automatically provided, at a level significantly better than an atomic test-and-set operation. If two concurrent transactions only access objects within a single ASE, then the level of concurrency control naturally provided by the single-threading suffices. When concurrent transactions access objects in multiple ASEs, a need may arise for provision of concurrency control in software, such as through "locking". The details of this higher level concurrency control mechanism have yet to be worked out.

8.3 Large objects

All the preceding discussion has assumed that an object is small enough that there are several at each ASE. While this is generally the case, there may occasionally be the need for truly large objects, which span multiple ASEs. To the extent that our set-of-objects construct can itself be viewed as an object, we already have some support for a large distributed object. However, we do not as yet have a robust model and compilation technique. Devising these requires further work.

8.4 Flexibility of object location

In our current system, a decision is made for a class at definition time, whether instances of the class are to be managed on the host or on SWIM. It may prove useful to have the flexibility to make this decision independently for each instance of the class. Doing so requires that code for class definition always be compiled both ways: through the regular C++ compiler for the host, and through the ASE microcode compiler for SWIM. Every time a new object is created, the user has to specify where it should be managed. The difficulty is that two instances of the same class are very different beasts where one is managed by the host and the other by SWIM. In effect, we have created two distinct types from one class definition. Support for this type mechanism may require a language extension, which we would like to avoid unless it proves absolutely essential.

9. Conclusions

SWIM is a medium-fine-grain MIMD multiprocessor system designed to perform intelligent object management. In this paper we showed how object-oriented computation can effectively make use of such back-end multi-processing, and present performance figures in support of our claims. We also showed how C++ could be implemented on this architecture, including some "less object-oriented" features of C++, that are really useful in a programming language, but not a good match for a truly object-oriented machine.

As of this writing, we have a prototype hardware and software system up and running. It is clear to us that significant performance benefits are possible for certain classes of object-oriented computation. Further work is underway to determine how broad-based these gains really are, and to characterize the circumstances in which our system provides a big win.

Appendix: C++ Code for a Graph Object

```
#define MAX_CHILDREN 4

const int DefaultKey=0;       // default key value for node
const int DefaultAttr=0;      // default attribute for node

class Node {      // one node in the graph
    int key;             // key
    int attr;            // attribute
    Node *child[MAX_CHILDREN];  // node's children
    int visit;    // visit mark for graph traversal
public:
                  // constructor
    Node(int k=DefaultKey, a=DefaultAttr);
                 // No user-specified destructor, ~Node()
    void add_child(Node*);          // add a child link
    void remove_child(Node*);       // add a child link
    Node *search(int k);            // look for first key
    void clean_search();            // reset visit marks
                                    //    after search
}

void          // set link from parent to child
Node::add_child(Node& cnode)
{
    int i;
    for (i=0; child[i] && i < MAX_CHILDREN; ++i) ;
    if (i < MAX_CHILDREN)
        child[i] = cnode;
}
```

```
Node&          // search for key k
Node::search(int k)
{
    int ccheck = 0;
    int csearch = NULL;  // result of recursive search

    if (visit)         // we already visited this node!
        return NULL;
    if (key == k)                   // we found it!
        return attr;
    visit = 1 ;
    for (ccheck = 0; child[ccheck] &&
                     ccheck < MAX_CHILDREN ; ++ccheck)
        if ((csearch=child[ccheck]->search(k)) != NULL)
            break;
    return csearch;
}

void
Node::clean_search()          // clean up after search
{
    int ccheck = 0;

    if (!visit)        // we already cleaned up this node
        return;
    visit = 0 ;
    for (ccheck = 0; child[ccheck] &&
                     ccheck < MAX_CHILDREN ; ++ccheck)
        child[ccheck]->clean_search() ;
    return ;
}

Node::Node(int k, int a)
{
    int i;
    visit = 0;
    key = k;
    attr = a;
    for (i=0; i < MAX_CHILDREN; ++i) child[i] = NULL ;
}
```

REFERENCES

[1] Agha A G, Hewitt C. "Concurrent Programming Using Actors." in Object-Oriented Concurrent Programming, A. Yonezawa and M. Takoro (ed.), MIT Press, Cambridge, MA, 1988.

[2] America A P. "Definition of the Programming Language POOL-T." ESPRIT Project 415, Doc. No. 0091, Philips Research Labs, Eindhoven, The Netherlands, June 1985.

[3] Asthana A, Jagadish H V, "Hardware Support for Debugging in a Small-Grain Parallel System." Proc. SIGPLAN/SIGOPS Workshop on Parallel and Distributed Debugging, Madison, WI, May 1988.

[4] Asthana A, Chandross J A, Jagadish H V, "The Trap as a Control Flow Mechanism." Proceedings of MICRO 21, the 21st Annual Workshop on Microprogramming and Micro-Architecture, San Diego, CA, Dec. 1988.

[5] Asthana A, Jagadish H V, Chandross J A, Lin D, Knauer S C, "A High Bandwith Intelligent Memory for Supercomputers." Proceedings Third International Conference on Supercomputing, 1988.

[6] Gehani N H, Roome W D. "Concurrent C." Software—Practice & Experience, 16(9), 1986, 821-844..

[7] Hewitt C. "Viewing Control Structures as Patterns of Passing Messages." Journal of Artificial Intelligence, 8(3), 1977, 323-364.

[8] Hornick M F, Zdonik S B. "A Shared Segemented Memory System for an Object-Oriented Database." ACM Trans. Office Information Systems, 5(1), Jan. 1987, 70-95.

[9] Jagadish H V, Rao S K, Kailath T, "Multiprocessor Architectures for Iterative Algorithms." IEEE Proceedings, Aug. 1987.

[10] Johnson G M. "Exploiting Paralleism in Computational Science." FGCS, 5(2-3), Sept. 1989.

[11] Krzyzanowski P, Asthana A, Jagadish H V. "SWIMCC – An Optimizing Compiler for the SWIM Processor." AT&T Bell Laboratories Technical Memorandum, 1991.

[12] Ozkarahan E A. "Evolution and Implementation ofthe RAP Database Machine." New Generation Computing, 3(3), 1985, 237-271.

[13] Slotnick D L. "Logic Per Track Devices." in Advances in Computers, vol. 10, Frantz Alt (ed.), Academic Press, New York, 1970, 291-296.

[14] Stroustrup B. "The C++ Programming Language". Addison-Wesley., 1986.

[15] Su S Y W, Copeland G P, Lipovsky G J. "The Architectural Features and Implementation Techniques of the Multi-Cell CASSM." IEEE Transactions on Computers, C-28(6), June 1979, 430-445.

[16] Yonezawa A, Briot J-P, Shibayama E, "Object Oriented Concurrent Programming in ABCL/1." Proc. 1st ACM Conf. on Object-Oriented Programming, Systems, Languages, and Applications, Portland, OR, Sept. 1986.

Author Index

Published in 1990

AI and Cognitive Science '89, Dublin City University, Eire, 14–15 September 1989
A. F. Smeaton and G. McDermott (Eds.)

Specification and Verification of Concurrent Systems, University of Stirling, Scotland, 6–8 July 1988
C. Rattray (Ed.)

Semantics for Concurrency, Proceedings of the International BCS-FACS Workshop, Sponsored by Logic for IT (S.E.R.C.), University of Leicester, UK, 23–25 July 1990
M. Z. Kwiatkowska, M. W. Shields and R. M. Thomas (Eds.)

Functional Programming, Glasgow 1989, Proceedings of the 1989 Glasgow Workshop, Fraserburgh, Scotland, 21–23 August 1989
K. Davis and J. Hughes (Eds.)

Persistent Object Systems, Proceedings of the Third International Workshop, Newcastle, Australia, 10–13 January 1989
J. Rosenberg and D. Koch (Eds.)

Z User Workshop, Oxford, 1989, Proceedings of the Fourth Annual Z User Meeting, Oxford, 15 December 1989
J. E. Nicholls (Ed.)

Formal Methods for Trustworthy Computer Systems (FM89), Halifax, Canada, 23–27 July 1989
Dan Craigen (Editor) and Karen Summerskill (Assistant Editor)

Security and Persistence, Proceedings of the International Workshop on Computer Architecture to Support Security and Persistence of Information, Bremen, West Germany, 8–11 May 1990
John Rosenberg and J. Leslie Keedy (Eds.)

Printing: Weihert-Druck GmbH, Darmstadt
Binding: Buchbinderei Schäffer, Grünstadt